William Wordsworth, Alexander Balloch Grosart

The Prose Works of William Wordsworth

Vol. II

William Wordsworth, Alexander Balloch Grosart

The Prose Works of William Wordsworth
Vol. II

ISBN/EAN: 9783744685856

Printed in Europe, USA, Canada, Australia, Japan

Cover: Foto ©Thomas Meinert / pixelio.de

More available books at **www.hansebooks.com**

THE PROSE WORKS

OF

WILLIAM WORDSWORTH.

FOR THE FIRST TIME COLLECTED,

WITH ADDITIONS FROM UNPUBLISHED MANUSCRIPTS.

Edited, with Preface, Notes and Illustrations,

BY THE

REV. ALEXANDER B. GROSART,
ST. GEORGE'S, BLACKBURN, LANCASHIRE.

IN THREE VOLUMES.

VOL. II.

ÆSTHETICAL AND LITERARY.

LONDON : EDWARD MOXON, SON, AND CO.
1 AMEN CORNER, PATERNOSTER ROW.
1876.

CONTENTS OF VOL. II.

† The Beaumont Letters are given from the originals, and in many cases, as
elsewhere, contain important additions and corrections. G.

ÆSTHETICAL AND LITERARY.

I. OF LITERARY BIOGRAPHY AND MONUMENTS.

NOTE.

For details on the several portions of this division, see the Preface in Vol. I. G.

A

LETTER

TO

A FRIEND OF ROBERT BURNS:

OCCASIONED BY

AN INTENDED REPUBLICATION

OF

THE ACCOUNT OF THE LIFE OF BURNS, BY DR. CURRIE;

AND

OF THE SELECTION MADE BY HIM FROM HIS LETTERS.

BY WILLIAM WORDSWORTH.

LONDON:

PRINTED FOR LONGMAN, HURST, REES, ORME, AND BROWN,
PATERNOSTER-ROW.

1816.

(a) A LETTER TO A FRIEND OF ROBERT BURNS.

TO JAMES GRAY, ESQ., EDINBURGH.

Dear Sir,

I have carefully perused the Review of the Life of your friend Robert Burns,* which you kindly transmitted to me; the author has rendered a substantial service to the poet's memory; and the annexed letters are all important to the subject. After having expressed this opinion, I shall not trouble you by commenting upon the publication; but will confine myself to the request of Mr. Gilbert Burns, that I would furnish him with my notions upon the best mode of conducting the defence of his brother's injured reputation; a favourable opportunity being now afforded him to convey his sentiments to the world, along with a republication of Dr. Currie's book, which he is about to superintend. From the respect which I have long felt for the character of the person who has thus honoured me, and from the gratitude which, as a lover of poetry, I owe to the genius of his departed relative, I should most gladly comply with this wish; if I could hope that any suggestions of mine would be of service to the cause. But, really, I feel it a thing of much delicacy, to give advice upon this occasion, as it appears to me, mainly, not a question of opinion, or of taste, but a matter of conscience. Mr. Gilbert Burns must know, if any man living does, what his brother was; and no one will deny that he, who possesses this knowledge, is a man of unimpeachable veracity. He has already spoken to the world in contradiction of the injurious assertions that have been made, and has told why he forbore to do this on their first appearance. If it be deemed ad-

* *A Review of the Life of Robert Burns, and of various Criticisms on his Character and Writings*, by Alexander Peterkin, 1814.

viseable to reprint Dr. Currie's narrative, without striking out such passages as the author, if he were now alive, would probably be happy to efface, let there be notes attached to the most obnoxious of them, in which the misrepresentations may be corrected, and the exaggerations exposed. I recommend this course, if Dr. Currie's Life is to be republished, as it now stands, in connexion with the poems and letters, and especially if prefixed to them; but, in my judgment, it would be best to copy the example which Mason has given in his second edition of Gray's works. There, inverting the order which had been properly adopted, when the Life and Letters were new matter, the poems are placed first; and the rest takes its place as subsidiary to them. If this were done in the intended edition of Burns's works, I should strenuously recommend, that a concise life of the poet be prefixed, from the pen of Gilbert Burns, who has already given public proof how well qualified he is for the undertaking. I know no better model as to proportion, and the degree of detail required, nor, indeed, as to the general execution, than the life of Milton by Fenton, prefixed to many editions of the *Paradise Lost.* But a more copious narrative would be expected from a brother; and some allowance ought to be made, in this and other respects, for an expectation so natural.

In this prefatory memoir, when the author has prepared himself by reflecting, that fraternal partiality may have rendered him, in some points, not so trust-worthy as others less favoured by opportunity, it will be incumbent upon him to proceed candidly and openly, as far as such a procedure will tend to restore to his brother that portion of public estimation, of which he appears to have been unjustly deprived. Nay, when we recal to mind the black things which have been written of this great man, and the frightful ones that have been insinuated against him; and, as far as the public knew, till lately, without complaint, remonstrance, or disavowal, from his nearest relatives; I am not sure that it would not be best, at this day, explicitly to declare to what degree Robert Burns had given way to pernicious habits, and, as nearly as may be, to fix the point to which his moral character had been degraded. It is a disgraceful feature of the times that this measure should be necessary; most painful to think that a *brother* should have such an office to perform. But, if Gilbert Burns be conscious that the subject will bear to be so treated, he has no choice; the duty has been imposed upon him by the errors into which the former biographer has fallen, in respect to the very principles upon which his work ought to have been conducted.

I well remember the acute sorrow with which, by my own fire-side, I first perused Dr. Currie's Narrative, and some of the letters, particularly of those composed in the latter part of the poet's life. If my pity for Burns was extreme, this pity did not preclude a strong indignation, of which he was not the object. If, said I, it were in the power of a biographer to relate the truth, the *whole* truth, and nothing *but* the truth, the friends and surviving kindred of the deceased, for the sake of general benefit to mankind, might endure that such heart-rending communication should be made to the world. But in no case is this possible; and, in the present, the opportunities of directly acquiring other than superficial knowledge have been most scanty; for the writer has barely seen the person who is the subject of his tale; nor did his avocations allow him to take the pains necessary for ascertaining what portion of the information conveyed to him was authentic. So much for facts and actions; and to what purpose relate them even were they true, if the narrative cannot be heard without extreme pain; unless they are placed in such a light, and brought forward in such order, that they shall explain their own laws, and leave the reader in as little uncertainty as the mysteries of our nature will allow, respecting the spirit from which they derived their existence, and which governed the agent? But hear on this pathetic and awful subject, the poet himself, pleading for those who have transgressed!

> One point must still be greatly dark,
> The moving *why* they do it,
> And just as lamely can ye mark
> How far, perhaps, they rue it.

> Who made the heart, 'tis *he* alone
> Decidedly can try us;
> He knows each chord—its various tone,
> Each spring, its various bias.

> Then at the balance let's be mute,
> We never can adjust it;
> What's done we partly may compute,
> But know not what's *resisted*.

How happened it that the recollection of this affecting passage did not check so amiable a man as Dr. Currie, while he was revealing to the world the infirmities of its author? He must have known enough of human nature to be assured that men would be eager to sit in judgment, and pronounce *decidedly* upon the guilt or innocence of Burns by his testimony; nay, that there were multitudes whose main interest in the allegations would be derived from the incitements which they found therein to undertake this presumptuous office. And where lies the collateral benefit, or what ultimate advantage can be expected, to counteract the injury that the many are thus tempted to do to their own minds; and to compensate the sorrow which must be fixed in the hearts of the considerate few, by language that proclaims so much, and provokes conjectures as unfavourable as imagination can furnish? Here, said I, being moved beyond what it would become me to express, here is a revolting account of a man of exquisite genius, and confessedly of many high moral qualities, sunk into the lowest depths of vice and misery! But the painful story, notwithstanding its minuteness, is incomplete,—in essentials it is deficient; so that the most attentive and sagacious reader cannot explain how a mind, so well established by knowledge, fell—and continued to fall, without power to prevent or retard its own ruin.

Would a bosom friend of the author, his counsellor and confessor, have told such things, if true, as this book contains? and who, but one possessed of the intimate knowledge which none but a bosom friend can acquire, could have been justified in making these avowals? Such a one, himself a pure spirit, having accompanied, as it were, upon wings, the pilgrim along the sorrowful road which he trod on foot; such a one, neither hurried down by its slippery descents, nor entangled among its thorns, nor perplexed by its windings, nor discomfited by its founderous passages—for the instruction of others—might have delineated, almost as in a map, the way which the afflicted pilgrim had pursued till the sad close of his diversified journey. In this manner the venerable spirit of Isaac Walton was qualified to have retraced the unsteady course of a highly-gifted man, who, in this lamentable point, and in versatility of genius, bore no unobvious resemblance to the Scottish bard; I mean his friend COTTON—whom, notwithstanding all that the sage must have disapproved in his life, he honoured with the title of son. Nothing like this, however, has the biographer of Burns accomplished; and, with his means of information, copious as in some respects they were, it would have been absurd to attempt it. The only motive, therefore, which could authorize the writing and publishing matter so distressing to read—is wanting!

Nor is Dr. Currie's performance censurable from these considerations alone; for information, which would have been of absolute worth if in his capacity of biographer and editor he had known when to stop short, is rendered unsatisfactory and inefficacious through the absence of this reserve, and from being coupled with statements of improbable and irreconcileable facts. We have the author's letters discharged upon us in showers; but how few readers will take the trouble of comparing those letters with each other, and with the other documents of the publication, in order to come at a genuine knowledge of the writer's character!—The life of Johnson by Boswell had broken through many pre-existing delicacies, and afforded the British public an opportunity of acquiring experience, which before it had happily wanted; nevertheless, at the time when the ill-selected medley of Burns's correspondence first appeared, little progress had been made (nor is it likely that, by the mass of mankind, much ever will be made) in determining what portion of these confidential communications escapes the pen in courteous, yet often innocent, compliance—to gratify the several tastes of correspondents; and as little towards distinguishing opinions and sentiments uttered for the momentary amusement merely of the writer's own fancy, from those which his judgment deliberately approves, and his heart faithfully cherishes. But the subject of this book was a man of extraordinary genius; whose birth, education, and employments had placed and kept him in a situation far below that in which the writers and readers of expensive volumes are usually found. Critics upon works of fiction have laid it down as a rule that remoteness of place, in fixing the choice of a subject, and in prescribing the mode of treating it, is equal in effect to distance of time;—restraints may be thrown off accordingly. Judge then of the delusions which artificial distinctions impose, when to a man like Doctor Currie, writing with views so honourable, the *social condition* of the individual of whom he was treating, could seem to place him at such a distance from the exalted reader, that ceremony might be discarded with him, and his memory sacrificed, as it were, almost without compunction. The poet was laid where these injuries could not reach him; but he had a parent, I understand, an admirable woman, still surviving ; a brother like Gilbert Burns!—a widow estimable for her virtues; and children, at that time infants, with the world before them, which they must face to obtain a maintenance ; who remembered their father probably with the tenderest affection;—and whose opening minds, as their years advanced, would become conscious of so many reasons for admiring him.—Ill-fated child of nature, too frequently thine own enemy,—unhappy favourite of genius, too often misguided,—this is indeed to be ' crushed beneath the fur- row's weight !'

Why, sir, do I write to you at this length, when all that I had to express in direct answer to the request, which occasioned this letter, lay in such narrow compass ?—Because having en- tered upon the subject, I am unable to quit it !—Your feelings, I trust, go along with mine ; and, rising from this individual case to a general view of the subject, you will probably agree with me in opinion that biography, though differing in some essentials from works of fiction, is nevertheless, like them, an *art*—an art, the laws of which are determined by the imperfec- tions of our nature, and the constitution of society. Truth is not here, as in the sciences, and in natural philosophy, to be sought without scruple, and promulgated for its own sake, upon the mere chance of its being serviceable ; but only for obviously justifying purposes, moral or intellectual.

Silence is a privilege of the grave, a right of the departed : let him, therefore, who infringes that right, by speaking pub- licly of, for, or against, those who cannot speak for themselves, take heed that he opens not his mouth without a sufficient sanc- tion. *De mortuis nil nisi bonum*, is a rule in which these senti- ments have been pushed to an extreme that proves how deeply humanity is interested in maintaining them. And it was wise to announce the precept thus absolutely ; both because there exist in that same nature, by which it has been dictated, so many temptations to disregard it,—and because there are powers and influences, within and without us, that will prevent its being literally fulfilled—to the suppression of profitable truth.

Penalties of law, conventions of manners, and personal fear, protect the reputation of the living; and something of this protection is extended to the recently dead,—who survive, to a certain degree, in their kindred and friends. Few are so insensible as not to feel this, and not to be actuated by the feeling. But only to philosophy enlightened by the affections does it belong justly to estimate the claims of the deceased on the one hand, and of the present age and future generations, on the other; and to strike a balance between them.—Such philosophy runs a risk of becoming extinct among us, if the coarse intrusions into the recesses, the gross breaches upon the sanctities, of domestic life, to which we have lately been more and more accustomed, are to be regarded as indications of a vigorous state of public feeling—favourable to the maintenance of the liberties of our country.—Intelligent lovers of freedom are from necessity bold and hardy lovers of truth; but, according to the measure in which their love is intelligent, is it attended with a finer discrimination, and a more sensitive delicacy. The wise and good (and all others being lovers of licence rather than of liberty are in fact slaves) respect, as one of the noblest characteristics of Englishmen, that jealousy of familiar approach, which, while it contributes to the maintenance of private dignity, is one of the most efficacious guardians of rational public freedom.

The general obligation upon which I have insisted, is especially binding upon those who undertake the biography of *authors.* Assuredly, there is no cause why the lives of that class of men should be pried into with the same diligent curiosity, and laid open with the same disregard of reserve, which may sometimes be expedient in composing the history of men who have borne an active part in the world. Such thorough knowledge of the good and bad qualities of these latter, as can only be obtained by a scrutiny of their private lives, conduces to explain not only their own public conduct, but that of those with whom they have acted. Nothing of this applies to authors, considered merely as authors. Our business is with their books, —to understand and to enjoy them. And, of poets more especially, it is true—that, if their works be good, they contain within themselves all that is necessary to their being comprehended and relished. It should seem that the ancients thought in this manner; for of the eminent Greek and Roman poets, few and scanty memorials were, I believe, ever prepared; and fewer still are preserved. It is delightful to read what, in the happy exercise of his own genius, Horace chooses to communicate of himself and his friends; but I confess I am not so much a lover of knowledge, independent of its quality, as to make it likely that it would much rejoice me, were I to hear that records of the Sabine poet and his contemporaries, composed upon the Boswellian plan, had been unearthed among the ruins of Herculaneum. You will interpret what I am writing, *liberally.* With respect to the light which such a discovery might throw upon Roman manners, there would be reasons to desire it: but I should dread to disfigure the beautiful ideal of the memories of those illustrious persons with incongruous features, and to sully the imaginative purity of their classical works with gross and trivial recollections.   The least weighty objection to heterogeneous details, is that they are mainly superfluous, and therefore an incumbrance.

But you will perhaps accuse me of refining too much; and it is, I own, comparatively of little importance, while we are engaged in reading the *Iliad*, the *Eneid*, the tragedies of *Othello* and *King Lear*, whether the authors of these poems were good or bad men; whether they lived happily or miserably.   Should a thought of the kind cross our minds, there would be no doubt, if irresistible external evidence did not decide the question unfavourably, that men of such transcendant genius were both good and happy: and if, unfortunately, it had been on record that they were otherwise, sympathy with the fate of their fictitious personages would banish the unwelcome truth whenever it obtruded itself, so that it would but slightly disturb our pleasure.   Far otherwise is it with that class of poets, the principal charm of whose writings depends upon the familiar knowledge which they convey of the personal feelings of their authors. This is eminently the case with the effusions of Burns;—in the small quantity of narrative that he has given, he himself bears no inconsiderable part, and he has produced no drama.   Neither the subjects of his poems, nor his manner of handling them, allow us long to forget their author.   On the basis of his human character he has reared a poetic one, which with more or less distinctness presents itself to view in almost every part of his earlier, and, in my estimation, his most valuable verses.   This poetic fabric, dug out of the quarry of genuine humanity, is airy and spiritual:—and though the materials, in some parts, are coarse, and the disposition is often fantastic and irregular, yet the whole is agreeable and strikingly attractive. Plague, then, upon your remorseless hunters after matter of fact (who, after all, rank among the blindest of human beings) when they would convince you that the foundations of this admirable edifice are hollow; and that its frame is unsound! Granting that all which has been raked up to the prejudice of Burns were literally true; and that it added, which it does not, to our better understanding of human nature and human life (for that genius is not incompatible with vice, and that vice leads to misery—the more acute from the sensibilities which are the elements of genius— we needed not those communications to inform us) how poor would have been the compensation for the deduction made, by this extrinsic knowledge, from the intrinsic efficacy of his poetry —to please, and to instruct!

In illustration of this sentiment, permit me to remind you that it is the privilege of poetic genius to catch, under certain restrictions of which perhaps at the time of its being exerted it is but dimly conscious, a spirit of pleasure wherever it can be found,—in the walks of nature, and in the business of men.—The poet, trusting to primary instincts, luxuriates among the felicities of love and wine, and is enraptured while he describes the fairer aspects of war: nor does he shrink from the company of the passion of love though immoderate—from convivial pleasure though intemperate—nor from the presence of war though savage, and recognized as the hand-maid of desolation. Frequently and admirably has Burns given way to these impulses of nature; both with reference to himself and in describing the condition of others. Who, but some impenetrable dunce or narrow-minded puritan in works of art, ever read without delight the picture which he has drawn of the convivial exaltation of the rustic adventurer, Tam o'Shanter? The poet fears not to tell the reader in the outset that his hero was a desperate and sottish drunkard, whose excesses were frequent as his opportunities. This reprobate sits down to his cups, while the storm is roaring, and heaven and earth are in confusion;—the night is driven on by song and tumultuous noise—laughter and jest thicken as the beverage improves upon the palate—conjugal fidelity archly bends to the service of general benevolence—selfishness is not absent, but wearing the mask of social cordiality—and, while these various elements of humanity are blended into one proud and happy composition of elated spirits, the anger of the tempest without doors only heightens and sets off the enjoyment within.—I pity him who cannot perceive that, in all this, though there was no moral purpose, there is a moral effect.

> Kings may be blest, but Tam was glorious,
> O'er a' the *ills* of life victorious.

What a lesson do these words convey of charitable indulgence for the vicious habits of the principal actor in this scene, and of those who resemble him !—Men who to the rigidly virtuous are objects almost of loathing, and whom therefore they cannot serve ! The poet, penetrating the unsightly and disgusting surfaces of things, has unveiled with exquisite skill the finer ties of imagination and feeling, that often bind these beings to practices productive of so much unhappiness to themselves, and to those whom it is their duty to cherish;—and, as far as he puts the reader into possession of this intelligent sympathy, he qualifies him for exercising a salutary influence over the minds of those who are thus deplorably enslaved.

Not less successfully does Burns avail himself of his own character and situation in society, to construct out of them a poetic self,—introduced as a dramatic personage—for the purpose of inspiriting his incidents, diversifying his pictures, recommending his opinions, and giving point to his sentiments. His brother can set me right if I am mistaken when I express a belief that, at the time when he wrote his story of *Death and Dr. Hornbook*, he had very rarely been intoxicated, or perhaps even much exhilarated by liquor. Yet how happily does he lead his reader into that track of sensations ! and with what lively humour does he describe the disorder of his senses and the confusion of his understanding, put to test by a deliberate attempt to count the horns of the moon !

> But whether she had three or four
> He could na' tell.

Behold a sudden apparition that disperses this disorder, and in a moment chills him into possession of himself ! Coming upon no more important mission than the grisly phantom was charged with, what mode of introduction could have been more efficient or appropriate ?

But, in those early poems, through the veil of assumed habits and pretended qualities, enough of the real man appears to show that he was conscious of sufficient cause to dread his own passions, and to bewail his errors ! We have rejected as false sometimes in the letter, and of necessity as false in the spirit, many of the testimonies that others have borne against him ; but, by his own hand—in words the import of which cannot be mistaken—it has been recorded that the order of his life but faintly corresponded with the clearness of his views. It is probable that he would have proved a still greater poet if, by strength of reason, he could have controlled the propensities which his sensibility engendered; but he would have been a poet of a different class : and certain it is, had that desirable restraint been early established, many peculiar beauties which enrich his verses could never have existed, and many accessary influences, which contribute greatly to their effect, would have been wanting. For instance, the momentous truth of the passage already quoted, ' One point must still be greatly dark,' &c. could not possibly have been conveyed with such pathetic force by any poet that ever lived, speaking in his own voice; unless it were felt that, like Burns, he was a man who preached from the text of his own errors ; and whose wisdom, beautiful as a flower that might have risen from seed sown from above, was in fact a scion from the root of personal suffering. Whom did the poet intend should be thought of as occupying that grave over which, after modestly setting forth the moral discernment and warm affections of its ' poor inhabitant,' it is supposed to be inscribed that`

> ——Thoughtless follies laid him low,
> And stained his name.

Who but himself,—himself anticipating the too probable termination of his own course ? Here is a sincere and solemn avowal —a public declaration *from his own will*—a confession at once devout, poetical, and human—a history in the shape of a prophecy ! What more was required of the biographer than to have put his seal to the writing, testifying that the foreboding had been realized, and that the record was authentic ?—Lastingly is it to be regretted in respect to this memorable being, that inconsiderate intrusion has not left us at liberty to enjoy his mirth, or his love; his wisdom or his wit; without an admixture of useless, irksome, and painful details, that take from his poems so much of that right—which, with all his carelessness, and frequent breaches of self-respect, he was not negligent to maintain for them—the right of imparting solid instruction through the medium of unalloyed pleasure.

You will have noticed that my observations have hitherto been confined to Dr. Currie's book: if, by fraternal piety, the poison can be sucked out of this wound, those inflicted by meaner hands may be safely left to heal of themselves. Of the other writers who have given their names, only one lays claim to even a slight acquaintance with the author, whose moral character they take upon them publicly to anatomize. The *Edinburgh* reviewer—and him I single out because the author of the vindication of Burns has treated his offences with comparative indulgence, to which he has no claim, and which, from whatever cause it might arise, has interfered with the dispensation of justice —the *Edinburgh* reviewer thus writes :* ' The *leading vice* in Burns's character, and the *cardinal deformity*, indeed, of ALL his productions, was his contempt, or affectation of contempt, for prudence, decency, and regularity, and his admiration of thoughtlessness, oddity, and vehement sensibility: his belief, in short, in the dispensing power of genius and social feeling in all matters of morality and common sense;' adding, that these vices and erroneous notions ' have communicated to a great part of his productions a character of immorality at once contemptible and hateful.' We are afterwards told, that he is *perpetually* making a parade of his thoughtlessness, inflammability, and imprudence; and, in the next paragraph, that he is *perpetually* doing something else; i.e. ' boasting of his own independence.' —Marvellous address in the commission of faults ! not less than Cæsar showed in the management of business ; who, it is said, could dictate to three secretaries upon three several affairs, at one and the same moment ! But, to be serious. When a man, self-elected into the office of a public judge of the literature and life of his contemporaries, can have the audacity to go these lengths in framing a summary of the contents of volumes that

---

* From Mr. Peterkin's pamphlet, who vouches for the accuracy of his citations; omitting, however, to apologize for their length.

are scattered over every quarter of the globe, and extant in almost every cottage of Scotland, to give the lie to his labours; we must not wonder if, in the plenitude of his concern for the interests of abstract morality, the infatuated slanderer should have found no obstacle to prevent him from insinuating that the poet, whose writings are to this degree stained and disfigured, was 'one of the sons of fancy and of song, who spend in vain superfluities the money that belongs of right to the pale industrious tradesman and his famishing infants; and who rave about friendship and philosophy in a tavern, while their wives' hearts,' &c. &c.

It is notorious that this persevering Aristarch,* as often as a work of original genius comes before him, avails himself of that opportunity to re-proclaim to the world the narrow range of his own comprehension. The happy self-complacency, the unsuspecting vain-glory, and the cordial *bonhommie*, with which this part of his duty is performed, do not leave him free to complain of being hardly dealt with if any one should declare the truth, by pronouncing much of the foregoing attack upon the intellectual and moral character of Burns, to be the trespass (for reasons that will shortly appear, it cannot be called the venial trespass) of a mind obtuse, superficial, and inept. What portion of malignity such a mind is susceptible of, the judicious admirers of the poet, and the discerning friends of the man, will not trouble themselves to enquire; but they will wish that this evil principle had possessed more sway than they are at liberty to assign to it; the offender's condition would not then have been so hopeless. For malignity *selects* its diet; but where is to be found the nourishment from which vanity will revolt? Malignity may be appeased by triumphs real or supposed, and will then sleep, or yield its place to a repentance producing dispositions of good will, and desires to make amends for past injury; but vanity is restless, reckless, intractable, unappeasable, insatiable. Fortunate is it for the world when this spirit incites only to actions that meet with an adequate pun-

° A friend, who chances to be present while the author is correcting the proof sheets, observes that Aristarchus is libelled by this application of his name, and advises that 'Zoilus' should be substituted. The question lies between spite and presumption; and it is not easy to decide upon a case where the claims of each party are so strong: but the name of Aristarch, who, simple man! would allow no verse to pass for Homer's which he did not approve of, is retained, for reasons that will be deemed cogent.

ishment in derision; such, as in a scheme of poetical justice,
would be aptly requited by assigning to the agents, when they
quit this lower world, a station in that not uncomfortable limbo
—the Paradise of Fools! But, assuredly, we shall have here
another proof that ridicule is not the test of truth, if it prevent
us from perceiving, that *depravity* has no ally more active, more
inveterate, nor, from the difficulty of divining to what kind and
degree of extravagance it may prompt, more pernicious than
self-conceit. Where this alliance is too obvious to be disputed,
the culprit ought not to be allowed the benefit of contempt—as
a shelter from detestation; much less should he be permitted
to plead, in excuse for his transgressions, that especial malevolence had little or no part in them. It is not recorded, that
the ancient, who set fire to the temple of Diana, had a particular
dislike to the goddess of chastity, or held idolatry in abhorrence:
he was a fool, an egregious fool, but not the less, on that account, a most odious monster. The tyrant who is described as
having rattled his chariot along a bridge of brass over the heads
of his subjects, was, no doubt, inwardly laughed at; but what
if this mock Jupiter, not satisfied with an empty noise of his
own making, had amused himself with throwing fire-brands upon
the house-tops, as a substitute for lightning; and, from his
elevation, had hurled stones upon the heads of his people, to
show that he was a master of the destructive bolt, as well as of
the harmless voice of the thunder!—The lovers of all that is
honourable to humanity have recently had occasion to rejoice
over the downfal of an intoxicated despot, whose vagaries furnish
more solid materials by which the philosopher will exemplify
how strict is the connection between the ludicrously, and the
terribly fantastic. We know, also, that Robespierre was one of
the vainest men that the most vain country upon earth has produced;—and from this passion, and from that cowardice which
naturally connects itself with it, flowed the horrors of his administration. It is a descent, which I fear you will scarcely
pardon, to compare these redoubtable enemies of mankind with
the anonymous conductor of a perishable publication. But the
moving spirit is the same in them all; and, as far as difference
of circumstances, and disparity of powers, will allow, manifests
itself in the same way; by professions of reverence for truth,
and concern for duty—carried to the giddiest heights of osten-

tation, while practice seems to have no other reliance than on the omnipotence of falsehood.

The transition from a vindication of Robert Burns to these hints for a picture of the intellectual deformity of one who has grossly outraged his memory, is too natural to require an apology : but I feel, sir, that I stand in need of indulgence for having detained you so long. Let me beg that you would impart to any judicious friends of the poet as much of the contents of these pages as you think will be serviceable to the cause ; but do not give publicity to any *portion* of them, unless it be thought probable that an open circulation of the whole may be useful.* The subject is delicate, and some of the opinions are of a kind, which, if torn away from the trunk that supports them, will be apt to wither, and, in that state, to contract poisonous qualities ; like the branches of the yew, which, while united by a living spirit to their native tree, are neither noxious, nor without beauty ; but, being dissevered and cast upon the ground, become deadly to the cattle that incautiously feed upon them.

To Mr. Gilbert Burns, especially, let my sentiments be conveyed, with my sincere respects, and best wishes for the success of his praise-worthy enterprize. And if, through modest apprehension, he should doubt of his own ability to do justice to his brother's memory, let him take encouragement from the assurance that the most odious part of the charges owed its credit to the silence of those who were deemed best entitled to speak ; and who, it was thought, would not have been mute, had they believed that they could speak beneficially. Moreover, it may be relied on as a general truth, which will not escape his recollection, that tasks of this kind are not so arduous as, to those who are tenderly concerned in their issue, they may at first appear to be ; for, if the many be hasty to condemn, there is a re-action of generosity which stimulates them—when forcibly summoned—to redress the wrong ; and, for the sensible part of mankind, *they* are neither dull to understand, nor slow to make allowance for, the aberrations of men, whose intellectual powers do honour to their species.

> I am, dear Sir, respectfully yours,
> WILLIAM WORDSWORTH.

Rydal Mount, January, 1816.

* It was deemed that it would be so, and the letter is published accordingly.

(b) OF MONUMENTS TO LITERARY MEN.

Letter to a Friend.

Rydal Mount, April 21. 1819.

SIR,

The letter with which you have honoured me, bearing date the 31st of March, I did not receive until yesterday; and, therefore, could not earlier express my regret that, notwithstanding a cordial approbation of the feeling which has prompted the undertaking, and a genuine sympathy in admiration with the gentlemen who have subscribed towards a Monument for Burns, I cannot unite my humble efforts with theirs in promoting this object.

Sincerely can I affirm that my respect for the motives which have swayed these gentlemen has urged me to trouble you with a brief statement of the reasons of my dissent.

In the first place : Eminent poets appear to me to be a class of men, who less than any others stand in need of such marks of distinction ; and hence I infer, that this mode of acknowledging their merits is one for which they would not, in general, be themselves solicitous. Burns did, indeed, erect a monument to Fergusson ; but I apprehend his gratitude took this course because he felt that Fergusson had been prematurely cut off, and that his fame bore no proportion to his deserts. In neither of these particulars can the fate of Burns justly be said to resemble that of his predecessor : his years were indeed few, but numerous enough to allow him to spread his name far and wide, and to take permanent root in the affections of his countrymen ; in short, he has raised for himself a monument so conspicuous, and of such imperishable materials, as to render a local fabric of stone superfluous, and, therefore, comparatively insignificant.

But why, if this be granted, should not his fond admirers be permitted to indulge their feelings, and at the same time to embellish the metropolis of Scotland ? If this may be justly objected to, and in my opinion it may, it is because the showy tributes to genius are apt to draw off attention from those efforts by which the interests of literature might be substantially promoted; and to exhaust public spirit in comparatively unprofitable exertions, when the wrongs of literary men are crying out for redress on all sides. It appears to me, that towards no class of his Majesty's subjects are the laws so unjust and oppressive. The attention of Parliament has lately been directed, by petition, to the exaction of copies of newly published works for certain libraries; but this is a trifling evil compared with the restrictions imposed upon the duration of copyright, which, in respect to works profound in philosophy, or elevated, abstracted, and refined in imagination, is tantamount almost to an exclusion of the author from all pecuniary recompence; and, even where works of imagination and manners are so constituted as to be adapted to immediate demand, as is the case of those of Burns, justly may it be asked, what reason can be assigned that an author who dies young should have the prospect before him of his children being left to languish in poverty and dependence, while booksellers are revelling in luxury upon gains derived from works which are the delight of many nations.

This subject might be carried much further, and we might ask, if the course of things insured immediate wealth, and accompanying rank and honours—honours and wealth often entailed on their families to men distinguished in the other learned professions,—why the laws should interfere to take away those pecuniary emoluments which are the natural inheritance of the posterity of authors, whose pursuits, if directed by genius and sustained by industry, yield in importance to none in which the members of a community can be engaged?

But to recur to the proposal in your letter. I would readily assist, according to my means, in erecting a monument to the memory of the Poet Chatterton, who, with transcendent genius, was cut off while he was yet a boy in years; this, could he have anticipated the tribute, might have soothed his troubled spirit, as an expression of general belief in the existence of those powers which he was too impatient and too proud to develope. At all events, it might prove an awful and a profitable warning. I should also be glad to see a monument erected on the banks of Loch Leven to the memory of the innocent and tender-hearted Michael Bruce, who, after a short life, spent in poverty and obscurity, was called away too early to have left behind him more than a few trustworthy promises of pure affections and unvitiated imagination.

Let the gallant defenders of our country be liberally rewarded with monuments ; their noble actions cannot speak for themselves, as the writings of men of genius are able to do. Gratitude in respect to them stands in need of admonition ; and the very multitude of heroic competitors which increases the demand for this sentiment towards our naval and military defenders, considered as a body, is injurious to the claims of individuals. Let our great statesmen and eminent lawyers, our learned and eloquent divines, and they who have successfully devoted themselves to the abstruser sciences, be rewarded in like manner ; but towards departed genius, exerted in the fine arts, and more especially in poetry, I humbly think, in the present state of things, the sense of our obligation to it may more satisfactorily be expressed by means pointing directly to the general benefit of literature.

Trusting that these opinions of an individual will be candidly interpreted, I have the honour to be

Your obedient servant,

W. WORDSWORTH.*

* *Memoirs*, ii. 88-91.

Letter to John Peace, Esq., City Library, Bristol.

Rydal Mount, April 8. 1844.

My DEAR MR. PEACE,

You have gratified me by what you say of Sir Thomas
Browne. I possess his *Religio Medici, Christian Morals, Vulgar
Errors,* &c. in separate publications, and value him highly as a
most original author. I almost regret that you did not add his
Treatise upon *Urn Burial* to your publication; it is not long,
and very remarkable for the vigour of mind that it displays.

Have you had any communication with Mr. Cottle upon the
subject of the subscription which he has set on foot for the
erection of a *Monument* to Southey in Bristol Cathedral? We
are all engaged in a like tribute to be placed in the parish church
of Keswick. For my own part, I am not particularly fond of
placing monuments in *churches*, at least in modern times. I
should prefer their being put in public places in the town with
which the party was connected by birth or otherwise; or in the
country, if he were a person who lived apart from the bustle of
the world. And in Southey's case, I should have liked better a
bronze bust, in some accessible and not likely to be disturbed
part of St. Vincent's Rocks, as a site, than the cathedral.

Thanks for your congratulations upon my birthday. I have
now entered, awful thought! upon my 75th year.

God bless you, and believe me, my dear friend,

Ever faithfully yours,

WM. WORDSWORTH.

Mrs. Wordsworth begs her kind remembrance, as does Miss
Fenwick, who is with us.*

° *Memoirs,* ii. 91-2.

II. UPON EPITAPHS.

(*a*) From ' The Friend.'
(*b* and *c*) From the Author's Mss.

(a) UPON EPITAPHS.

From ' The Friend,' Feb. 22, 1810.

IT needs scarcely be said, that an Epitaph presupposes a Monument, upon which it is to be engraven. Almost all Nations
have wished that certain external signs should point out the
places where their dead are interred. Among savage tribes un-
acquainted with letters this has mostly been done either by rude
stones placed near the graves, or by mounds of earth raised
over them. This custom proceeded obviously from a twofold
desire; first, to guard the remains of the deceased from irreverent approach or from savage violation : and, secondly, to preserve their memory. ' Never any,' says Camden, 'neglected
burial but some savage nations ; as the Bactrians, which cast
their dead to the dogs ; some varlet philosophers, as Diogenes,
who desired to be devoured of fishes ; some dissolute courtiers,
as Mæcenas, who was wont to say, Non tumulum curo ; sepelit
natura relictos.

I'm careless of a grave :—Nature her dead will save.

As soon as nations had learned the use of letters, epitaphs
were inscribed upon these monuments ; in order that their intention might be more surely and adequately fulfilled. I have
derived monuments and epitaphs from two sources of feeling :
but these do in fact resolve themselves into one. The invention of epitaphs, Weever, in his *Discourse of Funeral Monuments*, says rightly, ' proceeded from the presage of fore-feeling
of immortality, implanted in all men naturally, and is referred
to the scholars of Linus the Theban poet, who flourished about
the year of the world two thousand seven hundred ; who first
bewailed this Linus their Master, when he was slain, in doleful
verses, then called of him Œlina, afterwards Epitaphia, for that
they were first sung at burials, after engraved upon the sepul-
chres.'

And, verily, without the consciousness of a principle of immortality in the human soul, Man could never have had awakened

in him the desire to live in the remembrance of his fellows : mere love, or the yearning of kind towards kind, could not have produced it. The dog or horse perishes in the field, or in the stall, by the side of his companions, and is incapable of antici- pating the sorrow with which his surrounding associates shall bemoan his death, or pine for his loss ; he cannot pre-conceive this regret, he can form no thought of it ; and therefore cannot possibly have a desire to leave such regret or remembrance be- hind him. Add to the principle of love which exists in the in- ferior animals, the faculty of reason which exists in Man alone ; will the conjunction of these account for the desire ? Doubtless it is a necessary consequence of this conjunction ; yet not I think as a direct result, but only to be come at through an in- termediate thought, viz. that of an intimation or assurance within us, that some part of our nature is imperishable. At least the precedence, in order of birth, of one feeling to the other, is unquestionable. If we look back upon the days of childhood, we shall find that the time is not in remembrance when, with respect to our own individual Being, the mind was without this assurance ; whereas, the wish to be remembered by our friends or kindred after death, or even in absence, is, as we shall discover, a sensation that does not form itself till the *social* feelings have been developed, and the Reason has con- nected itself with a wide range of objects. Forlorn, and cut off from communication with the best part of his nature, must that man be, who should derive the sense of immortality, as it exists in the mind of a child, from the same unthinking gaiety or live- liness of animal spirits with which the lamb in the meadow, or any other irrational creature is endowed ; who should ascribe it, in short, to blank ignorance in the child ; to an inability arising from the imperfect state of his faculties to come, in any point of his being, into contact with a notion of death ; or to an unreflecting acquiescence in what had been instilled into him ! Has such an unfolder of the mysteries of nature, though he may have forgotten his former self, ever noticed the early, ob- stinate, and unappeasable inquisitiveness of children upon the subject of origination ? This single fact proves outwardly the monstrousness of those suppositions : for, if we had no direct external testimony that the minds of very young children medi- tate feelingly upon death and immortality, these inquiries, which we all know they are perpetually making concerning the *whence*, do necessarily include correspondent habits of interrogation concerning the *whither*. Origin and tendency are notions inseparably co-relative. Never did a child stand by the side of a running stream, pondering within himself what power was the feeder of the perpetual current, from what never-wearied sources the body of water was supplied, but he must have been inevitably propelled to follow this question by another : 'Towards what abyss is it in progress ? what receptacle can contain the mighty influx ?' And the spirit of the answer must have been, though the word might be sea or ocean, accompanied perhaps with an image gathered from a map, or from the real object in nature—these might have been the *letter*, but the *spirit* of the answer must have been *as* inevitably,—a receptacle without bounds or dimensions;—nothing less than infinity. We may, then, be justified in asserting, that the sense of immortality, if not a co-existent and twin birth with Reason, is among the earliest of her offspring : and we may further assert, that from these conjoined, and under their countenance, the human affections are gradually formed and opened out. This is not the place to enter into the recesses of these investigations ; but the subject requires me here to make a plain avowal, that, for my own part, it is to me inconceivable, that the sympathies of love towards each other, which grow with our growth, could ever attain any new strength, or even preserve the old, after we had received from the outward senses the impression of death, and were in the habit of having that impression daily renewed and its accompanying feeling brought home to ourselves, and to those we love ; if the same were not counteracted by those communications with our internal Being, which are anterior to all these experiences, and with which revelation coincides, and has through that coincidence alone (for otherwise it could not possess it) a power to affect us. I confess, with me the conviction is absolute, that, if the impression and sense of death were not thus counterbalanced, such a hollowness would pervade the whole system of things, such a want of correspondence and consistency, a disproportion so astounding betwixt means and ends, that there could be no repose, no joy. Were we to grow up unfostered by this genial warmth, a frost would chill the spirit, so penetrating and powerful, that there could be no motions of the life of love; and infinitely less could we have any wish to be remembered after we had passed away from a world in which each man had moved about like a shadow.—If, then, in a creature endowed with the faculties of foresight and reason, the social affections could not have unfolded themselves uncountenanced by the faith that Man is an immortal being; and if, consequently, neither could the individual dying have had a desire to survive in the remembrance of his fellows, nor on their side could they have felt a wish to preserve for future times vestiges of the departed; it follows, as a final inference, that without the belief in immortality, wherein these several desires originate, neither monuments nor epitaphs, in affectionate or laudatory commemoration of the deceased, could have existed in the world.

Simonides, it is related, upon landing in a strange country, found the corse of an unknown person lying by the sea-side; he buried it, and was honoured throughout Greece for the piety of that act. Another ancient Philosopher, chancing to fix his eyes upon a dead body, regarded the same with slight, if not with contempt; saying, ' See the shell of the flown bird !' But it is not to be supposed that the moral and tender-hearted Simonides was incapable of the lofty movements of thought, to which that other Sage gave way at the moment while his soul was intent only upon the indestructible being; nor, on the other hand, that he, in whose sight a lifeless human body was of no more value than the worthless shell from which the living fowl had departed, would not, in a different mood of mind, have been affected by those earthly considerations which had incited the philosophic Poet to the performance of that pious duty. And with regard to this latter we may be assured that, if he had been destitute of the capability of communing with the more exalted thoughts that appertain to human nature, he would have cared no more for the corse of the stranger than for the dead body of a seal or porpoise which might have been cast up by the waves. We respect the corporeal frame of Man, not merely because it is the habitation of a rational, but of an immortal Soul. Each of these Sages was in sympathy with the best feelings of our nature ; feelings which, though they seem opposite to each other, have another and a finer connection than that of contrast.—It is a connection formed through the subtle process by which, both in the natural and the moral world, qualities pass insensibly into their contraries, and things revolve upon each other. As, in sailing upon the orb of this planet, a voyage towards the regions where the sun sets, conducts gradually to the quarter where we have been accustomed to behold it come forth at its rising; and, in like manner, a voyage towards the east, the birth-place in our imagination of the morning, leads finally to the quarter where the sun is last seen when he departs from our eyes; so the contemplative Soul, travelling in the direction of mortality, advances to the country of everlasting life; and, in like manner, may she continue to explore those cheerful tracts, till she is brought back, for her advantage and benefit, to the land of transitory things—of sorrow and of tears.

On a midway point, therefore, which commands the thoughts and feelings of the two Sages whom we have represented in contrast, does the Author of that species of composition, the laws of which it is our present purpose to explain, take his stand. Accordingly, recurring to the twofold desire of guarding the remains of the deceased and preserving their memory, it may be said that a sepulchral monument is a tribute to a man as a human being; and that an epitaph (in the ordinary meaning attached to the word) includes this general feeling and something more; and is a record to preserve the memory of the dead, as a tribute due to his individual worth, for a satisfaction to the sorrowing hearts of the survivors, and for the common benefit of the living: which record is to be accomplished, not in a general manner, but, where it can, in *close connection with the bodily remains of the deceased:* and these, it may be added, among the modern nations of Europe, are deposited within, or contiguous to, their places of worship. In ancient times, as is well known, it was the custom to bury the dead beyond the walls of towns and cities; and among the Greeks and Romans they were frequently interred by the way-sides.

I could here pause with pleasure, and invite the Reader to indulge with me in contemplation of the advantages which must have attended such a practice. We might ruminate upon the beauty which the monuments, thus placed, must have borrowed from the surrounding images of nature—from the trees, the wild flowers, from a stream running perhaps within sight or hearing, from the beaten road stretching its weary length hard by. Many tender similitudes must these objects have presented to the mind of the traveller leaning upon one of the tombs, or reposing in the coolness of its shade, whether he had halted from weariness or in compliance with the invitation, 'Pause, Traveller!' so often found upon the monuments. And to its epitaph also must have been supplied strong appeals to visible appearances or immediate impressions, lively and affecting analogies of life as a journey—death as a sleep overcoming the tired wayfarer—of misfortune as a storm that falls suddenly upon him—of beauty as a flower that passeth away, or of innocent pleasure as one that may be gathered—of virtue that standeth firm as a rock against the beating waves;—of hope 'undermined insensibly like the poplar by the side of the river that has fed it,' or blasted in a moment like a pine-tree by the stroke of lightning upon the mountain-top—of admonitions and heart-stirring remembrances, like a refreshing breeze that comes without warning, or the taste of the waters of an unexpected fountain. These, and similar suggestions, must have given, formerly, to the language of the senseless stone a voice enforced and endeared by the benignity of that Nature with which it was in unison.—We, in modern times, have lost much of these advantages; and they are but in a small degree counterbalanced to the inhabitants of large towns and cities, by the custom of depositing the dead within, or contiguous to, their places of worship; however splendid or imposing may be the appearance of those edifices, or however interesting or salutary the recollections associated with them. Even were it not true that tombs lose their monitory virtue when thus obtruded upon the notice of men occupied with the cares of the world, and too often sullied and defiled by those cares, yet still, when death is in our thoughts, nothing can make amends for the want of the soothing influences of Nature, and for the absence of those types of renovation and decay, which the fields and woods offer to the notice of the serious and contemplative mind. To feel the force of this sentiment, let a man only compare in imagination the unsightly manner in which our monuments are crowded together in the busy, noisy, unclean, and almost grassless church-yard of a large town, with the still seclusion of a Turkish cemetery, in some remote place; and yet further sanctified by the grove of cypress in which it is embosomed. Thoughts in the same temper as these have already been expressed with true sensibility by an ingenuous Poet of the present day. The subject of his poem is 'All Saints Church, Derby :' he has been deploring the forbidding and unseemly appearance of its burial-ground, and uttering a wish, that in past times the practice had been adopted of interring the inhabitants of large towns in the country.—

> Then in some rural, calm, sequestered spot,
> Where healing Nature her benignant look
> Ne'er changes, save at that lorn season, when,
> With tresses drooping o'er her sable stole,
> She yearly mourns the mortal doom of man,
> Her noblest work, (so Israel's virgins erst,
> With annual moan upon the mountains wept
> Their fairest gone,) there in that rural scene,
> So placid, so congenial to the wish
> The Christian feels, of peaceful rest within
> The silent grave, I would have stayed :
>
> .   .   .   .   .   .
> —wandered forth, where the cold dew of heaven
> Lay on the humbler graves around, what time
> The pale moon gazed upon the turfy mounds,
> Pensive, as though like me, in lonely muse,
> Twere brooding on the dead inhumed beneath.
> There while with him, the holy man of Uz,
> O'er human destiny I sympathised,
> Counting the long, long periods prophecy
> Decrees to roll, ere the great day arrives
> Of resurrection, oft the blue-eyed Spring
> Had met me with her blossoms, as the Dove,
> Of old, returned with olive leaf, to cheer
> The Patriarch mourning o'er a world destroyed :
> And I would bless her visit ; for to me
> 'Tis sweet to trace the consonance that links
> As one, the works of Nature and the word
> Of God.—   JOHN EDWARDS.

A village church-yard, lying as it does in the lap of Nature, may indeed be most favourably contrasted with that of a town of crowded population ; and sepulture therein combines many of the best tendencies which belong to the mode practised by the Ancients, with others peculiar to itself. The sensations of pious cheerfulness, which attend the celebration of the sabbath-day in rural places, are profitably chastised by the sight of the graves of kindred and friends, gathered together in that general home towards which the thoughtful yet happy spectators themselves are journeying. Hence a parish-church, in the stillness of the country, is a visible centre of a community of the living and the dead; a point to which are habitually referred the nearest concerns of both.

As, then, both in cities and villages, the dead are deposited in close connection with our places of worship, with us the composition of an epitaph naturally turns, still more than among the nations of antiquity, upon the most serious and solemn affections of the human mind; upon departed worth—upon personal or social sorrow and admiration—upon religion, individual and social—upon time, and upon eternity. Accordingly, it suffices, in ordinary cases, to secure a composition of this kind from censure, that it contain nothing that shall shock or be inconsistent with this spirit. But, to entitle an epitaph to praise, more than this is necessary. It ought to contain some thought or feeling belonging to the mortal or immortal part of our nature touchingly expressed; and if that be done, however general or even trite the sentiment may be, every man of pure mind will read the words with pleasure and gratitude. A husband bewails a wife; a parent breathes a sigh of disappointed hope over a lost child; a son utters a sentiment of filial reverence for a departed father or mother; a friend perhaps inscribes an encomium recording the companionable qualities, or the solid virtues, of the tenant of the grave, whose departure has left a sadness upon his memory. This and a pious admonition to the living, and a humble expression of Christian confidence in immortality, is the language of a thousand church-yards; and it does not often happen that anything, in a greater degree discriminate or appropriate to the dead or to the living, is to be found in them. This want of discrimination has been ascribed by Dr. Johnson, in his Essay upon the epitaphs of Pope, to two causes; first, the scantiness of the objects of human praise; and, secondly, the want of variety in the characters of men; or, to use his own words, ' to the fact, that the greater part of mankind have no character at all.' Such language may be holden without blame among the generalities of common conversation; but does not become a critic and a moralist speaking seriously upon a serious subject. The objects of admiration in human nature are not scanty, but abundant: and every man has a character of his own, to the eye that has skill to perceive it. The real cause of the acknowledged want of discrimination in sepulchral memorials is this : That to analyse the characters of others, especially of those whom we love, is not a common or natural employment of men at any time. We are not anxious unerringly to understand the constitution of the minds of those who have soothed, who have cheered, who have supported us : with whom we have been long and daily pleased or delighted. The affections are their own justification. The light of love in our hearts is a satisfactory evidence that there is a body of worth in the minds of our friends or kindred, whence that light has proceeded. We shrink from the thought of placing their merits and defects to be weighed against each other in the nice balance of pure intellect; nor do we find much temptation to detect the shades by which a good quality or virtue is discriminated in them from an excellence known by the same general name as it exists in the mind of another ; and, least of all, do we incline to these refinements when under the pressure of sorrow, admiration, or regret, or when actuated by any of those feelings which incite men to prolong the memory of their friends and kindred, by records placed in the bosom of the all-uniting and equalising receptacle of the dead.

The first requisite, then, in an Epitaph is, that it should speak, in a tone which shall sink into the heart, the general language of humanity as connected with the subject of death— the source from which an epitaph proceeds—of death, and of life. To be born and to die are the two points in which all men feel themselves to be in absolute coincidence. This general language may be uttered so strikingly as to entitle an epitaph to high praise ; yet it cannot lay claim to the highest unless other excellencies be superadded. Passing through all intermediate steps, we will attempt to determine at once what these excellencies are, and wherein consists the perfection of this species of composition.—It will be found to lie in a due proportion of the common or universal feeling of humanity to sensations excited by a distinct and clear conception, conveyed to the reader's mind, of the individual, whose death is deplored and whose memory is to be preserved; at least of his character as, after death, it appeared to those who loved him and lament his loss. The general sympathy ought to be quickened, provoked, and diversified, by particular thoughts, actions, images,—circumstances of age, occupation, manner of life, prosperity which the deceased had known, or adversity to which he had been subject; and these ought to be bound together and solemnised into one harmony by the general sympathy. The two powers should temper, restrain, and exalt each other. The reader ought to know who and what the man was whom he is called upon to think of with interest. A distinct conception should be given (implicitly where it can, rather than explicitly) of the individual lamented. —But the writer of an epitaph is not an anatomist, who dissects the internal frame of the mind; he is not even a painter, who executes a portrait at leisure and in entire tranquillity; his delineation, we must remember, is performed by the side of the grave; and, what is more, the grave of one whom he loves and admires. What purity and brightness is that virtue clothed in, the image of which must no longer bless our living eyes! The character of a deceased friend or beloved kinsman is not seen, no—nor ought to be seen, otherwise than as a tree through a tender haze or a luminous mist, that spiritualises and beautifies it; that takes away, indeed, but only to the end that the parts which are not abstracted may appear more dignified and lovely; may impress and affect the more. Shall we say, then, that this is not truth, not a faithful image; and that, accordingly, the purposes of commemoration cannot be answered?—It *is* truth, and of the highest order; for, though doubtless things are not apparent which did exist; yet, the object being looked at through this medium, parts and proportions are brought into distinct view which before had been only imperfectly or unconsciously seen: it is truth hallowed by love—the joint offspring of the worth of the dead and the affections of the living! This may easily be brought to the test. Let one, whose eyes have been sharpened by personal hostility to discover what was amiss in the character of a good man, hear the tidings of his death, and what a change is wrought in a moment! Enmity melts away; and, as it disappears, unsightliness, disproportion, and deformity, vanish; and, through the influence of commiseration, a harmony of love and beauty succeeds. Bring such a man to the tombstone on which shall be inscribed an epitaph on his adversary, composed in the spirit which we have recommended. Would he turn from it as from an idle tale? No;—the thoughtful look, the sigh, and perhaps the involuntary tear, would testify that it had a sane, a generous, and good meaning; and that on the writer's mind had remained an impression which was a true abstract of the character of the deceased; that his gifts and graces were remembered in the simplicity in which they ought to be remembered. The composition and quality of the mind of a virtuous man, contemplated by the side of the grave where his body is mouldering, ought to appear, and be felt as something midway between what he was on earth walking about with his living frailties, and what he may be presumed to be as a spirit in heaven.

It suffices, therefore, that the trunk and the main branches of the worth of the deceased be boldly and unaffectedly represented. Any further detail, minutely and scrupulously pursued, especially if this be done with laborious and antithetic discriminations, must inevitably frustrate its own purpose; forcing the passing Spectator to this conclusion,—either that the dead did not possess the merits ascribed to him, or that they who have raised a monument to his memory, and must therefore be supposed to have been closely connected with him, were incapable of perceiving those merits; or at least during the act of composition had lost sight of them; for, the understanding having been so busy in its petty occupation, how could the heart of the mourner be other than cold? and in either of these cases, whether the fault be on the part of the buried person or the survivors, the memorial is unaffecting and profitless.

Much better is it to fall short in discrimination than to pursue it too far, or to labour it unfeelingly. For in no place are we so much disposed to dwell upon those points, of nature and condition, wherein all men resemble each other, as in the temple where the universal Father is worshipped, or by the side of the grave which gathers all human Beings to itself, and ' equalises the lofty and the low.' We suffer and we weep with the same heart; we love and are anxious for one another in one spirit; our hopes look to the same quarter; and the virtues by which we are all to be furthered and supported, as patience, meekness, good-will, justice, temperance, and temperate desires, are in an equal degree the concern of us all. Let an Epitaph, then, contain at least these acknowledgments to our common nature; nor let the sense of their importance be sacrificed to a balance of opposite qualities or minute distinctions in individual character; which if they do not, (as will for the most part be the case,) when examined, resolve themselves into a trick of words, will, even when they are true and just, for the most part be grievously out of place; for, as it is probable that few only have explored these intricacies of human nature, so can the tracing of them be interesting only to a few. But an epitaph is not a proud writing shut up for the studious: it is exposed to all—to the wise and the most ignorant; it is condescending, perspicuous, and lovingly solicits regard; its story and admonitions are brief, that the thoughtless, the busy, and indolent, may not be deterred, nor the impatient tired: the stooping old man cons the engraven record like a second horn-book;—the child is proud that he can read it;—and the stranger is introduced through its mediation to the company of a friend: it is concerning all, and for all:—in the church-yard it is open to the day; the sun looks down upon the stone, and the rains of heaven beat against it.

Yet, though the writer who would excite sympathy is bound in this case, more than in any other, to give proof that he himself has been moved, it is to be remembered, that to raise a monument is a sober and a reflective act; that the inscription which it bears is intended to be permanent, and for universal perusal; and that, for this reason, the thoughts and feelings expressed should be permanent also—liberated from that weakness and anguish of sorrow which is in nature transitory, and which with instinctive decency retires from notice. The passions should be subdued, the emotions controlled; strong, indeed, but nothing ungovernable or wholly involuntary. Seemliness requires this, and truth requires it also: for how can the narrator otherwise be trusted? Moreover, a grave is a tranquillising object: resignation in course of time springs up from it as naturally as the wild flowers, besprinkling the turf with which it may be covered, or gathering round the monument by which it is defended. The very form and substance of the monument which has received the inscription, and the appearance of the letters, testifying with what a slow and laborious hand they must have been engraven, might seem to reproach the author who had given way upon this occasion to transports of mind, or to quick turns of conflicting passion; though the same might constitute the life and beauty of a funeral oration or elegiac poem.

These sensations and judgments, acted upon perhaps unconsciously, have been one of the main causes why epitaphs so often personate the deceased, and represent him as speaking from his own tomb-stone. The departed Mortal is introduced telling you himself that his pains are gone ; that a state of rest is come ; and he conjures you to weep for him no longer. He admonishes with the voice of one experienced in the vanity of those affections which are confined to earthly objects, and gives a verdict like a superior Being, performing the office of a judge, who has no temptations to mislead him, and whose decision cannot but be dispassionate. Thus is death disarmed of its sting, and affliction unsubstantialised. By this tender fiction, the survivors bind themselves to a sedater sorrow, and employ the intervention of the imagination in order that the reason may speak her own language earlier than she would otherwise have been enabled to do. This shadowy interposition also harmoniously unites the two worlds of the living and the dead by their appropriate affections. And it may be observed, that here we have an additional proof of the propriety with which sepulchral inscriptions were referred to the consciousness of immortality as their primal source.

I do not speak with a wish to recommend that an epitaph should be cast in this mould preferably to the still more common one, in which what is said comes from the survivors directly ; but rather to point out how natural those feelings are which have induced men, in all states and ranks of society, so frequently to adopt this mode. And this I have done chiefly in order that the laws, which ought to govern the composition of the other, may be better understood. This latter mode, namely, that in which the survivors speak in their own persons, seems to me upon the whole greatly preferable : as it admits a wider range of notices ; and, above all, because, excluding the fiction which is the groundwork of the other, it rests upon a more solid basis.

Enough has been said to convey our notion of a perfect epitaph ; but it must be borne in mind that one is meant which will best answer the *general* ends of that species of composition. According to the course pointed out, the worth of private life, through all varieties of situation and character, will be most honourably and profitably preserved in memory. Nor would the model recommended less suit public men, in all instances save of those persons who by the greatness of their services in the employments of peace or war, or by the surpassing excellence of their works in art, literature, or science, have made themselves not only universally known, but have filled the heart of their country with everlasting gratitude. Yet I must here pause to correct myself. In describing the general tenor of thought which epitaphs ought to hold, I have omitted to say, that if it be the *actions* of a man, or even some *one* conspicuous or beneficial act of local or general utility, which have distinguished him, and excited a desire that he should be remembered, then, of course, ought the attention to be directed chiefly to those actions or that act: and such sentiments dwelt upon as naturally arise out of them or it. Having made this necessary distinction, I proceed.—The mighty benefactors of mankind, as they are not only known by the immediate survivors, but will continue to be known familiarly to latest posterity, do not stand in need of biographic sketches, in such a place; nor of delineations of character to individualise them. This is already done by their Works, in the memories of men. Their naked names, and a grand comprehensive sentiment of civic gratitude, patriotic love, or human admiration—or the utterance of some elementary principle most essential in the constitution of true virtue;—or a declaration touching that pious humility and self-abasement, which are ever most profound as minds are most susceptible of genuine exaltation—or an intuition, communicated in adequate words, of the sublimity of intellectual power;—these are the only tribute which can here be paid—the only offering that upon such an altar would not be unworthy.

> What needs my Shakspeare for his honoured bones
> The labour of an age in pilèd stones,
> Or that his hallowed reliques should be hid
> Under a star y-pointing pyramid?
> Dear Son of Memory, great Heir of Fame,
> What need'st thou such weak witness of thy name?
> Thou in our wonder and astonishment
> Hast built thyself a livelong monument,
> And so sepulchred, in such pomp dost lie,
> That kings for such a tomb would wish to die.

From the Author's Mss.

. Yet even these bones from insult to protect
Some frail memorial still erected nigh,
With uncouth rhymes and shapeless sculpture deck'd,
Implores the passing tribute of a sigh.
Their name, their years, spelt by the unletter'd Muse,
The place of fame and elegy supply,
And many a holy text around she strews,
That teach the rustic moralist to die.

WHEN a Stranger has walked round a Country Church-yard and
glanced his eye over so many brief chronicles, as the tomb-stones
usually contain, of faithful wives, tender husbands, dutiful
children, and good men of all classes ; he will be tempted to
exclaim in the language of one of the characters of a modern
Tale, in a similar situation, 'Where are all the *bad* people
buried ?' He may smile to himself an answer to this question,
and may regret that it has intruded upon him so soon. For my
own part such has been my lot ; and indeed a man, who is in
the habit of suffering his mind to be carried passively towards
truth as well as of going with conscious effort in search of it,
may be forgiven, if he has sometimes insensibly yielded to the
delusion of those flattering recitals, and found a pleasure in
believing that the prospect of real life had been as fair as it was
in that picture represented. And such a transitory oversight
will without difficulty be forgiven by those who have observed a
trivial fact in daily life, namely, how apt, in a series of calm
weather, we are to forget that rain and storms have been, and
will return to interrupt any scheme of business or pleasure which
our minds are occupied in arranging. Amid the quiet of a
church-yard thus decorated as it seemed by the hand of Memory,
and shining, if I may so say, in the light of love, I have been
affected by sensations akin to those which have risen in my mind

while I have been standing by the side of a smooth sea, on a Summer's day. It is such a happiness to have, in an unkind world, one enclosure where the voice of Detraction is not heard; where the traces of evil inclinations are unknown; where contentment prevails, and there is no jarring tone in the peaceful concert of amity and gratitude. I have been rouzed from this reverie by a consciousness suddenly flashing upon me, of the anxieties, the perturbations, and in many instances, the vices and rancorous dispositions, by which the hearts of those who lie under so smooth a surface and so fair an outside have been agitated. The image of an unruffled sea has still remained; but my fancy has penetrated into the depths of that sea,—with accompanying thoughts of shipwreck, of the destruction of the mariner's hopes, the bones of drowned men heaped together, monsters of the deep, and all the hideous and confused sights which Clarence saw in his dream.

Nevertheless, I have been able to return (and who may *not?*) to a steady contemplation of the benign influence of such a favourable Register lying open to the eyes of all. Without being so far lulled as to imagine I saw in a village church-yard the eye or central point of a rural Arcadia, I have felt that with all the vague and general expressions of love, gratitude, and praise, with which it is usually crowded, it is a far more faithful representation of homely life as existing among a community in which circumstances have not been untoward, than any report which might be made by a rigorous observer deficient in that spirit of forbearance and those kindly prepossessions, without which human life can in no condition be profitably looked at or described. For we must remember that it is the nature of vice to force itself upon notice, both in the act and by its consequences. Drunkenness, cruelty, brutal manners, sensuality and impiety, thoughtless prodigality and idleness, are obstreperous while they are in the height and heyday of their enjoyment; and when that is passed away, long and obtrusive is the train of misery which they draw after them. But on the contrary, the virtues, especially those of humble life, are retired; and many of the highest must be sought for or they will be overlooked. Industry, economy, temperance, and cleanliness, are indeed made obvious by flourishing fields, rosy complexions, and smiling countenances; but how few know anything of the trials to which men

in a lonely condition are subject, or of the steady and triumph-
ant manner in which those trials are often sustained, but they
themselves? The afflictions which peasants and rural citizens
have to struggle with are for the most part secret; the tears
which they wipe away, and the sighs which they stifle,—this is
all a labour of privacy. In fact their victories are to themselves
known only imperfectly; for it is inseparable from virtue, in the
pure sense of the word, to be unconscious of the might of her
own prowess. This is true of minds the most enlightened by
reflection; who have forecast what they may have to endure,
and prepared themselves accordingly. It is true even of these,
when they are called into action, that they necessarily lose sight
of their own accomplishments and support their conflicts in
self-forgetfulness and humility. That species of happy ignorance, which is the consequence of these noble qualities, must
exist still more frequently, and in a greater degree, in those persons to whom duty has never been matter of laborious specula-
tion, and who have no intimations of the power to act and to
resist which is in them, till they are summoned to put it forth.
I could illustrate this by many examples, which are now before
my eyes; but it would detain me too long from my principal
subject which was to suggest reasons for believing that the
encomiastic language of rural tomb-stones does not so far exceed
reality as might lightly be supposed. Doubtless, an inattentive
or ill-disposed Observer, who should apply to surrounding cottages the knowledge which he may possess of any rural neighbourhood, would upon the first impulse confidently report that
there was little in their living inhabitants which reflected the
concord and the virtue there dwelt upon so fondly. Much has
been said in a former Paper tending to correct this disposition;
and which will naturally combine with the present considerations. Besides, to slight the uniform language of these memorials as on that account not trustworthy would obviously be unjustifiable.

Enter a church-yard by the sea-coast, and you will be almost
sure to find the tomb-stones crowded with metaphors taken from
the sea and a sea-faring life. These are uniformly in the same
strain; but surely we ought not thence to infer that the words
are used of course, without any heartfelt sense of their propriety.
Would not the contrary conclusion be right? But I will adduce

a fact which more than a hundred analogical arguments will
carry to the mind a conviction of the strength and sanctity of
those feelings which persons in humble stations of society connect with their departed friends and kindred. We learn from
the Statistical Account of Scotland that in some districts, a
general transfer of inhabitants has taken place ; and that a
great majority of those who live, and labour, and attend public
worship in one part of the country, are buried in another.
Strong and unconquerable still continues to be the desire of all,
that their bones should rest by the side of their forefathers, and
very poor persons provide that their bodies should be conveyed
if necessary to a great distance to obtain that last satisfaction.
Nor can I refrain from saying that this natural interchange by
which the living inhabitants of a parish have small knowledge of
the dead who are buried in their church-yard is grievously to be
lamented, wherever it exists. For it cannot fail to preclude not
merely much but the best part of the wholesome influence of
that communion between living and dead which the conjunction
in rural districts of the place of burial and place of worship tends
so effectually to promote. Finally, let us remember that if it be
the nature of man to be insensible to vexations and afflictions
when they have passed away, he is equally insensible to the
height and depth of his blessings till they are removed from
him. An experienced and well-regulated mind, will not, therefore, be insensible to this monotonous language of sorrow and
affectionate admiration ; but will find under that veil a substance
of individual truth. Yet upon all men, and upon such a mind
in particular, an Epitaph must strike with a gleam of pleasure,
when the expression is of that kind which carries conviction
to the heart at once that the author was a sincere mourner, and
that the inhabitant of the grave deserved to be so lamented.
This may be done sometimes by a naked ejaculation ; as in an
instance which a friend of mine met with in a church-yard in
Germany, thus literally translated : ' Ah ! they have laid in the
grave a brave man : he was to me more than many !'

> Ach ! sie haben
> Einen Braven
> Mann begraben
> Mir war er mehr als viele.

An effect as pleasing is often produced by the recital of an affliction endured with fortitude, or of a privation submitted to with contentment; or by a grateful display of the temporal blessings with which Providence had favoured the deceased, and the happy course of life through which he had passed. And where these individualities are untouched upon, it may still happen that the estate of man in his helplessness, in his dependence upon his Maker, or some other inherent of his nature shall be movingly and profitably expressed. Every Reader will be able to supply from his own observation instances of all these kinds, and it will be more pleasing for him to refer to his memory than to have the page crowded with unnecessary quotations. I will however give one or two from an old book cited before. The following of general application, was a great favourite with our forefathers :

> Farwel my Frendys, the tyd abidyth no man,
>   I am departed hens, and so sal ye,
> But in this passage the best song I can
>   Is *Requiem Eternam*, now Jesu grant it me.
> When I have ended all myn adversity
> Grant me in Paradys to have a mansion
> That shedst Thy bloud for my redemption.

This epitaph might seem to be of the age of Chaucer, for it has the very tone and manner of the Prioress's Tale.

The next opens with a thought somewhat interrupting that complacency and gracious repose which the language and imagery of a church-yard tend to diffuse, but the truth is weighty and will not be less acceptable for the rudeness of the expression.

> When the bells be mearely roung
> And the Masse devoutly soung
> And the meate merrely eaten
> Then sall Robert Trappis his Wyffs and his Chyldren be
>   forgotten.
> Wherfor Iesu that of Mary sproung
> Set their soulys Thy Saynts among,
> Though it be undeservyd on their syde
> Yet good Lord let them evermor Thy mercy abyde!

It is well known how fond our ancestors were of a play upon the name of the deceased when it admitted of a double sense. The following is an instance of this propensity not idly indulged. It brings home a general truth to the individual by the medium of a pun, which will be readily pardoned for the sake of the image suggested by it, for the happy mood of mind in which the epitaph is composed, for the beauty of the language, and for the sweetness of the versification, which indeed, the date considered, is not a little curious. It is upon a man whose name was Palmer. I have modernized the spelling in order that its uncouthness may not interrupt the Reader's gratification.

> Palmers all our Fathers were .
> I a Palmer livèd here .
> And travelled still till worn with age
> I ended this world's pilgrimage,
> On the blest Ascension-day
> In the chearful month of May;
> One thousand with four hundred seven,
> And took my journey hence to heaven.

With this join the following, which was formerly to be seen upon a fair marble under the portraiture of one of the abbots of St. Albans.

> Hic quidem terra tegitur
> Peccati solvens debitum
> Cujus nomen non impositum
> In libro vitae sit inscriptum.

The spirit of it may be thus given : 'Here lies, covered by the earth, and paying his debt to sin, one whose name is not set forth : may it be inscribed in the Book of Life !'

But these instances, of the humility, the pious faith and simplicity of our forefathers, have led me from the scene of our contemplations—a Country Church-yard ! and from the memorials at this day commonly found in it. I began with noticing such as might be wholly uninteresting from the uniformity of the language which they exhibit ; because, without previously participating the truths upon which these general attestations are founded, it is impossible to arrive at that state of disposition of mind necessary to make those epitaphs thoroughly felt which have an especial recommendation. With the same view, I will venture to say a few words upon another characteristic of these compositions almost equally striking ; namely, the homeliness of some of the inscriptions, the strangeness of the illustrative images, the grotesque spelling, with the equivocal meaning often struck out by it, and the quaint jingle of the rhymes. These have often excited regret in serious minds, and provoked the unwilling to good-humoured laughter. Yet, for my own part, without affecting any superior sanctity, I must say that I have been better satisfied with myself, when in these evidences I have seen a proof how, deeply the piety of the rude forefathers of the hamlet, is seated in their natures; I mean how habitual and constitutional it is, and how awful the feeling which they attach to the situation of their departed friends,—a proof of this rather than of their ignorance or of a deadness in their faculties to a sense of the ridiculous. And that this deduction may be just, is rendered probable by the frequent occurrence of passages according to our present notion, full as ludicrous, in the writings of the most wise and learned men of former ages, divines and poets, who in the earnestness of their souls have applied metaphors and illustrations, taken either from Holy Writ or from the usages of their own country, in entire confidence that the sacredness of the theme they were discussing would sanctify the meanest object connected with it; or rather without ever conceiving it was possible that a ludicrous thought could spring up in any mind engaged in such meditations. And certainly, these odd and fantastic combinations are not confined to epitaphs of the peasantry, or of the lower orders of society, but are perhaps still more commonly produced among the higher, in a degree equally or more striking. For instance, what shall we say to this upon Sir George Vane, the noted Secretary of State to King Charles I. ?

> His Honour wonne i'th' field lies here in dust,
> His Honour got by grace shall never rust:
> The former fades, the latter shall fade never
> For why? He was Sʳ George once but Sᵗ George ever.

The date is 1679. When we reflect that the father of this personage must have had his taste formed in the punning Court of James I., and that the epitaph was composed at a time when our literature was stuffed with quaint or out-of-the-way thoughts, it will seem not unlikely that the author prided himself upon what he might call a clever hit: I mean his better affections were less occupied with the several associations belonging to the two ideas than his vanity delighted with that act of ingenuity by which they had been combined. But the first couplet consists of a just thought naturally expressed; and I should rather conclude the whole to be a work of honest simplicity; and that the

sense of worldly dignity associated with the title, in a degree
habitual to our ancestors, but which at this time we can but
feebly sympathize with, and the imaginative feeling involved—
viz. the saintly and chivalrous name of the cHampion of England, were unaffectedly linked together: and that both were
united and consolidated in the author's mind, and in the minds
of his contemporaries whom no doubt he had pleased, by a
devout contemplation of a happy immortality, the reward of the
just.

·At all events, leaving this particular case undecided, the
general propriety of these notices cannot be doubted ; and I gladly
avail myself of this opportunity to place in a clear view the
power and majesty of impassioned faith, whatever be its object :
to shew how it subjugates the lighter motions of the mind, and
sweeps away superficial difference in things.   And this I have
done, not to lower the witling and the worldling in their own
esteem, but with a wish to bring the ingenuous into still closer
communion with those primary sensations of the human heart,
which are the vital springs of sublime and pathetic composition,
in this and in every other kind.   And as from these primary sensations such composition speaks, so, unless correspondent ones
listen promptly and submissively in the inner cell of the mind
to whom it is addressed, the voice cannot be heard ; its highest
powers are wasted.

These suggestions may be further useful to establish a cri-
terion of sincerity, by which a writer may be judged ; and this
is of high import.   For, when a man is treating an interesting
subject, or one which he ought not to treat at all unless he be
interested, no faults have such a killing power as those which
prove that he is not in earnest, that he is acting a part, has
leisure for affectation, and feels that without it he could do
nothing.   This is one of the most odious of faults ; because it
shocks the moral sense, and is worse in a sepulchral inscription,
precisely in the same degree as that mode of composition calls
for sincerity more urgently than any other.   And indeed where
the internal evidence proves that the writer was moved, in other
words where this charm of sincerity lurks in the language of a
tombstone and secretly pervades it, there are no errors in style
or manner for which it will not be, in some degree, a recompence ; but without habits of reflection a test of this inward

simplicity cannot be come at; and as I have said, I am now writing with a hope to assist the well-disposed to attain it.

Let us take an instance where no one can be at a loss. The following lines are said to have been written by the illustrious Marquis of Montrose with the point of his sword, upon being informed of the death of his master, Charles I.:

> Great, good, and just, could I but rate
> My griefs, and thy so rigid fate;
> I'd weep the world to such a strain,
> As it should deluge once again.
> But since thy loud-tongued blood demands supplies,
> More from Briareus' hands than Argus' eyes, .
> I'll sing thy obsequies with trumpets' sounds
> And write thy epitaph with blood and wounds.

These funereal verses would certainly be wholly out of their place upon a tombstone; but who can doubt that the writer was transported to the height of the occasion? that he was moved as it became an heroic soldier, holding those principles and opinions, to be moved? His soul labours;—the most tremendous event in the history of the planet—namely, the deluge, is brought before his imagination by the physical image of tears,—a connection awful from its very remoteness and from the slender band that unites the ideas:—it passes into the region of fable likewise; for all modes of existence that forward his purpose are to be pressed into the service. The whole is instinct with spirit, and every word has its separate life; like the chariot of the Messiah, and the wheels of that chariot, as they appeared to the imagination of Milton aided by that of the prophet Ezekiel. It had power to move of itself, but was conveyed by cherubs.

> ————————with stars their bodies all
> And wings were set with eyes, with eyes the wheels
> Of beryl, and careering fires between.

Compare with the above verses of Montrose the following epitaph upon Sir Philip Sidney, which was formerly placed over his grave in St. Paul's Church.

> England, Netherland, the Heavens, and the Arts,
> The Soldiers, and the World, have made six parts
> Of noble Sidney; for who will suppose
> That a small heap of stones can Sidney enclose?

England hath his Body, for she it fed,
Netherland his Blood, in her defence shed :
The Heavens have his Soul, the Arts have his Fame,
The Soldiers the grief, the World his good Name.

There were many points in which the case of Sidney resembled
that of Charles I. He was a sovereign, but of a nobler kind—a
sovereign in the hearts of men ; and after his premature death
he was truly, as he hath been styled, 'the world-mourned
Sidney.' So fondly did the admiration of his contemporaries
settle upon him, that the sudden removal of a man so good,
great, and thoroughly accomplished, wrought upon many even
to repining, and to the questioning the dispensations of Providence. Yet he, whom Spenser and all the men of genius of
his age had tenderly bemoaned, is thus commemorated upon his
tomb-stone ; and to add to the indignity, the memorial is nothing more than the second-hand coat of a French commander !
It is a servile translation from a French epitaph, which says
Weever, 'was by some English Wit happily imitated and in-
geniously applied to the honour of our worthy chieftain.' Yet
Weever in a foregoing paragraph thus expresses himself upon
the same subject ; giving without his own knowledge, in my
opinion, an example of the manner in which an epitaph ought
to have been composed : 'But I cannot pass over in silence Sir
Philip Sidney, the elder brother, being (to use Camden's words)
the glorious star of this family, a lively pattern of virtue, and
the lovely joy of all the learned sort ; who fighting valiantly
with the enemy before Zutphen in Geldesland, dyed manfully.
This is that Sidney, whom, as God's will was, he should therefore be born into the world even to shew unto our age a sample
of ancient virtues : so His good pleasure was, before any man
looked for it, to call for him again and take him out of the world,
as being more worthy of heaven than earth. Thus we may see
perfect virtue suddenly vanisheth out of sight, and the best men
continue not long.'
    There can be no need to analyse this simple effusion of the
moment in order to contrast it with the laboured composition
before given ; the difference will flash upon the Reader at once.
But I may say it is not likely that such a frigid composition
as the former would have ever been applied to a man whose
death had so stirred up the hearts of his contemporaries, if it

had not been felt that something different from that nature which each man carried in his own breast was in his case requisite; and that a certain straining of mind was inseparable from the subject. Accordingly, an epitaph is adopted in which the Writer had turned from the genuine affections and their self-forgetting inspirations, to the end that his understanding, or the faculty designated by the word *head* as opposed to *heart*, might curiously construct a fabric to be wondered at. Hyperbole in the language of Montrose is a mean instrument made mighty because wielded by an afflicted soul, and strangeness is here the order of Nature. Montrose stretched after remote things, but was at the same time propelled towards them; the French Writer goes deliberately in search of them : no wonder then if what he brings home does not prove worth the carriage.

Let us return to an instance of common life. I quote it with reluctance, not so much for its absurdity as that the expression in one place will strike at first sight as little less than impious; and it is indeed, though unintentionally so, most irreverent. But I know no other example that will so forcibly illustrate the important truth I wish to establish. The following epitaph is to be found in a church-yard in Westmoreland; which the present Writer has reason to think of with interest as it contains the remains of some of his ancestors and kindred. The date is 1673.

> Under this Stone, Reader, inter'd doth lye,
>   Beauty and Virtue's true epitomy.
> At her appearance the noone-son
>   Blush'd and shrunk in 'cause quite outdon.
> In her concentered did all graces dwell:
>   God pluck'd my rose that He might take a smel.
> I'll say no more: but weeping wish I may
> Soone with thy dear chaste ashes com to lay.
>   Sic efflevit Maritus.

Can anything go beyond this in extravagance? yet, if the fundamental thoughts be translated into a natural style, they will be found reasonable and affecting—' The woman who lies here interred, was in my eyes a perfect image of beauty and virtue; she was to me a brighter object than the sun in heaven : God took her, who was my delight, from this earth to bring her nearer to Himself. Nothing further is worthy to be said than that weeping I wish soon to lie by thy dear chaste ashes. Thus did the husband pour out his tears.'

These verses are preceded by a brief account of the lady, in Latin prose, in which the little that is said is the uncorrupted language of affection. But, without this introductory communication I should myself have had no doubt, after recovering from the first shock of surprize and disapprobation, that this man, notwithstanding his extravagant expressions, was a sincere mourner; and that his heart, during the very act of composition, was moved. These fantastic images, though they stain the writing, stained not her soul,—they did not even touch it; but hung like globules of rain suspended above a green leaf, along which they may roll and leave no trace that they have passed over it. This simple-hearted man must have been betrayed by a common notion that what was natural in prose would be out of place in verse;—that it is not the Muse which puts on the garb but the garb which makes the Muse. And having adopted this notion at a time when vicious writings of this kind accorded with the public taste, it is probable that, in the excess of his modesty, the blankness of his inexperience, and the intensity of his affection, he thought that the further he wandered from Nature in his language the more would he honour his departed consort, who now appeared to him to have surpassed humanity in the excellence of her endowments. The quality of his fault and its very excess are both in favour of this conclusion.

Let us contrast this epitaph with one taken from a celebrated Writer of the last century.

To the memory of LUCY LYTTLETON, *Daughter &c. who departed this life &c. aged* 20. *Having employed the short time assigned to her here in the uniform practice of religion and virtue.*

> Made to engage all hearts, and charm all eyes,
> Though meek, magnanimous; though witty, wise;
> Polite, as all her life in Courts had been;
> Yet good, as she the world had never seen;
> The noble fire of an exalted mind,
> With gentle female tenderness combined.
> Her speech was the melodious voice of love,
> Her song the warbling of the vernal grove;
> Her eloquence was sweeter than her song,
> Soft as her heart, and as her reason strong;
> Her form each beauty of the mind express'd,
> Her mind was Virtue by the Graces drest.

The prose part of this inscription has the appearance of being intended for a tomb-stone; but there is nothing in the verse that would suggest such a thought. The composition is in the style of those laboured portraits in words which we sometimes see placed at the bottom of a print to fill up lines of expression which the bungling Artist had left imperfect. We know from other evidence that Lord Lyttleton dearly loved his wife; he has indeed composed a monody to her memory which proves this, and she was an amiable woman; neither of which facts could have been gathered from these inscriptive verses. This epitaph would derive little advantage from being translated into another style as the former was; for there is no under current; no skeleton or staminæ of thought and feeling. The Reader will perceive at once that nothing in the heart of the Writer had determined either the choice, the order or the expression, of the ideas; that there is no interchange of action from within and from without; that the connections are mechanical and arbitrary, and the lowest kind of these—heart and eyes: petty alliterations, as meek and magnanimous, witty and wise, combined with oppositions in thoughts where there is no necessary or natural opposition. Then follow voice, song, eloquence, form, mind—each enumerated by a separate act as if the Author had been making a *Catalogue Raisonné.*

These defects run through the whole; the only tolerable verse is,

Her speech was the melodious voice of love.

Observe, the question is not which of these epitaphs is better or worse; but which faults are of a worse kind. In the former case we have a mourner whose soul is occupied by grief and urged forward by his admiration. He deems in his simplicity that no hyperbole can transcend the perfections of her whom he has lost; for the version which I have given fairly demonstrates that, in spite of his outrageous expressions, the under current of his thoughts was natural and pure. We have therefore in him the example of a mind during the act of composition misled by false taste to the highest possible degree; and, in that of Lord Lyttleton, we have one of a feeling heart, not merely misled, but wholly laid asleep by the same power. Lord Lyttleton could not have written in this way upon such a subject, if he had not been seduced by the example of Pope, whose sparkling

and tuneful manner had bewitched the men of letters his contemporaries, and corrupted the judgment of the nation through
all ranks of society. So that a great portion of original genius
was necessary to embolden a man to write faithfully to Nature
upon any affecting subject if it belonged to a class of composition in which Pope had furnished examples.

I am anxious not to be misunderstood. It has already been
stated that in this species of composition above every other, our
sensations and judgments depend upon our opinion or feeling
of the Author's state of mind. Literature is here so far identi-
fied with morals, the quality of the act so far determined by our
notion of the aim and purpose of the agent, that nothing can
please us, however well executed in its kind, if we are persuaded
that the primary virtues of sincerity, earnestness and a moral
interest in the main object are wanting. Insensibility here
shocks us, and still more so if manifested by a Writer going
wholly out of his way in search of supposed beauties, which if
he were truly moved he could set no value upon, could not even
think of. We are struck in this case not merely with a sense
of disproportion and unfitness, but we cannot refrain from at-
tributing no small part of his intellectual to a moral demerit.
And here the difficulties of the question begin, namely in
ascertaining what errors in the choice of or the mode of expressing the thoughts, most surely indicate the want of that which
is most indispensible. Bad taste, whatever shape it may put
on, is injurious to the heart and the understanding. If a man
attaches much interest to the faculty of taste as it exists in himself and employs much time in those studies of which this
faculty (I use the word taste in its comprehensive though
most unjustifiable sense) is reckoned the arbiter, certain it is
his moral notions and dispositions must either be purified and
strengthened or corrupted and impaired. How can it be otherwise, when his ability to enter into the spirit of works in literature must depend upon his feelings, his imagination and his
understanding, that is upon his recipient, upon his creative or
active and upon his judging powers, and upon the accuracy and
compass of his knowledge, in fine upon all that makes up the
moral and intellectual man. What is true of individuals is
equally true of nations. Nevertheless a man called to a task in
which he is not practised, may have his expression thoroughly

defiled and clogged by the style prevalent in his age, yet still, through the force of circumstances that have roused him, his under feeling may remain strong and pure; yet this may be wholly concealed from common view. Indeed the favourite style of different ages is so different and wanders so far from propriety that if it were not that first rate Writers in all nations and tongues are governed by common principles, we might suppose that truth and nature were things not to be looked for in books; hence to an unpractised Reader the productions of every age will present obstacles in various degrees hard to surmount; a deformity of style not the worst in itself but of that kind with which he is least familiar will on the one hand be most likely to render him insensible to a pith and power which may be within, and on the other hand he will be the least able to see through that sort of falsehood which is most prevalent in the works of his own time. Many of my Readers, to apply these general observations to the present case, must have derived pleasure from the epitaph of Lord Lyttleton and no doubt will be startled at the comparison I have made; but bring it to the test recommended it will then be found that its faults, though not in degree so intolerable, are in kind more radical and deadly than those of the strange composition with which it has been compared.

The course which we have taken having brought us to the name of this distinguished Writer—Pope—I will in this place give a few observations upon his Epitaphs,—the largest collection we have in our language, from the pen of any Writer of eminence. As the epitaphs of Pope and also those of Chiabrera, which occasioned this dissertation, are in metre, it may be proper here to enquire how far the notion of a perfect epitaph, as given in a former Paper, may be modified by the choice of metre for the vehicle, in preference to prose. If our opinions be just, it is manifest that the basis must remain the same in either case; and that the difference can only lie in the superstructure; and it is equally plain, that a judicious man will be less disposed in this case than in any other to avail himself of the liberty given by metre to adopt phrases of fancy, or to enter into the more remote regions of illustrative imagery. For the occasion of writing an epitaph is matter-of-fact in its intensity, and forbids more authoritatively than any other species of composition all

modes of fiction, except those which the very strength of passion
has created ; which have been acknowledged by the human
heart, and have become so familiar that they are converted into
substantial realities. When I come to the epitaphs of Chiabrera,
I shall perhaps give instances in which I think he has not
written under the impression of this truth ; where the poetic
imagery does not elevate, deepen, or refine the human passion,
which it ought always to do or not to act at all, but excludes
it. In a far greater degree are Pope's epitaphs debased by
faults into which he could not I think have fallen if he had
written in prose as a plain man and not as a metrical Wit. I
will transcribe from Pope's Epitaphs the one upon Mrs. Corbet
(who died of a cancer), Dr. Johnson having extolled it highly
and pronounced it the best of the collection.

> Here rests a woman, good without pretence,
> Blest with plain reason and with sober sense ;
> No conquest she but o'er herself desir'd ;
> No arts essayed, but not to be admir'd.
> Passion and pride were to her soul unknown,
> Convinc'd that virtue only is our own.
> So unaffected, so compos'd a mind,
> So firm yet soft, so strong yet so refin'd,
> Heaven as its purest gold by tortures tried,
> The saint sustain'd it, but the woman died.

This *may* be the best of Pope's Epitaphs ; but if the standard
which we have fixed be a just one, it cannot be approved of.
First, it must be observed, that in the epitaphs of this Writer,
the true impulse is wanting, and that his motions must of
necessity be feeble. For he has no other aim than to give a
favourable portrait of the character of the deceased. Now mark
the process by which this is performed. Nothing is represented
implicitly, that is, with its accompaniment of circumstances, or
conveyed by its effects. The Author forgets that it is a living
creature that must interest us and not an intellectual existence,
which a mere character is. Insensible to this distinction the
brain of the Writer is set at work to report as flatteringly as he
may of the mind of his subject ; the good qualities are separately abstracted (can it be otherwise than coldly and unfeelingly ?)
and put together again as coldly and unfeelingly. The epitaph
now before us owes what exemption it may have from these
defects in its general plan to the excruciating disease of which

the lady died ; but it is liable to the same censure, and is, like
the rest, further objectionable in this ; namely, that the thoughts
have their nature changed and moulded by the vicious expression in which they are entangled, to an excess rendering them
wholly unfit for the place they occupy.

> Here rests a woman, good without pretence,
> Blest with plain reason—

from which *sober sense* is not sufficiently distinguishable. This
verse and a half, and the one ' so unaffected, so composed a
mind,' are characteristic, and the expression is true to nature ;
but they are, if I may take the liberty of saying it, the only
parts of the epitaph which have this merit. Minute criticism
is in its nature irksome, and as commonly practiced in books
and conversation, is both irksome and injurious. Yet every
mind must occasionally be exercised in this discipline, else it
cannot learn the art of bringing words rigorously to the test of
thoughts ; and these again to a comparison with things, their
archetypes, contemplated first in themselves, and secondly in
relation to each other ; in all which processes the mind must
be skilful, otherwise it will be perpetually imposed upon. In
the next couplet the word *conquest*, is applied in a manner that
would have been displeasing even from its triteness in a copy of
complimentary verses to a fashionable Beauty ; but to talk of
making conquests in an epitaph is not to be endured. ' No arts
essayed, but not to be admired,'—are words expressing that she
had recourse to artifices to conceal her amiable and admirable
qualities ; and the context implies that there was a merit in
this ; which surely no sane mind would allow. But the meaning of the Author, simply and honestly given, was nothing more
than that she shunned admiration, probably with a more apprehensive modesty than was common ; and more than this would
have been inconsistent with the praise bestowed upon her—that
she had an unaffected mind. This couplet is further objectionable, because the sense of love and peaceful admiration which
such a character naturally inspires, is disturbed by an oblique
and ill-timed stroke of satire. She is not praised so much as
others are blamed, and is degraded by the Author in thus
being made a covert or stalking-horse for gratifying a propensity
the most abhorrent from her own nature—' Passion and pride
were to her soul unknown.' It cannot be meant that she had

no passions, but that they were moderate and kept in subordination to her reason ; but the thought is not here expressed ; nor is it clear that a conviction in the understanding that 'virtue only is our own,' though it might suppress her pride, would be itself competent to govern or abate many other affections and passions to which our frail nature is, and ought in various degrees, to be subject. In fact, the Author appears to have had no precise notion of his own meaning. If she was 'good without pretence,' it seems unnecessary to say that she was not proud. Dr. Johnson, making an exception of the verse, 'Convinced that virtue only is our own,' praises this epitaph for 'containing nothing taken from common places.' Now in fact, as may be deduced from the principles of this discourse, it is not only no fault but a primary requisite in an epitaph that it shall contain thoughts and feelings which are in their substance common-place, and even trite. It is grounded upon the universal intellectual property of man,—sensations which all men have felt and feel in some degree daily and hourly;—truths whose very interest and importance have caused them to be unattended to, as things which could take care of themselves. But it is required that these truths should be instinctively ejaculated or should rise irresistibly from circumstances ; in a word that they should be uttered in such connection as shall make it felt that they are not adopted, not spoken by rote, but perceived in their whole compass with the freshness and clearness of an original intuition. The Writer must introduce the truth with such accompaniment as shall imply that he has mounted to the sources of things, penetrated the dark cavern from which the river that murmurs in every one's ear has flowed from generation to generation. The line 'Virtue only is our own,'—is objectionable, not from the common-placeness of the truth, but from the vapid manner in which it is conveyed. A similar sentiment is expressed with appropriate dignity in an epitaph by Chiabrera, where he makes the Archbishop of Albino say of himself, that he was

> ————smitten by the great ones of the world,
> But did not fall; for virtue braves all shocks,
> Upon herself resting immoveably.

'So firm yet soft, so strong yet so refined': These intellectual operations (while they can be conceived of as operations of intellect at all, for in fact one half of the process is mechanical, words doing their own work and one half of the line manufacturing the rest) remind me of the motions of a Posture-master, or of a man balancing a sword upon his finger, which must be kept from falling at all hazards. 'The saint sustained it, but the woman died.' Let us look steadily at this antithesis : the *saint*, that is her soul strengthened by religion, supported the anguish of her disease with patience and resignation ; but the *woman*, that is her body (for if anything else is meant by the word woman, it contradicts the former part of the proposition and the passage is nonsense), was overcome. Why was not this simply expressed; without playing with the Reader's fancy, to the delusion and dishonour of his understanding, by a trifling epigramatic point ? But alas ! ages must pass away before men will have their eyes open to the beauty and majesty of Truth, and will be taught to venerate Poetry no further than as she is a handmaid pure as her mistress—the noblest handmaid in her train !

(c) CELEBRATED EPITAPHS CONSIDERED.

From the Author's Mss.

I VINDICATE the rights and dignity of Nature ; and as long as I condemn nothing without assigning reasons not lightly given, I cannot suffer any individual, however highly and deservedly honoured by my countrymen, to stand in my way. If my notions are right, the epitaphs of Pope cannot well be too severely condemned; for not only are they almost wholly destitute of those universal feelings and simple movements of mind which we have called for as indispensible, but they are little better than a tisue of false thoughts, languid and vague expressions, unmeaning antithesis, and laborious attempts at discrimination. Pope's mind had been employed chiefly in observation upon the vices and follies of men. Now, vice and folly are in contradiction with the moral principle which can never be extinguished in the mind ; and therefore, wanting the contrast, are irregular, capricious, and inconsistent with them-selves. If a man has once said (see *Friend*, No. . . . . . .), 'Evil, be thou my good !' and has acted accordingly, however strenuous may have been his adherence to this principle, it will be well known by those who have had an opportunity of observing him narrowly that there have been perpetual obliquities in his course ; evil passions thwarting each other in various ways ; and now and then, revivals of his better nature, which check him for a short time or lead him to remeasure his steps :—not to speak of the various necessities of counterfeiting virtue, which the furtherance of his schemes will impose upon him, and the division which will be consequently introduced into his nature.

It is reasonable then that Cicero, when holding up Catiline to detestation ; and (without going to such an extreme case) that Dryden and Pope, when they are describing characters like Buckingham, Shaftsbury, and the Duchess of Marlborough, should represent qualities and actions at war with each other and with themselves; and that the page should be suitably crowded with antithetical expressions. But all this argues an

obtuse moral sensibility and a consequent want of knowledge,
if applied where virtue ought to be described in the language of
affectionate admiration. In the mind of the truly great and
good everything that is of importance is at peace with itself; all
is stillness, sweetness and stable grandeur. Accordingly the
contemplation of virtue is attended with repose. A lovely
quality, if its loveliness be clearly perceived, fastens the mind
with absolute sovereignty upon itself; permitting or inciting
it to pass, by smooth gradation or gentle transition, to some
other kindred quality. Thus a perfect image of meekness (I
refer to an instance before given) when looked at by a tender
mind in its happiest mood, might easily lead on to thoughts
of magnanimity; for assuredly there is nothing incongruous in
those virtues. But the mind would not then be separated from
the person who is the object of its thoughts; it would still be
confined to that person or to others of the same general character; that is, would be kept within the circle of qualities
which range themselves quietly by each other's sides. Whereas,
when meekness and magnanimity are represented antithetically,
the mind is not only carried from the main object, but is compelled to turn to a subject in which the quality exists divided
from some other as noble, its natural ally: a painful feeling!
that checks the course of love, and repels the sweet thoughts
that might be settling round the person whom it was the
Author's wish to endear to us; but for whom, after this interruption, we no longer care. If then a man, whose duty it is
to praise departed excellence not without some sense of regret
or sadness, to do this or to be silent, should upon all occasions
exhibit that mode of connecting thoughts, which is only natural
while we are delineating vice under certain relations, we may be
assured that the nobler sympathies are not alive in him; that
he has no clear insight into the internal constitution of virtue;
nor has himself been soothed, cheared, harmonized, by those
outward effects which follow everywhere her goings,—declaring
the presence of the invisible Deity. And though it be true that
the most admirable of them must fall far short of perfection,
and that the majority of those whose work is commemorated
upon their tomb-stones must have been persons in whom good
and evil were intermixed in various proportions and stood in
various degrees of opposition to each other, yet the Reader will

remember what has been said before upon that medium of love, sorrow and admiration, through which a departed friend is viewed : how it softens down or removes these harshnesses and contradictions, which moreover must be supposed never to have been grievous: for there can be no true love but between the good ; and no epitaph ought to be written upon a bad man, except for a warning.

The purpose of the remarks given in the last Essay was chiefly to assist the Reader in separating truth and sincerity from falsehood and affectation; presuming that if the unction of a devout heart be wanting everything else is of no avail. It was shewn that a current of just thought and feeling may flow under a surface of illustrative imagery so impure as to produce an effect the opposite of that which was intended. Yet, though this fault may be carried to an intolerable *degree*, the Reader will have gathered that in our estimation it is not *in kind* the most offensive and injurious. We have contrasted it in its excess with instances where the genuine current or vein was wholly wanting; where the thoughts and feelings had no vital union, but were artificially connected, or formally accumulated, in a manner that would imply discontinuity and feebleness of mind upon any occasion, but still more reprehensible here !

I will proceed to give milder examples not in this last kind but in the former ; namely of failure from various causes where the ground-work is good.

> Take holy earth! all that my soul holds dear:
> Take that best gift which Heaven so lately gave:
> To Bristol's fount I bore with trembling care,
> Her faded form.   She bow'd to taste the wave—
> And died.   Does youth, does beauty read the line?
> Does sympathetic fear their breasts alarm?
> Speak, dead Maria! breathe a strain divine;
> Even from the grave thou shalt have power to charm.
> Bid them in duty's sphere as meekly move:
> And if so fair, from vanity as free,
> As firm in friendship, and as fond in love;
> Tell them, tho 'tis an awful thing to die,
> ('Twas e'en to thee) yet, the dread path once trod;
> Heaven lifts its everlasting portals high,
> And bids ' the pure in heart behold their God.'

This epitaph has much of what we have demanded ; but it is debased in some instances by weakness of expression, in others by false prettiness. 'She bow'd to taste the wave, and died.' The plain truth was, she drank the Bristol waters which failed to restore her, and her death soon followed; but the expression involves a multitude of petty occupations for the fancy. 'She bow'd': was there any truth in this? 'to taste the wave': the water of a mineral spring which must have been drunk out of a goblet. Strange application of the word 'wave' and 'died': This would have been a just expression if the water had killed her; but, as it is, the tender thought involved in the disappoint-ment of a hope however faint is left unexpressed; and a shock of surprise is given, entertaining perhaps to a light fancy but to a steady mind unsatisfactory, because false. 'Speak! dead Maria, breathe a strain divine'! This sense flows nobly from the heart and the imagination; but perhaps it is not one of those impassioned thoughts which should be fixed in language upon a sepulchral stone. It is in its nature too poignant and transitory. A husband meditating by his wife's grave would throw off such a feeling, and would give voice to it; and it would be in its place in a Monody to her memory; but if I am not mistaken, ought to have been suppressed here, or uttered after a different manner. The implied impersonation of the de-ceased (according to the tenor of what has before been said) ought to have been more general and shadowy.

> And if so fair, from vanity as free,
> As firm in friendship and as fond in love;
> Tell them—

These are two sweet verses, but the word 'fair' is improper; for unquestionably it was not intended that their title to receive this assurance should depend at all upon their personal beauty. Moreover in this couplet and in what follows, the long suspen-sion of the sense excites the expectation of a thought less com-mon than the concluding one; and is an instance of a failure in doing what is most needful and most difficult in an epitaph to do; namely to give to universally received truths a pathos and spirit which shall re-admit them into the soul like revela-tions of the moment.

I have said that this excellence is difficult to attain; and why? Is it because nature is weak? No! Where the soul has been thoroughly stricken (and Heaven knows the course of life must have placed all men, at some time or other, in that condition) there is never a want of *positive* strength; but because the adversary of Nature (call that adversary Art or by what name you will) is *comparatively* strong. The far-searching influence of the power, which, for want of a better name, we will denominate Taste, is in nothing more evinced than in the changeful character and complexion of that species of composition which we have been reviewing. Upon a call so urgent, it might be expected that the affections, the memory, and the imagination would be *constrained* to speak their genuine language. Yet, if the few specimens which have been given in the course of this enquiry, do not demonstrate the fact, the Reader need only look into any collection of Epitaphs to be convinced, that the faults predominant in the literature of every age will be as strongly reflected in the sepulchral inscriptions as any where; nay perhaps more so, from the anxiety of the Author to do justice to the occasion: and especially if the composition be in verse; for then it comes more avowedly in the shape of a work of art; and of course, is more likely to be coloured by the work of art holden in most esteem at the time. In a bulky volume of Poetry entitled ELEGANT EXTRACTS IN VERSE, which must be known to most of my Readers, as it is circulated everywhere and in fact constitutes at this day the poetical library of our Schools, I find a number of epitaphs in verse, of the last century; and there is scarcely one which is not thoroughly tainted by the artifices which have over-run our writings in metre since the days of Dryden and Pope. Energy, stillness, grandeur, tenderness, those feelings which are the pure emanations of Nature, those thoughts which have the infinitude of truth, and those expressions which are not what the garb is to the body but what the body is to the soul, themselves a constituent part and power or function in the thought—all these are abandoned for their opposites,—as if our countrymen, through successive generations, had lost the sense of solemnity and pensiveness (not to speak of deeper emotions) and resorted to the tombs of their forefathers and contemporaries, only to be tickled and surprised. Would we not recoil from such gratification, in such a place, if the general literature of the country had not co-operated with other causes insidiously to weaken our sensibilities and deprave our judgments? Doubtless, there are shocks of event and circumstance, public and private, by which for all minds the truths of Nature will be elicited; but sorrow for that individual or people to whom these special interferences are necessary, to bring them into communion with the inner spirit of things! for such intercourse must be profitless in proportion as it is unfrequently irregular and transient. Words are too awful an instrument for good and evil, to be trifled with; they hold above all other external powers a dominion over thoughts. If words be not (recurring to a metaphor before used) an incarnation of the thought, but only a clothing for it, then surely will they prove an ill gift; such a one as those possessed vestments, read of in the stories of superstitious times, which had power to consume and to alienate from his right mind the victim who put them on. Language, if it do not uphold, and feed, and leave in quiet, like the power of gravitation or the air we breathe, is a counter-spirit, unremittingly and noiselessly at work, to subvert, to lay waste, to vitiate, and to dissolve. From a deep conviction then that the excellence of writing, whether in prose or verse, consists in a conjunction of Reason and Passion, a conjunction which must be of necessity benign; and that it might be deduced from what has been said that the taste, intellectual power and morals of a country are inseparably linked in mutual dependence, I have dwelt thus long upon this argument. And the occasion justifies me; for how could the tyranny of bad taste be brought home to the mind more aptly than by showing in what degree the feelings of nature yield to it when we are rendering to our friends the solemn testimony of our love? more forcibly than by giving proof that thoughts cannot, even upon this impulse, assume an outward life without a transmutation and a fall.

Epitaph on Miss Drummond in the Church of Broadsworth, Yorkshire.
MASON.

Here sleeps what once was beauty, once was grace;
Grace, that with tenderness and sense combin'd
To form that harmony of soul and face,
Where beauty shines, the mirror of the mind.
Such was the maid, that in the morn of youth,
In virgin innocence, in Nature's pride,
Blest with each art, that owes its charm to truth,
Sunk in her Father's fond embrace, and died.
He weeps: O venerate the holy tear!
Faith lends her aid to ease Affliction's load;

The parent mourns his child upon the bier,
The Christian yields an angel to his God.

The following is a translation from the Latin, communicated to a Lady in her childhood and by her preserved in memory. I regret that I have not seen the original.

She is gone—my beloved daughter Eliza is gone,
Fair, cheerful, benign, my child is gone.
Thee long to be regretted a Father mourns,
Regretted—but thanks to the most perfect God! not lost.
For a happier age approaches
When again, my child, I shall behold
And live with thee for ever.

Matthew Dobson to his dear, engaging, happy Eliza
Who in the 18th year of her age
Passed peaceably into heaven.

The former of these epitaphs is very far from being the worst of its kind, and on that account I have placed the two in contrast. Unquestionably, as the Father in the latter speaks in his own person, the situation is much more pathetic; but, making due allowance for this advantage, who does not here feel a superior truth and sanctity, which is not dependent upon this circumstance but merely the result of the expression and the connection of the thoughts? I am not so fortunate as to have any knowledge of the Author of this affecting composition, but I much fear if he had called in the assistance of English verse the better to convey his thoughts, such sacrifices would, from various influences, have been made *even by him*, that, though he might have excited admiration in thousands, he would have truly moved no one. The latter part of the following by Gray is almost the only instance among the metrical epitaphs in our language of the last century, which I remember, of affecting thoughts rising naturally and keeping themselves pure from vicious diction; and therefore retaining their appropriate power over the mind.

Epitaph on Mrs. Clark.

Lo! where the silent marble weeps,
A friend, a wife, a mother, sleeps;
A heart, within whose sacred cell
The peaceful virtues lov'd to dwell.
Affection warm, and love sincere,
And soft humanity were there.
In agony, in death resigned,
She felt the wound she left behind.

Her infant image, here below,
Sits smiling on a father's woe;
Whom what awaits, while yet he strays
Along the lonely vale of days?
A pang to secret sorrow dear;
A sigh, an unavailing tear,
Till time shall every grief remove,
With life, with meaning, and with love.

I have been speaking of faults which are aggravated by temptations thrown in the way of modern Writers when they compose in metre. The first six lines of this epitaph are vague and languid, more so than I think would have been possible had it been written in prose. Yet Gray, who was so happy in the remaining part, especially the last four lines, has grievously failed *in prose* upon a subject which it might have been expected would have bound him indissolubly to the propriety of Nature and comprehensive reason. I allude to the conclusion of the epitaph upon his mother, where he says, 'she was the careful tender mother of many children, one of whom alone had the misfortune to survive her.' This is a searching thought, but wholly out of place. Had it been said of an idiot, of a palsied child, or of an adult from any cause dependent upon his mother to a degree of helplessness which nothing but maternal tenderness and watchfulness could answer, that he had the misfortune to survive his mother, the thought would have been just. The same might also have been wrung from any man (thinking of himself) when his soul was smitten with compunction or remorse, through the consciousness of a misdeed from which he might have been preserved (as he hopes or believes) by his mother's prudence, by her anxious care if longer continued, or by the reverential fear of offending or disobeying her. But even then (unless accompanied with a detail of extraordinary circumstances), if transferred to her monument, it would have been misplaced, as being too peculiar, and for reasons which have been before alleged, namely, as too transitory and poignant. But in an ordinary case, for a man permanently and conspicuously to record that this was his fixed feeling; what is it but to run counter to the course of nature, which has made it matter of expectation and congratulation that parents should die before their children? What is it, if searched to the bottom, but lurking and sickly selfishness? Does not the regret include a wish that the mother should have survived all her offspring, have witnessed that bitter desolation where the order of things is disturbed and inverted? And finally, does it not withdraw the attention of the Reader from the subject to the Author of the Memorial, as one to be commiserated for his strangely unhappy condition, or to be condemned for the morbid constitution of his feelings, or for his deficiency in judgment? A fault of the same kind, though less in degree, is found in the epitaph of Pope upon Harcourt; of whom it is said that 'he never gave his father 'grief but when he died.' I need not point out how many situations there are in which such an expression of feeling would be natural and becoming; but in a permanent inscription things only should be admitted that have an enduring place in the mind; and a nice selection is required even among these. The Duke of Ormond said of his son Ossory, 'that he preferred his dead son to any living son in Christendom,'—a thought which (to adopt an expression used before) has the infinitude of truth! But though in this there is no momentary illusion, nothing fugitive, it would still have been unbecoming, had it been placed in open view over the son's grave; inasmuch as such expression of it would have had an ostentatious air, and would have implied a disparagement of others. The sublimity of the sentiment consists in its being the secret possession of the Father.

Having been engaged so long in the ungracious office of sitting in judgment where I have found so much more to censure than to approve, though, wherever it was in my power, I have placed good by the side of evil, that the Reader might intuitively receive the truths which I wished to communicate, I now turn back with pleasure to Chiabrera; of whose productions in this department the Reader of the *Friend* may be enabled to form a judgment who has attentively perused the few specimens only which have been given. 'An epitaph,' says Weever, 'is a superscription (either in verse or prose) or an astrict pithic diagram, writ, carved, or engraven upon the tomb, grave, or sepulchre of the defunct, briefly declaring (*and that with a kind of commiseration*) the name, the age, the deserts, the dignities, the state, *the praises both of body and minde*, the good and bad fortunes in the life, and the manner and time of the death of the person therein interred.' This account of an epitaph, which as far as it goes is just, was no doubt taken by Weever from the monuments of our own country, and it shews that in his conception an epitaph was not to be an abstract character of the deceased but an epitomized biography blended with description by which an impression of the character was to be conveyed. Bring forward the one incidental expression, a kind of commiseration, unite with it a concern on the part of the dead for the well-being of the living made known by exhortation and admonition, and let this commiseration and concern pervade and brood over the whole, so that what was peculiar to the individual shall still be subordinate to a sense of what he had in common with the species, our notion of a perfect epitaph would then be realized; and it pleases me to say that this is the very model upon which those of Chiabrera are for the most part framed. Observe how exquisitely this is exemplified in the one beginning ' Pause, courteous stranger! Balbi supplicates,' given in the *Friend* some weeks ago. The subject of the epitaph is introduced intreating, not directly in his own person but through the mouth of the author, that according to the religious belief of his country a prayer for his soul might be preferred to the Redeemer of the world: placed in counterpoize with this right which he has in common with all the dead, his individual earthly accomplishments appear light to his funeral Biographer as they did to the person of whom he speaks when alive, nor could Chiabrera have ventured to touch upon them but under the sanction of this person's acknowledgment. He then goes on to say how various and profound was his learning, and how deep a hold it took upon his affections, but that he weaned himself from these things as vanities, and was devoted in later life exclusively to the divine truths of the Gospel as the only knowledge in which he could find perfect rest. Here we are thrown back upon the introductory supplication and made to feel its especial propriety in this case; his life was long, and every part of it bore appropriate fruits. Urbina his birth-place might be proud of him, and the passenger who was entreated to pray for his soul has a wish breathed for his welfare. This composition is a perfect whole, there is nothing arbitrary or mechanical, but it is an organized body, of which the members are bound together by a common life and are all justly proportioned. If I had not gone so much into detail I should have given further instances of Chiabrera's Epitaphs, but I must content myself with saying that if he had abstained from the introduction of heathen mythology, of which he is lavish—an inexcusable fault for an inhabitant of a Christian country, yet admitting of some palliation in an Italian who treads classic soil and has before his eyes the ruins of the temples which were dedicated to those fictitious beings of objects of worship by the majestic people his ancestors—had omitted also some uncharacteristic particulars, and had not on some occasions forgotten that truth is the soul of passion, he would have left his Readers little to regret. I do not mean to say that higher and nobler thoughts may not be found in sepulchral inscriptions than his contain ; but he understood his work, the principles upon which he composed are just. The Reader of the *Friend* has had proofs of this : one shall be given of his mixed manner, exemplifying some of the points in which he has erred.

O Lelius beauteous flower of gentleness,
The fair Anglaia's friend above all friends :
O darling of the fascinating Loves
By what dire envy moved did Death uproot
Thy days e'er yet full blown, and what ill chance
Hath robbed Savona of her noblest grace?
She weeps for thee and shall for ever weep,
And if the fountain of her tears should fail
She would implore Sabete to supply
Her need : Sabete, sympathizing stream,
Who on his margin saw thee close thine eyes
On the chaste bosom of thy Lady dear,
Ah, what do riches, what does youth avail?
Dust are our hopes, I weeping did inscribe
In bitterness thy monument, and pray
Of every gentle spirit bitterly
To read the record with as copious tears.

This epitaph is not without some tender thoughts, but a comparison of it with the one upon the youthful Pozzobonelli (see *Friend*, No. . . .) will more clearly shew that Chiabrera has here neglected to ascertain whether the passions expressed were in kind and degree a dispensation of reason, or at least commodities issued under her licence and authority.

The epitaphs of Chiabrera are twenty-nine in number, all of them save two probably little known at this day in their own country and scarcely at all beyond the limits of it; and the

Reader is generally made acquainted with the moral and intellectual excellence which distinguished them by a brief history of the course of their lives or a selection of events and circumstances, and thus they are individualized; but in the two other instances, namely those of Tasso and Raphael, he enters into no particulars, but contents himself with four lines expressing one sentiment upon the principle laid down in the former part of this discourse, where the subject of an epitaph is a man of prime note.

> Torquato Tasso rests within this tomb :
> This figure weeping from her inmost heart
> Is Poesy : from such impassioned grief
> Let every one conclude what this man was.

The epitaph which Chiabrera composed for himself has also an appropriate brevity and is distinguished for its grandeur, the sentiment being the same as that which the Reader has before seen so happily enlarged upon.

As I am brought back to men of first rate distinction and public benefactors, I cannot resist the pleasure of transcribing the metrical part of an epitaph which formerly was inscribed in the church of St. Paul's to that Bishop of London who prevailed with William the Conqueror to secure to the inhabitants of the city all the liberties and privileges which they had enjoyed in the time of Edward the Confessor.

> These marble monuments to thee thy citizens assigne,
> Rewards (O Father) farre unfit to those deserts of thine :
> Thee unto them a faithful friend, thy London people found,
> And to this towne of no small weight, a stay both sure and sound.
> Their liberties restorde to them, by means of thee have beene,
> Their publicke weale by means of thee, large gifts have felt and seene :
> Thy riches, stocke, and beauty brave, one hour hath them supprest,
> Yet these thy virtues and good deeds with us for ever rest.

Thus have I attempted to determine what a sepulchral inscription ought to be, and taken at the same time a survey of what epitaphs are good and bad, and have shewn to what deficiencies in sensibility and to what errors in taste and judgement most commonly are to be ascribed. It was my intention to have given a few specimens from those of the ancients; but I have already I fear taken up too much of the Reader's time. I have not animadverted upon such, alas! far too numerous, as are reprehensible from the want of moral rectitude in those who have composed them or given it to be understood that they should be so composed; boastful and haughty panegyrics ludicrously contradicting the solid remembrance of those who knew the deceased; shocking the common sense of mankind by their extravagance, and affronting the very altar with their impious falshood. Those I leave to general scorn, not however without a general recommendation that they who have offended or may be disposed to offend in this manner, would take into serious thought the heinousness of their transgression.

Upon reviewing what has been written I think it better here to add a few favourable specimens such as are ordinarily found in our country church-yards at this day. If those primary sensations upon which I have dwelt so much be not stifled in the heart of the Reader, they will be read with pleasure, otherwise neither these nor more exalted strains can by him be truly interpreted.

Aged 87 *and* 83.

Not more with silver hairs than virtue crown'd
The good old pair take up this spot of ground:
Tread in their steps and you will surely find
Their Rest above, below their peace of mind.

At the Last Day I'm sure I shall appear,
To meet with Jesus Christ my Saviour dear:
Where I do hope to live with Him in bliss.
Oh, what a joy at my last hour was this!

Aged 3 *Months.*

What Christ said once He said to all,
Come unto Me, ye children small:
None shall do you any wrong,
For to My Kingdom you belong.

Aged 10 *Weeks.*

The Babe was sucking at the breast
When God did call him to his rest.

In an obscure corner of a country church-yard I once espied, half overgrown with hemlock and nettles, a very small stone laid upon the ground, bearing nothing more than the name of the deceased with the date of birth and death, importing that it was an infant which had been born one day and died the following. I know not how far the Reader may be in sympathy with me; but more awful thoughts of rights conferred, of hopes awakened, of remembrances stealing away or vanishing, were imparted to my mind by that inscription there before my eyes than by any other that it has ever been my lot to meet with upon a tomb-stone.

The most numerous class of sepulchral inscriptions do indeed record nothing else but the name of the buried person; but that he was born upon one day and died upon another. Addison in the *Spectator* making this observation says, 'that he cannot look upon those registers of existence, whether of brass or marble, but as a kind of satire upon the departed persons who had left no other memorial of them than that they were born and that they died.' In certain moods of mind this is a natural reflection; yet not perhaps the most salutary which the appearance might give birth to. As in these registers the name is mostly associated with others of the same family, this is a prolonged companionship, however shadowy: even a tomb like this is a shrine to which the fancies of a scattered family may return in pilgrimage; the thoughts of the individuals without any communication with each other must oftentimes meet here. Such a frail memorial then is not without its tendency to keep families together. It feeds also local attachment, which is the tap-root of the tree of Patriotism.

I know not how I can withdraw more satisfactorily from this long disquisition than by offering to the Reader as a farewell memorial the following Verses, suggested to me by a concise epitaph which I met with some time ago in one of the most retired vales among the mountains of Westmoreland. There is nothing in the detail of the poem which is not either founded upon the epitaph or gathered from enquiries concerning the deceased, made in the neighbourhood.

> Beneath that pine which rears its dusky head
> Aloft, and covered by a plain blue stone
> Briefly inscribed, a gentle Dalesman lies;
> From whom in early childhood was withdrawn
> The precious gift of hearing. He grew up
> From year to year in loneliness of soul;
> And this deep mountain valley was to him
> Soundless with all its streams. The bird of dawn
> Did never rouse this Cottager from sleep
> With startling summons; not for his delight

The vernal cuckoo shouted, not for him
Murmured the labouring bee. When stormy winds
Were working the broad bosom of the Lake
Into a thousand thousand sparkling waves,
Rocking the trees, or driving cloud on cloud
Along the sharp edge of yon lofty crags,
The agitated scene before his eye
Was silent as a picture; evermore
Were all things silent wheresoe'er he moved.
Yet by the solace of his own calm thoughts
Upheld, he duteously pursued the round
Of rural labours: the steep mountain side
Ascended with his staff and faithful dog;
The plough he guided and the scythe he swayed,
And the ripe corn before his sickle fell
Among the jocund reapers. For himself,
All watchful and industrious as he was,
He wrought not; neither field nor flock he owned :
No wish for wealth had place within his mind,
No husband's love nor father's hope or care;
Though born a younger brother, need was none
That from the floor of his paternal home
He should depart to plant himself anew;
And when mature in manhood he beheld
His parents laid in earth, no loss ensued
Of rights to him, but he remained well pleased ˙
By the pure bond of independent love,
An inmate of a second family,
The fellow-labourer and friend of him
To whom the small inheritance had fallen.
Nor deem that his mild presence was a weight
That pressed upon his brother's house; for books
Were ready comrades whom he could not tire;
Of whose society the blameless man
Was never satiate; their familiar voice
Even to old age with unabated charm
Beguiled his leisure hours, refreshed his thoughts,
Beyond its natural elevation raised
His introverted spirit, and bestowed
Upon his life an outward dignity
Which all acknowledged. The dark winter night,
The stormy day had each its own resource;
Song of the Muses, sage historic tale,.
Science severe, or word of Holy Writ
Announcing immortality and joy
To the assembled spirits of the just
From imperfection and decay secure :
Thus soothed at home, thus busy in the field,
To no perverse suspicion he gave way;

No languour, peevishness, nor vain complaint.
And they who were about him did not fail
In reverence or in courtesy; they prized
His gentle manners, and his peaceful smiles;
The gleams of his slow-varying countenance .
Were met with answering sympathy and love.
    At length when sixty years and five were told
A slow disease insensibly consumed
The powers of nature, and a few short steps
Of friends and kindred bore him from his home,
You cottage shaded by the woody cross,
To the profounder stillness of the grave.
Nor was his funeral denied the grace
Of many tears, virtuous and thoughtful grief,
Heart-sorrow rendered sweet by gratitude;
And now that monumental stone preserves
His name, and unambitiously relates
How long and by what kindly outward aids
And in what pure contentedness of mind
The sad privation was by him endured.
And yon tall pine-tree, whose composing sound
Was wasted on the good man's living ear,
Hath now its own peculiar sanctity,
And at the touch of every wandering breeze
Murmurs not idly o'er his peaceful grave.

III. ESSAYS, LETTERS, AND NOTES ELUCIDATORY AND CONFIRMATORY OF THE POEMS.

1798-1835.

(a) Of the Principles of Poetry and the 'Lyrical Ballads' (1798-1802).

(b) Of Poetic Diction.

(c) Poetry as a Study (1815).

(d) Of Poetry as Observation and Description, and Dedication of 1815.

(e) Of 'The Excursion:' Preface.

(f) Letters to Sir George and Lady Beaumont and Others on the Poems and related Subjects.

(g) Letter to Charles Fox with the 'Lyrical Ballads,' and his Answer, &c.

(h) Letter on the Principles of Poetry and his own Poems to (afterwards) Professor John Wilson.

NOTE.

Of the occasion and sources, &c. of the several portions of the present division see Preface in Vol. I.   G.

(a) OF THE PRINCIPLES OF POETRY AND THE 'LYRICAL BALLADS' (1798-1802).

The first Volume of these Poems has already been submitted to general perusal. It was published, as an experiment, which, I hoped, might be of some use to ascertain, how far, by fitting to metrical arrangement a selection of the real language of men in a state of vivid sensation, that sort of pleasure and that quantity of pleasure may be imparted, which a Poet may rationally endeavour to impart.

I had formed no very inaccurate estimate of the probable effect of those Poems: I flattered myself that they who should be pleased with them would read them with more than common pleasure: and, on the other hand, I was well aware, that by those who should dislike them, they would be read with more than common dislike. The result has differed from my expectation in this only, that a greater number have been pleased than I ventured to hope I should please.

.   .   .   .

Several of my Friends are anxious for the success of these Poems, from a belief, that, if the views with which they were composed were indeed realised, a class of Poetry would be produced, well adapted to interest mankind permanently, and not unimportant in the quality, and in the multiplicity of its moral relations: and on this account they have advised me to prefix a systematic defence of the theory upon which the Poems were written. But I was unwilling to undertake the task, knowing that on this occasion the Reader would look coldly upon my arguments, since I might be suspected of having been principally influenced by the selfish and foolish hope of *reasoning* him into an approbation of these particular Poems: and I was still more unwilling to undertake the task, because, adequately to display the opinions, and fully to enforce the arguments, would require a space wholly disproportionate to a preface. For, to treat the subject with the clearness and coherence of which it is susceptible, it would be necessary to give a full account of the present state of the public taste in this country, and to determine how far this taste is healthy or depraved ; which, again, could not be determined, without pointing out in what manner language and the human mind act and re-act on each other, and without re-tracing the revolutions, not of literature alone, but likewise of society itself. I have therefore altogether declined to enter regularly upon this defence ; yet I am sensible, that there would be something like impropriety in abruptly obtruding upon the Public, without a few words of introduction, Poems so materially different from those upon which general approbation is at present bestowed.

It is supposed, that by the act of writing in verse an Author makes a formal engagement that he will gratify certain known habits of association ; that he not only thus apprises the Reader that certain classes of ideas and expressions will be found in his book, but that others will be carefully excluded. This exponent or symbol held forth by metrical language must in different eras of literature have excited very different expectations : for example, in the age of Catullus, Terence, and Lucretius, and that of Statius or Claudian ; and in our own country, in the age of Shakspeare and Beaumont and Fletcher, and that of Donne and Cowley, or Dryden, or Pope. I will not take upon me to determine the exact import of the promise which, by the act of writing in verse, an Author in the present day makes to his reader : but it will undoubtedly appear to many persons that I have not ful-filled the terms of an engagement thus voluntarily contracted. They who have been accustomed to the gaudiness and inane phraseology of many modern writers, if they persist in reading this book to its conclusion, will, no doubt, frequently have to struggle with feelings of strangeness and awkwardness : they will look round for poetry, and will be induced to inquire by what species of courtesy these attempts can be permitted to as-sume that title. I hope therefore the reader will not censure me for attempting to state what I have proposed to myself to perform ; and also (as far as the limits of a preface will permit) to explain some of the chief reasons which have determined me in the choice of my purpose : that at least he may be spared any unpleasant feeling of disappointment, and that I myself may be protected from one of the most dishonourable accusations which can be brought against an Author ; namely, that of an indolence which prevents him from endeavouring to ascertain what is his duty, or, when his duty is ascertained, prevents him from performing it.

The principal object, then, proposed in these Poems was to choose incidents and situations from common life, and to relate or describe them, throughout, as far as was possible in a selection of language really used by men, and, at the same time, to throw over them a certain colouring of imagination, whereby ordinary things should be presented to the mind in an unusual aspect; and, further, and above all, to make these incidents and situations interesting by tracing in them, truly though not ostentatiously, the primary laws of our nature: chiefly, as far as regards the manner in which we associate ideas in a state of excitement. Humble and rustic life was generally chosen, because, in that condition, the essential passions of the heart find a better soil in which they can attain their maturity, are less under restraint, and speak a plainer and more emphatic language; because in that condition of life our elementary feelings co-exist in a state of greater simplicity, and, consequently, may be more accurately contemplated, and more forcibly communicated; because the manners of rural life germinate from those elementary feelings, and, from the necessary character of rural occupations, are more easily comprehended, and are more durable; and, lastly, because in that condition the passions of men are incorporated with the beautiful and permanent forms of Nature. The language, too, of these men has been adopted (purified indeed from what appear to be its real defects, from all lasting and rational causes of dislike or disgust) because such men hourly communicate with the best objects from which the best part of language is originally derived; and because, from their rank in society and the sameness and narrow circle of their intercourse, being less under the influence of social vanity, they convey their feelings and notions in simple and unelaborated expressions. Accordingly, such a language, arising out of repeated experience and regular feelings, is a more permanent, and a far more philosophical language, than that which is frequently substituted for it by Poets, who think that they are conferring honour upon themselves and their art, in proportion as they separate themselves from the sympathies of men, and indulge in arbitrary and capricious habits of expression, in order to furnish food for fickle tastes, and fickle appetites, of their own creation.*

I cannot, however, be insensible to the present outcry against the triviality and meanness, both of thought and language, which some of my contemporaries have occasionally introduced into their metrical compositions; and I acknowledge that this defect, where it exists, is more dishonourable to the Writer's own character than false refinement or arbitrary innovation, though I should contend at the same time, that it is far less pernicious in the sum of its consequences. From such verses the Poems in these volumes will be found distinguished at least by one mark of difference, that each of them has a worthy *purpose*. Not that I always began to write with a distinct purpose formally conceived; but habits of meditation have, I trust, so prompted and regulated my feelings, that my descriptions of such objects as strongly excite those feelings, will be found to carry along with them a *purpose*. If this opinion be erroneous, I can have little right to the name of a Poet. For all good poetry is the spontaneous overflow of powerful feelings: and though this be true, Poems to which any value can be attached were never produced on any variety of subjects but by a man who, being possessed of more than usual organic sensibility, had also thought long and deeply. For our continued influxes of feeling are modified and directed by our thoughts, which are indeed the representatives of all our past feelings; and, as by contemplating the relation of these general representatives to each other, we discover what is really important to men, so, by the repetition and continuance of this act, our feelings will be connected with important subjects, till at length, if we be originally possessed of much sensibility, such habits of mind will be produced, that, by obeying blindly and mechanically the impulses of those habits, we shall describe objects, and utter sentiments, of such a nature, and in such connection with each other, that the understanding of the Reader must necessarily be in some degree enlightened, and his affections strengthened and purified.

It has been said that each of these poems has a purpose. Another circumstance must be mentioned which distinguishes

---

* It is worth while here to observe, that the affecting parts of Chaucer are almost always expressed in language pure and universally intelligible even to this day.

these Poems from the popular Poetry of the day; it is this, that
the feeling therein developed gives importance to the action and
situation, and not the action and situation to the feeling.

A sense of false modesty shall not prevent me from asserting, that the Reader's attention is pointed to this mark of distinction, far less for the sake of these particular Poems than from
the general importance of the subject. The subject is indeed
important! For the human mind is capable of being excited
without the application of gross and violent stimulants; and he
must have a very faint perception of its beauty and dignity who
does not know this, and who does not further know, that one
being is elevated above another, in proportion as he possesses
this capability. It has therefore appeared to me, that to endeavour to produce or enlarge this capability is one of the best services in which, at any period, a Writer can be engaged; but this
service, excellent at all times, is especially so at the present day.
For a multitude of causes, unknown to former times, are now
acting with a combined force to blunt the discriminating powers
of the mind, and, unfitting it for all voluntary exertion, to re-
duce it to a state of almost savage torpor. The most effective
of these causes are the great national events which are daily taking place, and the increasing accumulation of men in cities,
where the uniformity of their occupations produces a craving for
extraordinary incident, which the rapid communication of intelligence hourly gratifies. To this tendency of life and manners the literature and theatrical exhibitions of the country have
conformed themselves. The invaluable works of our elder
writers, I had almost said the works of Shakspeare and Milton, are
driven into neglect by frantic novels, sickly and stupid German
Tragedies, and deluges of idle and extravagant stories in verse.
—When I think upon this degrading thirst after outrageous
stimulation, I am almost ashamed to have spoken of the feeble
endeavour made in these volumes to counteract it; and, reflecting upon the magnitude of the general evil, I should be oppressed with no dishonourable melancholy, had I not a deep impression of certain inherent and indestructible qualities of the
human mind, and likewise of certain powers in the great and
permanent objects that act upon it, which are equally inherent
and indestructible; and were there not added to this impression
a belief, that the time is approaching when the evil will be sys-

tematically opposed, by men of greater powers, and with far more distinguished success.

Having dwelt thus long on the subjects and aim of these Poems, I shall request the Reader's permission to apprise him of a few circumstances relating to their *style*, in order, among other reasons, that he may not censure me for not having performed what I never attempted. The Reader will find that personifications of abstract ideas rarely occur in these volumes; and are utterly rejected, as an ordinary device to elevate the style, and raise it above prose. My purpose was to imitate, and, as far as is possible, to adopt the very language of men; and assuredly such personifications do not make any natural or regular part of that language. They are, indeed, a figure of speech occasionally prompted by passion, and I have made use of them as such; but have endeavoured utterly to reject them as a mechanical device of style, or as a family language which Writers in metre seem to lay claim to by prescription. I have wished to keep the Reader in the company of flesh and blood, persuaded that by so doing I shall interest him. Others who pursue a different track will interest him likewise; I do not interfere with their claim, but wish to prefer a claim of my own. There will also be found in these volumes little of what is usually called poetic diction; as much pains has been taken to avoid it as is ordinarily taken to produce it; this has been done for the reason already alleged, to bring my language near to the language of men; and further, because the pleasure which I have proposed to myself to impart, is of a kind very different from that which is supposed by many persons to be the proper object of poetry. Without being culpably particular, I do not know how to give my Reader a more exact notion of the style in which it was my wish and intention to write, than by informing him that I have at all times endeavoured to look steadily at my subject; consequently, there is I hope in these Poems little falsehood of description, and my ideas are expressed in language fitted to their respective importance. Something must have been gained by this practice, as it is friendly to one property of all good poetry, namely, good sense: but it has necessarily cut me off from a large portion of phrases and figures of speech which from father to son have long been regarded as the common inheritance of Poets. I have also thought it expedient to restrict myself still further, having abstained from the use of many expressions, in themselves proper and beautiful, but which have been foolishly repeated by bad Poets, till such feelings of disgust are connected with them as it is scarcely possible by any art of association to overpower.

If in a poem there should be found a series of lines, or even a single line, in which the language, though naturally arranged, and according to the strict laws of metre, does not differ from that of prose, there is a numerous class of critics, who, when they stumble upon these prosaisms, as they call them, imagine that they have made a notable discovery, and exult over the Poet as over a man ignorant of his own profession. Now these men would establish a canon of criticism which the Reader will con- clude he must utterly reject, if he wishes to be pleased with these volumes. And it would be a most easy task to prove to him, that not only the language of a large portion of every good poem, even of the most elevated character, must necessarily, ex- cept with reference to the metre, in no respect differ from that of good prose, but likewise that some of the most interesting parts of the best poems will be found to be strictly the language of prose when prose is well written. The truth of this assertion might be demonstrated by innumerable passages from almost all the poetical writings, even of Milton himself. To illustrate the subject in a general manner, I will here adduce a short compo- sition of Gray, who was at the head of those who, by their rea- sonings, have attempted to widen the space of separation betwixt Prose and Metrical composition, and was more than any other man curiously elaborate in the structure of his own poetic diction.

> In vain to me the smiling mornings shine,
> And reddening Phœbus lifts his golden fire:
> The birds in vain their amorous descant join,
> Or cheerful fields resume their green attire.
> These ears, alas! for other notes repine;
> *A different object do these eyes require;*
> *My lonely anguish melts no heart but mine;*
> *And in my breast the imperfect joys expire;*
> Yet morning smiles the busy race to cheer,
> And new-born pleasure brings to happier men;
> The fields to all their wonted tribute bear;
> To warm their little loves the birds complain.
> *I fruitless mourn to him that cannot hear,*
> *And weep the more because I weep in vain.*

It will easily be perceived, that the only part of this Sonnet which is of any value is the lines printed in Italics; it is equally obvious, that, except in the rhyme, and in the use of the single word 'fruitless' for fruitlessly, which is so far a defect, the language of these lines does in no respect differ from that of prose.

By the foregoing quotation it has been shown that the language of Prose may yet be well adapted to Poetry; and it was previously asserted, that a large portion of the language of every good poem can in no respect differ from that of good Prose. We will go further. It may be safely affirmed, that there neither is, nor can be, any *essential* difference between the language of prose and metrical composition. We are fond of tracing the resemblance between Poetry and Painting, and, accordingly, we call them Sisters: but where shall we find bonds of connection sufficiently strict to typify the affinity betwixt metrical and prose composition? They both speak by and to the same organs; the bodies in which both of them are clothed may be said to be of the same substance, their affections are kindred, and almost identical, not necessarily differing even in degree; Poetry* sheds no tears 'such as Angels weep,' but natural and human tears; she can boast of no celestial ichor that distinguishes her vital juices from those of prose; the same human blood circulates through the veins of them both.

If it be affirmed that rhyme and metrical arrangement of themselves constitute a distinction which overturns what has just been said on the strict affinity of metrical language with that of prose, and paves the way for other artificial distinctions which the mind voluntarily admits, I answer that the language of such Poetry as is here recommended is, as far as is possible, a selection of the language really spoken by men; that this selection, wherever it is made with true taste and feeling, will of itself form a distinction far greater than would at first be imagined, and will entirely separate the composition from the vulgarity and meanness of ordinary life; and, if metre be super-

* I here use the word 'Poetry' (though against my own judgment) as opposed to the word Prose, and synonymous with metrical composition. But much confusion has been introduced into criticism by this contradistinction of Poetry and Prose, instead of the more philosophical one of Poetry and Matter of Fact, or Science. The only strict antithesis to Prose is Metre; nor is this, in truth, a *strict* antithesis, because lines and passages of metre so naturally occur in writing prose, that it would be scarcely possible to avoid them, even were it desirable

added thereto, I believe that a dissimilitude will be produced altogether sufficient for the gratification of a rational mind. What other distinction would we have ? Whence is it to come ? And where is it to exist ? Not, surely, where the Poet speaks through the mouths of his characters : it cannot be necessary here, either for elevation of style, or any of its supposed orna- ments : for, if the Poet's subject be judiciously chosen, it will naturally, and upon fit occasion, lead him to passions the lan- guage of which, if selected truly and judiciously, must neces- sarily be dignified and variegated, and alive with metaphors and figures. I forbear to speak of an incongruity which would shock the intelligent Reader, should the Poet interweave any foreign splendour of his own with that which the passion naturally suggests : it is sufficient to say that such addition is unneces- sary. And, surely, it is more probable that those passages, which with propriety abound with metaphors and figures, will have their due effect, if, upon other occasions where the passions are of a milder character, the style also be subdued and tem- perate.

But, as the pleasure which I hope to give by the Poems now presented to the Reader must depend entirely on just notions upon this subject, and, as it is in itself of high importance to our taste and moral feelings, I cannot content myself with these detached remarks. And if, in what I am about to say, it shall appear to some that my labour is unnecessary, and that I am like a man fighting a battle without enemies, such persons may be reminded, that, whatever be the language outwardly holden by men, a practical faith in the opinions which I am wishing to establish is almost unknown. If my conclusions are admitted, and carried as far as they must be carried if admitted at all, our judgments concerning the works of the greatest Poets both ancient and modern will be far different from what they are at present, both when we praise, and when we censure : and our moral feelings influencing and influenced by these judgments will, I believe, be corrected and purified.·

Taking up the subject, then, upon general grounds, let me ask, what is meant by the word Poet ? What is a Poet ? To whom does he address himself ? And what language is to be expected from him ?—He is a man speaking to men : a man, it is true, endowed with more lively sensibility, more enthusiasm and tenderness, who has a greater knowledge of human nature, and a more comprehensive soul, than are supposed to be common among mankind; a man pleased with his own passions and volitions, and who rejoices more than other men in the spirit of life that is in him; delighting to contemplate similar volitions and passions as manifested in the goings-on of the Universe, and habitually impelled to create them where he does not find them. To these qualities he has added a disposition to be affected more 'than other men by absent things as if they were present; an ability of conjuring up in himself passions, which are indeed far from being the same as those produced by real events, yet (especially in those parts of the general sympathy which are pleasing and delightful) do more nearly resemble the passions produced by real events, than anything which, from the motions of their own minds merely, other men are accustomed to feel in themselves :—whence, and from practice, he has acquired a greater readiness and power in expressing what he thinks and feels, and especially those thoughts and feelings which, by his own choice, or from the structure of his own mind, arise in him without immediate external excitement.

But whatever portion of this faculty we may suppose even the greatest Poet to possess, there cannot be a doubt that the language which it will suggest to him, must often, in liveliness and truth, fall short of that which is uttered by men in real life, under the actual pressure of those passions, certain shadows of which the Poet thus produces, or feels to be produced, in himself.

However exalted a notion we would wish to cherish of the character of a Poet, it is obvious, that while he describes and imitates passions, his employment is in some degree mechanical, compared with the freedom and power of real and substantial action and suffering. So that it will be the wish of the Poet to bring his feelings near to those of the persons whose feelings he describes, nay, for short spaces of time, perhaps, to let himself slip into an entire delusion, and even confound and identify his own feelings with theirs; modifying only the language which is thus suggested to him by a consideration that he describes for a particular purpose, that of giving pleasure. Here, then, he will apply the principle of selection which has been already insisted upon. He will depend upon this for removing what would otherwise be painful or disgusting in the passion ; he will feel that there is no necessity to trick out or to elevate nature : and, the more industriously he applies this principle, the deeper will be his faith that no words, which *his* fancy or imagination can suggest, will be to be compared with those which are the emanations of reality and truth.

But it may be said by those who do not object to the general spirit of these remarks, that, as it is impossible for the Poet to produce upon all occasions language as exquisitely fitted for the passion as that which the real passion itself suggests, it is proper that he should consider himself as in the situation of a translator, who does not scruple to substitute excellencies of another kind for those which are unattainable by him ; and endeavours occasionally to surpass his original, in order to make some amends for the general inferiority to which he feels that he must submit. But this would be to encourage idleness and unmanly despair. Further, it is the language of men who speak of what they do not understand ; who talk of Poetry as of a matter of amusement and idle pleasure ; who will converse with us as gravely about a *taste* for Poetry, as they express it, as if it were a thing as indifferent as a taste for rope-dancing, or Frontiniac or Sherry. Aristotle, I have been told, has said, that Poetry is the most philosophic of all writing : it is so : its object is truth, not individual and local, but general, and operative ; not standing upon external testimony, but carried alive into the heart by passion ; truth which is its own testimony, which gives competence and confidence to the tribunal to which it appeals, and receives them from the same tribunal. Poetry is the image of man and nature. The obstacles which stand in the way of the fidelity of the Biographer and Historian, and of their consequent utility, are incalculably greater than those which are to be encountered by the Poet who comprehends the dignity of his art. The Poet writes under one restriction only, namely, the necessity of giving immediate pleasure to a human Being possessed of that information which may be expected from him, not as a lawyer, a physician, a mariner, an astronomer, or a natural philosopher, but as a Man. Except this one restriction, there is no object standing between the Poet and the image of things ; between this, and the Biographer and Historian, there are a thousand.

Nor let this necessity of producing immediate pleasure be
considered as a degradation of the Poet's art.   It is far otherwise.   It is an acknowledgment of the beauty of the universe,
an acknowledgment the more sincere, because not formal, but
indirect; it is a task light and easy to him who looks at the
world in the spirit of love :· further, it is a homage paid to the
native and naked dignity of man, to the grand elementary principle of pleasure, by which he knows, and feels, and lives, and
moves.   We have no sympathy but what is propagated by pleasure : I would not be misunderstood; but wherever we sympathise with pain, it will be found that the sympathy is produced and carried on by subtle combinations with pleasure.   We
have no knowledge, that is, no general principles drawn from
the contemplation of particular facts, but what has been built
up by pleasure, and exists in us by pleasure alone.   The Man of
science, the Chemist and Mathematician, whatever ·difficulties
and disgusts they may have had to struggle with, know and feel
this.   However painful may be the objects with which the Anatomist's knowledge is connected, he feels that his knowledge is
pleasure; and where he has no pleasure he has no knowledge.
What then does the Poet ?· He considers man and the objects
that surround him as acting and re-acting upon each other, so
as to produce an infinite complexity of pain and pleasure; he
considers man in his own nature and in his ordinary life as
contemplating this with a certain quantity of immediate knowledge, with certain convictions, intuitions, and deductions, which
from habit acquire the quality of intuitions; he considers him
as looking upon this complex scene of ideas and sensations, and
finding every where objects that immediately excite in him sympathies which, from the necessities of his nature, are accompanied by an overbalance of enjoyment.

To this knowledge which all men carry about with them, and
to these sympathies in which, without any other discipline than
that of our daily life, we are fitted to take delight, the Poet
principally directs his attention.   He considers man and nature
as essentially adapted to each other, and the mind of man as
naturally the mirror of the fairest and most interesting properties of nature.   And thus the Poet, prompted by this feeling of
pleasure, which accompanies him through the whole course of
his studies, converses with general nature, with affections akin

to those, which, through labour and length of time, the Man of science has raised up in himself, by conversing with those particular parts of nature which are the objects of his studies. The knowledge both of the Poet and the Man of science is pleasure; but the knowledge of the one cleaves to us as a necessary part of our existence, our natural and unalienable inheritance; the other is a personal and individual acquisition, slow to come to us, and by no habitual and direct sympathy connecting us with our fellow-beings. The Man of science seeks truth as a remote and unknown benefactor; he cherishes and loves it in his solitude: the Poet, singing a song in which all human beings join with him, rejoices in the presence of truth as our visible friend and hourly companion. Poetry is the breath and finer spirit of all knowledge; it is the impassioned expression which is in the countenance of all Science. Emphatically may it be said of the Poet, as Shakspeare hath said of man, 'that he looks before and after.' He is the rock of defence for human nature; an upholder and preserver, carrying every where with him relationship and love. In spite of difference of soil and climate, of language and manners, of laws and customs: in spite of things silently gone out of mind, and things violently destroyed; the Poet binds together by passion and knowledge the vast empire of human society, as it is spread over the whole earth, and over all time. The objects of the Poet's thoughts are every where; though the eyes and senses of man are, it is true, his favourite guides, yet he will follow wheresoever he can find an atmosphere of sensation, in which to move his wings. Poetry is the first and last of all knowledge—it is as immortal as the heart of man. If the labours of Men of science should ever create any material revolution, direct or indirect, in our condition, and in the impressions which we habitually receive, the Poet will sleep then no more than at present; he will be ready to follow the steps of the Man of science, not only in those general indirect effects, but he will be at his side, carrying sensation into the midst of the objects of the science itself. The remotest discoveries of the Chemist, the Botanist, or Mineralogist, will be as proper objects of the Poet's art as any upon which it can be employed, if the time should ever come when these things shall be familiar to us, and the relations under which they are contemplated by the followers of these respective sciences shall be manifestly and palpably material to us as enjoying and suffering beings. If the time should ever come when what is now called science, thus familiarised to men, shall be ready to put on, as it were, a form of flesh and blood, the Poet will lend his divine spirit to aid the transfiguration, and will welcome the Being thus produced, as a dear and genuine inmate of the household of man.—It is not, then, to be supposed that any one, who holds that sublime notion of Poetry which I have attempted to convey, will break in upon the sanctity and truth of his pictures by transitory and accidental ornaments, and endeavour to excite admiration of himself by arts, the necessity of which must manifestly depend upon the assumed meanness of his subject.

What has been thus far said applies to Poetry in general; but especially to those parts of composition where the Poet speaks through the mouths of his. characters; and upon this point it appears to authorise the conclusion that there are few persons of good sense, who would not allow that the dramatic parts of composition are defective, in proportion as they deviate from the real language of nature, and are coloured by a diction of the Poet's own, either peculiar to him as an individual Poet or belonging simply to Poets in general; to a body of men who, from the circumstance of their composition being in metre, it is expected will employ a particular language.

It is not, then, in the dramatic parts of composition that we look for this distinction of language; but still it may be proper and necessary where the Poet speaks to us in his own person and character. To this I answer by referring the Reader to the description before given of a Poet. Among the qualities there enumerated as principally conducing to form a Poet, is implied nothing differing in kind from other men, but only in degree. The sum of what was said is, that the Poet is chiefly distinguished from other men by a greater promptness to think and feel without immediate external excitement, and a greater power in expressing such thoughts and feelings as are produced in him in that manner. But these passions and thoughts and feelings are the general passions and thoughts and feelings of men. And with what are they connected? Undoubtedly with our moral sentiments and animal sensations, and with the causes which excite these; with the operations of the elements, and the appearances of the visible universe; with storm and sunshine, with the revolutions of the seasons, with cold and heat, with loss of friends and kindred, with injuries and resentments, gratitude and hope, with fear and sorrow. These, and the like, are the sensations and objects which the Poet describes, as they are the sensations of other men, and the objects which interest them. The Poet thinks and feels in the spirit of human passions. How, then, can his language differ in any material degree from that of all other men who feel vividly and see clearly? It might be *proved* that it is impossible. But supposing that this were not the case, the Poet might then be allowed to use a peculiar language when expressing his feelings for his own gratification, or that of men like himself. But Poets do not write for Poets alone, but for men. Unless therefore we are advocates for that admiration which subsists upon ignorance, and that pleasure which arises from hearing what we do not understand, the Poet must descend from this supposed height; and, in order to excite rational sympathy, he must express himself as other men express themselves. To this it may be added, that while he is only selecting from the real language of men, or, which amounts to the same thing, composing accurately in the spirit of such selection, he is treading upon safe ground, and we know what we are to expect from him. Our feelings are the same with respect to metre; for, as it may be proper to remind the Reader, the distinction of metre is regular and uniform, and not, like that which is produced by what is usually called POETIC DICTION, arbitrary, and subject to infinite caprices, upon which no calculation whatever can be made. In the one case, the Reader is utterly at the mercy of the Poet, respecting what imagery or diction he may choose to connect with the passion; whereas, in the other, the metre obeys certain laws, to which the Poet and Reader both willingly submit because they are certain, and because no interference is made by them with the passion but such as the concurring testimony of ages has shown to heighten and improve the pleasure which co-exists with it.

It will now be proper to answer an obvious question, namely, Why, professing these opinions, have I written in verse? To this, in addition to such answer as is included in what has been already said, I reply, in the first place, Because, however I may have restricted myself, there is still left open to me what confessedly constitutes the most valuable object of all writing, whether in prose or verse; the great and universal passions of men, the most general and interesting of their occupations, and the entire world of nature before me—to supply endless combinations of forms and imagery. Now, supposing for a moment that whatever is interesting in these objects may be as vividly described in prose, why should I be condemned for attempting to superadd to such description, the charm which, by the consent of all nations, is acknowledged to exist in metrical language? To this, by such as are yet unconvinced, it may be answered that a very small part of the pleasure given by Poetry depends upon the metre, and that it is injudicious to write in metre, unless it be accompanied with the other artificial distinctions of style with which metre is usually accompanied, and that, by such deviation, more will be lost from the shock which will thereby be given to the Reader's associations than will be counterbalanced by any pleasure which he can derive from the general power of numbers. In answer to those who still contend for the necessity of accompanying metre with certain appropriate colours of style in order to the accomplishment of its appropriate end, and who also, in my opinion, greatly underrate the power of metre in itself, it might, perhaps, as far as relates to these Volumes, have been almost sufficient to observe, that poems are extant, written upon more humble subjects, and in a still more naked and simple style, which have continued to give pleasure from generation to generation. Now, if nakedness and simplicity be a defect, the fact here mentioned affords a strong presumption that poems somewhat less naked and simple are capable of affording pleasure at the present day; and, what I wished *chiefly* to attempt, at present, was to justify myself for having written under the impression of this belief.

But various causes might be pointed out why, when the style is manly, and the subject of some importance, words metrically arranged will long continue to impart such a pleasure to mankind as he who proves the extent of that pleasure will be desirous to impart. The end of Poetry is to produce excitement in co-existence with an overbalance of pleasure; but, by the supposition, excitement is an unusual and irregular state of the mind; ideas and feelings do not, in that state, succeed each other in accustomed order. If the words, however, by which this excitement is produced be in themselves powerful, or the images and feelings have an undue proportion of pain connected with them, there is some danger that the excitement may be carried beyond its proper bounds. Now the co-presence of something regular, something to which the mind has been accustomed in various moods and in a less excited state, cannot but have great efficacy in tempering and restraining the passion by an intertexture of ordinary feeling, and of feeling not strictly and necessarily connected with the passion. This is unquestionably true; and hence, though the opinion will at first appear paradoxical, from the tendency of metre to divest language, in a certain degree, of its reality, and thus to throw a sort of half-consciousness of unsubstantial existence over the whole composition, there can be little doubt but that more pathetic situations and sentiments, that is, those which have a greater proportion of pain connected with them, may be endured in metrical composition, especially in rhyme, than in prose. The metre of the old ballads is very artless; yet they contain many passages which would illustrate this opinion; and I hope, if the following Poems be attentively perused, similar instances will be found in them. This opinion may be further illustrated by appealing to the Reader's own experience of the reluctance with which he comes to the re-perusal of the distressful parts of *Clarissa Harlowe*, or the *Gamester;* while Shakspeare's writings, in the most pathetic scenes, never act upon us, as pathetic, beyond the bounds of pleasure—an effect which, in a much greater degree than might at first be imagined, is to be ascribed to small, but continual and regular impulses of pleasurable surprise from the metrical arrangement.—On the other hand (what it must be allowed will much more frequently happen) if the Poet's words should be incommensurate with the passion, and inadequate to raise the Reader to a height of desirable excitement, then, (unless the Poet's choice of his metre has been grossly injudicious) in the feelings of pleasure which the Reader has been accustomed to connect with metre in general, and in the feeling, whether cheerful or melancholy, which he has been accustomed to connect with that particular movement of metre, there will be found something which will greatly contribute to impart passion to the words, and to effect the complex end which the Poet proposes to himself.

If I had undertaken a SYSTEMATIC defence of the theory here

maintained, it would have been my duty to develop the various causes upon which the pleasure received from metrical language depends. Among the chief of these causes is to be reckoned a principle which must be well known to those who have made any of the Arts the object of accurate reflection; namely, the pleasure which the mind derives from the perception of similitude in dissimilitude. This principle is the great spring of the activity of our minds, and their chief feeder. From this principle the direction of the sexual appetite, and all the passions connected with it, take their origin: it is the life of our ordinary conversation; and upon the accuracy with which similitude in dissimilitude, and dissimilitude in similitude are perceived, depend our taste and our moral feelings. It would not be a useless employment to apply this principle to the consideration of metre, and to show that metre is hence enabled to afford much pleasure, and to point out in what manner that pleasure is produced. But my limits will not permit me to enter upon this subject, and I must content myself with a general summary.

I have said that poetry is the spontaneous overflow of powerful feelings: it takes its origin from emotion recollected in tranquillity: the emotion is contemplated till, by a species of re-action, the tranquillity gradually disappears, and an emotion, kindred to that which was before the subject of contemplation, is gradually produced, and does itself actually exist in the mind. In this mood successful composition generally begins, and in a mood similar to this it is carried on; but the emotion, of whatever kind, and in whatever degree, from various causes, is qualified by various pleasures, so that in describing any passions whatsoever, which are voluntarily described, the mind will, upon the whole, be in a state of enjoyment. If Nature be thus cautious to preserve in a state of enjoyment a being so employed, the Poet ought to profit by the lesson held forth to him, and ought especially to take care, that, whatever passions he communicates to his Reader, those passions, if his Reader's mind be sound and vigorous, should always be accompanied with an overbalance of pleasure. Now the music of harmonious metrical language, the sense of difficulty overcome, and the blind association of pleasure which has been previously received from. works of rhyme or metre of the same or similar construction, an indistinct perception perpetually renewed of language closely resembling that of real life, and yet, in the circumstance of metre, differing from it so widely—all these imperceptibly make up a complex feeling of delight, which is of the most important use in tempering the painful feeling always found intermingled with powerful descriptions of the deeper passions. This effect is always produced in pathetic and impassioned poetry; while, in lighter compositions, the ease and gracefulness with which the Poet manages his numbers are themselves confessedly a principal source of the gratification of the Reader. All that it is *necessary* to say, however, upon this subject, may be effected by affirming, what few persons will deny, that, of two descriptions, either of passions, manners, or characters, each of them equally well executed, the one in prose and the other in verse, the verse will be read a hundred times where the prose is read once.

Having thus explained a few of my reasons for writing in verse, and why I have chosen' subjects from common life, and endeavoured to bring my language near to the real language of men, if I have been too minute in pleading my own cause, I have at the same time been treating a subject of general interest; and for this reason a few words shall be added with reference solely to these particular poems, and to some defects which will probably be found in them. I am sensible that my associations must have sometimes been particular instead of general, and that, consequently, giving to things a false importance, I may have sometimes written upon unworthy subjects; but I am less apprehensive on this account, than that my language may frequently have suffered from those arbitrary connections of feelings and ideas with particular words and phrases, from which no man can altogether protect himself. Hence I have no doubt, that, in some instances, feelings, even of the ludicrous, may be given to my Readers by expressions which appeared to me tender and pathetic. Such faulty expressions, were I convinced they were faulty at present, and that they must necessarily continue to be so, I would willingly take all reasonable pains to correct. But it is dangerous to make these alterations on the simple authority of a few individuals, or even of certain classes of men; for where the understanding of an Author is not convinced, or his feelings altered, this cannot be done without great injury to himself: for his own feelings are his stay and support; and, if he set them aside in one instance, he may be induced to repeat this act till his mind shall lose all confidence in itself, and become utterly debilitated. To this it may be added, that the Critic ought never to forget that he is himself exposed to the same errors as the Poet, and, perhaps, in a much greater degree : for there can be no presumption in saying of most readers, that it is not probable they will be so well acquainted with the various stages of meaning through which words have passed, or with the fickleness or stability of the relations of particular ideas to each other; and, above all, since they are so much less interested in the subject, they may decide lightly and carelessly.

Long as the Reader has been detained, I hope he will permit me to caution him against a mode of false criticism which has been applied to Poetry, in which the language closely resembles that of life and nature. Such verses have been triumphed over in parodies, of which Dr. Johnson's stanza is a fair specimen :—

> I put my hat upon my head
> And walked into the Strand,
> And there I met another man
> Whose hat was in his hand.

Immediately under these lines let us place one of the most justly-admired stanzas of the ' Babes in the Wood.'

> These pretty Babes with hand in hand
> Went wandering up and down ;
> But never more they saw the Man
> Approaching from the Town.

In both these stanzas the words, and the order of the words, in no respect differ from the most unimpassioned conversation. There are words in both, for example, ' the Strand,' and ' the Town,' connected with none but the most familiar ideas; yet the one stanza we admit as admirable, and the other as a fair example of the superlatively contemptible. Whence arises this difference ? Not from the metre, not from the language, not from the order of the words; but the *matter* expressed in Dr. Johnson's stanza is contemptible. The proper method of treating trivial and simple verses, to which Dr. Johnson's stanza would be a fair parallelism, is not to say, this is a bad kind of poetry, or, this is not poetry; but, this wants sense ; it is neither interesting in itself, nor can *lead* to any thing interesting; the images neither originate in that sane state of feeling which arises out of thought, nor can excite thought or feeling in the Reader. This is the only sensible manner of dealing with such verses. Why trouble yourself about the species till you have previously decided upon the genus? Why take pains to prove that an ape is not a Newton, when it is self-evident that he is not a man?

One request I must make of my reader, which is, that in judging these Poems he would decide by his own feelings genuinely, and not by reflection upon what will probably be the judgment of others. How common is it to hear a person say, I myself do not object to this style of composition, or this or that expression, but, to such and such classes of people it will appear mean or ludicrous! This mode of criticism, so destructive of all sound unadulterated judgment, is almost universal: let the Reader then abide, independently, by his own feelings, and, if he finds himself affected, let him not suffer such conjectures to interfere with his pleasure.

If an Author, by any single composition, has impressed us with respect for his talents, it is useful to consider this as affording a presumption, that on other occasions where we have been displeased, he, nevertheless, may not have written ill or absurdly; and further, to give him so much credit for this one composition as may induce us to review what has displeased us, with more care than we should otherwise have bestowed upon it. This is not only an act of justice, but, in our decisions upon poetry especially, may conduce, in a high degree, to the improvement of our own taste: for an *accurate* taste in poetry, and in all the other arts, as Sir Joshua Reynolds has observed, is an *acquired* talent, which can only be produced by thought and a long-continued intercourse with the best models of composition. This is mentioned, not with so ridiculous a purpose as to prevent the most inexperienced Reader from judging for himself, (I have already said that I wish him to judge for himself;) but merely to temper the rashness of decision, and to suggest, that, if Poetry be a subject on which much time has not been bestowed, the judgment may be erroneous; and that, in many cases, it necessarily will be so.

Nothing would, I know, have so effectually contributed to

further the ond which I have in view, as to have shown of what
kind the pleasure is, and how that pleasure is produced, which
is confessedly produced by metrical composition essentially different from that which I have here endeavoured to recommend:
for the Reader will say that he has been pleased by such composition; and what more can be done for him? The power of
any art is limited; and he will suspect, that, if it be proposed
to furnish him with new friends, that can be only upon condition of his abandoning his old friends. Besides, as I have said,
the Reader is himself conscious of the pleasure which he has
received from such composition, composition to which he has
peculiarly attached the endearing name of Poetry; and all men
feel an habitual gratitude, and something of an honourable
bigotry, for the objects which have long continued to please
them: we not only wish to be pleased, but to be pleased in that
particular way in which we have been accustomed to be pleased.
There is in these feelings enough to resist a host of arguments;
and I should be the less able to combat them successfully, as I
am willing to allow, that, in order entirely to enjoy the Poetry
which I am recommending, it would be necessary to give up
much of what is ordinarily enjoyed. But, would my limits have
permitted me to point out how this pleasure is produced, many
obstacles might have been removed, and the Reader assisted in
perceiving that the powers of language are not so limited as he
may suppose; and that it is possible for Poetry to give other
enjoyments, of a purer, more lasting, and more exquisite nature.
This part of the subject has not been altogether neglected, but
it has not been so much my present aim to prove, that the interest excited by some other kinds of poetry is less vivid, and
less worthy of the nobler powers of the mind, as to offer reasons
for presuming, that if my purpose were fulfilled, a species of
poetry would be produced, which is genuine poetry; in its nature well adapted to interest mankind permanently, and likewise
important in the multiplicity and quality of its moral relations.

From what has been said, and from a perusal of the Poems,
the Reader will be able clearly to perceive the object which I
had in view: he will determine how far it has been attained;
and, what is a much more important question, whether it be
worth attaining: and upon the decision of these two questions
will rest my claim to the approbation of the Public.

'What is usually called Poetic Diction' (Essay i. page 84, line 22).

PERHAPS, as I have no right to expect that attentive perusal, without which, confined, as I have been, to the narrow limits of a Preface, my meaning cannot be thoroughly understood, I am anxious to give an exact notion of the sense in which the phrase poetic diction has been used; and for this purpose, a few words shall here be added, concerning the origin and characteristics of the phraseology, which I have condemned under that name.

The earliest poets of all nations generally wrote from passion excited by real events; they wrote naturally, and as men : feeling powerfully as they did, their language was daring, and figurative. In succeeding times, Poets, and Men ambitious of the fame of Poets, perceiving the influence of such language, and desirous of producing the same effect without being animated by the same passion, set themselves to a mechanical adoption of these figures of speech, and made use of them, sometimes with propriety, but much more frequently applied them to feelings and thoughts with which they had no natural connection whatsoever. A language was thus insensibly produced, differing materially from the real language of men in *any situation.* The Reader or Hearer of this distorted language found himself in a perturbed and unusual state of mind: when affected by the genuine language of passion he had been in a perturbed and unusual state of mind also : in both cases he was willing that his common judgment and understanding should be laid asleep, and he had no instinctive and infallible perception of the true to make him reject the false; the one served as a passport for the other. The emotion was in both cases delightful, and no wonder if he confounded the one with the other, and believed them both to be produced by the same, or similar causes. Besides, the Poet spake to him in the character of a man to be looked up to, a man of genius and authority. Thus, and from a variety of other causes, this distorted language was received with admiration; and Poets, it is probable, who had before contented themselves for the most part with misapplying only expressions which at first had been dictated by real passion, carried the abuse still further, and introduced phrases composed apparently in the spirit of the original figurative language of passion, yet altogether of their own invention, and characterised by various .degrees of wanton deviation from good sense and Nature.

It is indeed true, that the language of the earliest Poets was felt to differ materially from ordinary language, because it was the language of extraordinary occasions; but it was really spoken by men, language which the Poet himself had uttered when he had been affected by the events which he described, or which he had heard uttered by those around him. To this language it is probable that metre of some sort or other was early superadded. This separated the genuine language of Poetry still further from common life, so that whoever read or heard the poems of these earliest Poets felt himself moved in a way in which he had not been accustomed to be moved in real life, and by causes manifestly different from those which acted upon him in real life. This was the great temptation to all the corruptions which have followed: under the protection of this feeling succeeding Poets constructed a phraseology which had one thing, it is true, in common with the genuine language of poetry, namely, that it was not heard in ordinary conversation; that it was unusual. But the first Poets, as I have said, spake a language which, though unusual, was still the language of men. This circumstance, however, was disregarded by their successors; they found that they could please by easier means: they became proud of modes of expression which they themselves had invented, and which were uttered only by themselves. In process of time metre became a symbol or promise of this unusual language, and whoever took upon him to write in metre, according as he possessed more or less of true poetic genius, introduced less or more of this adulterated phraseology into his compositions, and the true and the false were inseparably inter-woven until, the taste of men becoming gradually perverted, this language was received as a natural language: and at length by the influence of books upon men, did to a certain degree really become so. Abuses of this kind were imported from one nation to another, and with the progress of refinement this diction became daily more and more corrupt, thrusting out of sight the plain humanities of Nature by a motley masquerade of, tricks, quaintnesses, hieroglyphics, and enigmas.

It would not be uninteresting to point out the causes of the pleasure given by this extravagant and absurd diction. It depends upon a great variety of causes, but upon none, perhaps, more than its influence in impressing a notion of the peculiarity and exaltation of the Poet's character, and in flattering the Reader's self-love by bringing him nearer to a sympathy with that character; an effect which is accomplished by unsettling ordinary habits of thinking, and thus assisting the Reader to approach to that perturbed and dizzy state of mind in which if he does not find himself, he imagines that he is *balked* of a peculiar enjoyment which poetry can and ought to bestow.

The sonnet quoted from Gray, in the Preface, except the lines printed in Italics, consists of little else but this diction, though not of the worst kind; and indeed, if one may be permitted to say so, it is far too common in the best writers both ancient and modern. Perhaps in no way, by positive example, could more easily be given a notion of what I mean by the phrase *poetic diction* than by referring to a comparison between the metrical paraphrase which we have of passages in the Old and New Testament, and those passages as they exist in our common Translation. See Pope's 'Messiah' throughout; Prior's 'Did sweeter sounds adorn my flowing tongue,' &c., &c., 'Though I speak with the tongues of men and of angels,' &c., &c. 1st Corinthians, chap. xiii. By way of immediate example, take the following of Dr. Johnson :

> Turn on the prudent Ant thy heedless eyes,
> Observe her labours, Sluggard, and be wise;
> No stern command, no monitory voice,
> Prescribes her duties, or directs her choice;
> Yet, timely provident, she hastes away
> To snatch the blessings of a plenteous day;
> When fruitful Summer loads the teeming plain,
> She crops the harvest, and she stores the grain.
> How long shall sloth usurp thy useless hours,
> Unnerve thy vigour, and enchain thy powers?
> While artful shades thy downy couch enclose,
> And soft solicitation courts repose,
> Amidst the drowsy charms of dull delight,
> Year chases year with unremitted flight,
> Till Want now following, fraudulent and slow,
> Shall spring to seize thee, like an ambush'd foe.

From this hubbub of words pass to the original. 'Go to the Ant, thou Sluggard, consider her ways, and be wise: which having no guide, overseer, or ruler, provideth her meat in the summer, and gathereth her food in the harvest. How long wilt thou sleep, O Sluggard? When wilt thou arise out of thy sleep? Yet a little sleep, a little slumber, a little folding of the hands to sleep. So shall thy poverty come as one that travelleth, and thy want as an armed man.' Proverbs, chap. vi.

One more quotation, and I have done. It is from Cowper's Verses supposed to be written by Alexander Selkirk :—

> Religion! what treasure untold
> Resides in that heavenly word!
> More precious than silver and gold,
> Or all that this earth can afford.
> But the sound of the church-going bell
> These valleys and rocks never heard,
> Ne'er sigh'd at the sound of a knell,
> Or smiled when a Sabbath appeared.
>
> Ye winds, that have made me your sport,
> Convey to this desolate shore
> Some cordial endearing report
> Of a land I must visit no more.
> My Friends, do they now and then send
> A wish or a thought after me?
> O tell me I yet have a friend,
> Though a friend I am never to see.

This passage is quoted as an instance of three different styles of composition. The first four lines are poorly expressed; some Critics would call the language prosaic; the fact is, it would be bad prose, so bad, that it is scarcely worse in metre. The epithet 'church-going' applied to a bell, and that by so chaste a writer as Cowper, is an instance of the strange abuses which Poets have introduced into their language, till they and their Readers take them as matters of course, if they do not single them out expressly as objects of admiration. The two lines 'Ne'er sigh'd at the sound,' &c., are, in my opinion, an instance of the language of passion wrested from its proper use, and, from the mere circumstance of the composition being in metre, applied upon an occasion that does not justify such violent expressions; and I should condemn the passage, though perhaps few Readers will agree with me, as vicious poetic diction.

The last stanza is throughout admirably expressed : it would be equally good whether in prose or verse, except that the Reader has an exquisite pleasure in seeing such natural language so naturally connected with metre. The beauty of this stanza tempts me to conclude with a principle which ought never to be lost sight of, and which has been my chief guide in all I have said,—namely, that in works *of imagination and sentiment*, for of these only have I been treating, in proportion as ideas and feelings are valuable, whether the composition be in prose or in verse, they require and exact one and the same language. Metre is but adventitious to composition, and the phraseology for which that passport is necessary, even where it may be graceful at all, will be little valued by the judicious.

WITH the young of both sexes, Poetry is, like love, a passion; but, for much the greater part of those who have been proud of its power over their minds, a necessity soon arises of breaking the pleasing bondage; or it relaxes of itself;—the thoughts being occupied in domestic cares, or the time engrossed by business. Poetry then becomes only an occasional recreation; while to those whose existence passes away in a course of fashionable pleasure, it is a species of luxurious amusement. In middle and declining age, a scattered number of serious persons resort to poetry, as to religion, for a protection against the pressure of trivial employments, and as a consolation for the afflictions of life. And, lastly, there are many, who, having been enamoured of this art in their youth, have found leisure, after youth was spent, to cultivate general literature; in which poetry has continued to be comprehended *as a study.*

Into the above classes the Readers of poetry may be divided; Critics abound in them all; but from the last only can opinions be collected of absolute value, and worthy to be depended upon, as prophetic of the destiny of a new work. The young, who in nothing can escape delusion, are especially subject to it in their intercourse with Poetry. The cause, not so obvious as the fact is unquestionable, is the same as that from which erroneous judgments in this art, in the minds of men of all ages, chiefly proceed; but upon Youth it operates with peculiar force. The appropriate business of poetry, (which, nevertheless, if genuine, is as permanent as pure science,) her appropriate employment, her privilege and her *duty,* is to treat of things not as they *are,* but as they *appear;* not as they exist in themselves, but as they *seem* to exist to the *senses,* and to the *passions.* What a world of delusion does this acknowledged obligation prepare for the inexperienced! what temptations to go astray are here held forth for them whose thoughts have been little disciplined by the understanding, and whose feelings revolt from the sway of reason!—When a juvenile Reader is in the height of his rapture with some vicious passage, should experience throw in doubts, or common-sense suggest suspicions, a lurking consciousness that the realities of the Muse are but shows, and that her live-liest excitements are raised by transient shocks of conflicting feeling and successive assemblages of contradictory thoughts—is ever at hand to justify extravagance, and to sanction ab-surdity. But, it may be asked, as these illusions are unavoid-able, and, no doubt, eminently useful to the mind as a process, what good can be gained by making observations, the tendency of which is to diminish the confidence of youth in its feelings, and thus to abridge its innocent and even profitable pleasures? The reproach implied in the question could not be warded off, if Youth were incapable of being delighted with what is truly excellent; or, if these errors always terminated of themselves in due season. But, with the majority, though their force be abated, they continue through life. Moreover, the fire of youth is too vivacious an element to be extinguished or damped by a philosophical remark; and, while there is no danger that what has been said will be injurious or painful to the ardent and the confident, it may prove beneficial to those who, being enthusi-astic, are, at the same time, modest and ingenuous. The intimation may unite with their own misgivings to regulate their sensibility, and to bring in, sooner than it would otherwise have arrived, a more discreet and sound judgment.

If it should excite wonder that men of ability, in later life, whose understandings have been rendered acute by practice in affairs, should be so easily and so far imposed upon when they happen to take up a new work in verse, this appears to be the cause;—that, having discontinued their attention to poetry, whatever progress may have been made in other departments of knowledge, they have not, as to this art, advanced in true dis-cernment beyond the age of youth. If, then, a new poem fall in their way, whose attractions are of that kind which would have enraptured them during the heat of youth, the judgment not being improved to a degree that they shall be disgusted, they are dazzled; and prize and cherish the faults for having had power to make the present time vanish before them, and to throw the mind back, as by enchantment, into the happiest season of life. As they read, powers seem to be revived, passions are re-generated, and pleasures restored. The Book was probably taken up after an escape from the burden of business, and with a wish to forget the world, and all its vexations and anxieties.

Having obtained this wish, and so much more, it is natural that they should make report as they have felt.

If Men of mature age, through want of practice, be thus easily beguiled into admiration of absurdities, extravagances, and misplaced ornaments, thinking it proper that their under-standings should enjoy a holiday, while they are unbending their minds with verse, it may be expected that such Readers will resemble their former selves also in strength of prejudice, and an inaptitude to be moved by the unostentatious beauties of a pure style. In the higher poetry, an enlightened Critic chiefly looks for a reflection of the wisdom of the heart and the grandeur of the imagination. Wherever these appear, simplicity accompanies them ; Magnificence herself, when legitimate, de-pending upon a simplicity of her own, to regulate her ornaments. But it is a well-known property of human nature, that our estimates are ever governed by comparisons, of which we are conscious with various degrees of distinctness. Is it not, then, inevitable (confining these observations to the effects of style merely) that an eye, accustomed to the glaring hues of diction by which such Readers are caught and excited, will for the most part be rather repelled than attracted by an original Work, the colouring of which is disposed according to a pure and refined scheme of harmony ? It is in the fine arts as in the affairs of life, no man can *serve* (i.e. obey with zeal and fidelity) two Masters.

As Poetry is most just to its own divine origin when it administers the comforts and breathes the spirit of religion, they who have learned to perceive this truth, and who betake them-selves to reading verse for sacred purposes, must be preserved from numerous illusions to which the two Classes of Readers, whom we have been considering, are liable. But, as the mind grows serious from the weight of life, the range of its passions is contracted accordingly ; and its sympathies become so exclu-sive, that many species of high excellence wholly escape, or but languidly excite its notice. Besides, men who read from reli-gious or moral inclinations, even when the subject is of that kind which they approve, are beset with misconceptions and mistakes peculiar to themselves. Attaching so much importance to the truths which interest them, they are prone to over-rate the Authors by whom those truths are expressed and enforced.

They come prepared to impart so much passion to the Poet's language, that they remain unconscious how little, in fact, they receive from it. And, on the other hand, religious faith is to him who holds it so momentous a thing, and error appears to be attended with such tremendous consequences, that, if opinions touching upon religion occur which the Reader condemns, he not only cannot sympathise with them, however animated the expression, but there is, for the most part, an end put to all satisfaction and enjoyment. Love, if it before existed, is converted into dislike; and the heart of the Reader is set against the Author and his book.—To these excesses, they, who from their professions ought to be the most guarded against them, are perhaps the most liable; I mean those sects whose religion, being from the calculating understanding, is cold and formal. For when Christianity, the religion of humility, is founded upon the proudest faculty of our nature, what can be expected but contradictions? Accordingly, believers of this cast are at one time contemptuous; at another, being troubled, as they are and must be, with inward misgivings, they are jealous and suspicious;—and at all seasons, they are under temptation to supply, by the heat with which they defend their tenets, the animation which is wanting to the constitution of the religion itself.

Faith was given to man that his affections, detached from the treasures of time, might be inclined to settle upon those of eternity:—the elevation of his nature, which this habit produces on earth, being to him a presumptive evidence of a future state of existence; and giving him a title to partake of its holiness. The religious man values what he sees chiefly as an 'imperfect shadowing forth' of what he is incapable of seeing. The concerns of religion refer to indefinite objects, and are too weighty for the mind to support them without relieving itself by resting a great part of the burthen upon words and symbols. The commerce between Man and his Maker cannot be carried on but by a process where much is represented in little, and the Infinite Being accommodates himself to a finite capacity. In all this may be perceived the affinity between religion and poetry; between religion—making up the deficiencies of reason by faith; and poetry—passionate for the instruction of reason; between religion—whose element is infinite, and whose ulti-

mate trust is the supreme of things, submitting herself to circum-
scription, and reconciled to substitutions; and poetry—ethereal
and transcendent, yet incapable to sustain her existence without
sensuous incarnation. In this community of nature may be
perceived also the lurking incitements of kindred error ;—so that
we shall find that no poetry has been more subject to distortion,
than that species, the argument and scope of which is religious;
and no lovers of the art have gone farther astray than the pious
and the devout.

Whither then shall we turn for that union of qualifications
which must necessarily exist before the decisions of a critic can
be of absolute value? For a mind at once poetical and philosophical; for a critic whose affections are as free and kindly as
the spirit of society, and whose understanding is severe as that
of dispassionate government? Where are we to look for that
initiatory composure of mind which no selfishness can disturb?
For a natural sensibility that has been tutored into correctness
without losing anything of its quickness; and for active faculties,
capable of answering the demands which an Author of original
imagination shall make upon them, associated with a judgment
that cannot be duped into admiration by aught that is unworthy
of it ?—among those and those only, who, never having suffered
their youthful love of poetry to remit much of its force, have applied to the consideration of the laws of this art the best power
of their understandings. At the same time it must be observed
—that, as this Class comprehends the only judgments which are
trustworthy, so does it include the most erroneous and perverse.
For to be mistaught is worse than to be untaught; and no per-
verseness equals that which is supported by system, no errors
are so difficult to root out as those which the understanding has
pledged its credit to uphold. In this Class are contained cen-
sors, who, if they be pleased with what is good, are pleased with
it only by imperfect glimpses, and upon false principles; who,
should they generalise rightly, to a certain point, are sure to
suffer for it in the end; who, if they stumble upon a sound rule,
are fettered by misapplying it, or by straining it too far; being
incapable of perceiving when it ought to yield to one of higher
order. In it are found critics too petulant to be passive to a
genuine poet, and too feeble to grapple with him; men, who
take upon them to report of the course which *he* holds whom

they are utterly unable to accompany,—confounded if he turn quick upon the wing, dismayed if he soar steadily 'into the region;'—men of palsied imaginations and indurated hearts; in whose minds all healthy action is languid, who therefore feed as the many direct them, or, with the many, are greedy after vicious provocatives;—judges, whose censure is auspicious, and whose praise ominous! In this class meet together the two extremes of best and worst.

The observations presented in the foregoing series are of too ungracious a nature to have been made without reluctance; and, were it only on this account, I would invite the reader to try them by the test of comprehensive experience. If the number of judges who can be confidently relied upon be in reality so small, it ought to follow that partial notice only, or neglect, perhaps long continued, or attention wholly inadequate to their merits—must have been the fate of most works in the higher departments of poetry; and that, on the other hand, numerous productions have blazed into popularity, and have passed away, leaving scarcely a trace behind them; it will be further found, that when Authors shall have at length raised themselves into general admiration and maintained their ground, errors and prejudices have prevailed concerning their genius and their works, which the few who are conscious of those errors and prejudices would deplore; if they were not recompensed by perceiving that there are select Spirits for whom it is ordained that their fame shall be in the world an existence like that of Virtue, which owes its being to the struggles it makes, and its vigour to the enemies whom it provokes;—a vivacious quality, ever doomed to meet with opposition, and still triumphing over it; and, from the nature of its dominion, incapable of being brought to the sad conclusion of Alexander, when he wept that there were no more worlds for him to conquer.

Let us take a hasty retrospect of the poetical literature of this Country for the greater part of the last two centuries, and see if the facts support these inferences.

Who is there that now reads the 'Creation' of Dubartas? Yet all Europe once resounded with his praise; he was caressed by kings; and, when his Poem was translated into our language, the 'Faery Queen' faded before it. The name of Spenser, whose genius is of a higher order than even that of Ariosto, is at this

day scarcely known beyond the limits of the British Isles. And
if the value of his works is to be estimated from the attention
now paid to them by his countrymen, compared with that which
they bestow on those of some other writers, it must be pronounced small indeed.

> The laurel, meed of mighty conquerors
> And poets *sage*—

are his own words; but his wisdom has, in this particular, been
his worst enemy: while its opposite, whether in the shape of
folly or madness, has been *their* best friend.   But he was a
great power, and bears a high name: the laurel has been awarded
to him.

A dramatic Author, if he write for the stage, must adapt
himself to the taste of the audience, or they will not endure
him; accordingly the mighty genius of Shakspeare was listened
to.   The people were delighted: but I am not sufficiently versed
in stage antiquities to determine whether they did not flock as
eagerly to the representation of many pieces of contemporary
Authors, wholly undeserving to appear upon the same boards.
Had there been a formal contest for superiority among dramatic
writers, that Shakspeare, like his predecessors Sophocles and
Euripides, would have often been subject to the mortification of
seeing the prize adjudged to sorry competitors, becomes too
probable, when we reflect that the admirers of Settle and Shad-
well were, in a later age, as numerous, and reckoned as respectable in point of talent, as those of Dryden.   At all events, that
Shakspeare stooped to accommodate himself to the People, is
sufficiently apparent; and one of the most striking proofs of
his almost omnipotent genius, is, that he could turn to such
glorious purpose those materials which the prepossessions of
the age compelled him to make use of.   Yet even this marvellous skill appears not to have been enough to prevent his rivals
from having some advantage over him in public estimation;
else how can we account for passages and scenes that exist in
his works, unless upon a supposition that some of the grossest
of them, a fact which in my own mind I have no doubt of, were
foisted in by the Players, for the gratification of the many?

But that his Works, whatever might be their reception upon
the stage, made but little impression upon the ruling Intellects
of the time, may be inferred from the fact that Lord Bacon, in

his multifarious writings, nowhere either quotes or alludes to him.*—His dramatic excellence enabled him to resume possession of the stage after the Restoration; but Dryden tells us that in his time two of the plays of Beaumont and Fletcher were acted for one of Shakspeare's. And so faint and limited was the perception of the poetic beauties of his dramas in the time of Pope, that, in his Edition of the Plays, with a view of rendering to the general reader a necessary service, he printed between inverted commas those passages which he thought most worthy of notice.

At this day, the French Critics have abated nothing of their aversion to this darling of our Nation : 'the English, with their bouffon de Shakspeare,' is as familiar an expression among them as in the time of Voltaire. Baron Grimm is the only French writer who seems to have perceived his infinite superiority to the first names of the French theatre; an advantage which the Parisian critic owed to his German blood and German education. The most enlightened Italians, though well acquainted with our language, are wholly incompetent to measure the proportions of Shakspeare. The Germans only, of foreign nations, are approaching towards a knowledge and feeling of what he is. In some respects they have acquired a superiority over the fellow-countrymen of the Poet : for among us it is a current, I might say, an established opinion, that Shakspeare is justly praised when he is pronounced to be ' a wild irregular genius, in whom great faults are compensated by great beauties.' How long may it be before this misconception passes away, and it becomes universally acknowledged that the judgment of Shakspeare in the selection of his materials, and in the manner in which he has made them, heterogeneous as they often are, constitute a unity of their own, and contribute all to one great end, is not less admirable than his imagination, his invention, and his intuitive knowledge of human Nature !

There is extant a small Volume of miscellaneous poems, in which Shakspeare expresses his own feelings in his own person. It is not difficult to conceive that the Editor, George

* The learned Hakewill (a third edition of whose book bears date 1635), writing to refute the error ' touching Nature's perpetual and universal decay,' cites triumphantly the names of Ariosto, Tasso, Bartas, and Spenser, as instances that poetic genius had not degenerated ; but he makes no mention of Shakspeare.

Steevens, should have been insensible to the beauties of one portion of that Volume, the Sonnets; though in no part of the writings of this Poet is found, in an equal compass, a greater number of exquisite feelings felicitously expressed. But, from regard to the Critic's own credit, he would not have ventured to talk of an* act of parliament not being strong enough to compel the perusal of those little pieces, if he had not known that the people of England were ignorant of the treasures contained in them: and if he had not, moreover, shared the too common propensity of human nature to exult over a supposed fall into the mire of a genius whom he had been compelled to regard with admiration, as an inmate of the celestial regions— 'there sitting where he durst not soar.'

Nine years before the death of Shakspeare, Milton was born: and early in life he published several small poems, which, though on their first appearance they were praised by a few of the judicious, were afterwards neglected to that degree, that Pope in his youth could borrow from them without risk of its being known. Whether these poems are at this day justly appreciated, I will not undertake to decide: nor would it imply a severe reflection upon the mass of readers to suppose the contrary; seeing that a man of the acknowledged genius of Voss, the German poet, could suffer their spirit to evaporate; and could change their character, as is done in the translation made by him of the most popular of those pieces. At all events, it is certain that these Poems of Milton are now much read, and loudly praised; yet were they little heard of till more than 150 years after their publication; and of the Sonnets, Dr. Johnson, as appears from Boswell's Life of him, was in the habit of thinking and speaking as contemptuously as Steevens wrote upon those of Shakspeare.

About the time when the Pindaric odes of Cowley and his imitators, and the productions of that class of curious thinkers whom Dr. Johnson has strangely styled metaphysical Poets, were beginning to lose something of that extravagant admiration which they had excited, the 'Paradise Lost' made its appearance. 'Fit audience find though few,' was the petition addressed by the Poet

° This flippant insensibility was publicly reprehended by Mr. Coleridge in a course of Lectures upon Poetry given by him at the Royal Institution. For the various merits of thought and language in Shakspeare's Sonnets, see Numbers 27, 29, 30, 32, 33, 54, 64, 66, 68, 73, 76, 86, 91, 92, 93, 97, 98, 105, 107, 108, 109, 111, 113, 114, 116, 117, 129, and many others.

to his inspiring Muse. I have said elsewhere that he gained
more than he asked; this I believe to be true; but Dr. Johnson
has fallen into a gross mistake when he attempts to prove, by the
sale of the work, that Milton's Countrymen were '*just* to it' upon
its first appearance. Thirteen hundred Copies were sold in two
years; an uncommon example, he asserts, of the prevalence of
genius in opposition to so much recent enmity as Milton's public
conduct had excited. But, be it remembered that, if Milton's
political and religious opinions, and the manner in which he announced them had raised him many enemies, they had procured
him numerous friends; who, as all personal danger was passed
away at the time of publication, would be eager to procure the
master-work of a man whom they revered, and whom they would
be proud of praising. Take, from the number of purchasers,
persons of this class, and also those who wished to possess the
Poem as a religious work, and but few I fear would be left who
sought for it on account of its poetical merits. The demand did
not immediately increase; 'for,' says Dr. Johnson, 'many more
readers' (he means persons in the habit of reading poetry) 'than
were supplied at first the Nation did not afford.' How careless
must a writer be who can make this assertion in the face of
so many existing title-pages to belie it! Turning to my own
shelves, I find the folio of Cowley, seventh edition, 1681. A book
near it is Flatman's Poems, fourth edition, 1686; Waller, fifth
edition, same date. The Poems of Norris of Bemerton not long
after went, I believe, through nine editions. What further demand there might be for these works I do not know; but I well
remember, that, twenty-five years ago, the booksellers' stalls in
London swarmed with the folios of Cowley. This is not mentioned in disparagement of that able writer and amiable man;
but merely to show—that, if Milton's work were not more read,
it was not because readers did not exist at the time. The early
editions of the 'Paradise Lost' were printed in a shape which
allowed them to be sold at a low price, yet only three thousand
copies of the Work were sold in eleven years; and the Nation,
says Dr. Johnson, had been satisfied from 1623 to 1664, that is,
forty-one years, with only two editions of the Works of Shakspeare; which probably did not together make one thousand
Copies; facts adduced by the critic to prove the 'paucity of
Readers.'—There were readers in multitudes; but their money

went for other purposes, as their admiration was fixed elsewhere.
We are authorized, then, to affirm, that the reception of the 'Paradise Lost,' and the slow progress of its fame, are proofs as striking as can be desired that the positions which I am attempting to establish are not erroneous.*—How amusing to shape to one's self such a critique as a Wit of Charles's days, or a Lord of the Miscellanies or trading Journalist of King William's time, would have brought forth, if he had set his faculties industriously to work upon this Poem, every where impregnated with *original* excellence.

So strange indeed are the obliquities of admiration, that they whose opinions are much influenced by authority will often be tempted to think that there are no fixed principles† in human nature for this art to rest upon. I have been honoured by being permitted to peruse in MS. a tract composed between the period of the Revolution and the close of that century. It is the Work of an English Peer of high accomplishments, its object to form the character and direct the studies of his son. Perhaps nowhere does a more beautiful treatise of the kind exist. The good sense and wisdom of the thoughts, the delicacy of the feelings, and the charm of the style, are, throughout, equally conspicuous. Yet the Author, selecting among the Poets of his own country those whom he deems most worthy of his son's perusal, particularises only Lord Rochester, Sir John Denham, and Cowley. Writing about the same time, Shaftesbury, an author at present unjustly depreciated, describes the English Muses as only yet lisping in their cradles.

The arts by which Pope, soon afterwards, contrived to procure to himself a more general and a higher reputation than perhaps any English Poet ever attained during his life-time, are known to the judicious. And as well known is it to them, that the undue exertion of those arts is the cause why Pope has for some time held a rank in literature, to which, if he had not been seduced by an over-love of immediate popularity, and had confided more in his native genius, he never could have descended.

* Hughes is express upon this subject: in his dedication of Spenser's Works to Lord Somers, he writes thus. 'It was your Lordship's encouraging a beautiful Edition of "Paradise Lost" that first brought that incomparable Poem to be generally known and esteemed.'

† This opinion seems actually to have been entertained by Adam Smith, the worst critic, David Hume not excepted, that Scotland, a soil to which this sort of weed seems natural, has produced.

He bewitched the nation by his melody, and dazzled it by his polished style, and was himself blinded by his own success. Having wandered from humanity in his Eclogues with boyish inexperience, the praise, which these compositions obtained, tempted him into a belief that Nature was not to be trusted, at least in pastoral Poetry. To prove this by example, he put his friend Gay upon writing those Eclogues which their author intended to be burlesque. The instigator of the work, and his admirers, could perceive in them nothing but what was ridiculous. Nevertheless, though these Poems contain some detestable passages, the effect, as Dr. Johnson well observes, ' of reality and truth became conspicuous even when the intention was to show them grovelling and degraded.' The Pastorals, ludicrous to such as prided themselves upon their refinement, in spite of those disgusting passages, ' became popular, and were read with delight, as just representations of rural manners and occupations.' •

Something less than sixty years after the publication of the ' Paradise Lost' appeared Thomson's 'Winter;' which was speedily followed by his other 'Seasons.' It is a work of inspiration ; much of it is written from himself, and nobly from himself. How was it received ? ' It was no sooner read,' says one of his contemporary biographers, ' than universally admired : those only excepted who had not been used to feel, or to look for any thing in poetry, beyond a *point* of satirical or epigrammatic wit, a smart *antithesis* richly trimmed with rhyme, or the softness of an *elegiac* complaint. To such his manly classical spirit could not readily commend itself ; till, after a more attentive perusal, they had got the better of their prejudices, and either acquired or affected a truer taste. A few others stood aloof, merely because they had long before fixed the articles of their poetical creed, and resigned themselves to an absolute despair of ever seeing any thing new and original. These were somewhat mortified to find their notions disturbed by the appearance of a poet, who seemed to owe nothing but to Nature and his own genius. But, in a short time, the applause became unanimous ; every one wondering how so many pictures, and pictures so familiar, should have moved them but faintly to what they felt in his descriptions. His digressions too, the overflowings of a tender benevolent heart, charmed the reader no less ; leaving him in doubt, whether he should more admire the Poet or love the Man.'

This case appears to bear strongly against us :—but we must distinguish between wonder and legitimate admiration. The subject of the work is the changes produced in the appearances of Nature by the revolution of the year : and, by undertaking to write in verse, Thomson pledged himself to treat his subject as became a Poet. Now it is remarkable that, excepting the nocturnal 'Reverie' of Lady Winchilsea, and a passage or two in the 'Windsor Forest' of Pope, the poetry of the period intervening between the publication of the 'Paradise Lost' and the 'Seasons' does not contain a single new image of external Nature ; and scarcely presents a familiar one from which it can be inferred that the eye of the Poet had been steadily fixed upon his object, much less that his feelings had urged him to work upon it in the spirit of genuine imagination. To what a low state knowledge of the most obvious and important phenomena had sunk, is evident from the style in which Dryden has executed a description of Night in one of his Tragedies, and Pope his translation of the celebrated moonlight scene in the 'Iliad.' A blind man, in the habit of attending accurately to descriptions casually dropped from the lips of those around him, might easily depict these appearances with more truth. Dryden's lines are vague, bombastic, and senseless ;* those of Pope, though he had Homer to guide him, are throughout false and contradictory. The verses of Dryden, once highly celebrated, are forgotten ; those of Pope still retain their hold upon public estimation,—nay, there is not a passage of descriptive poetry, which at this day finds so many and such ardent admirers. Strange to think of an enthusiast, as may have been the case with thousands, reciting those verses under the cope of a moonlight sky, without having his raptures in the least disturbed by a suspicion of their absurdity !—If these two distinguished writers could habitually think that the visible universe was of so little consequence to a

---

* CORTES *alone in a night-gown.*

All things are hush'd as Nature's self lay dead ;
The mountains seem to nod their drowsy head.
The little Birds in dreams their songs repeat,
And sleeping Flowers beneath the Night-dew sweat :
Even Lust and Envy sleep ; yet Love denies
Rest to my soul, and slumber to my eyes.
                                        DRYDEN's *Indian Emperor.*

poet, that it was scarcely necessary for him to cast his eyes upon it, we may be assured that those passages of the elder poets which faithfully and poetically describe the phenomena of Nature, were not at that time holden in much estimation, and that there was little accurate attention paid to those appearances.

Wonder is the natural product of Ignorance; and as the soil was *in such good condition* at the time of the publication of the 'Seasons,' the crop was doubtless abundant. Neither individuals nor nations become corrupt all at once, nor are they enlightened in a moment. Thomson was an inspired poet, but he could not work miracles; in cases where the art of seeing had in some degree been learned, the teacher would further the proficiency of his pupils, but he could do little *more;* though so far does vanity assist men in acts of self-deception, that many would often fancy they recognised a likeness when they knew nothing of the original. Having shown that much of what his biographer deemed genuine admiration must in fact have been blind wonderment—how is the rest to be accounted for?— Thomson was fortunate in the very title of his poem, which seemed to bring it home to the prepared sympathies of every one: in the next place, notwithstanding his high powers, he writes a vicious style; and his false ornaments are exactly of that kind which would be most likely to strike the undiscerning. He likewise abounds with sentimental common-places, that, from the manner in which they were brought forward, bore an imposing air of novelty. In any well-used copy of the 'Seasons' the book generally opens of itself with the rhapsody on love, or with one of the stories (perhaps 'Damon and Musidora'); these also are prominent in our collections of Extracts, and are the parts of his Work, which, after all, were probably most efficient in first recommending the author to general notice. Pope, repaying praises which he had received, and wishing to extol him to the highest, only styles him ' an elegant and philosophical poet;' nor are we able to collect any unquestionable proofs that the true characteristics of Thomson's genius as an imaginative poet* were perceived, till the elder Warton, almost forty years after the publication of the 'Seasons,' pointed them out by

* Since these observations upon Thomson were written, I have perused the second edition of his ' Seasons,' and find that even *that* does not contain the most striking passages which Warton points out for admiration; these, with other improvements, throughout the whole work, must have been added at a later period.

a note in his Essay on the Life and Writings of Pope. In the
'Castle of Indolence' (of which Gray speaks so coldly) these characteristics were almost as conspicuously displayed, and in verse
more harmonious, and diction more pure. Yet that fine poem
was neglected on its appearance, and is at this day the delight
only of a few !

When Thomson died, Collins breathed forth his regrets in
an Elegiac Poem, in which he pronounces a poetical curse upon
him who should regard with insensibility the place where the
Poet's remains were deposited. The Poems of the mourner
himself have now passed through innumerable editions, and are
universally known ; but if, when Collins died, the same kind of
imprecation had been pronounced by a surviving admirer, small
is the number whom it would not have comprehended. The
notice which his poems attained during his life-time was so
small, and of course the sale so insignificant, that not long
before his death he deemed it right to repay to the bookseller
the sum which he had advanced for them, and threw the edition
into the fire.

Next in importance to the 'Seasons' of Thomson, though at
considerable distance from that work in order of time, come the
Reliques of Ancient English Poetry ; collected, new-modelled,
and in many instances (if such a contradiction in terms may be
used) composed by the Editor, Dr. Percy. This work did not
steal silently into the world, as is evident from the number of
legendary tales, that appeared not long after its publication ;
and had been modelled, as the authors persuaded themselves,
after the old Ballad. The Compilation was however ill suited
to the then existing taste of city society ; and Dr. Johnson, 'mid
the little senate to which he gave laws, was not sparing in his
exertions to make it an object of contempt. The critic
triumphed, the legendary imitators were deservedly disregarded,
and, as undeservedly, their ill-imitated models sank, in this
country, into temporary neglect ; while Bürger, and other able
writers of Germany, were translating, or imitating these *Reliques,* and composing, with the aid of inspiration thence derived, poems which are the delight of the German nation. Dr.
Percy was so abashed by the ridicule flung upon his labours from
the ignorance and insensibility of the persons with whom he
lived, that, though while he was writing under a mask he had

not wanted resolution to follow his genius into the regions of true simplicity and genuine pathos (as is evinced by the exquisite ballad of ' Sir Cauline' and by many other pieces), yet when he appeared in his own person and character as a poetical writer, he adopted, as in the tale of the 'Hermit of Warkworth,' a diction scarcely in any one of its features distinguishable from the vague, the glossy, and unfeeling language of his day.   I mention this remarkable fact* with regret, esteeming the genius of Dr. Percy in this kind of writing superior to that of any other man by whom in modern times it has been cultivated.   That even Bürger (to whom Klopstock gave, in my hearing, a commendation which he denied to Goethe and Schiller, pronouncing him to be a genuine poet, and one of the few among the Germans whose works would last) had not the fine sensibility of Percy, might be shown from many passages, in which he has deserted his original only to go astray.   For example,

> Now daye was gone, and night was come,
> And all were fast asleepe,
> All save the Lady Emeline,
> Who sate in her bowre to weepe :
>
> And soone she heard her true Love's voice
> Low whispering at the walle,
> Awake, awake, my dear Ladye,
> 'Tis I thy true-love call.

Which is thus tricked out and dilated : .

> Als nun die Nacht Gebirg' und Thal
> Vermummt in Rabenschatten,
> Und Hochburgs Lampen überall
> Schon ausgeflimmert hatten,
> Und alles tief entschlafen war;
> Doch nur das Fräulein immerdar,
> Voll Fieberangst, noch wachte,
> Und seinen Ritter dachte :
> Da horch ! Ein süsser Liebeston
> Kam leis' empor geflogen.
> ' Ho, Trüdchen, ho ! Da bin ich schon !
> Frisch auf ! Dich angezogen !'

* Shenstone, in his ' Schoolmistress,' gives a still more remarkable instance of this timidity.   On its first appearance, (See D'Israeli's 2d Series of the *Curiosities of Literature*) the Poem was accompanied with an absurd prose commentary, showing, as indeed some incongruous expressions in the text imply that the whole was intended for burlesque.   In subsequent editions, the commentary was dropped, and the People have since continued to read in seriousness, doing for the Author what he had not courage openly to venture upon for himself.

But from humble ballads we must ascend to heroics.

All hail, Macpherson! hail to thee, Sire of Ossian! The Phantom was begotten by the smug embrace of an impudent Highlander upon a cloud of tradition—it travelled southward, where it was greeted with acclamation, and the thin Consistence took its course through Europe, upon the breath of popular applause. The Editor of the *Reliques* had indirectly preferred a claim to the praise of invention, by not concealing that his supplementary labours were considerable! how selfish his conduct, contrasted with that of the disinterested Gael, who, like Lear, gives his kingdom away, and is content to become a pensioner upon his own issue for a beggarly pittance!—Open this far-famed Book!—I have done so at random, and the beginning of the 'Epic Poem Temora,' in eight Books, presents itself. 'The blue waves of Ullin roll in light. The green hills are covered with day. Trees shake their dusky heads in the breeze. Grey torrents pour their noisy streams. Two green hills with aged oaks surround a narrow plain. The blue course of a stream is there. On its banks stood Cairbar of Atha. His spear supports the king; the red eyes of his fear are sad. Cormac rises on his soul with all his ghastly wounds.' Precious memorandums from the pocket-book of the blind Ossian!

If it be unbecoming, as I acknowledge that for the most part it is, to speak disrespectfully of Works that have enjoyed for a length of time a widely-spread reputation, without at the same time producing irrefragable proofs of their unworthiness, let me be forgiven upon this occasion.—Having had the good fortune to be born and reared in a mountainous country, from my very childhood I have felt the falsehood that pervades the volumes imposed upon the world under the name of Ossian. From what I saw with my own eyes, I knew that the imagery was spurious. In Nature everything is distinct, yet nothing defined into absolute independent singleness. In Macpherson's work, it is exactly the reverse; every thing (that is not stolen) is in this manner defined, insulated, dislocated, deadened,— yet nothing distinct. It will always be so when words are substituted for things. To say that the characters never could exist, that the manners are impossible, and that a dream has more substance than the whole state of society, as there depicted, is doing nothing more than pronouncing a censure which

Macpherson defied; when, with the steeps of Morven before his
eyes, he could talk so familiarly of his Car-borne heroes;—of
Morven, which, if one may judge from its appearance at the distance of a few miles, contains scarcely an acre of ground sufficiently accommodating for a sledge to be trailed along its surface.
—Mr. Malcolm Laing has ably shown that the diction of this
pretended translation is a motley assemblage from all quarters;
but he is so fond of making out parallel passages as to call poor
Macpherson to account for his '*ands*' and his '*buts*!' and he has
weakened his argument by conducting it as if he thought that
every striking resemblance was a *conscious* plagiarism. It is
enough that the coincidences are too remarkable for its being
probable or possible that they could arise in different minds
without communication between them. Now as the Translators
of the Bible, and Shakspeare, Milton, and Pope, could not be
indebted to Macpherson, it follows that he must have owed his
fine feathers to them; unless we are prepared gravely to assert,
with Madame de Staël, that many of the characteristic beauties
of our most celebrated English Poets are derived from the
ancient Fingallian; in which case the modern translator would
have been but giving back to Ossian his own.—It is consistent
that Lucien Buonaparte, who could censure Milton for having
surrounded Satan in the infernal regions with courtly and regal
splendour, should pronounce the modern Ossian to be the glory
of Scotland;—a country that has produced a Dunbar, a Buchanan, a Thomson, and a Burns! These opinions are of ill-
omen for the Epic ambition of him who has given them to the
world.

Yet, much as those pretended treasures of antiquity have
been admired, they have been wholly uninfluential upon the
literature of the Country. No succeeding writer appears to have
caught from them a ray of inspiration; no author, in the least
distinguished, has ventured formally to imitate them—except
the boy, Chatterton, on their first appearance. He had perceived, from the successful trials which he himself had made in
literary forgery, how few critics were able to distinguish between
a real ancient medal and a counterfeit of modern manufacture;
and he set himself to the work of filling a magazine with *Saxon
Poems*,—counterparts of those of Ossian, as like his as one of
his misty stars is to another. This incapability to amalgamate

with the literature of the Island, is, in my estimation, a decisive proof that the book is essentially unnatural ; nor should I require any other to demonstrate it to be a forgery, audacious as worthless.   Contrast, in this respect, the effect of Macpherson's publication with the *Reliques* of Percy, so unassuming, so modest in their pretensions !—I have already stated how much Germany is indebted to this latter work ; and for our own country, its poetry has been absolutely redeemed by it.   I do not think that there is an able writer in verse of the present day who would not be proud to acknowledge his obligations to the *Reliques ;* I know that it is so with my friends ; and, for myself, I am happy in this occasion to make a public avowal of my own.

Dr. Johnson, more fortunate in his contempt of the labours of Macpherson than those of his modest friend, was solicited not long after to furnish Prefaces biographical and critical for the works of some of the most eminent English Poets.   The booksellers took upon themselves to make the collection ; they referred probably to the most popular miscellanies, and, unquestionably, to their books of accounts ; and decided upon the claim of authors to be admitted into a body of the most eminent, from the familiarity of their names with the readers of that day, and by the profits, which, from the sale of his works, each had brought and was bringing to the Trade.   The Editor was allowed a limited exercise of discretion, and the Authors whom he recommended are scarcely to be mentioned without a smile.   We open the volume of Prefatory Lives, and to our astonishment the *first* name we find is that of Cowley !—What is become of the morning-star of English Poetry ?   Where is the bright Elizabethan constellation ?   Or, if names be more acceptable than images, where is the ever-to-be-honoured Chaucer ?   Where is Spenser ?   where Sidney ?   and, lastly, where he, whose rights as a poet, contradistinguished from those which he is universally allowed to possess as a dramatist, we have vindicated,—where Shakspeare ?—These, and a multitude of others not unworthy to be placed near them, their contemporaries and successors, we have *not*.   But in their stead, we have (could better be expected when precedence was to be settled by an abstract of reputation at any given period made, as in this case before us ?) Roscommon, and Stepney, and Phillips, and Walsh, and Smith, and Duke, and King, and Spratt—Halifax, Granville, Sheffield,

Congreve, Broome, and other reputed Magnates—metrical writers utterly worthless and useless, except for occasions like the present, when their productions are referred to as evidence what a small quantity of brain is necessary to procure a considerable stock of admiration, provided the aspirant will accommodate himself to the likings and fashions of his day.

As I do not mean to bring down this retrospect to our own times, it may with propriety be closed at the era of this distinguished event. From the literature of other ages and countries, proofs equally cogent might have been adduced, that the opinions announced in the former part of this Essay are founded upon truth. It was not an agreeable office, nor a prudent undertaking, to declare them ; but their importance seemed to render it a duty. It may still be asked, where lies the particular relation of what has been said to these Volumes ?—The question will be easily answered by the discerning Reader who is old enough to remember the taste that prevailed when some of these poems were first published, seventeen years ago ; who has also observed to what degree the poetry of this Island has since that period been coloured by them ; and who is further aware of the unremitting hostility with which, upon some principle or other, they have each and all been opposed. A sketch of my own notion of the constitution of Fame has been given ; and, as far as concerns myself, I have cause to be satisfied. The love, the admiration, the indifference, the slight, the aversion, and even the contempt, with which these Poems have been received, knowing, as I do, the source within my own mind, from which they have proceeded, and the labour and pains, which, when labour and pains appeared needful, have been bestowed upon them, must all, if I think consistently, be received as pledges and tokens, bearing the same general impression, though widely different in value ;—they are all proofs that for the present time I have not laboured in vain ; and afford assurances, more or less authentic, that the products of my industry will endure.

If there be one conclusion more forcibly pressed upon us than another by the review which has been given of the fortunes and fate of poetical Works, it is this,—that every author, as far as he is great and at the same time *original*, has had the task of *creating* the taste by which he is to be enjoyed; so has it been, so will it continue to be. This remark was long since

made to me by the philosophical Friend for the separation of
whose poems from my own I have previously expressed my
regret. The predecessors of an original Genius of a high order
will have smoothed the way for all that he has in common with
them ;—and much he will have in common; but, for what is
peculiarly his own, he will be called upon to clear and often to
shape his own road :—he will be in the condition of Hannibal
among the Alps.

And where lies the real difficulty of creating that taste by
which a truly original poet is to be relished ? Is it in breaking
the bonds of custom, in overcoming the prejudices of false refinement, and displacing the aversions of inexperience ? Or,
if he labour for an object which here and elsewhere I have proposed to myself, does it consist in divesting the reader of the
pride that induces him to dwell upon those points wherein men
differ from each other, to the exclusion of those in which all
men are alike, or the same ; and in making him ashamed of
the vanity that renders him insensible of the appropriate excellence which civil arrangements, less unjust than might appear,
and Nature illimitable in her bounty, have conferred on men
who may stand below him in the scale of society? Finally,
does it lie in establishing that dominion over the spirits of
readers by which they are to be humbled and humanised, in
order that they may be purified and exalted ?

If these ends are to be attained by the mere communication
of *knowledge*, it does *not* lie here.—TASTE, I would remind the
reader, like IMAGINATION, is a word which has been forced to
extend its services far beyond the point to which philosophy
would have confined them. It is a metaphor, taken from a
passive sense of the human body, and transferred to things
which are in their essence *not* passive,—to intellectual *acts* and
operations. The word, Imagination, has been overstrained,
from impulses honourable to mankind, to meet the demands of
the faculty which is perhaps the noblest of our nature. In the
instance of Taste, the process has been reversed ; and from the
prevalence of dispositions at once injurious and discreditable,
being no other than that selfishness which is the child of apathy,
—which, as Nations decline in productive and creative power,
makes them value themselves upon a presumed refinement of
judging. Poverty of language is the primary cause of the use

which we make of the word, Imagination; but the word, Taste, has been stretched to the sense which it bears in modern Europe by habits of self-conceit, inducing that inversion in the order of things whereby a passive faculty is made paramount among the faculties conversant with the fine arts. Proportion and congruity, the requisite knowledge being supposed, are sub- jects upon which taste may be trusted; it is competent to this office ;—for in its intercourse with these the mind is *passive,* and is affected painfully or pleasurably as by an instinct. But the profound and the exquisite in feeling, the lofty and universal in thought and imagination; or, in ordinary language, the pathetic and the sublime ;—are neither of them, accurately speaking, objects of a faculty which could ever without a sinking in the spirit of Nations have been designated by the metaphor— *Taste.* And why? Because without the exertion of a co-operating *power* in the mind of the Reader, there can be no adequate sympathy with either of these emotions: without this auxiliary impulse, elevated or profound passion cannot exist.

Passion, it must be observed, is derived from a word which signifies *suffering;* but the connection which suffering has with effort, with exertion, and *action,* is immediate and inseparable. How strikingly is this property of human nature exhibited by the fact, that, in popular language, to be in a passion, is to be angry! —But, Anger in hasty *words* or *blows* Itself discharges on its foes.

To be moved, then, by a passion, is to be excited, often to ex-ternal, and always to internal, effort: whether for the continuance and strengthening of the passion, or for its suppression, accordingly as the course which it takes may be painful or pleasurable. If the latter, the soul must contribute to its support, or it never becomes vivid,—and soon languishes, and dies. And this brings us to the point. If every great poet with whose writings men are familiar, in the highest exercise of his genius, before he can be thoroughly enjoyed, has to call forth and to communicate *power*, this service, in a still greater degree, falls upon an original writer, at his first appearance in the world.—Of genius the only proof is, the act of doing well what is worthy to be done, and what was never done before: Of genius, in the fine arts, the only infallible sign is the widening the sphere of human sensibility, for the delight, honour, and benefit of human nature.

Genius is the introduction of a new element into the intellectual universe : or, if that be not allowed, it is the application of powers to objects on which they had not before been exercised, or the employment of them in such a manner as to produce effects hitherto unknown. What is all this but an advance, or a conquest, made by the soul of the poet ? Is it to be supposed that the reader can make progress of this kind, like an Indian prince or general—stretched on his palanquin, and borne by his slaves ? No ; he is invigorated and inspirited by his leader, in order that he may exert himself; for he cannot proceed in quiescence, he cannot be carried like a dead weight. Therefore to create taste is to call forth and bestow power, of which knowledge is the effect ; and *there* lies the true difficulty.

As the pathetic participates of an *animal* sensation, it might seem—that, if the springs of this emotion were genuine, all men, possessed of competent knowledge of the facts and circumstances, would be instantaneously affected. And, doubtless, in the works of every true poet will be found passages of that species of excellence, which is proved by effects immediate and universal. But there are emotions of the pathetic that are simple and direct, and others—that are complex and revolutionary ; some—to which the heart yields with gentleness ; others—against which it struggles with pride ; these varieties are infinite as the combinations of circumstance and the constitutions of character. Remember, also, that the medium through which, in poetry, the heart is to be affected—is language ; a thing subject to endless fluctuations and arbitrary associations. The genius of the poet melts these down for his purpose ; but they retain their shape and quality to him who is not capable of exerting, within his own mind, a corresponding energy. There is also a meditative, as well as a human, pathos ; an enthusiastic, as well as an ordinary, sorrow ; a sadness that has its seat in the depths of reason, to which the mind cannot sink gently of itself—but to which it must descend by treading the steps of thought. And for the sublime,—if we consider what are the cares that occupy the passing day, and how remote is the practice and the course of life from the sources of sublimity in the soul of Man, can it be wondered that there is little existing preparation for a poet charged with a new mission to extend its kingdom, and to augment and spread its enjoyments ?

Away, then, with the senseless iteration of the word *popular*, applied to new works in poetry, as if there were no test of excellence in this first of the fine arts but that all men should run after its productions, as if urged by an appetite, or constrained by a spell!—The qualities of writing best fitted for eager reception are either such as startle the world into attention by their audacity and extravagance ; or they are chiefly of a superficial kind lying upon the surfaces of manners ; or arising out of a selection and arrangement of incidents, by which the mind is kept upon the stretch of curiosity and the fancy amused without the trouble of thought. But in every thing which is to send the soul into herself, to be admonished of her weakness, or to be made conscious of her power :—wherever life and Nature are described as operated upon by the creative or abstracting virtue of the imagination ; wherever the instinctive wisdom of antiquity and her heroic passions uniting, in the heart of the poet, with the meditative wisdom of later ages, have produced that accord of sublimated humanity, which is at once a history of the remote past and a prophetic enunciation of the remotest future, *there*, the poet must reconcile himself for a season to few and scattered hearers.—Grand thoughts (and Shakspeare must often have sighed over this truth), as they are most naturally and most fitly conceived in solitude, so can they not be brought forth in the midst of plaudits, without some violation of their sanctity. Go to a silent exhibition of the productions of the Sister Art, and be convinced that the qualities which dazzle at first sight, and kindle the admiration of the multitude, are essentially different from those by which permanent influence is secured. Let us not shrink from following up these principles as far as they will carry us, and conclude with observing—that there never has been a period, and perhaps never will be, in which vicious poetry, of some kind or other, has not excited more zealous admiration, and been far more generally read, than good ; but this advantage attends the good, that the *individual*, as well as the species, survives from age to age ; whereas, of the depraved, though the species be immortal, the individual quickly *perishes ;* the object of present admiration vanishes, being supplanted by some other as easily produced ; which, though no better, brings with it at least the irritation of novelty,—with adaptation, more or less skilful, to the changing humours of the majority of those who are most at leisure to regard poetical works when they first solicit their attention.

Is it the result of the whole, that, in the opinion of the Writer, the judgment of the People is not to be respected ? The thought is most injurious ; and, could the charge be brought against him, he would repel it with indignation. The People have already been justified, and their eulogium pronounced by implication, when it was said, above—that, of *good* poetry, the *individual*, as well as the species, *survives*. And how does it survive but through the People ? What preserves it but their intellect and their wisdom ?

> ——Past and future, are the wings
> On whose support, harmoniously conjoined, .
> Moves the great Spirit of human knowledge——ms.

The voice that issues from this Spirit, is that Vox Populi which the Deity inspires. Foolish must he be who can mistake for this a local acclamation, or a transitory outcry—transitory though it be for years, local though from a Nation. Still more lamentable is his error who can believe that there is any thing of divine infallibility in the clamour of that small though loud portion of the community, ever governed by factitious influence, which, under the name of the PUBLIC, passes itself, upon the unthinking, for the PEOPLE. Towards the Public, the Writer hopes that he feels as much deference as it is entitled to : but to the People, philosophically characterised, and to the embodied spirit of their knowledge, so far as it exists and moves, at the present, faithfully supported by its two wings, the past and the future, his devout respect, his reverence, is due. He offers it willingly and readily ; and, this done, takes leave of his Readers, by assuring them—that, if he were not persuaded that the contents of these Volumes, and the Work to which they are subsidiary, evince something of the ' Vision and the Faculty divine ;' and that, both in words and things, they will operate in their degree, to extend the domain of sensibility for the delight, the honour, and the benefit of human nature, notwithstanding the many happy hours which he has employed in their composition, and the manifold comforts and enjoyments they have procured to him, he would not, if a wish could do it, save them from immediate destruction ;—from becoming at this moment, to the world, as a thing that had never been.

1815.

(d) OF POETRY AS OBSERVATION AND DESCRIPTION.

THE powers requisite for the production of poetry are: first, those of Observation and Description,—*i. e.*, the ability to observe with accuracy things as they are in themselves, and with fidelity to describe them, unmodified by any passion or feeling existing in the mind of the describer: whether the things depicted be actually present to the senses, or have a place only in the memory. This power, though indispensable to a Poet, is one which he employs only in submission to necessity, and never for a continuance of time: as its exercise supposes all the higher qualities of the mind to be passive, and in a state of subjection to external objects, much in the same way as a translator or engraver ought to be to his original. 2ndly, Sensibility,—which, the more exquisite it is, the wider will be the range of a poet's perceptions; and the more will he be incited to observe objects, both as they exist in themselves, and as re-acted upon by his own mind. (The distinction between poetic and human sensibility has been marked in the character of the Poet delineated in the original preface.) 3dly, Reflection,—which makes the Poet acquainted with the value of actions, images, thoughts, and feelings; and assists the sensibility in perceiving their connection with each other. 4thly, Imagination and Fancy,—to modify, to create, and to associate. 5thly, Invention,—by which characters are composed out of materials supplied by observation; whether of the Poet's own heart and mind, or of external life and nature; and such incidents and situations produced as are most impressive to the imagination, and most fitted to do justice to the characters, sentiments, and passions, which the Poet undertakes to illustrate. And, lastly, Judgment,—to decide how and where, and in what degree, each of these faculties ought to be exerted; so that the less shall not be sacrificed to the greater; nor the greater, slighting the less, arrogate, to its own injury, more than its due. By judgment, also, is determined what are the laws and appropriate graces of every species of composition.*

* As sensibility to harmony of numbers, and the power of producing it, are invariably attendants upon the faculties above specified, nothing has been said upon those requisites.

The materials of Poetry, by these powers collected and produced, are cast, by means of various moulds, into divers forms.
The moulds may be enumerated, and the forms specified, in the
following order. 1st, The Narrative,—including the Epopœia,
the Historic Poem, the Tale, the Romance, the Mock-Heroic,
and, if the spirit of Homer will tolerate such neighbourhood,
that dear production of our days, the metrical Novel. Of this
class, the distinguishing mark is, that the Narrator, however
liberally his speaking agents be introduced, is himself the source
from which every thing primarily flows. Epic Poets, in order
that their mode of composition may accord with the elevation of
their subject, represent themselves as *singing* from the inspiration of the Muse, 'Arma virumque *cano ;*' but this is a fiction,
in modern times, of slight value ; the 'Iliad' or the 'Paradise Lost'
would gain little in our estimation by being chanted. The other
poets who belong to this class are commonly content to *tell* their
tale ;—so that of the whole it may be affirmed that they neither
require nor reject the accompaniment of music.

2ndly, The Dramatic, — consisting of Tragedy, Historic
Drama, Comedy, and Masque, in which the poet does not appear
at all in his own person, and where the whole action is carried
on by speech and dialogue of the agents ; music being admitted
only incidentally and rarely. The Opera may be placed here,
inasmuch as it proceeds by dialogue ; though depending, to the
degree that it does, upon music, it has a strong claim to be
ranked with the lyrical. The characteristic and impassioned
Epistle, of which Ovid and Pope have given examples, considered
as a species of monodrama, may, without impropriety, be placed
in this class.•

3dly, The Lyrical,—containing the Hymn, the Ode, the
Elegy, the Song, and the Ballad ; in all which, for the production of their *full* effect, an accompaniment of music is indispensable.

4thly, The Idyllium,—descriptive chiefly either of the processes and appearances of external nature, as the 'Seasons' of
Thomson ; or of characters, manners, and sentiments, as are
Shenstone's 'Schoolmistress,' 'The Cotter's Saturday Night' of
Burns, 'The Twa Dogs' of the same Author ; or of these in conjunction with the appearances of Nature, as most of the pieces
of Theocritus, the 'Allegro' and 'Penseroso' of Milton, Beattie's

'Minstrel,' Goldsmith's 'Deserted Village.' The Epitaph, the Inscription, the Sonnet, most of the epistles of poets writing in their own persons, and all loco-descriptive poetry, belong to this class.

5thly, Didactic,—the principal object of which is direct instruction ; as the Poem of Lucretius, the 'Georgics' of Virgil, ' The Fleece' of Dyer, Mason's ' English Garden,' &c.

And, lastly, philosophical Satire, like that of Horace and Juvenal ; personal and occasional Satire rarely comprehending sufficient of the general in the individual to be dignified with the name of poetry.

Out of the three last has been constructed a composite order, of which Young's ' Night Thoughts,' and Cowper's ' Task,' are excellent examples.

It is deducible from the above, that poems, apparently miscellaneous, may with propriety be arranged either with reference to the powers of mind *predominant* in the production of them ; or to the mould in which they are cast ; or, lastly, to the subjects to which they relate. From each of these considerations, the following Poems have been divided into classes ; which, that the work may more obviously correspond with the course of human life, and for the sake of exhibiting in it the three requisites of a legitimate whole, a beginning, a middle, and an end, have been also arranged, as far as it was possible, according to an order of time, commencing with Childhood, and terminating with Old Age, Death, and Immortality. My guiding wish was, that the small pieces of which these volumes consist, thus discriminated, might be regarded under a twofold view ; as composing an entire work within themselves, and as adjuncts to the philosophical Poem, ' The Recluse.' This arrangement has long presented itself habitually to my own mind. Nevertheless, I should have preferred to scatter the contents of these volumes at random, if I had been persuaded that, by the plan adopted, any thing material would be taken from the natural effect of the pieces, individually, on the mind of the unreflecting Reader. I trust there is a sufficient variety in each class to prevent this ; while, for him who reads with reflection, the arrangement will serve as a commentary unostentatiously directing his attention to my purposes, both particular and general. But, as I wish to guard against the possibility of misleading by this classification, it is proper first to remind the Reader, that certain poems are placed according to the powers of mind, in the Author's conception, predominant in the production of them; *predominant,* which implies the exertion of other faculties in less degree. Where there is more imagination than fancy in a poem, it is placed under the head of imagination, and *vice versâ.* Both the above classes might without impropriety have been enlarged from that consisting of 'Poems founded on the Affections;' as might this latter from those, and from the class 'proceeding from Sentiment and Reflection.' The most striking characteristics of each piece, mutual illustration, variety, and proportion, have governed me throughout.

None of the other Classes, except those of Fancy and Imagination, require any particular notice. But a remark of general application may be made. All Poets, except the dramatic, have been in the practice of feigning that their works were composed to the music of the harp or lyre: with what degree of affectation this has been done in modern times, I leave to the judicious to determine. For my own part, I have not been disposed to violate probability so far, or to make such a large demand upon the Reader's charity. Some of these pieces are essentially lyrical; and, therefore, cannot have their due force without a supposed musical accompaniment; but, in much the greatest part, as a substitute for the classic lyre or romantic harp, I require nothing more than an animated or impassioned recitation, adapted to the subject. Poems, however humble in their kind, if they be good in that kind, cannot read themselves; the law of long syllable and short must not be so inflexible,— the letter of metre must not be so impassive to the spirit of versification,—as to deprive the Reader of all voluntary power to modulate, in subordination to the sense, the music of the poem; —in the same manner as his mind is left at liberty, and even summoned, to act upon its thoughts and images. But, though the accompaniment of a musical instrument be frequently dispensed with, the true Poet does not therefore abandon his privilege distinct from that of the mere Proseman;

> He murmurs near the running brooks
> A music sweeter than their own.

Let us come now to the consideration of the words Fancy and Imagination, as employed in the classification of the following Poems. 'A man,' says an intelligent author, 'has imagination in proportion as he can distinctly copy in idea the impressions of sense : it is the faculty which *images* within the mind the phenomena of sensation. A man has fancy in proportion as he can call up, connect, or associate, at pleasure, those internal images (φαντάζειν is to cause to appear) so as to complete ideal representations of absent objects. Imagination is the power of depicting, and fancy of evoking and combining. The imagination is formed by patient observation ; the fancy by a voluntary activity in shifting the scenery of the mind. The more accurate the imagination, the more safely may a painter, or a poet, undertake a delineation, or a description, without the presence of the objects to be characterised. The more versatile the fancy, the more original and striking will be the decorations produced.'—*British Synonyms discriminated, by W. Taylor.*

Is not this as if a man should undertake to supply an account of a building, and be so intent upon what he had discovered of the foundation, as to conclude his task without once looking up at the superstructure ? Here, as in other instances throughout the volume, the judicious Author's mind is enthralled by Etymology ; he takes up the original word as his guide and escort, and too often does not perceive how soon he becomes its prisoner, without liberty to tread in any path but that to which it confines him. It is not easy to find out how imagination, thus explained, differs from distinct remembrance of images ; or fancy from quick and vivid recollection of them : each is nothing more than a mode of memory. If the two words bear the above meaning and no other, what term is left to designate that faculty of which the Poet is ' all compact ;' he whose eye glances from earth to heaven, whose spiritual attributes body forth what his pen is prompt in turning to shape ; or what is left to characterise Fancy, as insinuating herself into the heart of objects with creative activity ? Imagination, in the sense of the word as giving title to a class of the following Poems, has no reference to images that are merely a faithful copy, existing in the mind, of absent external objects ; but is a word of higher import, denoting operations of the mind upon those objects and processes of creation or of composition, governed by certain fixed laws. I proceed to illustrate my meaning by instances. A parrot *hangs* from the wires of his cage by his beak or by his claws ; or a

monkey from the bough of a tree by his paws or his tail. Each
creature does so literally and actually. In the first Eclogue of
Virgil, the shepherd, thinking of the time when he is to take
leave of his farm, thus addresses his goats :—

> Non ego vos posthac viridi projectus in antro
> Dumosa *pendere* procul de rupe videbo.

> ———— half way down
> *Hangs* one who gathers samphire,

is the well-known expression of Shakspeare, delineating an ordinary image upon the cliffs of Dover. In these two instances
is a slight exertion of the faculty which I denominate imagination, in the use of one word : 'neither the goats nor the samphire-
gatherer do literally hang, as does the parrot or the monkey ;
but, presenting to the senses something of such an appearance,
the mind in its activity, for its own gratification, contemplates
them as hanging.

> As when far off at sea a fleet descried
> *Hangs* in the clouds, by equinoctial wind ;
> Close sailing from Bengala, or the isles
> Of Ternate or Tidore, whence merchants bring
> Their spicy drugs ; they on the trading flood
> Through the wide Ethiopian to the Cape
> Ply, stemming nightly toward the Pole ; so seemed
> Far off the flying Fiend.

Here is the full strength of the imagination involved in the
word *hangs*, and exerted upon the whole image : First, the fleet,
an aggregate of many ships, is represented as one mighty person,
whose track, we know and feel, is upon the waters ; but, taking
advantage of its appearance to the senses, the Poet dares to represent it as *hanging in the clouds*, both for the gratification of
the mind in contemplating the image itself, and in reference to
the motion and appearance of the sublime objects to which it is
compared.

From impressions of sight we will pass to those of sound ;
which, as they must necessarily be of a less definite character,
shall be selected from these volumes :

> Over his own sweet voice the Stock-dove *broods ;*

of the same bird,

> His voice was *buried* among trees,
> Yet to be come at by the breeze ;

> O, Cuckoo ! shall I call thee *Bird*,
> Or but a wandering *Voice ?*

The stock-dove is said to *coo*, a sound well imitating the note of the bird; but, by the intervention of the metaphor *broods*, the affections are called in by the imagination to assist in marking the manner in which the bird reiterates and prolongs her soft note, as if herself delighting to listen to it, and participating of a still and quiet satisfaction, like that which may be supposed inseparable from the continuous process of incubation. ' His voice was buried among the trees,' a metaphor expressing the love of *seclusion* by which this Bird is marked; and characterising its note as not partaking of the shrill and the piercing, and therefore more easily deadened by the intervening shade; yet a note so peculiar and withal so pleasing,.that the breeze, gifted with that love of the sound which the Poet feels, penetrates the shades in which it is entombed, and conveys it to the ear of the listener.

> Shall I call thee Bird,
> Or but a wandering Voice?

This concise interrogation characterises the seeming ubiquity of the voice of the cuckoo, and dispossesses the creature almost of a corporeal existence; the Imagination being tempted to this exertion of her power by a consciousness in the memory that the cuckoo is almost perpetually heard throughout the season of spring, but seldom becomes an object of sight.

Thus far of images independent of each other, and immediately endowed by the mind with properties that do not inhere in them, upon an incitement from properties and qualities the existence of which is inherent and obvious. These processes of imagination are carried on either by conferring additional properties upon an object, or abstracting from it some of those which it actually possesses, and thus enabling it to re-act upon the mind which hath performed the process, like a new existence.

I pass from the Imagination acting upon an individual image to a consideration of the same faculty employed upon images in a conjunction by which they modify each other. The Reader has already had a fine instance before him in the passage quoted from Virgil, where the apparently perilous situation of the goat, hanging upon the shaggy precipice, is contrasted with that of the shepherd contemplating it from the seclusion of the cavern in which he lies stretched at ease and in security. Take these

images separately, and how unaffecting the picture compared
with that produced by their being thus connected with, and opposed to, each other!

> As a huge stone is sometimes seen to lie
> Couched on the bald top of an eminence,
> Wonder to all who do the same espy
> By what means it could thither come, and whence,
> So that it seems a thing endued with sense,
> Like a sea-beast crawled forth, which on a shelf
> Of rock or sand reposeth, there to sun himself.

> Such seemed this Man; not all alive or dead
> Nor all asleep, in his extreme old age.

>   .   .   .   .   .   .
> Motionless as a cloud the old Man stood,
> That heareth not the loud winds when they call,
> And moveth altogether if it move at all.

In these images, the conferring, the abstracting, and the modifying powers of the Imagination, immediately and mediately acting, are all brought into conjunction. The stone is endowed
with something of the power of life to approximate it to the sea-
beast; and the sea-beast stripped of some of its vital qualities
to assimilate it to the stone; which intermediate image is thus
treated for the purpose of bringing the original image, that of
the stone, to a nearer resemblance to the figure and condition of
the aged Man; who is divested of so much of the indications of
life and motion as to bring him to the point where the two objects unite and coalesce in just comparison. After what has
been said, the image of the cloud need not be commented upon.

Thus far of an endowing or modifying power: but the Imagination also shapes and *creates*; and how? By innumerable
processes; and in none does it more delight than in that of con-
solidating numbers into unity, and dissolving and separating
unity into number,—alternations proceeding from, and governed
by, a sublime consciousness of the soul in her own mighty and
almost divine powers. Recur to the passage already cited from
Milton. When the compact Fleet, as one Person, has been introduced 'Sailing from Bengala.' 'They,' *i.e.* the 'merchants,'
representing the fleet resolved into a multitude of ships, 'ply'
their voyage towards the extremities of the earth: 'So' (referring to the word 'As' in the commencement) 'seemed the flying
Fiend;' the image of his person acting to recombine the multi-

tude of ships into one body,—the point from which the comparison set out. ' So seemed,' and to whom seemed ? To the heavenly Muse who dictates the poem, to the eye of the Poet's mind, and to that of the Reader, present at one moment in the wide Ethiopian, and the next in the solitudes, then first broken in upon, of the infernal regions !

> Modo me Thebis, modo ponit Athenis.

Here again this mighty Poet,—speaking of the Messiah going forth to expel from heaven the rebellious angels,

> Attended by ten thousand thousand Saints
> He onward came : far off his coming shone,—

the retinue of Saints, and the Person of the Messiah himself, lost almost and merged in the splendour of that indefinite abstraction ' His coming !'

As I do not mean here to treat this subject further than to throw some light upon the present Volumes, and especially upon one division of them, I shall spare myself and the Reader the trouble of considering the Imagination as it deals with thoughts and sentiments, as it regulates the composition of characters, and determines the course of actions : I will not consider it (more than I have already done by implication) as that power which, in the language of one of my most esteemed Friends, ' draws all things to one; which makes things animate or inanimate, beings with their attributes, subjects with their accessories, take one colour and serve to one effect.'* The grand store-houses of enthusiastic and meditative Imagination, of poetical, as contradistinguished from human and dramatic Imagination, are the prophetic and lyrical parts of the Holy Scriptures, and the works of Milton ; to which I cannot forbear to add those of Spenser. I select these writers in preference to those of ancient Greece and Rome, because the anthropomorphitism of the Pagan religion subjected the minds of the greatest poets in those countries too much to the bondage of definite form ; from which the Hebrews were preserved by their abhorrence of idolatry. This abhorrence was almost as strong in our great epic Poet, both from circumstances of his life, and from the constitution of his mind. However imbued the surface might be with classical literature, he was a Hebrew in soul; and all

* Charles Lamb upon the genius of Hogarth.

things tended in him towards the sublime. Spenser, of a gentler nature, maintained his freedom by aid of his allegorical spirit, at one time inciting him to create persons out of abstractions ; and, at another, by a superior effort of genius, to give the universality and permanence of abstractions to his human beings, by means of attributes and emblems that belong to the highest moral truths and the purest sensations,—of which his character of Una is a glorious example. Of the human and dramatic Imagination the works of Shakspeare are an inexhaustible source.

> I tax not you, ye Elements, with unkindness,
> I never gave you kingdoms, call'd you Daughters !

And if, bearing in mind the many Poets distinguished by this prime quality, whose names I omit to mention ; yet justified by recollection of the insults which the ignorant, the incapable and the presumptuous, have heaped upon these and my other writings, I may be permitted to anticipate the judgment of posterity upon myself, I shall declare (censurable, I grant, if the notoriety of the fact above stated does not justify me) that I have given in these unfavourable times, evidence of exertions of this faculty upon its worthiest objects, the external universe, the moral and religious sentiments of Man, his natural affections, and his acquired passions ; which have the same ennobling tendency as the productions of men, in this kind, worthy to be holden in undying remembrance.

To the mode in which Fancy has already been characterised as the power of evoking and combining, or, as my friend Mr. Coleridge has styled it, ' the aggregative and associative power,' my objection is only that the definition is too general. To aggregate and to associate, to evoke and to combine, belong as well to the Imagination as to the Fancy ; but either the materials evoked and combined are different; or they are brought together under a different law, and for a different purpose. Fancy does not require that the materials which she makes use of should be susceptible of change in their constitution, from her touch ; and, where they admit of modification, it is enough for her purpose if it be slight, limited, and evanescent. · Directly the reverse of these, are the desires and demands of the Imagination. She recoils from every thing but the plastic, the pliant, and the indefinite. She leaves it to Fancy to describe Queen Mab as coming,

In shape no bigger than an agate-stone
On the fore-finger of an alderman.

Having to speak of stature, she does not tell you that her gigantic Angel was as tall as Pompey's Pillar ; much less that he was
twelve cubits, or twelve hundred cubits high ; or that his dimensions equalled those of Teneriffe or Atlas ;—because these,
and if they were a million times as high it would be the same,
are bounded : The expression is, ' His stature reached the sky !'
the illimitable firmament !—When the Imagination frames a
comparison, if it does not strike on the first presentation, a sense
of the truth of the likeness, from the moment that it is perceived, grows—and continues to grow—upon the mind ; the resemblance depending less upon outline of form and feature, than
upon expression and effect ; less upon casual and outstanding,
than upon inherent and internal, properties : moreover, the images invariably modify each other.—The law under which the
processes of Fancy are carried on is as capricious as the accidents of things, and the effects are surprising, playful, ludicrous,
amusing, tender, or pathetic, as the objects happen to be appo-
sitely produced or fortunately combined.   Fancy depends upon
the rapidity and profusion with which she scatters her thoughts
and images ; trusting that their number, and the felicity with
which they are linked together, will make amends for the want of
individual value : or she prides herself upon the curious subtilty
and the successful elaboration with which she can detect their
lurking affinities.   If she can win you over to her purpose, and
impart to you her feelings, she cares not how unstable or transitory may be her influence, knowing that it will not be out of her
power to resume it upon an apt occasion.   But the Imagination
is conscious of an indestructible dominion ;—the Soul may fall
away from it, not being able to sustain its grandeur ; but, if
once felt and acknowledged, by no act of any other faculty of the
mind can it be relaxed, impaired, or diminished.—Fancy is given
to quicken and to beguile the temporal part of our nature, Imagination to incite and to support the eternal.—Yet is it not the
less true that Fancy, as she is an active, is also, under her own
laws and in her own spirit, a creative faculty.   In what manner
Fancy ambitiously aims at a rivalship with Imagination, and
Imagination stoops to work with materials of Fancy, might be
illustrated from the compositions of all eloquent writers, whether

in prose or verse ; and chiefly from those of our own Country. Scarcely a page of the impassioned parts of Bishop Taylor's Works can be opened that shall not afford examples.—Referring the Reader to those inestimable volumes, I will content myself with placing a conceit (ascribed to Lord Chesterfield) in contrast with a passage from the 'Paradise Lost :'—

> The dews of the evening most carefully shun,
> They are the tears of the sky for the loss of the sun.

After the transgression of Adam, Milton, with other appearances of sympathising Nature, thus marks the immediate consequence,

> Sky lowered, and, muttering thunder, some sad drops
> Wept at completion of the mortal sin.

The associating link is the same in each instance : Dew and rain, not distinguishable from the liquid substance of tears, are employed as indications of sorrow. A flash of surprise is the effect in the former case ; a flash of surprise, and nothing more ; for the nature of things does not sustain the combination. In the latter, the effects from the act, of which there is this immediate consequence and visible sign, are so momentous, that the mind acknowledges the justice and reasonableness of the sympathy in nature so manifested ; and the sky weeps drops of water as if with human eyes, as 'Earth had before trembled from her entrails, and Nature given a second groan.'

Finally, I will refer to Cotton's 'Ode upon Winter,' an admirable composition, though stained with some peculiarities of the age in which he lived, for a general illustration of the characteristics of Fancy. The middle part of this ode contains a most lively description of the entrance of Winter, with his retinue, as 'A palsied king,' and yet a military monarch,—advancing for conquest with his army ; the several bodies of which, and their arms and equipments, are described with a rapidity of detail, and a profusion of *fanciful* comparisons, which indicate on the part of the poet extreme activity of intellect, and a correspondent hurry of delightful feeling. Winter retires from the foe into his fortress, where

> ———— a magazine
> Of sovereign juice is collared in ;
> Liquor that will the siege maintain
> Should Phœbus ne'er return again.

Though myself a water-drinker, I cannot resist the pleasure of transcribing what follows, as an instance still more happy of Fancy employed in the treatment of feeling than, in its preceding passages, the Poem supplies of her management of forms.

'Tis that, that gives the poet rage,
And thaws the gelly'd blood of age;
Matures the young, restores the old,
And makes the fainting coward bold.

It lays the careful head to rest,
Calms palpitations in the breast,
Renders our lives' misfortune sweet:

. . . . . .

Then let the chill Sirocco blow,
And gird us round with hills of snow,
Or else go whistle to the shore,
And make the hollow mountains roar.

Whilst we together jovial sit
Careless, and crowned with mirth and wit,
Where, though bleak winds confine us home,
Our fancies round the world shall roam.

We'll think of all the Friends we know,
And drink to all worth drinking to;
When having drunk all thine and mine,
We rather shall want healths than wine.

But where Friends fail us, we'll supply
Our friendships with our charity;
Men that remote in sorrows live,
Shall by our lusty brimmers thrive.

We'll drink the wanting into wealth,
And those that languish into health,
The afflicted into joy; th' opprest
Into security and rest.

The worthy in disgrace shall find
Favour return again more kind,
And in restraint who stifled lie,
Shall taste the air of liberty.

The brave shall triumph in success,
The lovers shall have mistresses,
Poor unregarded Virtue, praise,
And the neglected Poet, bays.

Thus shall our healths do others good,
Whilst we ourselves do all we would;
For, freed from envy and from care,
What would we be but what we are?

When I sate down to write this Preface, it was my intention to have made it more comprehensive; but, thinking that I ought rather to apologise for detaining the reader so long, I will here conclude.

DEDICATION: PREFIXED TO THE EDITION OF 1815.

To Sir George Howland Beaumont, Bart.

MY DEAR SIR GEORGE,

Accept my thanks for the permission given me to dedicate these Volumes to you. In addition to a lively pleasure derived from general considerations, I feel a particular satisfaction; for, by inscribing these Poems with your Name, I seem to myself in some degree to repay, by an appropriate honour, the great obligation which I owe to one part of the Collection—as having been the means of first making us personally known to each other. Upon much of the remainder, also, you have a peculiar claim,—for some of the best pieces were composed under the shade of your own groves, upon the classic ground of Coleorton; where I was animated by the recollection of those illustrious Poets of your name and family, who were born in that neighbourhood; and, we may be assured, did not wander with indifference by the dashing stream of Grace Dieu, and among the rocks that diversify the forest of Charnwood.—Nor is there any one to whom such parts of this Collection as have been inspired or coloured by the beautiful Country from which I now address you, could be presented with more propriety than to yourself—to whom it has suggested so many admirable pictures. Early in life, the sublimity and beauty of this region excited your admiration; and I know that you are bound to it in mind by a still strengthening attachment.

Wishing and hoping that this Work, with the embellishments it has received from your pencil, may survive as a lasting memorial of a friendship which I reckon among the blessings of my life,

I have the honour to be, my dear Sir George,

Yours most affectionately and faithfully,

WILLIAM WORDSWORTH.

RYDAL MOUNT, WESTMORELAND,
February 1, 1815.

THE Title-page announces that this is only a portion of a poem; and the Reader must be here apprised that it belongs to the second part of a long and laborious Work, which is to consist of three parts.—The Author will candidly acknowledge that, if the first of these had been completed, and in such a manner as to satisfy his own mind, he should have preferred the natural order of publication, and have given that to the world first; but, as the second division of the Work was designed to refer more to passing events, and to an existing state of things, than the others were meant to do, more continuous exertion was naturally bestowed upon it, and greater progress made here than in the rest of the poem; and as this part does not depend upon the preceding, to a degree which will materially injure its own peculiar interest, the Author, complying with the earnest entreaties of some valued Friends, presents the following pages to the Public.

It may be proper to state whence the poem, of which ' The Excursion' is a part, derives its Title of THE RECLUSE.—Several years ago, when the Author retired to his native mountains, with the hope of being enabled to construct a literary Work that might live, it was a reasonable thing that he should take a review of his own mind, and examine how far Nature and Education had qualified him for such employment. As subsidiary to this preparation, he undertook to record, in verse, the origin and progress of his own powers, as far as he was acquainted with them. That Work, addressed to a dear Friend, most distinguished for his knowledge and genius, and to whom the Author's Intellect is deeply indebted, has been long finished; ̖and the result of the investigation which gave rise to it was a determination to compose a philosophical poem, containing views of Man, Nature, and Society; and to be entitled, ' The Recluse;' as having for its principal subject the sensations and opinions of a poet living in retirement.—The preparatory poem is biographical, and conducts the history of the Author's mind · to the point when he was emboldened to hope that his faculties were sufficiently matured for entering upon the arduous labour which he had proposed to himself: and the two Works have the same kind of relation to each other, if he may so express himself, as the ante-chapel has to the body of a gothic church. Continuing this allusion, he may be permitted to add, that his minor Pieces, which have been long before the Public, when they shall be properly arranged, will be found by the attentive Reader to have such connection with the main Work as may give them claim to be likened to the little cells, oratories, and sepulchral recesses, ordinarily included in those edifices.

The Author would not have deemed himself justified in saying, upon this occasion, so much of performances either unfinished, or unpublished, if he had not thought that the labour bestowed by him upon what he has heretofore and now laid before the Public entitled him to candid attention for such a statement as he thinks necessary to throw light upon his endeavours to please and, he would hope, to benefit his countrymen.—Nothing further need be added, than that the first and third parts of 'The Recluse' will consist chiefly of meditations in the Author's own person; and that in the intermediate part ('The Excursion') the intervention of characters speaking is employed, and something of a dramatic form adopted.

It is not the Author's intention formally to announce a system: it was more animating to him to proceed in a different course; and if he shall succeed in conveying to the mind clear thoughts, lively images, and strong feelings, the Reader will have no difficulty in extracting the system for himself. And in the mean time the following passage, taken from the conclusion of the first book of 'The Recluse,' may be acceptable as a kind of *Prospectus* of the design and scope of the whole Poem.

> On Man, on Nature, and on Human Life,
> Musing in solitude, I oft perceive
> Fair trains of imagery before me rise,
> Accompanied by feelings of delight
> Pure, or with no unpleasing sadness mixed;
> And I am conscious of affecting thoughts
> And dear remembrances, whose presence soothes
> Or elevates the Mind, intent to weigh
> The good and evil of our mortal state.
> —To these emotions, whencesoe'er they come,
> Whether from breath of outward circumstance,
> Or from the Soul—an impulse to herself—

I would give utterance in numerous verse.
Of Truth, of Grandeur, Beauty, Love, and Hope,
And melancholy Fear subdued by Faith;
Of blessed consolations in distress;
Of moral strength, and intellectual Power;
Of joy in widest commonalty spread;
Of the individual Mind that keeps her own
Inviolate retirement, subject there
To Conscience only, and the law supreme
Of that Intelligence which governs all—
I sing:—' fit audience let me find though few!'

    So prayed, more gaining than he asked, the Bard—
In holiest mood. Urania, I shall need
Thy guidance, or a greater Muse, if such
Descend to earth or dwell in highest heaven!
For I must tread on shadowy ground, must sink
Deep—and, aloft ascending, breathe in worlds
To which the heaven of heavens is but a veil.
All strength—all terror, single or in bands,
That ever was put forth in personal form—
Jehovah—with His thunder, and the choir
Of shouting Angels, and the empyreal thrones—
I pass them unalarmed. Not Chaos, not
The darkest pit of lowest Erebus,
Nor aught of blinder vacancy, scooped out
By help of dreams—can breed such fear and awe
As fall upon us often when we look
Into our Minds, into the Mind of Man—
My haunt, and the main region of my song.
—Beauty—a living Presence of the earth,
Surpassing the most fair ideal Forms
Which craft of delicate Spirits hath composed
From earth's materials—waits upon my steps;
Pitches her tents before me as I move,
An hourly neighbour. Paradise, and groves
Elysian, Fortunate Fields—like those of old
Sought in the Atlantic Main—why should they be
A history only of departed things,
Or a mere fiction of what never was?
For the discerning intellect of Man,
When wedded to this goodly universe
In love and holy passion, shall find these
A simple produce of the common day.
—I, long before the blissful hour arrives,
Would chant, in lonely peace, the spousal verse
Of this great consummation:—and, by words
Which speak of nothing more than what we are,
Would I arouse the sensual from their sleep
Of Death, and win the vacant and the vain

To noble raptures; while my voice proclaims
How exquisitely the individual Mind
(And the progressive powers perhaps no less
Of the whole species) to the external World
Is fitted:—and how exquisitely, too—
Theme this but little heard of among men—
The external World is fitted to the Mind;
And the creation (by no lower name
Can it be called) which they with blended might
Accomplish:—this is our high argument.
—Such grateful haunts foregoing, if I oft
Must turn elsewhere—to travel near the tribes
And fellowships of men, and see ill sights
Of madding passions mutually inflamed;
Must hear Humanity in fields and groves
Pipe solitary anguish; or must hang
Brooding above the fierce confederate storm
Of sorrow, barricadoed evermore
Within the walls of cities—may these sounds
Have their authentic comment; that even these
Hearing, I be not downcast or forlorn!—
Descend, prophetic Spirit! that inspir'st
The human Soul of universal earth,
Dreaming on things to come; and dost possess
A metropolitan temple in the hearts
Of mighty Poets: upon me bestow
A gift of genuine insight; that my Song
With star-like virtue in its place may shine,
Shedding benignant influence, and secure,
Itself, from all malevolent effect
Of those mutations that extend their sway
Throughout the nether sphere!—And if with this
I mix more lowly matter: with the thing
Contemplated, describe the Mind and Man
Contemplating: and who, and what he was—
The transitory Being that beheld
This Vision: when and where, and how he lived;
Be not this labour useless. If such theme
May sort with highest objects, then—dread Power!
Whose gracious favour is the primal source
Of all illumination—may my Life
Express the image of a better time,
More wise desires, and simpler manners;—nurse
My Heart in genuine freedom:—all pure thoughts
Be with me;—so shall Thy unfailing love
Guide, and support, and cheer me to the end!

(/) LETTERS TO SIR GEORGE AND LADY BEAUMONT AND OTHERS ON THE POEMS AND RELATED SUBJECTS.

GRATITUDE FOR KINDNESSES, DIFFICULTY OF LETTER-WRITING, &c.

Letter to Sir George H. Beaumont, Bart.

Grasmere, 14th October, 1803.

DEAR SIR GEORGE,

If any Person were to be informed of the particulars of your kindness to me,—if it were described to him in all its delicacy and nobleness,—and he should afterwards be told that I suffered eight weeks to elapse without writing to you one word of thanks or acknowledgment, he would deem it a thing absolutely *impossible*. It is nevertheless true. This is, in fact, the first time that I have taken up a pen, not for writing letters, but on any account whatsoever, except once, since Mr. Coleridge showed me the writings of the Applethwaite Estate, and told me the little history of what you had done for me, the motives, &c. I need not say that it gave me the most heartfelt pleasure, not for my own sake chiefly, though in that point of view it might well be most highly interesting to me, but as an act which, considered in all its relations as to matter and manner, it would not be too much to say, did honour to human nature; at least, I felt it as such, and it overpowered me.

Owing to a set of painful and uneasy sensations which I have, more or less, at all times about my chest, from a disease which chiefly affects my nerves and digestive organs, and which makes my aversion from writing little less than madness, I deferred writing to you, being at first made still more uncomfortable by travelling, and loathing to do violence to myself, in what ought to be an act of pure pleasure and enjoyment, viz., the expression of my deep sense of your goodness. This feeling was, indeed, so strong in me, as to make me look upon the act of writing to you, not as the work of a moment, but as a business with some-

thing little less than awful in it, a task, a duty, a thing not to
be done but in my best, my purest, and my happiest moments.
Many of these I had, but then I had not my pen and ink [and]
my paper before me, my conveniences, 'my appliances and means
to boot;' all which, the moment that I thought of them, seemed
to disturb and impair the sanctity of my pleasure.   I contented
myself with thinking over my complacent feelings, and breathing forth solitary gratulations and thanksgivings, which I did
in many a sweet and many a wild place, during my late Tour.
In this shape, procrastination became irresistible to me; at last
I said, I will write at home from my own fireside, when I shall
be at ease and in comfort.   I have now been more than a fortnight at home, but the uneasiness in my chest has made me
beat off the time when the pen was to be taken up.   I do not
know from what cause it is, but during the last three years
I have never had a pen in my hand for five minutes, before my
whole frame becomes one bundle of uneasiness; a perspiration
starts out all over me, and my chest is oppressed in a manner
which I cannot describe.   This is a sad weakness; for I am
sure, though it is chiefly owing to the state of my body, that by
exertion of mind I might in part control it.   So, however, it is;
and I mention it, because I am sure when you are made acquainted with the circumstances, though the extent to which it
exists nobody can well conceive, you will look leniently upon
my silence, and rather pity than blame me; though I must still
continue to reproach myself, as I have done bitterly every day
for these last eight weeks.   One thing in particular has given me
great uneasiness: it is, least in the extreme delicacy of your
mind, which is well known to me, you for a moment may have
been perplexed by a single apprehension that there might be
any error, anything which I might misconceive, in your kindness
to me.   When I think of the possibility of this, I am vexed
beyond measure that I had not resolution to write immediately.
But I hope that these fears are all groundless, and that you have
(as I know your nature will lead you to do) suspended your judgment upon my silence, blaming me indeed but in that qualified
way in which a good man blames what he believes will be found
an act of venial infirmity, when it is fully explained.   But I have
troubled you far too much with this.   Such I am however, and
deeply I regret that I am such.   I shall conclude with solemnly

assuring you, late as it is, that nothing can wear out of my heart, as long as my faculties remain, the deep feeling which I have of your delicate and noble conduct towards me.

It is now high time to speak of the estate, and what is to be done with it. It is a most delightful situation, and few things would give me greater pleasure than to realise the plan which you had in view for me, of building a house there. But I am afraid, I am sorry to say, that the chances are very much against this, partly on account of the state of my own affairs, and still more from the improbability of Mr. Coleridge's continuing in the country. The writings are at present in my possession, and what I should wish is, that I might be considered at present as steward of the land, with liberty to lay out the rent in planting, or any other improvement which might be thought advisable, with a view to building upon it. And if it should be out of my power to pitch my own tent there, I would then request that you would give me leave to restore the property to your own hands, in order that you might have the opportunity of again presenting it to some worthy person who might be so fortunate as to be able to make that pleasant use of it which it was your wish that I should have done.

Mr. Coleridge informed me, that immediately after you left Keswick, he had, as I requested, returned you thanks for those two elegant drawings which you were so good as to leave for me. The present is valuable in itself, and I consider it as a high honour conferred on me. How often did we wish for five minutes' command of your pencil while we were in Scotland! or rather that you had been with us. Sometimes I am sure you would have been highly delighted. In one thing Scotland is superior to every country I have travelled in; I mean the graceful beauty of the dresses and figures. There is a tone of imagination about them beyond anything I have seen elsewhere.

Mr. Coleridge, I understand, has written to you several times lately ; so of course he will have told you when and why he left us. I am glad he did, as I am sure the solitary part of his tour did him much the most service. He is still unwell, though wonderfully strong. He is attempting to bring on a fit of the gout, which he is sure will relieve him greatly. I was at Keswick last Sunday and saw both him and Mr. Southey, whom I liked very much. Coleridge looks better, I think, than when you saw

him ; and is, I also think, upon the whole, much better. Lady
Beaumont will be pleased to hear that our carriage (though it
did not suit Mr. Coleridge, the noise of it being particularly
unpleasant to him) answered wonderfully well for my sister and
me, and that the whole tour far surpassed our most sanguine
expectations.

They are sadly remiss at Keswick in putting themselves to
trouble in defence of the country; they came forward very cheer-
fully some time ago, but were so thwarted by the orders and
counter-orders of the ministry and their servants, that they have
thrown up the whole in disgust. At Grasmere, we have turned
out almost to a man. We are to go to Ambleside on Sunday to
be mustered, and put on, for the first time, our military apparel.
I remain, dear Sir George, with the most affectionate and respectful regard for you and Lady Beaumont,

Yours sincerely,
W. WORDSWORTH.

My sister will transcribe three sonnets,* which I do not send
you from any notion I have of their merit, but merely because
they are the only verses I have written since I had the pleasure
of seeing you and Lady Beaumont. At the sight of Kilchurn
Castle, an ancient residence of the Breadalbanes, upon an island
in Loch Awe, I felt a real poetical impulse : but I did not proceed. I began a poem (apostrophising the castle) thus :

> Child of loud-throated war ! the mountain stream
> Roars in thy hearing ; but thy hour of rest
> Is come, and thou art silent in thine age ;

but I stopp'd.†

° Written at Needpath, (near Peebles,) a mansion of the Duke of Queensbury : ' Now as I live, I pity that great Lord,' &c. [*Memorials of a Tour in
Scotland*, xii.] To the Men of Kent : ' Vanguard of Liberty, ye Men of Kent !'
[*Poems dedicated to National Independence and Liberty*, xxiii.] Anticipation :
' Shout, for a mighty victory is won !' [*Ibid.* xxvi.] &c. If you think, either you
or Lady Beaumont, that these two last Sonnets are worth publication, would you
have the goodness to circulate them in any way you like. [On *various readings*
in these Sonnets, see our Notes and Illustrations. G.]

† *Memoirs*, vol. i. pp. 260-4, with important additions from the original. G.

OF SIR JOSHUA REYNOLDS, &c.

Letter to Sir George H. Beaumont, Bart.

Grasmere, July 20. 1804.

DEAR SIR GEORGE,

Lady Beaumont in a letter to my sister told her some time ago that it was your intention to have written to me, but knowing my aversion to letter writing you were unwilling to impose upon me the trouble of answering. I am much obliged to you for the honour you intended me, and deeply sensible of your delicacy. If a man were what he ought to be, with such feelings and such motives as I have, it would be as easy for him to write to Sir George Beaumont as to take his food when he was hungry or his repose when he was weary. But we suffer bad habits to grow upon us, and that has been the case with me, as you have had reason to find and forgive already. I cannot quit the subject without regretting that any weakness of mine should have prevented my hearing from you, which would always give me great delight, and though I cannot presume to say that I should be a *punctual* correspondent, I am sure I should not be insensible of your kindness, but should also do my best to deserve it.

A few days ago I received from Mr. Southey your very acceptable present of Sir Joshua Reynolds's Works, which, with the Life, I have nearly read through. Several of the Discourses I had read before, though never regularly together: they have very much added to the high opinion which I before entertained of Sir Joshua Reynolds. Of a great part of them, never having had an opportunity of *studying* any pictures whatsoever, I can be but a very inadequate judge; but of such parts of the Discourses as relate to general philosophy, I may be entitled to speak with more confidence; and it gives me great pleasure to say to you, knowing your great regard for Sir Joshua, that they appear to me highly honourable to him. The sound judgment universally displayed in these Discourses is truly admirable,—I mean the deep conviction of the necessity of unwearied labour and diligence, the reverence for the great men of his art, and the comprehensive and unexclusive character of his taste. Is it not a pity, Sir George, that a man with such a high sense of the *dignity* of his art, and with such industry, should not have given more of his time to the nobler departments of painting? I do not say this so much on account of what the world would have gained by the superior excellence and interest of his pictures, though doubtless that would have been very considerable, but for the sake of example. It is such an animating sight to see a man of genius, regardless of temporary gains, whether of money or praise, fixing his attention solely upon what is intrinsically interesting and permanent, and finding his happiness in an entire devotion of himself to such pursuits as shall most ennoble human nature. We have not yet seen enough of this in modern times; and never was there a period in society when such examples were likely to do more good than at present. The industry and love of truth which distinguish Sir Joshua's mind are most admirable; but he appears to me to have lived too much for the age in which he lived, and the people among whom he lived, though this in an infinitely less degree than his friend Burke, of whom Goldsmith said, with such truth, long ago, that—

> Born for the universe, he narrowed his mind,
> And to party gave up what was meant for mankind.

I should not have said thus much of Reynolds, which I have not said without pain, but because I have so great a respect for his character, and because he lived at a time when, being the first Englishman distinguished for excellence in the higher department of painting, he had the field fairly open for him to have given an example, upon which all eyes needs must have been fixed, of a man preferring the cultivation and exertion of his own powers in the highest possible degree to any other object of regard. My writing is growing quite illegible. I must therefore either mend it, or throw down the pen.

How sorry we all are under this roof that we cannot have the pleasure of seeing you and Lady Beaumont down this summer! The weather has been most glorious, and the country, of course, most delightful. Our own valley in particular was last night, by the light of the full moon, and in the perfect stillness of the lake, a scene of loveliness and repose as affecting as was ever beheld by the eye of man. We have had a day and a half of Mr. Davy's company at Grasmere, and no more: he seemed to leave us with great regret, being post-haste on his way to Edinburgh. I went with him to Paterdale, on his road to Penrith, where he would take coach. We had a deal of talk about you and Lady Beaumont: he was in your debt a letter, as I found, and exceedingly sorry that he had not been able to get over to see you, having been engaged at Mr. Coke's sheep-shearing, which had not left him time to cross from the Duke of Bedford's to your place. We had a very pleasant interview, though far too short. He is a most interesting man, whose views are fixed upon worthy objects.

That Loughrigg Tarn, beautiful pool of water as it is, is a perpetual mortification to me when I think that you and Lady Beaumont were so near having a summer-nest there. This is often talked over among us; and we always end the subject with a heigh ho! of regret. But I must think of concluding. My sister thanks Lady Beaumont for her last letter, and will write to her in a few days; but I must say to her myself how happy I was to hear that her sister had derived any consolation from Coleridge's poems and mine. I must also add how much pleasure it gives me that Lady Beaumont is so kindly, so affectionately disposed to my dear and good sister, and also to the other unknown parts of my family. Could we but have Coleridge back among us again! There is no happiness in this life but in intellect and virtue. Those were very pretty verses which Lady Beaumont sent; and we were much obliged to her for them.

What shocking bad writing I have sent you; I don't know [how] it is, but [it] seems as if I could not write any better.

Farewell. Believe me, with the sincerest love and affection for you and Lady Beaumont,

Yours,

WM. WORDSWORTH.*

✗ FAMILY NEWS, REYNOLDS, &c.

Letter to Sir George H. Beaumont, Bart.

Grasmere, August 30. (?) 1804.

DEAR SIR GEORGE,

Wednesday last, Mrs. Coleridge, as she may, perhaps, herself have informed you or Lady Beaumont, received

---

* *Memoirs*, vol. i. pp. 267-70, with important additions from the original. G.

a letter from Coleridge. I happened to be at Keswick when it arrived; and she has sent it over to us to-day. I will transcribe the most material parts of it, first assuring you, to remove anxiety on your part, that the contents are, we think, upon the whole, promising. He begins thus (date, June 5. 1804, Tuesday noon; Dr. Stoddart's, Malta) :—' I landed, in more than usual health, in the harbour of Valetta, about four o'clock, Friday afternoon, April 18. Since then I have been waiting, day after day, for the departure of Mr. Laing, tutor of the only child of Sir A. Ball, our civil governor.'

.   .   .   .

My sister has to thank Lady Beaumont for a letter; but she is at present unable to write, from a violent inflammation in her eyes, which I hope is no more than the complaint going about : but as she has lately been over-fatigued, and is in other respects unwell, I am not without fear that the indisposition in her eyes may last some time. As soon as she is able, she will do herself the pleasure of writing to Lady Beaumont. Mrs. Wordsworth and Lady B.'s little god-daughter* are both doing very well. Had the child been a boy, we should have persisted in our right to avail ourselves of Lady Beaumont's goodness in offering to stand sponsor for it. The name of *Dorothy;* obsolete as it is now grown, had been so long devoted in my own thoughts to the first daughter that I might have, that I could not break this promise to myself—a promise in which my wife participated; though the name of *Mary*, to my ear the most musical and truly English in sound we have, would have otherwise been most welcome to me, including, as it would, Lady Beaumont and its mother. This last sentence, though in a letter to you, Sir George, is intended for Lady Beaumont.

.   .   .   .

When I ventured to express my regret at Sir Joshua Rey-nolds giving so much of his time to portrait-painting and to his friends, I did not mean to recommend absolute solitude and se-clusion from the world as an advantage to him or anybody else. I think it a great evil; and indeed, in the case of a painter, fre-quent intercourse with the living world seems absolutely neces-sary to keep the mind in health and vigour. I spoke, in some respects, in compliment to Sir Joshua Reynolds, feeling deeply,

* Dora Wordsworth, born Aug. 16. 1804.

as I do, the power of his genius, and loving passionately the labours of genius in every way in which I am capable of comprehending them. Mr. Malone, in the account prefixed to the Discourses, tells us that Sir Joshua generally passed the time from eleven till four every day in portrait-painting. This it was that grieved me, as a sacrifice of great things to little ones. It will give me great pleasure to hear from you at your leisure. I am anxious to know that you are satisfied with the site and intended plan of your house. I suppose no man ever built a house without finding, when it was finished, that something in it might have been better done. *Internal* architecture seems to have arrived at great excellence in England; but, I don't know how it is, I scarcely ever see the *outside* of a new house that pleases me. But I must break off. Believe me, with best remembrances from my wife and sister to yourself and Lady Beaumont,

Yours,

With the greatest respect and regard,

W. WORDSWORTH.

My poetical labours have been entirely suspended during the last two months: I am most anxious to return to them.*

OF NATURE AND ART, &c.

Letter to Sir George H. Beaumont.

August 28. 1811, Cottage, 7 minutes' walk from
the seaside, near Bootle, Cumberland.

MY DEAR SIR GEORGE,

How shall I appear before you again after so long an interval? It seems that now I ought rather to begin with an apology for writing, than for not having written during a space of almost twelve months. I have blamed myself not a little; yet not so much as I should have done had I not known that the main cause of my silence has been the affection I feel for you; on which account it is not so easy to me to write upon trifling or daily occurrences to you as it would be to write to another whom I loved less. Accordingly these have not had power to tempt me to take up the pen; and in the mean while,

* *Memoirs*, vol. i. pp. 270-2. G.

from my more intimate concerns I have abstained, partly because I do not, in many cases, myself like to see the reflection of them upon paper, and still more because it is my wish at all times, when I think of the state in which your health and spirits may happen to be, that my letter should be wholly free from melancholy, and breathe nothing but cheerfulness and pleasure. Having made this avowal, I trust that what may be wanting to my justification will be made up by your kindness and forgiving disposition.

It was near about this time last year that we were employed in our pleasant tour to the Leasowes and Hagley. The twelve months that have elapsed have not impaired the impressions which those scenes made upon me, nor weakened my remembrance of the delight which the places and objects, and the conversations they led to, awakened in our minds.

.   .   .   .

It is very late to mention, that when in Wales, last autumn, I contrived to pass a day and a half with your friend Price at Foxley. He was very kind, and took due pains to show me all the beauties of his place. I should have been very insensible not to be pleased with, and grateful for, his attentions; and certainly I was gratified by the sight of the scenes through which he conducted me.

.   .   .   .   .   .

I was less able to do justice in my own mind to the scenery of Foxley. You will, perhaps, think it a strange fault that I am going to find with it, considering the acknowledged taste of the owner, viz. that, small as it is compared with hundreds of places, the domain is too extensive for the character of the country. Wanting both rock and water, it necessarily wants variety; and in a district of this kind, the portion of a gentleman's estate which he keeps exclusively to himself, and which he devotes, wholly or in part, to ornament, may very easily exceed the proper bounds,—not, indeed, as to the preservation of wood, but most easily as to every thing else. A man by little and little becomes so delicate and fastidious with respect to forms in scenery, where he has a power to exercise a control over them, that if they do not exactly please him in all moods and every point of view, his power becomes his law; he banishes one, and then rids himself of another; impoverishing and *mono-*

tonising landscapes, which, if not originally distinguished by the bounty of Nature, must be ill able to spare the inspiriting varieties which art, and the occupations and wants of life in a country left more to itself, never fail to produce. This relish of humanity Foxley wants, and is therefore to me, in spite of all its recommendations, a melancholy spot,—I mean that part of it which the owner keeps to himself, and has taken so much pains with. I heard the other day of two artists who thus expressed themselves upon the subject of a scene among our lakes: 'Plague upon those vile enclosures!' said one; 'they spoil every thing.' 'Oh,' said the other, 'I never *see* them.' Glover was the name of this last. Now, for my part, I should not wish to be either of these gentlemen; but to have in my own mind the power of turning to advantage, wherever it is possible, every object of art and nature as they appear before me. What a noble instance, as you have often pointed out to me, has Rubens given of this in that picture in your possession, where he has brought, as it were, a whole county into one landscape, and made the most formal partitions of cultivation, hedgerows of pollard willows, conduct the eye into the depths and distances of his picture; and thus, more than by any other means, has given it that appearance of immensity which is so striking. As I have slipped into the subject of painting, I feel anxious to inquire whether your pencil has been busy last winter in the solitude and uninterrupted quiet of Dunmow. Most likely you know that we have changed our residence in Grasmere, which I hope will be attended with a great overbalance of advantages. One we are certain of—that we have at least one sitting-room clear of smoke, I trust, in all winds. . . . Over the chimney-piece is hung your little picture, from the neighbourhood of Coleorton. In our other house, on account of the frequent fits of smoke from the chimneys, both the pictures which I have from your hand were confined to bed-rooms. A few days after I had enjoyed the pleasure of seeing, in different moods of mind, your Coleorton landscape from my fire-side, it *suggested* to me the following sonnet, which, having walked out to the side of Grasmere brook, where it murmurs through the meadows near the church, I composed immediately:

> Praised be the art whose subtle power could stay
> Yon cloud, and fix it in that glorious shape;

> Nor would permit the thin smoke to escape,
> Nor those bright sunbeams to forsake the day;
> Which stopped that band of travellers on their way,
> Ere they were lost within the shady wood;
> And showed the bark upon the glassy flood
> For ever anchored in her sheltering bay.

.   .   .   .

The images of the smoke and the travellers are taken from your picture; the rest were added, in order to place the thought in a clear point of view, and for the sake of variety. I hope Coleorton continues to improve upon you and Lady Beaumont; and that Mr. Taylor's new laws and regulations are at least *peaceably* submitted to. Mrs. W. and I return in a few days to Grasmere. We cannot say that the child for whose sake we came down to the sea-side has derived much benefit from the bathing. The weather has been very unfavourable: we have, however, contrived to see every thing that lies within a reasonable walk of our present residence; among other places, Mulcaster—at least as much of it as can be seen from the public road; but the noble proprietor has contrived to shut himself up so with plantations and chained gates and locks, that whatever prospects he may command from his stately prison, or rather fortification, can only be guessed at by the passing traveller. In the state of blindness and unprofitable peeping in which we were compelled to pursue our way up a long and steep hill, I could not help observing to my companion that the Hibernian peer had completely given the lie to the poet Thomson, when, in a strain of proud enthusiasm, he boasts,

> I care not, Fortune, what you me deny,
>   You cannot rob me of free Nature's grace;
> You cannot shut the windows of the sky,
>   Through which Aurora shows her brightening face;
> You cannot bar my constant feet to trace
>   The woods and lawns by living stream, &c.
>   (*Castle of Indolence.*)

The *windows of the sky* were not *shut*, indeed, but the business was done more thoroughly; for the sky was nearly shut out altogether. This is like most others, a bleak and treeless coast, but abounding in corn-fields, and with a noble beach, which is delightful either for walking or riding. The Isle of Man is right opposite our window; and though in this unsettled weather often invisible, its appearance has afforded us great amusement.

One afternoon, above the whole length of it was stretched a body of clouds, shaped and coloured like a magnificent grove in winter when whitened with snow and illuminated by the morning sun, which, having melted the snow in part, has intermingled black masses among the brightness. The whole sky was scattered over with fleecy dark clouds, such as any sunshiny day produces, and which were changing their shapes and position every moment. But this line of clouds immoveably attached themselves to the island, and manifestly took their shape from the influence of its mountains. There appeared to be just span enough of sky to allow the hand to slide between the top of Snâfell, the highest peak in the island, and the base of this glorious forest, in which little change was noticeable for more than the space of half an hour. We had another fine sight one evening, walking along a rising ground, about two miles distant from the shore. It was about the hour of sunset, and the sea was perfectly calm; and in a quarter where its surface was indistinguishable from the western sky, hazy, and luminous with the setting sun, appeared a tall sloop-rigged vessel, magnified by the atmosphere through which it was viewed, and seeming rather to hang in the air than to float upon the waters. Milton compares the appearance of Satan to a *fleet* descried far off at sea. The visionary grandeur and beautiful form of this *single* vessel, could words have conveyed to the mind the picture which nature presented to the eye, would have suited his purpose as well as the largest company of vessels that ever associated together with the help of a trade wind in the wide ocean; yet not exactly so, and for this reason, that his image is a permanent one, not dependent upon accident.

I have not left myself room to assure you how sincerely I remain, Your affectionate friend,

W. WORDSWORTH.*

———

'THE RECLUSE,' REYNOLDS, &c.

To Sir George Beaumont, Bart.

Grasmere, Dec. 25th. 1804.

MY DEAR SIR GEORGE,

Long since ought I to have thanked you for your last affectionate letter; but I knew how indulgent you were, and

* *Memoirs*, vol. i. pp. 272-8. G.

therefore fell, I won't say more easily, but surely with far less pain to myself, into my old trick of procrastination. I was deeply sensible of your kindness in inviting me to Grosvenor Square, and then felt and still feel a strong inclination to avail myself of the opportunity of cultivating your friendship and that of Lady Beaumont, and of seeing a little of the world at the same time.   But as the wish is strong there are also strong obstacles against it; first, though I have lately been tolerably industrious, I am far behind-hand with my appointed work; and next, my nervous system is so apt to be deranged by going from home, that I am by no means sure that I should not be so much of a dependent invalid, I mean a person obliged to manage himself, as to make it absolutely improper for me to obtrude myself where neither my exertions of mind or body, could enable me to be tolerable company.   I say nothing of my family, because a short absence would be abundantly recompensed by the pleasure of a 'sweet return.'   At all events, I must express my sincere thanks for your kindness and the pleasure which I received from your letter, breathing throughout such favourable dispositions, I may say, such earnest friendship towards me.

I think we are completely agreed upon the subject of Sir Joshua, that is, we both regret that he did not devote more of his time to the higher branches of the Art, and further, I think you join with me in lamenting to a certain degree at least that he did not live more to himself.   I have since read the rest of his Discourses, with which I have been greatly pleased, and wish most heartily that I could have an opportunity of seeing in your company your own collection of pictures and some others in town, Mr. Angerstein's, for instance, to have pointed out to me some of those finer and peculiar beauties of painting which I am afraid I shall never have an occasion of becoming sufficiently familiar with pictures to discover of myself.   There is not a day in my life when I am at home in which that exquisite little drawing of yours of Applethwaite does not affect me with a sense of harmony and grace, which I cannot describe.   Mr. Edridge, an artist whom you know, saw this drawing along with a Mr. Duppa, another artist, who published *Hints from Raphael and Michael Angelo;* and they were both most enthusiastic in their praise of it, to my great delight.   By the bye, I thought Mr. Edridge a man of very mild and pleasing manners, and as far as I could judge, of delicate feelings, in the province of his Art. Duppa is publishing a life of Michael Angelo, and I received from him a few days ago two proof-sheets of an Appendix which contains the poems of M. A., which I shall read, and translate one or two of them, if I can do it with decent success. I have peeped into the Sonnets, and they do not appear at all unworthy of their great Author.

You will be pleased to hear that I have been advancing with my work: I have written upwards of 2000 verses during the last ten weeks. I do not know if you are exactly acquainted with the plan of my poetical labour: it is twofold; first, a Poem, to be called ' The Recluse ;' in which it will be my object to express in verse my most interesting feelings concerning man, nature, and society; and next, a poem (in which I am at present chiefly engaged) on my earlier life, or the growth of my own mind, taken up upon a large scale. This latter work I expect to have finished before the month of May; and then I purpose to fall with all my might on the former, which is the chief object upon which my thoughts have been fixed these many years. Of this poem, that of ' The Pedlar,'* which Coleridge read you, is part, and I may have written of it altogether about 2000 lines. It will consist, I hope, of about ten or twelve thousand.

May we not hope for the pleasure of seeing you and Lady Beaumont down here next Summer? I flatter myself that Coleridge will then be return'd, and though we would not [on] any account that he should fix himself in this rainy part of England, yet perhaps we may have the happiness of meeting all together for a few weeks. We have lately built in our little rocky orchard, a little circular Hut, lined with moss, like a wren's nest, and coated on the outside with heath, that stands most charmingly, with several views from the different sides of it, of the Lake, the Valley, and the Church—sadly spoiled, however, lately by being white-washed. The little retreat is most delightful, and I am sure you and Lady Beaumont would be highly pleased with it. Coleridge has never seen it. What a happiness would it be to us to see him there, and entertain you all next Summer in our homely way under its shady thatch. I will

* ' The Excursion.' ' The Pedlar' was the title once proposed, from the character of the Wanderer, but abandoned. [*Memoirs,* vol. i. p. 304.]

copy a dwarf inscription which I wrote for it the other day, before the building was entirely finished, which indeed it is not yet.

> No whimsy of the purse is here,
> No Pleasure-House forlorn;
> Use, comfort, do this roof endear:
> A tributary Shed to chear
> The little Cottage that is near,
> To help it and adorn.

I hope the young Roscius, if he go on as he has begun, will rescue the English theatre from the infamy that has fallen upon it, and restore the reign of good sense and nature. From what you have seen, Sir George, do you think he could manage a character of Shakspeare? Neither Selin nor Douglas require much power; but even to perform them as he does, talents and genius I should think must be necessary. I had very little hope I confess, thinking it very natural that a theatre which had brought a dog upon the stage as a principal performer, would catch at a wonder whatever shape it might put on.

We have had no tidings of Coleridge these several months. He spoke of papers which he had sent by private hands, none of which *we* have received. It must be most criminal neglect somewhere if the fever be suffered to enter Malta. Farewell, and believe me, my dear Sir George, your affectionate and sincere friend,   W. Wordsworth.*

'THE RECLUSE,' YOUNG ROSCIUS, &c.

Letter to Sir George H. Beaumont, Bart.

Grasmere, May 1st. 1805.

My dear Sir George,

I have wished to write to you every day this long time, but I have also had another wish, which has interfered to prevent me; I mean the wish to resume my poetical labours: time was stealing away fast from me, and nothing done, and my mind still seeming unfit to do anything. At first I had a strong impulse to write a poem that should record my brother's virtues, and be worthy of his memory. I began to give vent to my feelings, with this view, but I was overpowered by my subject, and could not proceed. I composed much, but it is all lost except

* *Memoirs*, vol. i. p. 304 *et seq.*, with important additions from the original. G.

a few lines, as it came from me in such a torrent that I was unable to remember it. I could not hold the pen myself, and the subject was such that I could not employ Mrs. Wordsworth or my sister as my amanuensis. This work must therefore rest awhile till I am something calmer; I shall, however, never be at peace till, as far as in me lies, I have done justice to my departed brother's memory. His heroic death (the particulars of which I have now accurately collected from several of the survivors) exacts this from me, and still more his singularly interesting character, and virtuous and innocent life.

Unable to proceed with this work, I turned my thoughts again to the Poem on my own Life, and you will be glad to hear that I have added 300 lines to it in the course of last week. Two books more will conclude it. It will be not much less than 9000 lines,—not hundred but thousand lines long,—an alarming length! and a thing unprecedented in literary history that a man should talk so much about himself. It is not self-conceit, as you will know well, that has induced me to do this, but real humility. I began the work because I was unprepared to treat any more arduous subject, and diffident of my own powers. Here, at least, I hoped that to a certain degree I should be sure of succeeding, as I had nothing to do but describe what I had felt and thought; therefore could not easily be bewildered. This might certainly have been done in narrower compass by a man of more address; but I have done my best. If, when the work shall be finished, it appears to the judicious to have redundancies, they shall be lopped off, if possible; but this is very difficult to do, when a man has written with thought; and this defect, whenever I have suspected it or found it to exist in any writings of mine, I have always found incurable. The fault lies too deep, and is in the first conception. If you see Coleridge before I do, do not speak of this to him, as I should like to have his judgment unpreoccupied by such an apprehension. I wish much to have your further opinion of the young Roscius, above all of his 'Hamlet.' It is certainly impossible that he should understand the character, that is, the composition of the character. But many of the sentiments which are put into Hamlet's mouth he may be supposed to be capable of feeling, and to a certain degree of entering into the spirit of some of the situations. I never saw 'Hamlet' acted myself, nor do I know what kind of a play they make of it.   I think I have heard that some parts which I consider among the finest are omitted : in particular, Hamlet's wild language after the ghost has disappeared.   The players have taken intolerable liberties with Shakspeare's Plays, especially with ' Richard the Third,' which, though a character admirably conceived and drawn, is in some scenes bad enough in Shakspeare himself; but the play, as it is now acted, has always appeared to me a disgrace to the English stage.   ' Hamlet,' I suppose, is treated by them with more reverence.   They are both characters far, far above the abilities of any actor whom I have ever seen.   Henderson was before my time, and, of course, Garrick.

We are looking anxiously for Coleridge : perhaps he may be with you now.   We were afraid that he might have had to hear other bad news of our family, as Lady Beaumont's little goddaughter has lately had that dangerous complaint, the croup, particularly dangerous here, where we are thirteen miles from any medical advice on which we can have the least reliance. Her case has been a mild one, but sufficient to alarm us much, and Mrs. Wordsworth and her aunt have undergone much fatigue in sitting up, as for nearly a fortnight she had very bad nights. She yet requires much care and attention.

Is your building going on ? I was mortified that the sweet little valley, of which you spoke some time ago, was no longer in the possession of your family : it is the place, I believe, where that illustrious and most extraordinary man, Beaumont the Poet, and his brother, were born.   One is astonished when one thinks of that man having been only eight-and-twenty years of age, for I believe he was no more, when he died.   Shakspeare, we are told, had scarcely written a single play at that age.   I hope, for the sake of poets, you are proud of these men.

Lady Beaumont mentioned some time ago that you were painting a picture from ' The Thorn :' is it finished?   I should like to see it ; the poem is a favourite with me, and I shall love it the better for the honour you have done it.   We shall be most happy to have the other drawing which you promised us some time ago.   The dimensions of the Applethwaite one are eight inches high, and a very little above ten broad ; this, of course, exclusive of the margin.

I am anxious to know how your health goes on : we are better than we had reason to expect. When we look back upon this Spring, it seems like a dreary dream to us. But I trust in God that we shall yet 'bear up and steer right onward.'

Farewell. I am, your affectionate friend,

W. WORDSWORTH.

My sister thanks Lady Beaumont for her letter, the short one of the other day, and hopes to be able to write soon. Have you seen Southey's 'Madoc'? We have it in the house, but have deferred reading it, having been too busy with the child. I should like to know how it pleases you.*

PORTRAIT OF COLERIDGE: 'THE EXCURSION' FINISHED: SOUTHEY'S 'MADOC,' &c.

Letter to Sir George H. Beaumont, Bart.

Grasmere, June 3d. 1805.

MY DEAR SIR GEORGE,

I write to you from the moss-hut at the top of my orchard, the sun just sinking behind the hills in front of the entrance, and his light falling upon the green moss of the side opposite me. A linnet is singing in the tree above, and the children of some of our neighbours, who have been to-day little John's visitors, are playing below equally noisy and happy. The green fields in the level area of the vale, and part of the lake, lie before me in quietness. I have just been reading two news-papers, full of factious brawls about Lord Melville and his delin-quencies, ravage of the French in the West Indies, victories of the English in the East, fleets of ours roaming the sea in search of enemies whom they cannot find, &c. &c. &c.; and I have asked myself more than once lately, if my affections can be in the right place, caring as I do so little about what the world seems to care so much for. All this seems to me, 'a tale told by an idiot, full of sound and fury, signifying nothing.' It is pleasant in such a mood to turn one's thoughts to a good man and a dear friend. I have, therefore, taken up the pen to write to you. And, first, let me thank you (which I ought to have done long

* *Memoirs*, vol. i. pp. 305-8. G.

ago, and should have done, but that I knew I had a licence from you to procrastinate) for your most acceptable present of Coleridge's portrait, welcome in itself, and more so as coming from you. It is as good a resemblance as I expect to see of Coleridge, taking it all together, for I consider C.'s as a face absolutely impracticable. Mrs. Wordsworth was overjoyed at the sight of the print; Dorothy and I much pleased. We think it excellent about the eyes and forehead, which are the finest parts of C.'s face, and the general contour of the face is well given ; but, to my sister and me, it seems to fail sadly about the middle of the face, particularly at the bottom of the nose. Mrs. W. feels this also ; and my sister so much, that, except when she covers the whole of the middle of the face, it seems to her so entirely to alter the expression, as rather to confound than revive in her mind the remembrance of the original. We think, as far as mere likeness goes, Hazlitt's is better; but the expression in Hazlitt's is quite dolorous and funereal; that in this is much more pleasing, though certainly falling far below what one would wish to see infused into a picture of C. Mrs. C. received a day or two ago a letter from a friend who had letters from Malta, not from Coleridge, but a Miss Stoddart, who is there with her brother. These letters are of the date of the fifth of March, and speak of him as looking well and quite well, and talking of coming home, but doubtful whether by land or sea.

I have the pleasure to say, that I finished my poem about a fortnight ago. I had looked forward to the day as a most happy one ; and I was indeed grateful to God for giving me life to complete the work, such as it is. But it was not a happy day for me ; I was dejected on many accounts : when I looked back upon the performance, it seemed to have a dead weight about it,—the reality so far short of the expectation. It was the first long labour that I had finished ; and the doubt whether I should ever live to write 'The Recluse,' and the sense which I had of this poem being so far below what I seemed capable of executing, depressed me much ; above all, many heavy thoughts of my poor departed brother hung upon me, the joy which I should have had in showing him the manuscript, and a thousand other vain fancies and dreams. I have spoken of this, because it was a state of feeling new to me, the occasion being new. This work may be considered as a sort of *portico* to 'The Recluse,' part of the same building, which I hope to be able, ere long, to begin with in earnest; and if I am permitted to bring it to a conclusion, and to write, further, a narrative poem of the epic kind, I shall consider the task of my life as over. I ought to add, that I have the satisfaction of finding the present poem not quite of so alarming a length as I apprehended.

I wish much to hear from you, if you have leisure; but as you are so indulgent to me, it would be the highest injustice were I otherwise to you.

We have read 'Madoc,' and been highly pleased with it. It abounds in beautiful pictures and descriptions, happily introduced, and there is an animation diffused through the whole story, though it cannot, perhaps, be said that any of the characters interest you much, except, perhaps, young Llewellyn, whose situation is highly interesting, and he appears to me the best conceived and sustained character in the piece. His speech to his uncle at their meeting in the island is particularly interesting. The poem fails in the highest gifts of the poet's mind, imagination in the true sense of the word, and knowledge of human nature and the human heart. There is nothing that shows the hand of the great master; but the beauties in description are innumerable; for instance, that of the figure of the bard, towards the beginning of the convention of the bards, receiving the poetic inspiration; that of the wife of Tlalala, the savage, going out to meet her husband; that of Madoc, and the Atzecan king with a long name, preparing for battle; everywhere, indeed, you have beautiful descriptions, and it is a work which does the author high credit, I think. I should like to know your opinion of it. Farewell! Best remembrances and love to Lady Beaumont. Believe me,

My dear Sir George,

Your most sincere friend,

W. Wordsworth.

My sister thanks Lady Beaumont for her letter, and will write in a few days. I find that Lady B. has been pleased much by 'Madoc.'*

* *Memoirs*, vol. i. pp. 309-12. G.

COLERIDGE: VISIT TO COLEORTON: HOUBRAKEN:
'MADOC,' &c.

To Sir George H. Beaumont, Bart.

Grasmere, July 29th. [1805.]

MY DEAR SIR GEORGE,

We have all here been made happy in hearing that
you are so much better. I write now chiefly on account of a mistake
which you seem to be under concerning Coleridge.   I guess from
your letter that you suppose him to be appointed to the place of
Secretary to Sir A. Ball.   This is by no means the case.   He is
merely an occasional substitute for Mr. Chapman, who is secretary, and no doubt must have resumed his office long before this;
as he had been expected every day some time before the date of
C.'s last letter.   The paragraph in the Paper (which we also
saw) positively states that C. is appointed Secretary.   This is
an error, and has been merely put in upon common rumour.

When you were ill I had a thought which I will mention to
you.   It was this : I wished to know how you were at present
situated as to house-room at Coleorton, that is, whether you could
have found a corner for me to put my head in, in case I could
have contrived to have commanded three weeks' time, or so.   I
am at present, and shall be for some time, engaged with a sick
Friend, who has come all the way from Bristol on purpose to see
us, and has taken lodgings in the Village; but should you be
unwell again, and my company be like to tend in the least to
exhilarate you, I should like to know, that were it in my power
to go and see you, I might have the liberty to do so.

Having such reason to expect Coleridge at present (were we
at liberty in other respects), I cannot think of taking my family
a tour, agreeable to your kind suggestion.   Something has,
however, already been added by your means to our comforts, in
the way of Books, and probably we shall be able to make an
excursion ere the Summer be over.

By the bye, are you possessed of Houbraken and Vertue's
Heads of Illustrious Persons, with anecdotes of their Lives by
Birch ?   I had an opportunity of purchasing a handsome copy
(far below the price at which it now sells, I believe, in London)
at Penrith, a few weeks ago; and if you have not a copy, and think

the work has any merit, you would please me greatly by giving it a place in your Library.

I am glad you like the passage in ' Madoc' about Llewellyn. Southey's mind does not seem strong enough to draw the picture of a hero. The character of Madoc is often very insipid and contemptible; for instance, when he is told that the Foemen have surprised Caer, Madoc, and of course (he has reason to believe) butchered or carried away all the women and children, what does the Author make him do? Think of Goervyl and Llayan very tenderly forsooth; but not a word about his people! In short, according to my notion, the character is throughout languidly conceived, and, as you observe, the contrast between her and Llewellyn makes him look very mean. I made a mistake when I pointed out a beautiful passage as being in the beginning of the meeting of the bards; it occurs before, and ends thus:

> ———— His eyes were closed;
> His head, as if in reverence to receive
> The inspiration, bent; and as he raised
> His glowing countenance and brighter eye
> And swept with passionate hands the ringing harp.

The verses of your ancestor Francis Beaumont, the younger, are very elegant and harmonious, and written with true feeling. Is this the only poem of his extant? There are some pleasing Verses (I think by Corbet, Bishop of Norwich) on the death of Francis Beaumont the elder. They end, I remember, thus, alluding to his short life:

> ———— by whose sole death appears,
> Wit's a disease consumes men in few years.

I have never seen the works of the brother of the dramatic Poet; but I know he wrote a poem upon the Battle of Bosworth Field. Probably it will be in the volume which you have found, which it would give me great pleasure to see, as also Charnwood Rocks, which must have a striking effect in that country. I am highly flattered by Lady Beaumont's favourable opinion of me and my poems.

My Sister will answer her affectionate letter very soon; she would have done it before now, but she has been from home three days and unwell, or entirely engrossed with some visitors whom we have had, the rest of her time.

The letter which you will find accompanying this is from an

acquaintance of ours to his wife.   He lives at Patterdale, and she was over at Grasmere.   We thought it would interest you. Farewell.   I remain, in hopes of good news of your health, your affectionate and sincere friend,

W. WORDSWORTH.

From Mr. Luff of Patterdale to his Wife.

Patterdale, July 23d. [1805.]

AN event happened here last night which has greatly affected the whole village, and particularly myself.

The body, or more properly speaking, bones of a poor fellow were yesterday found by Willy Harrison, in the rocks at the head of red Tarn.   It appears that he was attempting to descend the Pass from Helvellyn to the Tarn, when he lost his footing and was dashed to pieces.

His name appears to have been Charles Gough.   Several things were found in his pockets; fishing tackle, memorandums, a gold watch, silver pencil, Claude Lorraine glasses, &c.

Poor fellow!   It is very strange, but we met him when we were last reviewed in April; and he then wanted John Harrison to turn back with him and go to the Tarn ; but he was told that his request could not be complied with.   It appears that he proceeded [forward] and met his fate.

You will be much interested to know that a spaniel bitch was found alive by his side, where she has remained upwards of three months, guarding the bones of her master ; but she had become so wild that it was with difficulty she was taken.   She is in good condition ; and what is more odd, had whelped a pup, which from its size must have lived some weeks, but when found was lying dead by the bones.   The bones are as completely freed from flesh as if they had been anatomised, and perfectly white and dry.   The head can nowhere be found.   The arms, one thigh and a leg were all that remained in the clothes.   All the rest were scattered about here and there.

When I reflect on my own wanderings and the many dangerous situations I have found myself in, in the pursuit of game, I cannot help thanking Providence that I am now here to relate to you this melancholy tale.   I wonder whether poor Fan's affection would under similar circumstances have equalled that of the little spaniel.

OF LORD NELSON AND 'THE HAPPY WARRIOR,' AND PITT; AND ON BUILDING, GARDENING, &c.

Letter to Sir George H. Beaumont, Bart.

Grasmere, Feb. 11th. 1806.

MY DEAR SIR GEORGE,

Upon opening this letter, you must have seen that it is accompanied with a copy of verses.* I hope they will give you some pleasure, as it will be the best way in which they can repay me for a little vexation, of which they have been the cause. They were written several weeks ago, and I wished to send them to you, but could not muster up resolution, as I felt that they were so unworthy of the subject. Accordingly, I kept them by me from week to week, with a hope (which has proved vain) that, in some happy moment, a new fit of inspiration would help me to mend them ; and hence my silence, which, with your usual goodness, I know you will excuse.

You will find that the verses are allusive to Lord Nelson ; and they will show that I must have sympathised with you in admiration of the man, and sorrow for our loss. Yet, considering the matter coolly, there was little to regret. The state of Lord Nelson's health, I suppose, was such, that he could not have lived long ; and the first burst of exultation upon landing in his native country, and his reception here, would have been dearly bought, perhaps, by pain and bodily weakness, and distress among his friends, which he could neither remove nor alleviate. Few men have ever died under circumstances so likely to make their deaths of benefit to their country : it is not easy to see what his life could have done comparable to it. The loss of such men as Lord Nelson is, indeed, great and real ; but surely not for the reason which makes most people grieve, a supposition that no other such man is in the country. The old ballad has taught us how to feel on these occasions :

> I trust I have within my realm
> Five hundred good as he.

But this is the evil, that nowhere is merit so much under the power of what (to avoid a more serious expression) one may call that of fortune, as in military and naval service ; and it is

* 'The Happy Warrior.'

five hundred to one that such men will not have attained situations where they can show themselves, so that the country may know in whom to trust. Lord Nelson had attained that situation; and, therefore, I think (and not for the other reason), ought we chiefly to lament that he is taken from us.

Mr. Pitt is also gone! by tens of thousands looked upon in like manner as a great loss. For my own part, as probably you know, I have never been able to regard his political life with complacency. I believe him, however, to have been as disinterested a man, and as true a lover of his country, as it was possible for so ambitious a man to be. His first wish (though probably unknown to himself) was that his country should prosper under his administration; his next that it should prosper. Could the order of these wishes have been reversed, Mr. Pitt would have avoided many of the grievous mistakes into which, I think, he fell. I know, my dear Sir George, you will give me credit for speaking without arrogance; and I am aware it is not unlikely you may differ greatly from me in these points. But I like, in some things, to differ with a friend, and that he should *know* I differ from him; it seems to make a more healthy friendship, to act as a relief to those notions and feelings which we have in common, and to give them a grace and spirit which they could not otherwise possess.

There were some parts in the long letter which I wrote about laying out grounds, in which the expression must have been left imperfect. I like splendid mansions in their proper places, and have no objection to large or even obtrusive houses in themselves. My dislike is to that system of gardening which, because a house happens to be large or splendid, and stands at the head of a large domain, establishes it therefore as a principle that the house ought to *dye* all the surrounding country with a strength of colouring and to an extent proportionate to its own importance. This system, I think, is founded in false taste, false feeling, and its effects disgusting in the highest degree. The reason you mention as having induced you to build was worthy of you, and gave me the highest pleasure. But I hope God will grant you and Lady Beaumont life to enjoy yourselves the fruit of your exertions for many years.

We have lately had much anxiety about Coleridge. What can have become of him? It must be upwards of three months since he landed at Trieste. Has he returned to Malta think you, or what can have befallen him? He has never since been heard of.

Lady Beaumont spoke of your having been ill of a cold; I hope you are better. We have all here been more or less deranged in the same way.

We have to thank you for a present of game, which arrived in good time.

Never have a moment's uneasiness about answering my letters. We are all well at present, and unite in affectionate wishes to you and Lady Beaumont. Believe me,

Your sincere friend,

W. WORDSWORTH.

I have thoughts of sending the Verses to a Newspaper.*

OF HIS OWN POEMS AS FALSELY CRITICISED.

Letter to Lady Beaumont.

Coleorton, May 21. 1807.

MY DEAR LADY BEAUMONT,

Though I am to see you so soon, I cannot but write a word or two, to thank you for the interest you take in my poems, as evinced by your solicitude about their immediate reception. I write partly to thank you for this, and to express the pleasure it has given me, and partly to remove any uneasiness from your mind which the disappointments you sometimes meet with, in this labour of love, may occasion. I see that you have many battles to fight for me,—more than, in the ardour and confidence of your pure and elevated mind, you had ever thought of being summoned to; but be assured that this opposition is nothing more than what I distinctly foresaw that you and my other friends would have to encounter. I say this, not to give myself credit for an eye of prophecy, but to allay any vexatious thoughts on my account which this opposition may have produced in you.

It is impossible that any expectations can be lower than

---

* *Memoirs*, vol. i. p. 321 *et seq.*, with important additions from the original. By a curious inadvertence this letter is dated 1796—quite plainly—for 1806, as shown by the post-mark outside. G.

mine concerning the immediate effect of this little work upon what is called the public. I do not here take into consideration the envy and malevolence, and all the bad passions which always stand in the way of a work of any merit from a living poet; but merely think of the pure, absolute, honest ignorance in which all worldlings of every rank and situation must be enveloped, with respect to the thoughts, feelings, and images, on which the life of my poems depends. The things which I have taken, whether from within or without, what have they to do with routs, dinners, morning calls, hurry from door to door, from street to street, on foot or in carriage; with Mr. Pitt or Mr. Fox, Mr. Paul or Sir Francis Burdett, the Westminster election or the borough of Honiton? In a word—for I cannot stop to make my way through the hurry of images that present themselves to me—what have they to do with endless talking about things nobody cares any thing for except as far as their own vanity is concerned, and this with persons they care nothing for but as their vanity or *selfishness* is concerned?—what have they to do (to say all at once) with a life without love? In such a life there can be no thought; for we have no thought (save thoughts of pain) but as far as we have love and admiration.

It is an awful truth, that there neither is, nor can be, any genuine enjoyment of poetry among nineteen out of twenty of those persons who live, or wish to live, in the broad light of the world—among those who either are, or are striving to make themselves, people of consideration in society. This is a truth, and an awful one, because to be incapable of a feeling of poetry, in my sense of the word, is to be without love of human nature and reverence for God.

Upon this I shall insist elsewhere; at present let me confine myself to my object, which is to make you, my dear friend, as easy-hearted as myself with respect to these poems. Trouble not yourself upon their present reception; of what moment is that compared with what I trust is their destiny?—to console the afflicted; to add sunshine to daylight, by making the happy happier; to teach the young and the gracious of every age to see, to think, and feel, and, therefore, to become more actively and securely virtuous] this is their office, which I trust they will faithfully perform, long after we (that is, all that is mortal of us) are mouldered in our graves. I am well aware how far it would seem to many I overrate my own exertions, when I speak in this way, in direct connection with the volume I have just made public.

I am not, however, afraid of such censure, insignificant as probably the majority of those poems would appear to very respectable persons. I do not mean London wits and witlings, for these have too many foul passions about them to be respectable, even if they had more intellect than the benign laws of Providence will allow to such a heartless existence as theirs is; but grave, kindly-natured, worthy persons, who would be pleased if they could. I hope that these volumes are not without some recommendations, even for readers of this class : but their imagination has slept ; and the voice which is the voice of my poetry, without imagination, cannot be heard. Leaving these, I was going to say a word to such readers as Mr. ——. Such ! —how would he be offended if he knew I considered him only as a representative of a class, and not an unique ! ‘ Pity,’ says Mr. —— ‘ that so many trifling things should be admitted to obstruct the view of those that have merit.’ Now, let this candid judge take, by way of example, the sonnets, which, probably, with the exception of two or three other poems, for which I will not contend, appear to him the most trifling, as they are the shortest. I would say to him, omitting things of higher consideration, there is one thing which must strike you at once, if you will only read these poems,—that those ‘ to Liberty,’ at least, have a connection with, or a bearing upon, each other ; and, therefore, if individually they want weight, perhaps, as a body, they may not be so deficient. At least, this ought to induce you to suspend your judgment, and qualify it so far as to allow that the writer aims at least at comprehensiveness.

But, dropping this, I would boldly say at once, that these sonnets, while they each fix the attention upon some important sentiment, separately considered, do, at the same time, collectively make a poem on the subject of civil liberty and national independence, which, either for simplicity of style or grandeur of moral sentiment, is, alas ! likely to have few parallels in the poetry of the present day. Again, turn to the ‘ Moods of my own Mind.’ There is scarcely a poem here of above thirty lines, and very trifling these poems will appear to many ; but, omitting to speak of them individually, do they not, taken collectively, fix the attention upon a subject eminently poetical, viz., the interest which objects in Nature derive from the predominance of certain affections, more or less permanent, more or less capable of salutary renewal in the mind of the being contemplating these objects? This is poetic, and essentially poetic. And why? Because it is creative.

But I am wasting words, for it is nothing more than you know; and if said to those for whom it is intended, it would not be understood.

I see by your last letter, that Mrs. Fermor has entered into the spirit of these 'Moods of my own Mind.' Your transcript from her letter gave me the greatest pleasure; but I must say that even she has something yet to receive from me. I say this with confidence, from her thinking that I have fallen below myself in the sonnet, beginning,

> With ships the sea was sprinkled far and nigh.

As to the other which she objects to, I will only observe, that there is a misprint in the last line but two,

> And *though* this wilderness,

for

> And *through* this wilderness,

that makes it unintelligible. This latter sonnet, for many reasons (though I do not abandon it), I will not now speak of; but upon the other, I could say something important in conversation, and will attempt now to illustrate it by a comment, which, I feel, will be inadequate to convey my meaning. There is scarcely one of my poems which does not aim to direct the attention to some moral sentiment, or to some general principle, or law of thought, or of our intellectual constitution. For instance, in the present case, who is there that has not felt that the mind can have no rest among a multitude of objects, of which it either cannot make one whole, or from which it cannot single out one individual whereupon may be concentrated the attention, divided among or distracted by a multitude? After a certain time, we must either select one image or object, which must put out of view the rest wholly, or must subordinate them to itself while it stands forth as a head:

> How glowed the firmament
> With living sapphires! Hesperus, that *led*
> The starry host, rode brightest; till the moon,

Rising in clouded majesty, at length,
Apparent *Queen*, unveiled *her peerless* light,
And o'er the dark her silver mantle threw.

Having laid this down as a general principle, take the case before us. I am represented in the sonnet as casting my eyes over the sea, sprinkled with a multitude of ships, like the heavens with stars. My mind may be supposed to float up and down among them, in a kind of dreamy indifference with respect either to this or that one, only in a pleasurable state of feeling with respect to the whole prospect. 'Joyously it showed.' This continued till that feeling may be supposed to have passed away, and a kind of comparative listlessness or apathy to have succeeded, as at this line,

Some veering up and down, one knew not why.

All at once, while I am in this state, comes forth an object, an individual; and my mind, sleepy and unfixed, is awakened and fastened in a moment.

Hesperus, that *led*
The starry host,

is a poetical object, because the glory of his own nature gives him the pre-eminence the moment he appears. · He calls forth the poetic faculty, receiving its exertions as a tribute. But this ship in the sonnet may, in a manner still more appropriate, be said to come upon a mission of the poetic spirit, because, in its own appearance and attributes, it is barely sufficiently distinguished to rouse the creative faculty of the human mind, to exertions at all times welcome, but doubly so when they come upon us when in a state of remissness. The mind being once fixed and roused, all the rest comes from itself; it is merely a lordly ship, nothing more :

This ship was nought to me, nor I to her,
Yet I pursued her with a lover's look.

My mind wantons with grateful joy in the exercise of its own powers, and, loving its own creation,

This ship to all the rest I did prefer,

making her a sovereign or a regent, and thus giving body and life to all the rest; mingling up this idea with fondness and praise—

where she comes the winds must stir;

and concluding the whole with,

On went she, and due north her journey took;

thus taking up again the reader with whom I began, letting
him know how long I must have watched this favourite vessel,
and inviting him to rest his mind as mine is resting.

Having said so much upon mere fourteen lines, which Mrs.
Fermor did not approve, I cannot but add a word or two upon
my satisfaction in finding that my mind has so much in common
with hers, and that we participate so many of each other's
pleasures. I collect this from her having singled out the two
little poems, 'The Daffodils,' and 'The Rock crowned with
Snowdrops.' I am sure that whoever is much pleased with
either of these quiet and tender delineations must be fitted to
walk through the recesses of my poetry with delight, and will
there recognise, at every turn, something or other in which,
and over which, it has that property and right which knowledge
and love confer. The line,

Come, blessed barrier, &c.

in the 'Sonnet upon Sleep,' which Mrs. F. points out, had
before been mentioned to me by Coleridge, and, indeed, by
almost every body who had heard it, as eminently beautiful.
My letter (as this second sheet, which I am obliged to take,
admonishes me) is growing to an enormous length; and yet,
saving that I have expressed my calm confidence that these
poems will live, I have said nothing which has a particular
application to the object of it, which was to remove all disquiet
from your mind on account of the condemnation they may at
present incur from that portion of my contemporaries who are
called the public. I am sure, my dear Lady Beaumont, if you
attach any importance to it, it can only be from an apprehension
that it may affect me, upon which I have already set you at
ease; or from a fear that this present blame is ominous of their
future or final destiny. If this be the case, your tenderness for
me betrays you. Be assured that the decision of these persons
has nothing to do with the question; they are altogether incompetent judges. These people, in the senseless hurry of their
idle lives, do not *read* books, they merely snatch a glance at
them, that they may talk about them. And even if this were
not so, never forget what, I believe, was observed to you by
Coleridge, that every great and original writer, in proportion as
he is great or original, must himself create the taste by which
he is to be relished; he must teach the art by which he is to

be seen; this, in a certain degree, even to all persons, however wise and pure may be their lives, and however unvitiated their taste. But for those who dip into books in order to give an opinion of them, or talk about them to take up an opinion—for this multitude of unhappy, and misguided, and misguiding beings, an entire regeneration must be produced; and if this be possible, it must be a work *of time.* To conclude, my ears are stone-dead to this idle buzz, and my flesh as insensible as iron to these petty stings; and, after what I have said, I am sure yours will be the same. I doubt not that you will share with me an invincible confidence that my writings (and among them these little poems) will co-operate with the benign tendencies in human nature and society, wherever found; and that they will, in their degree, be efficacious in making men wiser, better, and happier. Farewell! I will not apologise for this letter, though its length demands an apology. Believe me, eagerly wishing for the happy day when I shall see you and Sir George here,

Most affectionately yours,

W. WORDSWORTH.

Do not hurry your coming hither on our account: my sister regrets that she did not press this upon you, as you say in your letter, ' we cannot *possibly* come before the first week in June ;' from which we infer that your kindness will induce you to make sacrifices for our sakes. Whatever pleasure we may have in thinking of Grasmere, we have no impatience to be gone, and think with full as much regret of leaving Coleorton. I had, for myself, indeed, a wish to be at Grasmere with as much of the summer before me as might be; but to this I attach no importance whatever, as far as the gratification of that wish interferes with any inclination or duty of yours. I could not be satisfied without seeing you here, and shall have great pleasure in waiting.[*]

[*] *Memoirs,* vol. i. pp. 331-40.

OF 'PETER BELL,' AND OTHER POEMS.

Letter to Sir George H. Beaumont, Bart.

MY DEAR SIR GEORGE,

I am quite delighted to hear of your picture for 'Peter Bell;' I was much pleased with the sketch, and I have no doubt that the picture will surpass it as far as a picture ought to do. I long much to see it. I should approve of any engraver approved by you. But remember that no poem of mine will ever be popular; and I am afraid that the sale of 'Peter' would not carry the expence of the engraving, and that the poem, in the estimation of the public, would be a weight upon the print. I say not this in modest disparagement of the poem, but in sorrow for the sickly taste of the public in verse. The *people* would love the poem of 'Peter Bell,' but the *public* (a very different being) will never love it. Thanks for dear Lady B.'s transcript from your friend's letter; it is written with candour, but I must say a word or two not in praise of it. 'Instances of what I mean,' says your friend, 'are to be found in a poem on a Daisy' (by the by, it is on *the* Daisy, a mighty difference!) 'and on *Daffodils reflected in the Water.*' Is this accurately transcribed by Lady Beaumont? If it be, what shall we think of criticism or judgment founded upon, and exemplified by, a poem which must have been so inattentively perused? My language is precise; and, therefore, it would be false modesty to charge myself with blame.

> Beneath the trees,
> Ten thousand dancing in the *breeze*.
> The *waves beside* them danced, but they
> Outdid the *sparkling waves* in glee.

Can expression be more distinct? And let me ask your friend how it is possible for flowers to be *reflected* in water where there are *waves?* They may, indeed, in *still* water; but the very object of my poem is the trouble or agitation, both of the flowers and the water. I must needs respect the understanding of every one honoured by your friendship; but sincerity compels me to say that my poems must be more nearly looked at, before they can give rise to any remarks of much value, even from the strongest minds. With respect to this individual poem, Lady

B. will recollect how Mrs. Fermor expressed herself upon it. A letter also was sent to me, addressed to a friend of mine, and by him communicated to me, in which this identical poem was singled out for fervent approbation. What then shall we say? Why, let the poet first consult his own heart, as I have done, and leave the rest to posterity,—to, I hope, an improving posterity. The fact is, the English *public* are at this moment in the same state of mind with respect to my poems, if small things may be compared with great, as the French are in respect to Shakspeare, and not the French alone, but almost the whole Continent. In short, in your friend's letter, I am condemned for the very thing for which I ought to have been praised, viz., that I have not written down to the level of superficial observers and unthinking minds. Every great poet is a teacher: I wish either to be considered as a teacher, or as nothing.

To turn to a more pleasing subject. Have you painted anything else beside this picture from 'Peter Bell?' Your two oil-paintings (and, indeed, everything I have of yours) have been much admired by the artists who have seen them. And, for our own parts, we like them better every day; this, in particular, is the case with the small picture from the neighbourhood of Coleorton, which, indeed, pleased me much at the first sight, but less impressed the rest of our household, who now see as many beauties in it as I do myself. Havill, the water-colour painter, was much pleased with these things; he is painting at Ambleside, and has done a view of Rydal Water, looking down upon it from Rydal Park, of which I should like to know your opinion; it will be exhibited in the Spring, in the water-colour Exhibition. I have purchased a black-lead pencil sketch of Mr. Green, of Ambleside, which, I think, has great merit, the materials being uncommonly picturesque, and well put together: I should dearly like to have the same subject (it is the cottage at Glencoign, by Ulleswater) treated by you. In the poem I have just written, you will find one situation which, if the work should ever become familiarly known, would furnish as fine a subject for a picture as any thing I remember in poetry ancient or modern. I need not mention what it is, as when you read the poem you cannot miss it. We have at last had, by the same post, two letters from Coleridge, long and melancholy; and also, from Keswick, an account so depressing as to the state of his health, that I should have set off immediately to London, to see him, if I had not myself been confined by indisposition.

I hope that Davy is by this time perfectly restored to health.
Believe me, my dear Sir George,

Most sincerely yours,

W. Wordsworth.[*]

OF BUILDING AND GARDENING AND LAYING OUT OF GROUNDS.

Letter to Sir George H. Beaumont, Bart.

Grasmere, October 17th. 1805.

My dear Sir George,

I was very glad to learn that you had room for me at Coleorton, and far more so, that your health was so much mended.   Lady Beaumont's last letter to my sister has made us wish that you were fairly through your present engagements with workmen and builders, and, as to improvements, had smoothed over the first difficulties, and gotten things into a way of improving themselves.   I do not suppose that any man ever built a house, without finding in the progress of it obstacles that were unforeseen, and something that might have been better planned ; things teazing and vexatious when they come, however the mind may have been made up at the outset to a general expectation of the kind.

With respect to the grounds, you have there the advantage of being in good hands, namely, those of Nature ; and, assuredly, whatever petty crosses from contrariety of opinion or any other cause you may now meet with, these will soon disappear, and leave nothing behind but satisfaction and harmony.   Setting out from the distinction made by Coleridge which you mentioned, that your house will belong to the country, and not the country be an appendage to your house, you cannot be wrong. Indeed, in the present state of society, I see nothing interesting either to the imagination or the heart, and, of course, nothing which true taste can approve, in any interference with Nature, grounded upon any other principle.   In times when the feudal

* *Memoirs*, vol. i. pp. 340-3.

system was in its vigor, and the personal importance of every chieftain might be said to depend entirely upon the extent of his landed property and rights of seignory; when the king, in the habits of people's minds, was considered as the primary and true proprietor of the soil, which was granted out by him to different lords, and again by them to their several tenants under them, for the joint defence of all; there might have been something imposing to the imagination in the whole face of a district, testifying, obtrusively even, its dependence upon its chief. Such an image would have been in the spirit of the society, implying power, grandeur, military state, and security; and, less directly, in the person of the chief, high birth, and knightly education and accomplishments; in short, the most of what was then deemed interesting or affecting. Yet, with the exception of large parks and forests, nothing of this kind was known at that time, and these were left in their wild state, so that such display of ownership, so far from taking from the beauty of Nature, was itself a chief cause of that beauty being left unspoiled and unimpaired. The *improvements*, when the place was sufficiently tranquil to admit of any, though absurd and monstrous in themselves, were confined (as our present Laureate has observed, I remember, in one of his essays) to an acre or two about the house in the shape of garden with terraces, &c. So that Nature had greatly the advantage in those days, when what has been called English gardening was unheard of. This is now beginning to be perceived, and we are setting out to travel backwards. Painters and poets have had the credit of being reckoned the fathers of English gardening; they will also have, hereafter, the better praise of being fathers of a better taste. Error is in general nothing more than getting hold of good things, as every thing has two handles, by the wrong one. It was a misconception of the meaning and principles of poets and painters which gave countenance to the modern system of gardening, which is now, I hope, on the decline; in other words, we are submitting to the rule which you at present are guided by, that of having our houses belong to the country, which will of course lead us back to the simplicity of Nature. And leaving your own individual sentiments and present work out of the question, what good can come of any other guide, under any circumstances? We have, indeed, distinctions of

rank, hereditary legislators, and large landed proprietors; but
from numberless causes the state of society is so much altered,
that nothing of that lofty or imposing interest, formerly attached to large property in land, can now exist; none of the
poetic pride, and pomp, and circumstance; nor anything that
can be considered as making amends for violation done to the
holiness of Nature. Let us take an extreme case, such as a
residence of a Duke of Norfolk, or Northumberland : of course
you would expect a mansion, in some degree answerable to their
consequence, with all conveniences. The names of Howard and
Percy will always stand high in the regards of Englishmen ;
but it is degrading, not only to such families as these, but to
every really interesting one, to suppose that their importance
will be most felt where most displayed, particularly in the way
I am now alluding to. This is contracting a general feeling
into a local one. Besides, were it not so, as to what concerns
the Past, a man would be sadly astray, who should go, for example, to modernise Alnwick and its dependencies, with his
head full of the ancient Percies : he would find nothing there
which would remind him of them, except by contrast; and of
that kind of admonition he would, indeed, have enough. But
this by the bye, for it is against the principle itself I am contending, and not the misapplication of it. After what was said
above, I may ask, if anything connected with the families of
Howard and Percy, and their rank and influence, and thus with
the state of government and society, could, in the present age,
be deemed a recompence for their thrusting themselves in between us and Nature. Surely it is a substitution of little things
for great when we would put a whole country into a nobleman's
livery. I know nothing which to me would be so pleasing or
affecting, as to be able to say when I am in the midst of a large
estate—This man is not the victim of his condition ; he is not
the spoiled child of worldly grandeur; the thought of himself
does not take the lead in his enjoyments; he is, where he ought
to be, lowly-minded, and has human feelings; he has a true
relish of simplicity, and therefore stands the best chance of being
happy; at least, without it there is no happiness, because there
can be no true sense of the bounty and beauty of the creation,
or insight into the constitution of the human mind. Let a man
of wealth and influence shew, by the appearance of the country

in his neighbourhood, that he treads in the steps of the good sense of the age, and occasionally goes foremost; let him give countenance to improvements in agriculture, steering clear of the pedantry of it, and showing that its grossest utilities will connect themselves harmoniously with the more intellectual arts, and even thrive the best under such connection; let him do his utmost to be surrounded with tenants living comfortably, which will bring always with it the best of all graces which a country can have—flourishing fields and happy-looking houses; and, in that part of his estate devoted to park and pleasure-ground, let him keep himself as much out of sight as possible; let Nature be all in all, taking care that everything done by man shall be in the way of being adopted by her. If people chuse that a great mansion should be the chief figure in a country, let this kind of keeping prevail through the picture, and true taste will find no fault.

I am writing now rather for writing's sake than anything else, for I have many remembrances beating about in my head which you would little suspect. I have been thinking of you, and Coleridge, and our Scotch Tour, and Lord Lowther's grounds, and Heaven knows what. I have had before me the tremendously long ell-wide gravel walks of the Duke of Athol, among the wild glens of Blair, Bruar Water, and Dunkeld, brushed neatly, without a blade of grass or weed upon them, or anything that bore traces of a human footstep; much indeed of human hands, but wear or tear of foot was none. Thence I pass'd to our neighbour, Lord Lowther. You know that his predecessor, greatly, without doubt, to the advantage of the place, left it to take care of itself. The present lord seems disposed to do something, but not much. He has a neighbour, a Quaker, an amiable, inoffensive man,* and a little of a poet too, who has amused himself, upon his own small estate upon the Emont, in twining pathways along the banks of the river, making little cells and bowers with inscriptions of his own writing, all very pretty as not spreading far. This man is at present Arbiter Elegantiarum, or master of the grounds, at Lowther, and what he has done hitherto is very well, as it is little more than making accessible what could not before be got at. You know something of Lowther. I believe a more delightful spot is not

* Mr. Thomas Wilkinson. See poem, ' To his Spade.'

under the sun. Last summer I had a charming walk along the
river, for which I was indebted to this man, whose intention is
to carry the walk along the river-side till it joins the great road
at Lowther Bridge, which you will recollect, just under Brougham,
about a mile from Penrith. This to my great sorrow! for the
manufactured walk, which was absolutely necessary in many
places, will in one place pass through a few hundred yards of
forest ground, and will there efface the most beautiful specimen
of a forest pathway ever seen by human eyes, and which I have
paced many an hour, when I was a youth, with some of those I
best love. This path winds on under the trees with the wan-
tonness of a river or a living creature; and even if I may say
so with the subtlety of a spirit, contracting or enlarging itself,
visible or invisible as it likes. There is a continued opening
between the trees, a narrow slip of green turf besprinkled with
flowers, chiefly daisies, and here it is, if I may use the same
kind of language, that this pretty path plays its pranks, wearing away the turf and flowers at its pleasure. When I took
the walk I was speaking of, last summer, it was Sunday. I met
several of the people of the country posting to and from church,
in different parts; and in a retired spot by the river-side were
two musicians (belonging probably to some corps of volunteers)
playing upon the hautboy and clarionet. You may guess I was
not a little delighted; and as you had been a visiter at Lowther,
I could not help wishing you were with me. And now I am
brought to the sentiment which occasioned this detail; I may
say, brought back to my subject, which is this,—that all just
and solid pleasure in natural objects rests upon two pillars,
God and Man. Laying out grounds, as it is called, may be considered as a liberal art, in some sort like poetry and painting;
and its object, like that of all the liberal arts, is, or ought to be,
to move the affections under the controul of good sense; that
is, those of the best and wisest: but, speaking with more precision, it is to assist Nature in moving the affections, and,
surely, as I have said, the affections of those who have the
deepest perception of the beauty of Nature; who have the most
valuable feelings, that is, the most permanent, the most independent, the most ennobling, connected with Nature and human
life. No liberal art aims merely at the gratification of an individual or a class: the painter or poet is degraded in proportion

as he does so; the true servants of the Arts pay homage to the human kind as impersonated in unwarped and enlightened minds. If this be so when we are merely putting together words or colours, how much more ought the feeling to prevail when we are in the midst of the realities of things; of the beauty and harmony, of the joy and happiness of living creatures; of men and children, of birds and beasts, of hills and streams, and trees and flowers; with the changes of night and day, evening and morning, summer and winter; and all their unwearied actions and energies, as benign in the spirit that animates them as they are beautiful and grand in that form and clothing which is given to them for the delight of our senses! But I must stop, for you feel these things as deeply as I; more deeply, if it were only for this, that you have lived longer. What then shall we say of many great mansions with their unqualified expulsion of human creatures from their neighbourhood, happy or not; houses, which do what is fabled of the upas tree, that they breathe out death and desolation! I know you will feel with me here, both as a man and a lover and professor of the arts. I was glad to hear from Lady Beaumont that you did not think of removing your village. Of course much here will depend upon circumstances, above all, with what kind of inhabitants, from the nature of the employments in that district, the village is likely to be stocked. But, for my part, strip my neighbourhood of human beings, and I should think it one of the greatest privations I could undergo. You have all the poverty of solitude, nothing of its elevation. In a word, if I were disposed to write a sermon (and this is something like one) upon the subject of taste in natural beauty, I should take for my text the little pathway in Lowther Woods, and all which I had to say would begin and end in the human heart, as under the direction of the Divine Nature, conferring value on the objects of the senses, and pointing out what is valuable in them.

I began this subject with Coleorton in my thoughts, and a confidence, that whatever difficulties or crosses (as of many good things it is not easy to chuse the best) you might meet with in the practical application of your principles of Taste, yet, being what they are, you will soon be pleased and satisfied. Only (if I may take the freedom to say so) do not give way too much to others: considering what your studies and pursuits have been, your own judgment must be the best: professional men may suggest hints, but I would keep the decision to myself.

Lady Beaumont utters something like an apprehension that the slowness of workmen or other impediments may prevent our families meeting at Coleorton next summer. We shall be sorry for this, the more so, as the same cause will hinder your coming hither. At all events, we shall depend upon her frankness, which we take most kindly indeed; I mean, on the promise she has made, to let us know whether you are gotten so far through your work as to make it comfortable for us all to be together.

I cannot close this letter without a word about myself. I am sorry to say I am not yet settled to any serious employment. The expectation of Coleridge not a little unhinges me, and, still more, the number of visitors we have had; but winter is approaching, and I have good hopes. I mentioned Michael Angelo's poetry some time ago; it is the most difficult to construe I ever met with, but just what you would expect from such a man, shewing abundantly how conversant his soul was with great things. There is a mistake in the world concerning the Italian language; the poetry of Dante and Michael Angelo proves, that if there be little majesty and strength in Italian verse, the fault is in the authors, and not in the tongue. I can translate, and have translated, two books of Ariosto, at the rate, nearly, of 100 lines a day; but so much meaning has been put by Michael Angelo into so little room, and that meaning sometimes so excellent in itself, that I found the difficulty of translating him insurmountable. I attempted, at least, fifteen of the sonnets, but could not anywhere succeed. I have sent you the only one I was able to finish : it is far from being the best, or most characteristic, but the others were too much for me.*

I began this letter about a week ago, having been interrupted. I mention this, because I have on this account to apologise to Lady Beaumont, and to my sister also, whose intention it was to have written, but being very much engaged, she put it off as I was writing. We have been weaning Dorothy, and since, she has had a return of the croup from an imprudent exposure on a very cold day. But she is doing well again; and

* 'Yes, Hope may with my strong desire keep pace,' &c.

my sister will write very soon. Lady Beaumont inquired how game might be sent us. There is a direct conveyance from Manchester to Kendal by the mail, and a parcel directed for me, to be delivered at Kendal, immediately, to John Brockbank, Ambleside, postman, would, I dare say, find its way to us expeditiously enough; only you will have the goodness to mention in your letters when you do send anything, otherwise we may not be aware of any mistake.

I am glad the Houbraken will be acceptable, and will send it any way you shall think proper, though perhaps, as it would only make a small parcel, there might be some risk in trusting it to the waggon or mail, unless it could be conveniently inquired after. No news of Coleridge. The length of this letter is quite formidable; forgive it. Farewell, and believe me, my dear Sir George,

Your truly affectionate friend,

W. WORDSWORTH.*

X. OF THE INSCRIPTIONS AT COLEORTON.

Letter to Sir George H. Beaumont, Bart.

MY DEAR SIR GEORGE,

Had there been room at the end of the small avenue of lime-trees for planting a spacious circle of the same trees, the urn might have been placed in the centre, with the inscription thus altered:

> Ye lime-trees, ranged around this hallowed urn,
> Shoot forth with lively power at Spring's return!
>
> Here may some painter sit in future days,
> Some future poet meditate his lays!
> Not mindless of that distant age, renowned,
> When inspiration hovered o'er this ground,
> The haunt of him who sang, how spear and shield
> In civil conflict met on Bosworth field,
> And of that famous youth (full soon removed
> From earth!) by mighty Shakespear's self approved,
> Fletcher's associate, Jonson's friend beloved.

The first couplet of the above, as it before stood, would have appeared ludicrous, if the stone had remained after the

---

* *Memoirs*, vol. i. pp. 345-54, with very important additions from the original. G.

tree might have been gone.   The couplet relating to the household virtues did not accord with the painter and the poet; the former being allegorical figures; the latter, living men.

What follows, I composed yesterday morning, thinking there might be no impropriety in placing it, so as to be *visible only to a person sitting within the niche* which we hollowed out of the sandstone in the winter-garden.   I am told that this is, in the present form of the niche, impossible; but I shall be most ready, when I come to Coleorton, to scoop out a place for it, if Lady Beaumont think it worth while.

INSCRIPTION.

Oft is the medal faithful to its trust
When temples, columns, towers, are laid in dust;
And 'tis a common ordinance of fate
That things obscure and small outlive the great.
Hence, &c.

These inscriptions have all one fault, they are too long; but I was unable to do justice to the thoughts in less room.   The second has brought Sir John Beaumont and his brother Francis so lively to my mind, that I recur to the plan of republishing the former's poems, perhaps in connection with those of Francis. Could any further *search* be made after the ' Crown of Thorns?' If I recollect right, Southey applied without effect to the numerous friends he has among the collectors.   The best way, perhaps, of managing this republication would be, to print it in a very elegant type and paper, and not many copies, to be sold high, so that it might be prized by the collectors as a curiosity. Bearing in mind how many excellent things there are in Sir John Beaumont's little volume, I am somewhat mortified at this mode of honouring his memory; but in the present state of the taste of this country, I cannot flatter myself that poems of that character would win their way into general circulation. Should it appear advisable, another edition might afterwards be published, upon a plan which would place the book within the reach of those who have little money to spare.   I remain, my dear Sir George,

Your affectionate friend,
W. WORDSWORTH.*

* *Memoirs*, vol. i. pp. 358-60.

X　　　　OF POEMS, COLERIDGE, &c. &c.

Letter to Sir George H. Beaumont, Bart.

Grasmere, Sat., Nov. 16. 1811.

MY DEAR SIR GEORGE,

I have to thank you for two letters. Lady Beaumont also will accept my acknowledgments for the interesting letter with which she favoured me. "

.　　　.　　　.　　　.　　　.　　　.　　　.

I learn from Mrs. Coleridge, who has lately heard from C——, that Alston, the painter, has arrived in London. Coleridge speaks of him as a most interesting person. He has brought with him a few pictures from his own pencil, among others, a Cupid and Psyche, which, in C.'s opinion, has not, for colouring, been surpassed since Titian. C. is about to deliver a Course of Lectures upon Poetry, at some Institution in the city. He is well, and I learn that the 'Friend' has been a good deal inquired after lately. For ourselves, we never hear from him.

I am glad that the inscriptions please you. It did always appear to me, that inscriptions, particularly those in verse, or in a dead language, were never supposed *necessarily* to be the composition of those in whose name they appeared. If a more striking, or more dramatic effect could be produced, I have always thought, that in an epitaph or memorial of any kind, a father, or husband, &c. might be introduced, speaking, without any absolute deception being intended: that is, the reader is understood to be at liberty to say to himself,—these verses, or this Latin, may be the composition of some unknown person, and not that of the father, widow, or friend, from whose hand or voice they profess to proceed. If the composition be natural, affecting, or beautiful, it is all that is required. This, at least, was my view of the subject, or I should not have adopted that mode. However, in respect to your scruples, which I feel are both delicate and reasonable, I have altered the verses; and I have only to regret that the alteration is not more happily done. But I never found anything more difficult. I wished to preserve the expression *patrimonial grounds*, but I found this impossible, on account of the awkwardness of the pronouns, he

.and his, as applied to Reynolds, and to yourself. This, even where it does not produce confusion, is always inelegant. I was, therefore, obliged to drop it; so that we must be content, I fear, with the inscription as it stands below. As you mention that the first copy was mislaid, I will transcribe the first part from that; but you can either choose the Dome or the Abbey as you like.

> Ye lime-trees, ranged before this hallowed urn,
> Shoot forth with lively power at Spring's return;
> And be not slow a stately growth to rear
> Of pillars, branching off from year to year,
> Till ye have framed, at length, a darksome aisle,
> Like a recess within that sacred pile
> Where Reynolds, 'mid our country's noblest dead,
> In the last sanctity of fame is laid, &c. &c.

I hope this will do: I tried a hundred different ways, but cannot hit upon anything better. I am sorry to learn from Lady Beaumont, that there is reason to believe that our cedar is already perished. I am sorry for it. The verses upon that subject you and Lady B. praise highly; and certainly, if they have merit, as I cannot but think they have, your discriminating praises have pointed it out. The alteration in the beginning, I think with you, is a great improvement, and the first line is, to my ear, very rich and grateful. As to the 'Female and Male,' I know not how to get rid of it; for that circumstance gives the recess an appropriate interest. I remember, Mr. Bowles, the poet, objected to the word ravishment at the end of the sonnet to the winter-garden; yet it has the authority of all the first-rate poets, for instance, Milton:

> In whose sight all things joy, with *ravishment*,
> Attracted by thy beauty still to gaze.

Objections upon these grounds merit more attention in regard to inscriptions than any other sort of composition; and on this account, the lines (I mean those upon the niche) had better be suppressed, for it is not improbable that the altering of them might cost me more trouble than writing a hundred fresh ones.

We were happy to hear that your mother, Lady Beaumont, was so surprisingly well. You do not mention the school at Coleorton. Pray how is Wilkie in health, and also as to progress in his art? I do not doubt that I shall like Arnold's picture; but he would have been a better painter, if his genius had led him to *read* more in the early part of his life. Wilkie's style of painting does not require that the mind should be fed from books; but I do not think it possible to *excel* in *landscape* painting without a strong tincture of the poetic spirit.*

X   OF THE INSCRIPTIONS AT COLEORTON.

Letter to Lady Beaumont.

Grasmere, Wednesday, Nov. 20. 1811.

MY DEAR LADY BEAUMONT,

When you see this you will think I mean to overrun you with inscriptions : I do not mean to tax you with putting them up, only with reading them. The following I composed yesterday morning, in a walk from Brathway, whither I had been to accompany my sister.

FOR A SEAT IN THE GROVES OF COLEORTON.

Beneath yon eastern ridge, the craggy bound
Rugged and high of Charnwood's forest-ground,
Stand yet, but, Stranger! hidden from thy view,
The ivied ruins of forlorn Grace Dieu, &c. &c.

I hope that neither you nor Sir George will think that the above takes from the effect of the mention of Francis Beaumont in the poem upon the cedar. Grace Dieu is itself so interesting a spot, and has naturally and historically such a connection with Coleorton, that I could not deny myself the pleasure of paying it this mark of attention. The thought of writing the inscription occurred to me many years ago. I took the liberty of transcribing for Sir George an alteration which I had made in the inscription for St. Herbert's island; I was not then quite satisfied with it; I have since retouched it, and will trouble you to read him the following, which I hope will give you pleasure.

This island, guarded from profane approach
By mountains high and waters widely spread,
Gave to St. Herbert a benign retreat, &c. &c.

I ought to mention, that the line,

And things of holy use unhallowed lie,

is taken from the following of Daniel,

Strait all that holy was unhallowed lies.

* *Memoirs*, vol. i. pp. 360-3.

I will take this occasion of recommending to you (if you happen
to have Daniel's poems) to read the epistle addressed to the
Lady Margaret, Countess of Cumberland, beginning,

> He that of such a height hath built his mind.

The whole poem is composed in a strain of meditative morality
more dignified and affecting than anything of the kind I ever
read.   It is, besides, strikingly applicable to the revolutions of
the present times.

My dear Lady Beaumont, your letter and the accounts it
contains of the winter-garden, gave me great pleasure.   I cannot but think, that under your care, it will grow up into one of
the most beautiful and interesting spots in England.   We all
here have a longing desire to see it.   I have mentioned the
high opinion we have of it to a couple of my friends, persons
of taste living in this country, who are determined, the first
time they are called up to London, to turn aside to visit it;
which I said they might without scruple do, if they mentioned
my name to the gardener.   My sister begs me to say, that she
is aware how long she has been in your debt, and that she
should have written before now, but that, as I have, latterly,
been in frequent communication with Coleorton, she thought it
as well to defer answering your letter.   Do you see the *Courier*
newspaper at Dunmow?   I ask on account of a little poem
upon the comet, which I have read in it to-day.   Though with
several defects, and some feeble and constrained expressions, it
has great merit, and is far superior to the run, not merely of
newspaper, but of modern poetry in general.   I half suspect it
to be Coleridge's, for though it is, in parts, inferior to him, I
know no other writer of the day who can do so well.   It consists
of five stanzas, in the measure of the ' Fairy Queen.'   It is to be
found in last Saturday's paper, November 16th.   If you don't
see the *Courier* we will transcribe it for you.   As so much of
this letter is taken up with my verses, I will e'en trespass still.
further on your indulgence, and conclude with a sonnet, which
I wrote some time ago upon the poet, John Dyer.   If you have
not read the ' Fleece,' I would strongly recommend it to you.
The character of Dyer, as a patriot, a citizen, and a tender-
hearted friend of humanity was, in some respects, injurious to
him as a poet, and has induced him to dwell, in his poem, upon

processes which, however important in themselves, were unsusceptible of being poetically treated.   Accordingly, his poem is, in several places, dry and heavy; but its beauties are innumerable, and of a high order.   In point of *imagination* and purity of style, I am not sure that he is not superior to any writer in verse since the time of Milton.

SONNET.

Bard of the Fleece! whose skilful genius made
That work a living landscape fair and bright;
Nor hallowed less by musical delight
Than those soft scenes through which thy childhood strayed,
Those southern tracts of Cambria, deep embayed, &c. &c.

In the above is one whole line from the 'Fleece,' and two other expressions.   When you read the 'Fleece' you will recognise them.   I remain, my dear Lady Beaumont,

Your sincere friend,

W. WORDSWORTH.*

EXCURSION IN NORTH WALES.

Letter to Sir George H. Beaumont.

Hindwell, Radnor, Sept. 20. 1824.

MY DEAR SIR GEORGE,   -

After a three weeks' ramble in North Wales, Mrs. Wordsworth, Dora, and myself are set down quietly here for three weeks more.   The weather has been delightful, and everything to our wishes.   On a beautiful day we took the steampacket at Liverpool, passed the mouth of the Dee, coasted the extremity of the Vale of Clwyd, sailed close under Great Orm's Head, had a noble prospect of Penmaenmawr, and having almost touched upon Puffin's Island, we reached Bangor Ferry, a little after six in the afternoon.   We admired the stupendous preparations for the bridge over the Menai; and breakfasted next morning at Carnarvon.   We employed several hours in exploring the interior of the noble castle, and looking at it from different points of view in the neighbourhood.   At half-past four we departed for Llanberris, having fine views as we looked back of C. Castle, the sea, and Anglesey.   A little before sunset

* *Memoirs*, vol. i. pp. 363-6.

we came in sight of Llanberris Lake, Snowdon, and all the craggy hills and mountains surrounding it; the foreground a beautiful contrast to this grandeur and desolation—a green sloping hollow, furnishing a shelter for one of the most beautiful collections of lowly Welsh cottages, with thatched roofs, overgrown with plants, anywhere to be met with : the hamlet is called Cum-y-glo.   And here we took boat, while the solemn lights of evening were receding towards the tops of the mountains.   As we advanced, Dolbardin Castle came in view, and Snowdon opened upon our admiration.   It was almost dark when we reached the quiet and comfortable inn at Llanberris.

.   .   .   .

There being no carriage-road, we undertook to walk by the Pass of Llanberris, eight miles, to Capel Cerig; this proved fatiguing, but it was the only oppressive exertion we made during the course of our tour.   We arrived at Capel Cerig in time for a glance at the Snowdonian range, from the garden of the inn, in connection with the lake (or rather pool) reflecting the crimson clouds of evening. The outline of Snowdon is perhaps seen nowhere to more advantage than from this place. Next morning, five miles down a beautiful valley to the banks of the Conway, which stream we followed to Llanrwst; but the day was so hot that we could only make use of the morning and evening.   Here we were joined, according to previous arrangement, by Bishop Hobart, of New York, who remained with us till two o'clock next day, and left us to complete his hasty tour through North and South Wales.   In the afternoon arrived my old college friend and youthful companion among the Alps, the Rev. R. Jones, and in his car we all proceeded to the Falls of the Conway, thence up that river to a newly-erected inn on the Irish road, where we lodged; having passed through bold and rocky scenery along the banks of a stream which is a feeder of the Dee. Next morning we turned from the Irish road three or four miles to visit the 'Valley of Meditation' (Glyn Mavyr) where Mr. Jones has, at present, a curacy, with a comfortable parsonage.   We slept at Corwen, and went down the Dee to Llangollen, which you and dear Lady B. know well.   Called upon the celebrated Recluses,* who hoped that you and Lady B. had not forgotten them; they certainly had not forgotten you, and

* The Lady E. Butler, and the Hon. Miss Ponsonby.

they begged us to say that they retained a lively remembrance of you both. We drank tea and passed a couple of hours with them in the evening, having visited the aqueduct over the Dee and Chirk Castle in the afternoon. Lady E. has not been well, and has suffered much in her eyes, but she is surprisingly lively for her years. Miss P. is apparently in unimpaired health. Next day I sent them the following sonnet from Ruthin, which was conceived, and in a great measure composed, in their grounds.

> A stream, to mingle with your favourite Dee,
> Along the *Vale of Meditation* flows ;
> So named by those fierce Britons, pleased to see
> In Nature's face the expression of repose, &c. &c.

.   .   .   .

We passed three days with Mr. Jones's friends in the vale of Clwyd, looking about us, and on the Tuesday set off again, accompanied by our friend, to complete our tour. We dined at Conway, walked to Bennarth, the view from which is a good deal choked up with wood. A small part of the castle has been demolished for the sake of the new road to communicate with the suspension-bridge, which they are about to make to the small island opposite the castle, to be connected by a long embankment with the opposite shore. The bridge will, I think, prove rather ornamental when time has taken off the newness of its supporting masonry ; but the mound deplorably impairs the majesty of the water at high-tide ; in fact it destroys its lake-like appearance. Our drive to Aber in the evening was charming ; sun setting in glory. We had also a delightful walk next morning up the vale of Aber, terminated by a lofty waterfall ; not much in itself, but most striking as a closing accompaniment to the secluded valley. Here, in the early morning, I saw an odd sight—fifteen milk-maids together, laden with their brimming pails. How cheerful and happy they appeared ! and not a little inclined to joke after the manner of the pastoral persons in Theocritus. That day brought us to Capel Cerig again, after a charming drive up the banks of the Ogwen, having previously had beautiful views of Bangor, the sea, and its shipping. From Capel Cerig down the justly celebrated vale of Nant Gwynant to Bethgelart. In this vale are two small lakes, the higher of which is the only Welsh lake which has any pretensions to compare with our own ; and it has one great advantage over them, that it remains wholly free from intrusive objects. We saw it early in the morning ; and with the green-ness of the meadows at its head, the steep rocks on one of its shores, and the bold mountains at *both* extremities, a feature almost peculiar to itself, it appeared to us truly enchanting. The village of Bethgelart is much altered for the worse : new and formal houses have, in a great measure, supplanted the old rugged and tufted cottages, and a smart hotel has taken the lead of the lowly public-house in which I took refreshment almost thirty years ago, previous to a midnight ascent to the summit of Snowdon. At B. we were agreeably surprised by the appearance of Mr. Hare, of New College, Oxford. We slept at Tan-y-bylch, having employed the afternoon in exploring the beauties of the vale of Festiniog. Next day to Barmouth, whence, the following morning, we took boat and rowed up its sublime estuary, which may compare with the finest of Scotland, having the advantage of a superior climate. From Dolgelly we went to Tal-y-llyn, a solitary and very interesting lake under Cader Idris. Next day, being Sunday, we heard service per-formed in Welsh, and in the afternoon went part of the way down a beautiful valley to Machynleth, next morning to Aberyst-with, and up the Rhydiol to the Devil's Bridge, where we passed the following day in exploring those two rivers, and Hafod in the neighbourhood. I had seen these things long ago, but either my memory or my powers of observation had not done them justice. It rained heavily in the night, and we saw the waterfalls in perfection. While Dora was attempting to make a sketch from the chasm in the rain, I composed by her side the following address to the torrent :

> How art thou named ? In search of what strange land,
> From what huge height descending ? Can such force
> Of water issue from a British source?

Next day, viz. last Wednesday, we reached this place, and found all our friends well, except our good and valuable friend, Mr. Monkhouse, who is here, and in a very alarming state of health. His physicians have ordered him to pass the winter in Devonshire, fearing a consumption ; but he is certainly not suffering under a regular hectic pulmonary decline : his pulse is good, so is his appetite, and he has no fever, but is deplor-ably emaciated. He is a near relation of Mrs. W., and one, as you know, of my best friends. I hope to see Mr. Price, at Foxley, in a few days. Mrs. W.'s brother is about to change his present residence for a farm close by Foxley.

Now, my dear Sir George, what chance is there of your being in Wales during any part of the autumn? I would strain a point to meet you anywhere, were it only for a couple of days. Write immediately, or should you be absent without Lady B. she will have the goodness to tell me of your movements. I saw the Lowthers just before I set off, all well. You probably have heard from my sister. It is time to make an end of this long letter, which might have been somewhat less dry if I had not wished to make you master of our whole route. Except ascending one of the high mountains, Snowdon or Cader Idris, we omitted nothing, and saw as much as the shortened days would allow. With love to Lady B. and yourself, dear Sir George, from us all, I remain, ever,

Most faithfully yours,

WM. WORDSWORTH.*

* *Memoirs*, vol. ii. pp. 121-7.

(y) LETTER TO THE RIGHT HON. CHARLES JAMES FOX.

With the 'Lyrical Ballads' (1801): with critical Remarks on his Poems.

Grasmere, Westmoreland, January 14th. 1801.

SIR,

It is not without much difficulty that I have summoned the courage to request your acceptance of these volumes. Should I express my real feelings, I am sure that I should seem to make a parade of diffidence and humility.

Several of the poems contained in these volumes are written upon subjects which are the common property of all poets, and which, at some period of your life, must have been interesting to a man of your sensibility, and perhaps may still continue to be so. It would be highly gratifying to me to suppose that even in a single instance the manner in which I have treated these general topics should afford you any pleasure ; but such a hope does not influence me upon the present occasion ; in truth I do not feel it. Besides, I am convinced that there must be many things in this collection which may impress you with an unfavourable idea of my intellectual powers. I do not say this with a wish to degrade myself, but I am sensible that this must be the case, from the different circles in which we have moved, and the different objects with which we have been conversant.

Being utterly unknown to you as I am, I am well aware that if I am justified in writing to you at all, it is necessary my letter should be short ; but I have feelings within me, which I hope will so far show themselves, as to excuse the trespass which I am afraid I shall make.

In common with the whole of the English people, I have observed in your public character a constant predominance of sensibility of heart. Necessitated as you have been from your public situation to have much to do with men in bodies, and in classes, and accordingly to contemplate them in that relation, it has been your praise that you have not thereby been prevented from looking upon them as individuals, and that you have habitually left your heart open to be influenced by them in that capacity. This habit cannot but have made you dear to poets ; and I am sure that if, since your first entrance into public life, there has been a single true poet living in England, he must have loved you.

But were I assured that I myself had a just claim to the title of a poet, all the dignity being attached to the word which belongs to it, I do not think that I should have ventured for that reason to offer these volumes to you ; at present it is solely on account of two poems in the second volume, the one entitled ' The Brothers,' and the other ' Michael,' that I have been emboldened to take this liberty.

It appears to me that the most calamitous effect which has followed the measures which have lately been pursued in this country, is, a rapid decay of the domestic affections among the lower orders of society. This effect the present rulers of this country are not conscious of, or they disregard it. For many years past, the tendency of society, amongst almost all the nations of Europe, has been to produce it; but recently, by the spreading of manufactures through every part of the country, by the heavy taxes upon postage, by workhouses, houses of industry, and the invention of soup-shops, &c., superadded to the increasing disproportion between the price of labour and that of the necessaries of life, the bonds of domestic feeling among the poor, as far as the influence of these things has extended, have been weakened, and in innumerable instances entirely destroyed. The evil would be the less to be regretted, if these institutions were regarded only as palliatives to a disease; but the vanity and pride of their promoters are so subtly interwoven with them, that they are deemed great discoveries and blessings to humanity. In the meantime, parents are separated from their children, and children from their parents ; the wife no longer prepares, with her own hands, a meal for her husband, the produce of his labour ; there is little doing in his house in which his affections can be interested, and but little left in it that he can love. I have two neighbours, a man and his wife, both upwards of eighty years of age. They live alone. The husband has been confined to his bed many months, and has never had, nor till within these few weeks has ever needed, any body to attend to him but his wife. She has recently been seized with a lameness which has often prevented her from being able to carry him his food to his bed. The neighbours fetch water for her from the well, and do other kind offices for them both. But her infirmities increase. She told my servant two days ago, that she was afraid they must both be boarded out among some other poor of the parish (they have long been supported by the parish); but she said it was hard, having kept house together so long, to come to this, and she was sure that 'it would burst her heart.' I mention this fact to show how deeply the spirit of independence is, even yet, rooted in some parts of the country. These people could not express themselves in this way without an almost sublime conviction of the blessings of independent domestic life. If it is true, as I believe, that this spirit is rapidly disappearing, no greater curse can befall a Land.

I earnestly entreat your pardon for having detained you so long. In the two poems, 'The Brothers,' and 'Michael,' I have attempted to draw a picture of the domestic affections, as I know they exist among a class of men who are now almost confined to the north of England. They are small independent *proprietors* of land, here called statesmen, men of respectable education, who daily labour on their own little properties. The domestic affections will always be strong amongst men who live in a country not crowded with population, if these men are placed above poverty. But if they are proprietors of small estates, which have descended to them from their ancestors, the power, which these affections will acquire amongst such men, is inconceivable by those who have only had an opportunity of observing hired labourers, farmers, and the manufacturing poor. Their little tract of land serves as a kind of permanent rallying point for their domestic feelings, as a tablet upon which they are written, which makes them objects of memory in a thousand instances, when they would otherwise be forgotten. It is a fountain fitted to the nature of social man, from which supplies of affection, as pure as his heart was intended for, are daily drawn. This class of men is rapidly disappearing. You, Sir, have a consciousness, upon which every good man will congratulate you, that the whole of your public conduct has, in one way or other, been directed to the preservation of this class of men, and those who hold similar situations. You have felt that the most sacred of all property is the property of the poor. The two poems, which I have mentioned, were written with a view to show that men who do not wear fine clothes can feel deeply. 'Pectus enim est quod disertos facit, et vis mentis. Ideoque imperitis quoque, si modo sint aliquo affectu concitati, verba non desunt.' The poems are faithful copies from Nature; and I hope whatever effect they may have upon you, you will at least be able to perceive that they may excite profitable sympathies in many kind and good hearts, and may in some small degree enlarge our feelings of reverence for our species, and our knowledge of human nature, by showing that our best qualities are possessed by men whom we are too apt to consider, not with reference to the points in which they resemble us, but to those in which they manifestly differ from us. I thought, at a time when these feelings are sapped in so many ways, that the two poems might co-operate, however feebly, with the illustrious efforts which you have made to stem this and other evils with which the country is labouring; and it is on this account alone that I have taken the liberty of thus addressing you.

Wishing earnestly that the time may come when the country may perceive what it has lost by neglecting your advice, and hoping that your latter days may be attended with health and comfort,

I remain,
With the highest respect and admiration,
Your most obedient and humble servant,
W. WORDSWORTH.[*]

Fox's reply was as follows:

SIR,

I owe you many apologies for having so long deferred thanking you for your poems, and your obliging letter accompanying them, which I received early in March. The poems have given me the greatest pleasure; and if I were obliged to choose out of them, I do not know whether I should not say that 'Harry Gill,' 'We are Seven,' 'The Mad Mother,' and 'The Idiot,' are my favourites. I read with particular attention the two you pointed out; but whether it be from early prepossessions, or whatever other cause, I am no great friend to blank verse for subjects which are to be treated of with simplicity.

[*] *Memoirs,* vol. i. pp. 166-171.

You will excuse my stating my opinion to you so freely, which I should not do if I did not really admire many of the poems in the collection, and many parts even of those in blank verse. Of the poems which you state not to be yours, that entitled 'Love' appears to me to be the best, and I do not know who is the author. 'The Nightingale' I understand to be Mr. Coleridge's, who combats, I think, very successfully, the mistaken prejudice of the nightingale's note being melancholy. I am, with great truth,

Sir,

Your most obedient servant,

C. J. Fox.*

St. Ann's Hill, May 25. [1801.]

In connection with the above the following observations addressed by Wordsworth to some friends fitly find a place here.

Speaking of the poem of the *Leech-Gatherer,*† sent in MS., he says:

'It is not a matter of indifference whether you are pleased with his figure and employment, it may be comparatively whether you are pleased with *this Poem;* but it is of the utmost importance that you should have had pleasure in contemplating the fortitude, independence, persevering spirit, and the general moral dignity of this old man's character.'

And again, on the same poem:

'I will explain to you, in prose, my feelings in writing *that* poem. . . I describe myself as having been exalted to the highest pitch of delight by the joyousness and beauty of Nature; and then as depressed, even in the midst of those beautiful objects, to the lowest dejection and despair. A young poet in the midst of the happiness of Nature is described as overwhelmed by the thoughts of the miserable reverses which have befallen the happiest of all men, viz. poets. I think of this till I am so deeply impressed with it, that I consider the manner in which I was rescued from my dejection and despair almost as an interposition of Providence. A person reading the poem with feelings like mine will have been awed and controlled, expecting something spiritual or supernatural. What is brought forward? A

* *Memoirs*, vol. i. pp. 171-2.   † Entitled 'Resolution and Independence.'

lonely place, "a pond, by which an old man *was*, far from all house or home :" not *stood*, nor *sat*, but *was*—the figure presented in the most naked simplicity possible. This feeling of spirituality or supernaturalness is again referred to as being strong in my mind in this passage.   How came he here? thought I, or what can he be doing?   I then describe him, whether ill or well is not for me to judge with perfect confidence ; but this I *can* confidently affirm, that though I believe God has given me a strong imagination, I cannot conceive a figure more impressive than that of an old man like this, the survivor of a wife and ten children, travelling alone among the mountains and all lonely places, carrying with him his own fortitude and the necessities which an unjust state of society has laid upon him.   You speak of his speech as tedious.   Everything is tedious when one does not read with the feelings of the author.   "The Thorn" is tedious to hundreds ; and so is the "Idiot Boy" to hundreds.   It is in the character of the old man to tell his story, which an impatient reader must feel tedious.   But, good heavens! such a figure, in such a place ; a pious, self-respecting, miserably infirm and pleased old man telling such a tale !

'Your feelings upon the "Mother and the Boy, with the Butterfly," were not indifferent : it was an affair of whole continents of moral sympathy.'

'I am for the most part uncertain about my success in *altering* poems ; but in this case,' speaking of an insertion, 'I am sure I have produced a great improvement.'*

* *Memoirs*, vol. i. pp. 166-174.

Letter to (afterwards) Professor John Wilson [' Christopher North'].

To ———————.

MY DEAR SIR,

Had it not been for a very amiable modesty you could not have imagined that your letter could give me any offence. It was on many accounts highly grateful to me. I was pleased to find that I had given so much pleasure to an ingenuous and able mind, and I further considered the enjoyment which you had had from my Poems as an earnest that others might be delighted with them in the same, or a like manner. It is plain from your letter that the pleasure which I have given you has not been blind or unthinking; you have studied the poems, and prove that you have entered into the spirit of them. They have not given you a cheap or vulgar pleasure; therefore, I feel that you are entitled to my kindest thanks for having done some violence to your natural diffidence in the communication which you have made to me.

There is scarcely any part of your letter that does not deserve particular notice; but partly from some constitutional infirmities, and partly from certain habits of mind, I do not write any letters unless upon business, not even to my dearest friends. Except during absence from my own family I have not written five letters of friendship during the last five years. I have mentioned this in order that I may retain your good opinion, should my letter be less minute than you are entitled to expect. You seem to be desirous of my opinion on the influence of natural objects in forming the character of Nations. This cannot be understood without first considering their influence upon men in general, first, with reference to such objects as are common to all countries; and, next, such as belong exclusively to any particular country, or in a greater degree to it than to another. Now it is manifest that no human being can be so besotted and debased by oppression, penury, or any other evil which unhumanises man, as to be utterly insensible to the colours, forms,

or smell of flowers, the [voices*] and motions of birds and
beasts, the appearances of the sky and heavenly bodies, the
general warmth of a fine day, the terror and uncomfortableness
of a storm, &c. &c. How dead soever many full-grown men
may outwardly seem to these things, all are more or less affected by them; and in childhood, in the first practice and
exercise of their senses, they must have been not the nourishers
merely, but often the fathers of their passions. There cannot
be a doubt that in tracts of country where images of danger,
melancholy, grandeur, or loveliness, softness, and ease prevail,
that they will make themselves felt powerfully in forming the
characters of the people, so as to produce an uniformity or national character, where the nation is small and is not made up
of men who, inhabiting different soils, climates, &c., by their
civil usages and relations materially interfere with each other.
It was so formerly, no doubt, in the Highlands of Scotland;
but we cannot perhaps observe much of it in our own island at
the present day, because, even in the most sequestered places,
by manufactures, traffic, religion, law, interchange of inhabitants, &c., distinctions are done away, which would otherwise
have been strong and obvious. This complex state of society
does not, however, prevent the characters of individuals from
frequently receiving a strong bias, not merely from the impressions of general Nature, but also from local objects and images.
But it seems that to produce these effects, in the degree in which
we frequently find them to be produced, there must be a peculiar sensibility of original organisation combining with moral
accidents, as is exhibited in ' THE BROTHERS' and in ' RUTH ;' I
mean, to produce this in a marked degree ; not that I believe
that any man was ever brought up in the country without loving it, especially in his better moments, or in a district of particular grandeur or beauty without feeling some stronger attachment to it on that account than he would otherwise have felt.
I include, you will observe, in these considerations, the influence
of climate, changes in the atmosphere and elements, and the
labours and occupations which particular districts require.

You begin what you say upon the ' Idiot Boy,' with this observation, that nothing is a fit subject for poetry which does not

* Parts of this letter have been torn, and words have been lost; some of
which are here conjecturally supplied between brackets.

please. But here follows a question, Does not please whom? Some have little knowledge of natural imagery of any kind, and, of course, little relish for it; some are disgusted with the very mention of the words pastoral poetry, sheep or shepherds; some cannot tolerate a poem with a ghost or any supernatural agency in it; others would shrink from an animated description of the pleasures of love, as from a thing carnal and libidinous; some cannot bear to see delicate and refined feelings ascribed to men in low conditions in society, because their vanity and self-love tell them that these belong only to themselves, and men like themselves in dress, station, and way of life; others are disgusted with the naked language of some of the most interesting passions of men, because either it is indelicate, or gross, or vulgar; as many fine ladies could not bear certain expressions in the 'Mother' and the 'Thorn,' and, as in the instance of Adam Smith, who, we are told, could not endure the ballad of 'Clym of the Clough,' because the author had not written like a gentleman. Then there are professional and national prejudices for evermore. Some take no interest in the description of a particular passion or quality, as love of solitariness, we will say, genial activity of fancy, love of Nature, religion, and so forth, because they have [little or] nothing of it in themselves; and so on without end. I return then to [the] question, please whom? or what? I answer, human nature as it has been [and ever] will be. But where are we to find the best measure of this? I answer, [from with] in; by stripping our own hearts naked, and by looking out of ourselves to [wards men] who lead the simplest lives, and most according to Nature; men who have never known false refinements, wayward and artificial desires, false criticisms, effeminate habits of thinking and feeling, or who having known these things have outgrown them. This latter class is the most to be depended upon, but it is very small in number. People in our rank in life are perpetually falling into one sad mistake, namely, that of supposing that human nature and the persons they associate with are one and the same thing. Whom do we generally associate with? Gentlemen, persons of fortune, professional men, ladies, persons who can afford to buy, or can easily procure books of half-a-guinea price, hot-pressed, and printed upon superfine paper. These persons are, it is true, a part of human nature, but we err lamentably if we suppose them to be fair representatives of the vast mass of human existence. And yet few ever consider books but with reference to their power of pleasing these persons and men of a higher rank; few descend lower, among cottages and fields, and among children. A man must have done this habitually before his judgment upon the 'Idiot Boy' would be in any way decisive with me. I *know* I have done this myself habitually; I wrote the poem with exceeding delight and pleasure, and whenever I read it I read it with pleasure. You have given me praise for having reflected faithfully in my Poems the feelings of human nature. I would fain hope that I have done so. But a great Poet ought to do more than this; he ought, to a certain degree, to rectify men's feelings, to give them new compositions of feeling, to render their feelings more sane, pure, and permanent, in short, more consonant to Nature, that is, to eternal Nature, and the great moving Spirit of things. He ought to travel before men occasionally as well as at their sides. I may illustrate this by a reference to natural objects. What false notions have prevailed from generation to generation of the true character of the Nightingale. As far as my Friend's Poem, in the 'Lyrical Ballads,' is read, it will contribute greatly to rectify these. You will recollect a passage in Cowper, where, speaking of rural sounds, he says,

> And *even* the boding Owl
> That hails the rising moon has charms for me.

Cowper was passionately fond of natural objects, yet you see he mentions it as a marvellous thing that he could connect pleasure with the cry of the owl. In the same poem he speaks in the same manner of that beautiful plant, the gorse; making in some degree an amiable boast of his loving it '*unsightly*' and unsmooth as it is. There are many aversions of this kind, which, though they have some foundation in nature, have yet so slight a one, that, though they may have prevailed hundreds of years, a philosopher will look upon them as accidents. So with respect to many moral feelings, either of love or dislike. What excessive admiration was paid in former times to personal prowess and military success; it is so with the latter even at the present day, but surely not nearly so much as heretofore. So with regard to birth, and innumerable other modes of sentiment, civil and religious. But you will be inclined to ask by this time how all this applies to the 'Idiot Boy.' To this I can only say that the loathing and disgust which many people have at the sight of an idiot, is a feeling which, though having some foundation in human nature, is not necessarily attached to it in any virtuous degree, but is owing in a great measure to a false delicacy, and, if I may say it without rudeness, a certain want of comprehensiveness of thinking and feeling. Persons in the lower classes of society have little or nothing of this: if an idiot is born in a poor man's house, it must be taken care of, and cannot be boarded out, as it would be by gentlefolks, or sent to a public or private receptacle for such unfortunate beings. [Poor people] seeing frequently among their neighbours such objects, easily [forget] whatever there is of natural disgust about them, and have [therefore] a sane state, so that without pain or suffering they [perform] their duties towards them. I could with pleasure pursue this subject, but I must now strictly adopt the plan which I proposed to myself when I began to write this letter, namely, that of setting down a few hints or memorandums, which you will think of for my sake.

I have often applied to idiots, in my own mind, that sublime expression of Scripture that ' *their life is hidden with God.*' They are worshipped, probably from a feeling of this sort, in several parts of the East. Among the Alps, where they are numerous, they are considered, I believe, as a blessing to the family to which they belong. I have, indeed, often looked upon the conduct of fathers and mothers of the lower classes of society towards idiots as the great triumph of the human heart. It is there that we see the strength, disinterestedness, and grandeur of love; nor have I ever been able to contemplate an object that calls out so many excellent and virtuous sentiments without finding it hallowed thereby, and having something in me which bears down before it, like a deluge, every feeble sensation of disgust and aversion.

There are, in my opinion, several important mistakes in the latter part of your letter which I could have wished to notice; but I find myself much fatigued. These refer both to the Boy and the Mother. I must content myself simply with observing that it is probable that the principal cause of your dislike to this particular poem lies in the *word* Idiot. If there had been any such word in our language, *to which we had attached passion,* as

lack-wit, half-wit, witless, &c., I should have certainly employed
it in preference; but there is no such word. Observe (this is
entirely in reference to this particular poem), my 'Idiot' is not
one of those who cannot articulate, and such as are usually disgusting in their persons:

> *Whether in cunning or in joy,*
> *And then his words were not a few, &c.*

and the last speech at the end of the poem. The 'Boy' whom
I had in my mind was by no means disgusting in his appearance, quite the contrary; and I have known several with imperfect faculties, who are handsome in their persons and features.
There is one, at present, within a mile of my own house, re-
markably so, though [he has something] of a stare and vacancy
in his countenance. A friend of mine, knowing that some
persons had a dislike to the poem, such as you have expressed,
advised me to add a stanza, describing the person of the Boy
[so as] entirely to separate him in the imaginations of my
readers from that class of idiots who are disgusting in their
persons; but the narration in the poem is so rapid and impassioned, that I could not find a place in which to insert the
stanza without checking the progress of it, and [so leaving] a
deadness upon the feeling. This poem has, I know, frequently
produced the same effect as it did upon you and your friends;
but there are many also to whom it affords exquisite delight,
and who, indeed, prefer it to any other of my poems. This
proves that the feelings there delineated are such as men *may*
sympathise with. This is enough for my purpose. It is not
enough for me as a Poet, to delineate merely such feelings as
all men *do* sympathise with; but it is also highly desirable to
add to these others, such as all men *may* sympathise with, and
such as there is reason to believe they would be better and more
moral beings if they did sympathise with.

I conclude with regret, because I have not said one half of
[what I intended] to say; but I am sure you will deem my
excuse sufficient, [when I] inform you that my head aches
violently, and I am in other respects unwell. I must, however,
again give you my warmest thanks for your kind letter. I shall
be happy to hear from you again: and do not think it unrea-
sonable that I should request a letter from you, when I feel
that the answer which I may make to it will not perhaps be

above three or four lines.   This I mention to you with frankness, and you will not take it ill after what I have before said of
my remissness in writing letters.

I am, dear Sir,

With great respect,

Yours sincerely,

W. Wordsworth.*

* *Memoirs*, vol. i. pp. 192-200.

IV. DESCRIPTIVE.

(*a*) A GUIDE THROUGH THE DISTRICT OF THE LAKES.

(*b*) LETTERS, &c. ON KENDAL AND WINDERMERE RAILWAY.

NOTE.

See Preface in Vol. I. for details on the ' Guide' and these Letters.   G.

A

GUIDE

THROUGH THE

DISTRICT OF THE LAKES

IN

𝔈𝔥𝔢 North of England,

WITH

A DESCRIPTION OF THE SCENERY, &c.

FOR THE USE OF

TOURISTS AND RESIDENTS.

FIFTH EDITION,
WITH CONSIDERABLE ADDITIONS.

By WILLIAM WORDSWORTH.

KENDAL:

PUBLISHED BY HUDSON AND NICHOLSON,

AND IN LONDON BY

LONGMAN & CO., MOXON, AND WHITTAKER & CO.

1835.

CONTENTS.

In preparing this Manual, it was the Author's principal wish to furnish a Guide or Companion for the *Minds* of Persons of taste, and feeling for Landscape, who might be inclined to explore the District of the Lakes with that degree of attention to which its beauty may fairly lay claim. For the more sure attainment, however, of this primary object, he will begin by undertaking the humble and tedious task of supplying the Tourist with directions how to approach the several scenes in their best, or most convenient, order. But first, supposing the approach to be made from the south, and through Yorkshire, there are certain interesting spots which may be confidently recommended to his notice, if time can be spared before entering upon the Lake District; and the route may be changed in returning.

There are three approaches to the Lakes through Yorkshire ; the least adviseable is the great north road by Catterick and Greta Bridge, and onwards to Penrith. The Traveller, however, taking this route, might halt at Greta Bridge, and be well recompenced if he can afford to give an hour or two to the banks of the Greta, and of the Tees, at Rokeby. Barnard Castle also, about two miles up the Tees, is a striking object, and the main North Road might be rejoined at Bowes. Every one has heard. of the great Fall of the Tees above Middleham, interesting for its grandeur, as the avenue of rocks that leads to it, is to the geologist. But this place lies so far out of the way as scarcely to be within the compass of our notice. It might, however, be visited by a Traveller on foot, or on horseback, who could rejoin the main road upon Stanemoor.

The second road leads through a more interesting tract of country, beginning at Ripon, from which place see Fountain's Abbey, and thence by Hackfall, and Masham, to Jervaux Abbey, and up the vale of Wensley ; turning aside before Askrigg is reached, to see Aysgarth-force, upon the Ure ; and again, near Hawes, to Hardraw Scar, of which, with its waterfall, Turner has a fine drawing. Thence over the fells to Sedbergh, and Kendal.

The third approach from Yorkshire is through Leeds. Four miles beyond that town are the ruins of Kirkstall Abbey, should that road to Skipton be chosen; but the other by Otley may be made much more interesting by turning off at Addington to Bolton Bridge, for the sake of visiting the Abbey and grounds. It would be well, however, for a party previously to secure beds, if wanted, at the inn, as there is but one, and it is much resorted to in summer.

The Traveller on foot, or horseback, would do well to follow the banks of the Wharf upwards, to Burnsall, and thence cross over the hills to Gordale—a noble scene, beautifully described in Gray's Tour, and with which no one can be disappointed. Thence to Malham, where there is a respectable village inn, and so on, by Malham Cove, to Settle.

Travellers in carriages must go from Bolton Bridge to Skipton, where they rejoin the main road; and should they be inclined to visit Gordale, a tolerable road turns off beyond Skipton. Beyond Settle, under Giggleswick Scar, the road passes an ebbing and flowing well, worthy the notice of the Naturalist. Four miles to the right of Ingleton, is Weathercote Cave, a fine object, but whoever diverges for this, must return to Ingleton. Near Kirkby Lonsdale observe the view from the bridge over the Lune, and descend to the channel of the river, and by no means omit looking at the Vale of Lune from the Church-yard.

The journey towards the Lake country through Lancashire, is, with the exception of the Vale of the Ribble, at Preston, uninteresting; till you come near Lancaster, and obtain a view of the fells and mountains of Lancashire and Westmorland; with Lancaster Castle, and the Tower of the Church seeming to make part of the Castle, in the foreground.

They who wish to see the celebrated ruins of Furness Abbey, and are not afraid of crossing the Sands, may go from Lancaster to Ulverston; from which place take the direct road to Dalton; but by all means return through Urswick, for the sake of the view from the top of the hill, before descending into the grounds of Conishead Priory. From this quarter the Lakes would be advantageously approached by Coniston; thence to Hawkshead, and by the Ferry over Windermere, to Bowness:

a much better introduction than by going direct from Coniston to Ambleside, which ought not to be done, as that would greatly take off from the effect of Windermere.

Let us now go back to Lancaster. The direct road thence to Kendal is 22 miles, but by making a circuit of eight miles, the Vale of the Lune to Kirkby Lonsdale will be included. The whole tract is pleasing; there is one view mentioned by Gray and Mason especially so. In West's Guide it is thus pointed out :—' About a quarter of a mile beyond the third mile-stone, where the road makes a turn to the right, there is a gate on the left which leads into a field where the station meant, will be found.' Thus far for those who approach the Lakes from the South.

Travellers from the North would do well to go from Carlisle by Wigton, and proceed along the Lake of Bassenthwaite to Keswick; or, if convenience should take them first to Penrith, it would still be better to cross the country to Keswick, and begin with that vale, rather than with Ulswater. It is worth while to mention, in this place, that the banks of the river Eden, about Corby, are well worthy of notice, both on account of their natural beauty, and the viaducts which have recently been carried over the bed of the river, and over a neighbouring ravine. In the Church of Wetherby, close by, is a fine piece of monumental sculpture by Nollekens. The scenes of Nunnery, upon the Eden, or rather that part of them which is upon Croglin, a mountain stream there falling into the Eden, are, in their way, unrivalled. But the nearest road thither, from Corby, is so bad, that no one can be advised to take it in a carriage. Nunnery may be reached from Corby by making a circuit and crossing the Eden at Armathwaite bridge. A portion of this road, however, is bad enough.

As much the greatest number of Lake Tourists begin by passing from Kendal to Bowness, upon Windermere, our notices shall commence with that Lake. Bowness is situated upon its eastern side, and at equal distance from each extremity of the Lake of

WINDERMERE.

The lower part of this Lake is rarely visited, but has many interesting points of view, especially at Storr's Hall and at Fellfoot, where the Coniston Mountains peer nobly over the western

barrier, which elsewhere, along the whole Lake, is comparatively tame. To one also who has ascended the hill from Grath-
waite on the western side, the Promontory called Rawlinson's
Nab, Storr's Hall, and the Troutbeck Mountains, about sun-set,
make a splendid landscape. The view from the Pleasure-house
of the Station near the Ferry has suffered much from Larch
plantations ; this mischief, however, is gradually disappearing,
and the Larches, under the management of the proprietor, Mr.
Curwen, are giving way to the native wood. Windermere ought
to be seen both from its shores and from its surface. None of
the other Lakes unfold so many fresh beauties to him who sails
upon them. This is owing to its greater size, to the islands,
and to its having *two* vales at the head, with their accompanying
mountains of nearly equal dignity. Nor can the grandeur of
these two terminations be seen at once from any point, except
from the bosom of the Lake. The Islands may be explored at
any time of the day ; but one bright unruffled evening, must,
if possible, be set apart for the splendour, the stillness, and
solemnity of a three hours' voyage upon the higher division of
the Lake, not omitting, towards the end of the excursion, to
quit the expanse of water, and peep into the close and calm
River at the head ; which, in its quiet character, at such a time,
appears rather like an overflow of the peaceful Lake itself, than
to have any more immediate connection with the rough mountains whence it has descended, or the turbulent torrents by
which it is supplied. Many persons content themselves with
what they see of Windermere during their progress in a boat
from Bowness to the head of the Lake, walking thence to Ambleside. But the whole road from Bowness is rich in diversity
of pleasing or grand scenery ; there is scarcely a field on the
road side, which, if entered, would not give to the landscape
some additional charm. Low-wood Inn, a mile from the head
of Windermere, is a most pleasant halting-place ; no inn in
the whole district is so agreeably situated for water views and
excursions ; and the fields above it, and the lane that leads to
Troutbeck, present beautiful views towards each extremity of
the Lake. From this place, and from

AMBLESIDE,

Rides may be taken in numerous directions, and the interesting walks are inexhaustible;* a few out of the main road may be particularized;—the lane that leads from Ambleside to Skelgill; the ride, or walk by Rothay Bridge, and up the stream under Loughrigg Fell, continued on the western side of Rydal Lake, and along the fell to the foot of Grasmere Lake, and thence round by the church of Grasmere; or, turning round Loughrigg Fell by Loughrigg Tarn and the River Brathay, back to Ambleside. From Ambleside is another charming excursion by Clappersgate, where cross the Brathay, and proceed with the river on the right to the hamlet of Skelwith-fold; when the houses are passed, turn, before you descend the hill, through a gate on the right, and from a rocky point is a fine view of the Brathay River, Langdale Pikes, &c.; then proceed to Colwith-force, and up Little Langdale to Blea Tarn. The scene in which this small piece of water lies, suggested to the Author the following description, (given in his Poem of the 'Excursion') supposing the spectator to look down upon it, not from the road, but from one of its elevated sides.

> ' Behold!
> Beneath our feet, a little lowly Vale,
> A lowly Vale, and yet uplifted high
> Among the mountains; even as if the spot
> Had been, from eldest time by wish of theirs,
> So placed, to be shut out from all the world!
> Urn-like it was in shape, deep as an Urn;
> With rocks encompassed, save that to the South
> Was one small opening, where a heath-clad ridge
> Supplied a boundary less abrupt and close;
> A quiet treeless nook,† with two green fields,
> A liquid pool that glittered in the sun,
> And one bare Dwelling; one Abode, no more!
> It seemed the home of poverty and toil,
> Though not of want: the little fields, made green
> By husbandry of many thrifty years,
> Paid cheerful tribute to the moorland House.
> —There crows the Cock, single in his domain:
> The small birds find in Spring no thicket there
> To shroud them; only from the neighbouring Vales
> The Cuckoo, straggling up to the hill tops,
> Shouteth faint tidings of some gladder place.'

* Mr. Green's Guide to the Lakes, in two vols., contains a complete Magazine of minute and accurate information of this kind, with the names of mountains, streams, &c.

† No longer strictly applicable, on account of recent plantations.

From this little Vale return towards Ambleside by Great Langdale, stopping, if there be time, to see Dungeon-ghyll waterfall.

The Lake of

CONISTON

May be conveniently visited from Ambleside, but is seen to most advantage by entering the country over the Sands from Lancaster. The Stranger, from the moment he sets his foot on those Sands, seems to leave the turmoil and traffic of the world behind him ; and, crossing the majestic plain whence the sea has retired, he beholds, rising apparently from its base, the cluster of mountains among which he is going to wander, and towards whose recesses, by the Vale of Coniston, he is gradually and peacefully led. From the Inn at the head of Coniston Lake, a leisurely Traveller might have much pleasure in looking into Yewdale and Tilberthwaite, returning to his Inn from the head of Yewdale by a mountain track which has the farm of Tarn Hows, a little on the right: by this road is seen much the best view of Coniston Lake from the south. At the head of Coniston Water there is an agreeable Inn, from which an enterprising Tourist might go to the Vale of the Duddon, over Walna Scar, down to Seathwaite, Newfield, and to the rocks where the river issues from a narrow pass into the broad Vale. The Stream is very interesting for the space of a mile above this point, and below, by Ulpha Kirk, till it enters the Sands, where it is overlooked by the solitary Mountain Black Comb, the summit of which, as that experienced surveyor, Colonel Mudge, declared, commands a more extensive view than any point in Britain. Ireland he saw more than once, but not when the sun was above the horizon.

> Close by the Sea, lone sentinel,
>   Black-Comb his forward station keeps ;
> He breaks the sea's tumultuous swell,—
>   And ponders o'er the level deeps.
>
> He listens to the bugle horn,
>   Where Eskdale's lovely valley bends ;
> Eyes Walney's early fields of corn ;
>   Sea-birds to Holker's woods he sends.
>
> Beneath his feet the sunk ship rests,
> In Duddon Sands, its masts all bare :
> *   *   *   *   *
>   *The Minstrels of Windermere,* by Chas. Farish, B.D.

The Tourist may either return to the Inn at Coniston by Broughton, or, by turning to the left before he comes to that town, or, which would be much better, he may cross from

ULPHA KIRK

Over Birker moor, to Birker-force, at the head of the finest ravine in the country; and thence up the Vale of the Esk, by Hardknot and Wrynose, back to Ambleside. Near the road, in ascending from Eskdale, are conspicuous remains of a Roman fortress. Details of the Duddon and Donnerdale are given in the Author's series of Sonnets upon the Duddon and in the accompanying Notes. In addition to its two Vales at its head, Windermere communicates with two lateral Vallies; that of Troutbeck, distinguished by the mountains at its head—by picturesque remains of cottage architecture; and, towards the lower part, by bold foregrounds formed by the steep and winding banks of the river. This Vale, as before mentioned, may be most conveniently seen from Low Wood. The other lateral Valley, that of Hawkshead, is visited to most advantage, and most conveniently, from Bowness; crossing the Lake by the Ferry—then pass the two villages of Sawrey, and on quitting the latter, you have a fine view of the Lake of Esthwaite, and the cone of one of the Langdale Pikes in the distance.

Before you leave Ambleside give three minutes to looking at a passage of the brook which runs through the town; it is to be seen from a garden on the right bank of the stream, a few steps above the bridge—the garden at present is rented by Mrs. Airey. —Stockgill-force, upon the same stream, will have been mentioned to you as one of the sights of the neighbourhood. And by a Tourist halting a few days in Ambleside, the *Nook* also might be visited; a spot where there is a bridge over Scandale-beck, which makes a pretty subject for the pencil. Lastly, for residents of a week or so at Ambleside, there are delightful rambles over every part of Loughrigg Fell and among the enclosures on its sides; particularly about Loughrigg Tarn, and on its eastern side about Fox How and the properties adjoining to the northwards.

ROAD FROM AMBLESIDE TO KESWICK.

The Waterfalls of Rydal are pointed out to every one. But it ought to be observed here, that Rydal-mere is no where seen

to advantage from the *main road*. Fine views of it may be had
from Rydal Park; but these grounds, as well as those of Rydal
Mount and Ivy Cottage, from which also it is viewed to advantage, are private. A foot road passing behind Rydal Mount and
under Nab Scar to Grasmere, is very favourable to views of the
Lake and the Vale, looking back towards Ambleside. The horse
road also, along the western side of the Lake, under Loughrigg
fell, as before mentioned, does justice to the beauties of this
small mere, of which the Traveller who keeps the high road is
not at all aware.

GRASMERE.

There are two small Inns in the Vale of Grasmere, one near
the Church, from which it may be conveniently explored in every
direction, and a mountain walk taken up Easedale to Easedale
Tarn, one of the finest tarns in the country, thence to Stickle
Tarn, and to the top of Langdale Pikes. (See also the Vale of
Grasmere from Butterlip How. A boat is kept by the innkeeper,
and this circular Vale, in the solemnity of a fine evening, will
make, from the bosom of the Lake, an impression that will be
scarcely ever effaced.

The direct road from Grasmere to Keswick does not (as has
been observed of Rydal Mere) shew to advantage Thirlmere, or
Wythburn Lake, with its surrounding mountains. By a Traveller proceeding at leisure, a deviation ought to be made from
the main road, when he has advanced a little beyond the sixth
mile-stone short of Keswick, from which point there is a noble
view of the Vale of Legberthwaite, with Blencathra (commonly
called Saddle-back) in front. Having previously enquired, at the
Inn near Wythburn Chapel, the best way from this mile-stone
to the bridge that divides the Lake, he must cross it, and proceed with the Lake on the right, to the hamlet a little beyond
its termination, and rejoin the main road upon Shoulthwaite
Moss, about four miles from Keswick; or, if on foot, the Tourist
may follow the stream that issues from Thirlmere down the romantic Vale of St. John's, and so (enquiring the way at some
cottage) to Keswick, by a circuit of little more than a mile. A
more interesting tract of country is scarcely any where to be
seen, than the road between Ambleside and Keswick, with the
deviations that have been pointed out. Helvellyn may be conveniently ascended from the Inn at Wythburn.

THE VALE OF KESWICK.

This Vale stretches, without winding, nearly North and South, from the head of Derwent Water to the foot of Bassenthwaite Lake. It communicates with Borrowdale on the South; with the river Greta, and Thirlmere, on the East, with which the Traveller has become acquainted on his way from Ambleside; and with the Vale of Newlands on the West—which last Vale he may pass through, in going to, or returning from, Buttermere. The best views of Keswick Lake are from Crow Park; Frier's Crag; the Stable-field, close by; the Vicarage, and from various points in taking the circuit of the Lake. More distant views, and perhaps full as interesting, are from the side of Latrigg, from Ormathwaite, and Applethwaite; and thence along the road at the foot of Skiddaw towards Bassenthwaite, for about a quarter of a mile. [There are fine bird's eye views from the Castle-hill; from Ashness, on the road to Watenlath, and by following the Watenlath stream downwards to the Cataract of Lodore.] This Lake also, if the weather be fine, ought to be circumnavigated. There are good views along the western side of Bassenthwaite Lake, and from Armathwaite at its foot; but the eastern side from the high road has little to recommend it. The Traveller from Carlisle, approaching by way of Ireby, has, from the old road on the top of Bassenthwaite-hawse, much the most striking view of the Plain and Lake of Bassenthwaite, flanked by Skiddaw, and terminated by Wallowcrag on the south-east of Derwent Lake; the same point commands an extensive view of Solway Frith and the Scotch Mountains. They who take the circuit of Derwent Lake, may at the same time include BORROWDALE, going as far as Bowder-stone, or Rosthwaite. Borrowdale is also conveniently seen on the way to Wastdale over Styhead; or, to Buttermere, by Seatoller and Honister Crag; or, going over the Stake, through Langdale, to Ambleside. Buttermere may be visited by a shorter way through Newlands, but though the descent upon the Vale of Buttermere, by this approach, is very striking, as it also is to one entering by the head of the Vale, under Honister Crag, yet, after all, the best entrance from Keswick is from the lower part of the Vale, having gone over Whinlater to Scale Hill, where there is a roomy Inn, with very good accommodation. [The Mountains of the Vale of

BUTTERMERE AND CRUMMOCK

are no where so impressive as from the bosom of Crummock Water. Scale-force, near it, is a fine chasm, with a lofty, though but slender, Fall of water.

From Scale Hill a pleasant walk may be taken to an eminence in Mr. Marshall's woods, and another by crossing the bridge at the foot of the hill, upon which the Inn stands, and turning to the right, after the opposite hill has been ascended a little way, then follow the road for half a mile or so that leads towards Lorton, looking back upon Crummock Water, &c., between the openings of the fences. Turn back and make your way to

LOWESWATER.

But this small Lake is only approached to advantage from the other end; therefore any Traveller going by this road to Wastdale, must look back upon it. This road to Wastdale, after passing the village of Lamplugh Cross, presents suddenly a fine view of the Lake of Ennerdale, with its Mountains; and, six or seven miles beyond, leads down upon Calder Abbey. Little of this ruin is left, but that little is well worthy of notice. At Calder Bridge are two comfortable Inns, and, a few miles beyond, accommodations may be had at the Strands, at the foot of Wastdale. Into

WASTDALE

are three horse-roads, viz. over the Stye, from Borrowdale; a short cut from Eskdale by Burnmore Tarn, which road descends upon the head of the Lake; and the principal entrance from the open country by the Strands at its foot. This last is much the best approach. Wastdale is well worth the notice of the Traveller who is not afraid of fatigue; no part of the country is more distinguished by sublimity. Wastwater may also be visited from Ambleside; by going up Langdale, over Hardknot and Wrynose—down Eskdale and by Irton Hall to the Strands; but this road can only be taken on foot, or on horseback, or in a cart.

We will conclude with

ULLSWATER,

as being, perhaps, upon the whole, the happiest combination of beauty and grandeur, which any of the Lakes affords. It lies not more than ten miles from Ambleside, and the Pass of Kirkstone and the descent from it are very impressive; but, notwithstanding, this Vale, like the others, loses much of its effect by being entered from the head: so that it is better to go from Keswick through Matterdale, and descend upon Gowbarrow Park; you are thus brought at once upon a magnificent view of the two higher reaches of the Lake. Ara-force thunders down the Ghyll on the left, at a small distance from the road. If Ullswater be approached from Penrith, a mile and a half brings you to the winding vale of Eamont, and the prospects increase in interest till you reach Patterdale; but the first four miles along Ullswater by this road are comparatively tame; and in order to see the lower part of the Lake to advantage, it is necessary to go round by Pooley Bridge, and to ride at least three miles along the Westmorland side of the water, towards Martindale. (The views, especially if you ascend from the road into the fields, are magnificent; yet this is only mentioned that the transient Visitant may know what exists; for it would be inconvenient to go in search of them. They who take this course of three or four miles *on foot*, should have a boat in readiness at the end of the walk, to carry them across to the Cumberland side of the Lake, near Old Church, thence to pursue the road upwards to Patterdale. The Church-yard Yew-tree still survives at Old Church, but there are no remains of a Place of Worship, a New Chapel having been erected in a more central situation, which Chapel was consecrated by the then Bishop of Carlisle, when on his way to crown Queen Elizabeth, he being the only Prelate who would undertake the office. It may be here mentioned that Bassenthwaite Chapel yet stands in a bay as sequestered as the Site of Old Church; such situations having been chosen in disturbed times to elude marauders.

The Trunk, or Body of the Vale of Ullswater need not be further noticed, as its beauties show themselves: but the curious Traveller may wish to know something of its tributary Streams.

At Dalemain, about three miles from Penrith, a Stream is crossed called the Dacre, or Dacor, which name it bore as early as the time of the Venerable Bede. This stream does not enter the Lake, but joins the Eamont a mile below. It rises in the moorish Country about Penruddock, flows down a soft sequestered Valley, passing by the ancient mansions of Hutton John and Dacre Castle. The former is pleasantly situated, though of a character somewhat gloomy and monastic, and from some of the fields near Dalemain, Dacre Castle, backed by the jagged summit of Saddleback, with the Valley and Stream in front, forms a grand picture.   There is no other stream that conducts to any glen or valley worthy of being mentioned, till we reach that which leads up to Ara-force, and thence into Matterdale, before spoken of. Matterdale, though a wild and interesting spot, has no peculiar features that would make it worth the Stranger's while to go in search of them; but, in Gowbarrow Park, the lover of Nature might linger for hours. Here is a powerful Brook, which dashes among rocks through a deep glen, hung on every side with a rich and happy intermixture of native wood; here are beds of luxuriant fern, aged hawthorns, and hollies decked with honey-suckles; and fallow-deer glancing and bounding over the lawns and through the thickets. These are the attractions of the re-tired views, or constitute a foreground for ever-varying pictures of the majestic Lake, forced to take a winding course by bold promontories, and environed by mountains of sublime form, towering above each other.   At the outlet of Gowbarrow Park, we reach a third stream, which flows through a little recess called Glencoin, where lurks a single house, yet visible from the road.   Let the Artist or leisurely Traveller turn aside to it, for the buildings and objects around them are romantic and pic-turesque.   Having passed under the steeps of Styebarrow Crag, and the remains of its native woods, at Glenridding Bridge, a fourth Stream is crossed.

The opening on the side of Ullswater Vale, down which this Stream flows, is adorned with fertile fields, cottages, and natural groves, that agreeably unite with the transverse views of the Lake; and the Stream, if followed up after the enclosures are left behind, will lead along bold water-breaks and waterfalls to a silent Tarn in the recesses of Helvellyn.   This desolate spot was formerly haunted by eagles, that built in the precipice which forms its western barrier.   These birds used to wheel and hover round the head of the solitary angler.   It also derives a melan-choly interest from the fate of a young man, a stranger, who perished some years ago, by falling down the rocks in his at-tempt to cross over to Grasmere.   His remains were discovered by means of a faithful dog that had lingered here for the space of three months, self-supported, and probably retaining to the last an attachment to the skeleton of its master. But to return to the road in the main Vale of Ullswater.—At the head of the Lake (being now in Patterdale) we cross a fifth Stream, Grisdale Beck : this would conduct through a woody steep, where may be seen some unusually large ancient hollies, up to the level area of the Valley of Grisdale ; hence there is a path for foot-travellers, and along which a horse may be led to Grasmere. A sublime combination of mountain forms appears in front while ascending the bed of this valley, and the impression increases till the path leads almost immediately under the projecting masses of Helvellyn. Having retraced the banks of the Stream to Patterdale, and pursued the road up the main Dale, the next considerable stream would, if ascended in the same manner, conduct to Deep-dale, the character of which Valley may be conjectured from its name. It is terminated by a cove, a craggy and gloomy abyss, with precipitous sides ; a faithful receptacle of the snows that are driven into it, by the west wind, from the summit of Fairfield. Lastly, having gone along the western side of Brotherswater and passed Hartsop Hall, a Stream soon after issues from a cove richly decorated with native wood. This spot is, I believe, never explored by Travellers ; but, from these sylvan and rocky recesses, whoever looks back on the gleaming surface of Brotherswater, or forward to the precipitous sides and lofty ridges of Dove Crag, &c., will be equally pleased with the beauty, the grandeur, and the wildness of the scenery.

Seven Glens or Vallies have been noticed, which branch off from the Cumberland side of the Vale. The opposite side has only two Streams of any importance, one of which would lead up from the point where it crosses the Kirkstone-road, near the foot of Brotherswater, to the decaying hamlet of Hartsop, remarkable for its cottage architecture, and thence to Hayswater, much frequented by anglers. The other, coming down Martindale, enters Ullswater at Sandwyke, opposite to Gowbarrow Park. No persons but such as come to Patterdale, merely to pass through it, should fail to walk as far as Blowick, the only enclosed land which on this side borders the higher part of the Lake. The axe has here indiscriminately levelled a rich wood of birches and oaks, that divided this favoured spot into a hun-

dred pictures. It has yet its land-locked bays, and rocky promontories ; but those beautiful woods are gone, which *perfected*
its seclusion ; and scenes, that might formerly have been compared to an inexhaustible volume, are now spread before the eye
in a single sheet,—magnificent indeed, but seemingly perused
in a moment! From Blowick a narrow track conducts along
the craggy side of Place-fell, richly adorned with juniper, and
sprinkled over with birches, to the village of Sandwyke, a few
straggling houses, that with the small estates attached to them,
occupy an opening opposite to Lyulph's Tower and Gowbarrow
Park. In Martindale,* the road loses sight of the Lake, and
leads over a steep hill, bringing you again into view of Ullswater. Its lowest reach, four miles in length, is before you;
and the view terminated by the long ridge of Cross Fell in the
distance. Immediately under the eye is a deep-indented bay,
with a plot of fertile land, traversed by a small brook, and rendered cheerful by two or three substantial houses of a more ornamented and showy appearance than is usual in those wild spots.

From Pooley Bridge, at the foot of the Lake, Haweswater
may be conveniently visited. Haweswater is a lesser Ullswater,
with this advantage, that it remains undefiled by the intrusion
of bad taste.

Lowther Castle is about four miles from Pooley Bridge, and,
if during this Tour the Stranger has complained, as he will have
had reason to do, of a want of majestic trees, he may be abundantly recompensed for his loss in the far-spreading woods which
surround that mansion. Visitants, for the most part, see little
of the beauty of these magnificent grounds, being content with
the view from the Terrace; but the whole course of the Lowther, from Askham to the bridge under Brougham Hall, presents almost at every step some new feature of river, woodland, and rocky landscape. A portion of this tract has, from its
beauty, acquired the name of the Elysian Fields ;—but the course
of the stream can only be followed by the pedestrian.

NOTE.—*Vide* p. 227.—About 200 yards beyond the last house on the
Keswick side of Rydal village the road is cut through a low wooded rock,
called Thrang Crag. The top of it, which is only a few steps on the
south side, affords the best view of the Vale which is to be had by a
Traveller who confines himself to the public road.

* See page 308.

SECTION FIRST.

VIEW OF THE COUNTRY AS FORMED BY NATURE.

AT Lucerne, in Switzerland, is shewn a Model of the Alpine country which encompasses the Lake of the four Cantons. The Spectator ascends a little platform, and sees mountains, lakes, glaciers, rivers, woods, waterfalls, and vallies, with their cottages, and every other object contained in them, lying at his feet; all things being represented in their appropriate colours. It may be easily conceived that this exhibition affords an exquisite delight to the imagination, tempting it to wander at will from valley to valley, from mountain to mountain, through the deepest recesses of the Alps. But it supplies also a more substantial pleasure: for the sublime and beautiful region, with all its hidden treasures, and their bearings and relations to each other, is thereby comprehended and understood at once.

Something of this kind, without touching upon minute details and individualities which would only confuse and embarrass, will here be attempted, in respect to the Lakes in the north of England, and the vales and mountains enclosing and surrounding them. The delineation, if tolerably executed, will, in some instances, communicate to the traveller, who has already seen the objects, new information; and will assist in giving to his recollections a more orderly arrangement than his own opportunities of observing may have permitted him to make; while it will be still more useful to the future traveller, by directing his attention at once to distinctions in things which, without such previous aid, a length of time only could enable him to discover. It is hoped, also, that this Essay may become generally serviceable, by leading to habits of more exact and considerate observation than, as far as the writer knows, have hitherto been applied to local scenery.

To begin, then, with the main outlines of the country;—I know not how to give the reader a distinct image of these more readily, than by requesting him to place himself with me, in imagination, upon some given point ; let it be the top of either of the mountains, Great Gavel, or Scawfell ; or, rather, let us suppose our station to be a cloud hanging midway between those two mountains, at not more than half a mile's distance from the summit of each, and not many yards above their highest elevation ; we shall then see stretched at our feet a number of vallies, not fewer than eight, diverging from the point, on which we are supposed to stand, like spokes from the nave of a wheel. First, we note, lying to the south-east, the vale of Langdale,* which will conduct the eye to the long lake of Winandermere, stretched nearly to the sea; or rather to the sands of the vast bay of Morcamb, serving here for the rim of this imaginary wheel ;— let us trace it in a direction from the south-east towards the south, and we shall next fix our eyes upon the vale of Coniston, running up likewise from the sea, but not (as all the other vallies do) to the nave of the wheel, and therefore it may be not inaptly represented as a broken spoke sticking in the rim. Looking forth again, with an inclination towards the west, we see immediately at our feet the vale of Duddon, in which is no lake, but a copious stream, winding among fields, rocks, and mountains, and terminating its course in the sands of Duddon. The fourth vale, next to be observed, viz. that of the Esk, is of the same general character as the last, yet beautifully discriminated from it by peculiar features. Its stream passes under the woody steep upon which stands Muncaster Castle, the ancient seat of the Penningtons, and after forming a short and narrow æstuary enters the sea below the small town of Ravenglass. Next, almost due west, look down into, and along the deep valley of Wastdale, with its little chapel and half a dozen neat dwellings scattered upon a plain of meadow and corn-ground intersected with stone walls apparently innumerable, like a large piece of lawless patch-work, or an array of mathematical figures, such as in the ancient schools of geometry might have been sportively and fantastically traced out upon sand. Beyond this little fertile plain lies, within a bed of steep mountains, the long, narrow, stern, and desolate lake of Wastdale ; and, beyond this, a dusky

---

* Anciently spelt Langden, and so called by the old inhabitants to this day— *dean,* from which the latter part of the word is derived, being in many parts of England a name for a valley.

tract of level ground conducts the eye to the Irish Sea. The stream that issues from Wast-water is named the Irt, and falls into the æstuary of the river Esk. Next comes in view Ennerdale, with its lake of bold and somewhat savage shores. Its stream, the Ehen or Enna, flowing through a soft and fertile country, passes the town of Egremont, and the ruins of the castle,—then, seeming, like the other rivers, to break through the barrier of sand thrown up by the winds on this tempestuous coast, enters the Irish Sea. The vale of Buttermere, with the lake and village of that name, and Crummock-water, beyond, next present themselves. We will follow the main stream, the Coker, through the fertile and beautiful vale of Lorton, till it is lost in the Derwent, below the noble ruins of Cockermouth Castle. Lastly, Borrowdale, of which the vale of Keswick is only a continuation, stretching due north, brings us to a point nearly opposite to the vale of Winandermere with which we began. From this it will appear, that the image of a wheel, thus far exact, is little more than one half complete; but the deficiency on the eastern side may be supplied by the vales of Wytheburn, Ulswater, Hawswater, and the vale of Grasmere and Rydal; none of these, however, run up to the central point between Great Gavel and Scawfell. From this, hitherto our central point, take a flight of not more than four or five miles eastward to the ridge of Helvellyn, and you will look down upon Wytheburn and St. John's Vale, which are a branch of the vale of Keswick; upon Ulswater, stretching due east:—and not far beyond to the south-east (though from this point not visible) lie the vale and lake of Hawswater; and lastly, the vale of Grasmere, Rydal, and Ambleside, brings you back to Winandermere, thus completing, though on the eastern side in a somewhat irregular manner, the representative figure of the wheel.

Such, concisely given, is the general topographical view of the country of the Lakes in the north of England; and it may be observed, that, from the circumference to the centre, that is, from the sea or plain country to the mountain stations specified, there is—in the several ridges that enclose these vales, and divide them from each other, I mean in the forms and surfaces, first of the swelling grounds, next of the hills and rocks, and lastly of the mountains—an ascent of almost regular gradation, from elegance and richness, to their highest point of grandeur

and sublimity.   It follows therefore from this, first, that these
rocks, hills, and mountains, must present themselves to view
in stages rising above each other, the mountains clustering together towards the central point ; and next, that an observer
familiar with the several vales, must, from their various position
in relation to the sun, have had before his eyes every possible
embellishment of beauty, dignity, and splendour, which light
and shadow can bestow upon objects so diversified.   For example, in the vale of Winandermere, if the spectator looks for
gentle and lovely scenes, his eye is turned towards the south ;
if for the grand, towards the north : in the vale of Keswick,
which (as hath been said) lies almost due north of this, it is
directly the reverse.   Hence, when the sun is setting in summer far to the north-west, it is seen, by the spectator from the
shores or breast of Winandermere, resting among the summits
of the loftiest mountains, some of which will perhaps be half or
wholly hidden by clouds, or by the blaze of light which the orb
diffuses around it ; and the surface of the lake will reflect before
the eye correspondent colours through every variety of beauty,
and through all degrees of splendour.   In the vale of Keswick,
at the same period, the sun sets over the humbler regions of
the landscape, and showers down upon *them* the radiance which
at once veils and glorifies,—sending forth, meanwhile, broad
streams of rosy, crimson, purple, or golden light, towards the
grand mountains in the south and south-east, which, thus illuminated, with all their projections and cavities, and with an
intermixture of solemn shadows, are seen distinctly through a
cool and clear atmosphere.   Of course, there is as marked a
difference between the *noontide* appearance of these two opposite
vales.   The bedimming haze that overspreads the south, and
the clear atmosphere and determined shadows of the clouds
in the north, at the same time of the day, are each seen in these
several vales, with a contrast as striking.   The reader will easily
conceive in what degree the intermediate vales partake of a
kindred variety.

   I do not indeed know any tract of country in which, within so
narrow a compass, may be found an equal variety in the influences of light and shadow upon the sublime or beautiful features
of landscape ; and it is owing to the combined circumstances to
which the reader's attention has been directed.   From a point

between Great Gavel and Scawfell, a shepherd would not require more than an hour to descend into any one of eight of the principal vales by which he would be surrounded; and all the others lie (with the exception of Hawswater) at but a small distance. Yet, though clustered together, every valley has its distinct and separate character : in some instances, as if they had been formed in studied contrast to each other, and in others with the united pleasing differences and resemblances of a sisterly rivalship. This concentration of interest gives to the country a decided superiority over the most attractive districts of Scotland and Wales, especially for the pedestrian traveller. In Scotland and Wales are found, undoubtedly, individual scenes, which, in their several kinds, cannot be excelled. But, in Scotland, particularly, what long tracts of desolate country intervene! so that the traveller, when he reaches a spot deservedly of great celebrity, would find it difficult to determine how much of his pleasure is owing to excellence inherent in the landscape itself; and how much to an instantaneous recovery from an oppression left upon his spirits by the barrenness and desolation through which he has passed.

But to proceed with our survey ;—and, first, of the MOUNTAINS. Their *forms* are endlessly diversified, sweeping easily or boldly in simple majesty, abrupt and precipitous, or soft and elegant. In magnitude and grandeur they are individually inferior to the most celebrated of those in some other parts of this island; but, in the combinations which they make, towering above each other, or lifting themselves in ridges like the waves of a tumultuous sea, and in the beauty and variety of their surfaces and colours, they are surpassed by none.

The general *surface* of the mountains is turf, rendered rich and green by the moisture of the climate. Sometimes the turf, as in the neighbourhood of Newlands, is little broken, the whole covering being soft and downy pasturage. In other places rocks predominate; the soil is laid bare by torrents and burstings of water from the sides of the mountains in heavy rains; and not unfrequently their perpendicular sides are seamed by ravines (formed also by rains and torrents) which, meeting in angular points, entrench and scar the surface with numerous figures like the letters W. and Y.

In the ridge that divides Eskdale from Wasdale, granite is

found ; but the MOUNTAINS are for the most part composed of the stone by mineralogists termed schist, which, as you approach the plain country, gives place to limestone and freestone; but schist being the substance of the mountains, the predominant *colour* of their *rocky* parts is bluish, or hoary grey—the general tint of the lichens with which the bare stone is encrusted. With this blue or grey colour is frequently intermixed a red tinge, proceeding from the iron that interveins the stone, and impregnates the soil. The iron is the principle of decomposition in these rocks ; and hence, when they become pulverized, the elementary particles crumbling down, overspread in many places the steep and almost precipitous sides of the mountains with an intermixture of colours, like the compound hues of a dove's neck. When in the heat of advancing summer, the fresh green tint of the herbage has somewhat faded, it is again revived by the appearance of the fern profusely spread over the same ground : and, upon this plant, more than upon anything else, do the changes which the seasons make in the colouring of the mountains depend. About the first week in October, the rich green, which prevailed through the whole summer, is usually passed away. The brilliant and various colours of the fern are then in harmony with the autumnal woods; bright yellow or lemon colour, at the base of the mountains, melting gradually, through orange, to a dark russet brown towards the summits, where the plant, being more exposed to the weather, is in a more advanced state of decay. Neither heath nor furze are *generally* found upon the *sides* of these mountains, though in many places they are adorned by those plants, so beautiful when in flower. We may add, that the mountains are of height sufficient to have the surface towards the summit softened by distance, and to imbibe the finest aërial hues. In common also with other mountains, their apparent forms and colours are perpetually changed by the clouds and vapours which float round them : the effect indeed of mist or haze, in a country of this character, is like that of magic. I have seen six or seven ridges rising above each other, all created in a moment by the vapours upon the side of a mountain, which, in its ordinary appearance, shewed not a projecting point to furnish even a hint for such an operation.

I will take this opportunity of observing, that they who have studied the appearances of Nature feel that the superiority,

in point of visual interest, of mountainous over other countries
—is more strikingly displayed in winter than in summer. This,
as must be obvious, is partly owing to the *forms* of the mountains, which, of course, are not affected by the seasons; but
also, in no small degree, to the greater variety that exists in
their winter than their summer *colouring*. This variety is such,
and so harmoniously preserved, that it leaves little cause of
regret when the splendour of autumn is passed away. The oak-
coppices, upon the sides of the mountains, retain russet leaves;
the birch stands conspicuous with its silver stem and puce-
coloured twigs; the hollies, with green leaves and scarlet berries,
have come forth to view from among the deciduous trees, whose
summer foliage had concealed them; the ivy is now plentifully
apparent upon the stems and boughs of the trees, and upon the
steep rocks. In place of the deep summer-green of the herbage
and fern, many rich colours play into each other over the surface
of the mountains; turf (the tints of which are interchangeably
tawny-green, olive, and brown), beds of withered fern, and grey
rocks, being harmoniously blended together. The mosses and
lichens are never so fresh and flourishing as in winter, if it be
not a season of frost; and their minute beauties prodigally adorn
the foreground. Wherever we turn, we find these productions
of Nature, to which winter is rather favourable than unkindly,
scattered over the walls, banks of earth, rocks, and stones, and
upon the trunks of trees, with the intermixture of several species
of small fern, now green and fresh; and, to the observing
passenger, their forms and colours are a source of inexhaustable
admiration. Add to this the hoar-frost and snow, with all the
varieties they create, and which volumes would not be sufficient
to describe. I will content myself with one instance of the
colouring produced by snow, which may not be uninteresting
to painters. It is extracted from the memorandum-book of a
friend; and for its accuracy I can speak, having been an eye-
witness of the appearance. 'I observed,' says he, 'the beautiful
effect of the drifted snow upon the mountains, and the perfect
tone of colour. From the top of the mountains downwards a
rich olive was produced by the powdery snow and the grass,
which olive was warmed with a little brown, and in this way
harmoniously combined, by insensible gradations, with the white.
The drifting took away the monotony of snow; and the whole

vale of Grasmere, seen from the terrace walk in Easedale, was as varied, perhaps more so, than even in the pomp of autumn. In the distance was Loughrigg-Fell, the basin-wall of the lake : this, from the summit downward, was a rich orange-olive ; then the lake of a bright olive-green, nearly the same tint as the snow-powdered mountain tops and high slopes in Easedale ; and lastly, the church, with its firs, forming the centre of the view. Next to the church came nine distinguishable hills, six of them with woody sides turned towards us, all of them oak-copses with their bright red leaves and snow-powdered twigs ; these hills—so variously situated in relation to each other, and to the view in general, so variously powdered, some only enough to give the herbage a rich brown tint, one intensely white and lighting up all the others—were yet so placed, as in the most inobtrusive manner to harmonise by contrast with a perfect naked, snow-less bleak summit in the far distance.'

Having spoken of the forms, surface, and colour of the mountains, let us descend into the VALES. Though these have been represented under the general image of the spokes of a wheel, they are, for the most part, winding; the windings of many being abrupt and intricate. And, it may be observed, that, in one circumstance, the general shape of them all has been determined by that primitive conformation through which so many became receptacles of lakes. For they are not formed, as are most of the celebrated Welsh vallies, by an approximation of the sloping bases of the opposite mountains towards each other, leaving little more between than a channel for the passage of a hasty river ; but the bottom of these vallies is mostly a spacious and gently declining area, apparently level as the floor of a temple, or the surface of a lake, and broken in many cases, by rocks and hills, which rise up like islands from the plain. In such of the vallies as make many windings, these level areas open upon the traveller in succession, divided from each other sometimes by a mutual approximation of the hills, leaving only passage for a river, sometimes by correspondent windings, without such approximation ; and sometimes by a bold advance of one mountain towards that which is opposite it. It may here be observed with propriety that the several rocks and hills, which have been described as rising up like islands from the level area of the vale, have regulated the choice of the inhabitants in the situation of their dwellings. Where none of these are found, and the inclination of the ground is not sufficiently rapid easily to carry off the waters, (as in the higher part of Langdale, for instance,) the houses are not sprinkled over the middle of the vales, but confined to their sides, being placed merely so far up the mountain as to be protected from the floods. But where these rocks and hills have been scattered over the plain of the vale, (as in Grasmere, Donnerdale, Eskdale, &c.) the beauty which they give to the scene is much heightened by a single cottage, or cluster of cottages, that will be almost always found under them, or upon their sides; dryness and shelter having tempted the Dalesmen to fix their habitations there.

I shall now speak of the LAKES of this country. The form of the lake is most perfect when, like Derwent-water, and some of the smaller lakes, it least resembles that of a river ;—I mean, when being looked at from any given point where the whole may be seen at once, the width of it bears such proportion to the length, that, however the outline may be diversified by far-receding bays, it never assumes the shape of a river, and is contemplated with that placid and quiet feeling which belongs peculiarly to the lake—as a body of still water under the influence of no current ; reflecting therefore the clouds, the light, and all the imagery of the sky and surrounding hills ; expressing also and making visible the changes of the atmosphere, and motions of the lightest breeze, and subject to agitation only from the winds—

> ————The visible scene
> Would enter unawares into his mind
> With all its solemn imagery, its rocks,
> Its woods, and that uncertain heaven received
> Into the bosom of the *steady* lake !

It must be noticed, as a favourable characteristic of the lakes of this country, that, though several of the largest, such as Winandermere, Ulswater, Hawswater, do, when the whole length of them is commanded from an elevated point, loose somewhat of the peculiar form of the lake, and assume the resemblance of a magnificent river ; yet, as their shape is winding, (particularly that of Ulswater and Hawswater) when the view of the whole is obstructed by those barriers which determine the windings, and the spectator is confined to one reach, the appropriate feeling is revived ; and one lake may thus in succession present to the eye the essential characteristic of many. But, though the forms of the large lakes have this advantage, it is nevertheless favourable to the beauty of the country that the largest of them are comparatively small; and that the same vale generally furnishes a succession of lakes, instead of being filled with one. The vales in North Wales, as hath been observed, are not formed for the reception of lakes; those of Switzerland, Scotland, and this part of the North of England, *are* so formed; but, in Switzerland and Scotland, the proportion of diffused water is often too great, as at the lake of Geneva for instance, and in most of the Scotch lakes. No doubt it sounds magnificent and flatters the imagination, to hear at a distance of expanses of water so many leagues in length and miles in width; and such ample room may be delightful to the fresh-water sailor, scudding with a lively breeze amid the rapidly-shifting scenery. But, who ever travelled along the banks of Loch-Lomond, variegated as the lower part is by islands, without feeling that a speedier termination of the long vista of blank water would be acceptable; and without wishing for an interposition of green meadows, trees, and cottages, and a sparkling stream to run by his side? In fact, a notion, of grandeur, as connected with magnitude, has seduced persons of taste into a general mistake upon this subject. It is much more desirable, for the purposes of pleasure, that lakes should be numerous, and small or middle-sized, than large, not only for communication by walks and rides, but for variety, and for recurrence of similar appearances. To illustrate this by one instance:—how pleasing is it to have a ready and frequent opportunity of watching, at the outlet of a lake, the stream pushing its way among the rocks in lively contrast with the stillness from which it has escaped; and how amusing to compare its noisy and turbulent motions with the gentle playfulness of the breezes, that may be starting up or wandering here and there over the faintly-rippled surface of the broad water! I may add, as a general remark, that, in lakes of great width, the shores cannot be distinctly seen at the same time, and therefore contribute little to mutual illustration and ornament; and, if the opposite shores are out of sight of each other, like those of the American and Asiatic lakes, then unfortunately the traveller is reminded of a nobler object; he has the blankness of a sea-prospect without the grandeur and accompanying sense of power.

As the comparatively small size of the lakes in the North of England is favourable to the production of variegated landscape, their *boundary-line* also is for the most part gracefully or boldly indented. That uniformity which prevails in the primitive frame of the lower grounds among all chains or clusters of mountains where large bodies of still water are bedded, is broken by the *secondary* agents of Nature, ever at work to supply the deficiences of the mould in which things were originally cast. Using the word *deficiences*, I do not speak with reference to those stronger emotions which a region of mountains is peculiarly fitted to excite. The bases of those huge barriers may run for a long space in straight lines, and these parallel to each other; the opposite sides of a profound vale may ascend as exact counterparts, or in mutual reflection, like the billows of a troubled sea; and the impression be, from its very simplicity, more awful and sublime. Sublimity is the result of Nature's first great dealings with the superficies of the Earth; but the general tendency of her subsequent operations is towards the production of beauty; by a multiplicity of symmetrical parts uniting in a consistent whole. This is every where exemplified along the margins of these lakes. Masses of rock, that have been precipitated from the heights into the area of waters, lie in some places like stranded ships; or have acquired the compact structure of jutting piers; or project in little peninsulas crested with native wood. The smallest rivulet—one whose silent influx is scarcely noticeable in a season of dry weather—so faint is the dimple made by it on the surface of the smooth lake—will be found to have been not useless in shaping, by its deposits of gravel and soil in time of flood, a curve that would not otherwise have existed. But the more powerful brooks, encroaching upon the level of the lake, have, in course of time, given birth to ample promontories of sweeping outline that contrast boldly with the longitudinal base of the steeps on the opposite shore; while their flat or gently-sloping surfaces never fail to introduce, into the midst of desolation and barrenness, the elements of fertility, even where the habitations of men may not have been raised. These alluvial promontories, however, threaten, in some places, to bisect the waters which they have long adorned; and, in course of ages, they will cause some of the lakes to dwindle into numerous and insignificant pools; which, in their turn, will finally be filled up. But, checking these intrusive calculations, let us rather be content with appearances as they are, and pursue in imagination the meandering shores, whether rugged steeps, admitting of no cultivation, descend into the water; or gently-sloping lawns and woods, or flat and fertile meadows, stretch between the margin of the lake and the mountains. Among minuter recommendations will be noticed, especially along bays exposed to the setting-in of strong winds, the curved rim of fine blue gravel, thrown up in course of time by the waves, half of it perhaps gleaming from under the water, and the corresponding half of a lighter hue; and in other parts bordering the lake, groves, if I may so call them, of reeds and bulrushes; or plots of water-lilies lifting up their large target-shaped leaves to the breeze, while the white flower is heaving upon the wave.

3 To these may naturally be added the birds that enliven the waters. Wild-ducks in spring-time hatch their young in the islands, and upon reedy shores;—the sand-piper, flitting along the stony margins, by its restless note attracts the eye to motions as restless:—upon some jutting rock, or at the edge of a smooth meadow, the stately heron may be descried with folded wings, that might seem to have caught their delicate hue from the blue waters, by the side of which she watches for her sustenance. In winter, the lakes are sometimes resorted to by wild swans; and in that season habitually by widgeons, goldings, and other aquatic fowl of the smaller species. Let me be allowed the aid of verse to describe the evolutions which these visitants sometimes perform, on a fine day towards the close of winter.

> Mark how the feather'd tenants of the flood,
> With grace of motion that might scarcely seem
> Inferior to angelical, prolong
> Their curious pastime! shaping in mid air
> (And sometimes with ambitious wing that soars
> High as the level of the mountain tops,)
> A circuit ampler than the lake beneath,
> Their own domain;—but ever, while intent
> On tracing and retracing that large round,
> Their jubilant activity evolves
> Hundreds of curves and circlets, to and fro,
> Upward and downward, progress intricate
> Yet unperplex'd, as if one spirit swayed
> Their indefatigable flight.—'Tis done—
> Ten times, or more, I fancied it had ceased;

But lo! the vanish'd company again
Ascending;—they approach—I hear their wings
Faint, faint, at first, and then an eager sound
Past in a moment—and as faint again!
They tempt the sun to sport amid their plumes;
They tempt the water or the gleaming ice,
To shew them a fair image;—'tis themselves,
Their own fair forms, upon the glimmering plain,
Painted more soft and fair as they descend
Almost to touch;—then up again aloft,
Up with a sally and a flash of speed,
As if they scorn'd both resting-place and rest!

The ISLANDS, dispersed among these lakes, are neither so numerous nor so beautiful as might be expected from the account that has been given of the manner in which the level areas of the vales are so frequently diversified by rocks, hills, and hillocks, scattered over them; nor are they ornamented (as are several of the lakes in Scotland and Ireland) by the remains of castles or other places of defence; nor with the still more interesting ruins of religious edifices. Every one must regret that scarcely a vestige is left of the Oratory, consecrated to the Virgin, which stood upon Chapel-Holm in Windermere, and that the Chauntry has disappeared, where mass used to be sung, upon St. Herbert's Island, Derwent-water. The islands of the last-mentioned lake are neither fortunately placed nor of pleasing shape; but if the wood upon them were managed with more taste, they might become interesting features in the landscape. There is a beautiful cluster on Winandermere; a pair pleasingly contrasted upon Rydal; nor must the solitary green island of Grasmere be forgotten. In the bosom of each of the lakes of Ennerdale and Devockwater is a single rock, which, owing to its neighbourhood to the sea, is—

The haunt of cormorants and sea-mews' clang,

a music well suited to the stern and wild character of the several scenes! It may be worth while here to mention (not as an object of beauty, but of curiosity) that there occasionally appears above the surface of Derwent-water, and always in the same place, a considerable tract of spongy ground covered with aquatic plants, which is called the Floating, but with more propriety might be named the Buoyant, Island; and, on one of the pools near the lake of Esthwaite, may sometimes be seen a mossy

Islet, with trees upon it, shifting about before the wind, a *lusus naturæ* frequent on the great rivers of America, and not unknown in other parts of the world.

—————fas habeas invisere Tiburis arva,
Albuneaeque lacum, atque umbras terrasque natantes.*

This part of the subject may be concluded with observing—that, from the multitude of brooks and torrents that fall into these lakes, and of internal springs by which they are fed, and which circulate through them like veins, they are truly living lakes, ' *vivi lacus ;*' and are thus discriminated from the stagnant and sullen pools frequent among mountains that have been formed by volcanoes, and from the shallow meres found in flat and fenny countries. The water is also of crystalline purity; so that, if it were not for the reflections of the incumbent mountains by which it is darkened, a delusion might be felt, by a person resting quietly in a boat on the bosom of Winandermere or Derwent-water, similar to that which Carver so beautifully describes when he was floating alone in the middle of lake Erie or Ontario, and could almost have imagined that his boat was suspended in an element as pure as air, or rather that the air and water were one.

Having spoken of Lakes I must not omit to mention, as a kindred feature of this country, those bodies of still water called TARNS. In the economy of Nature these are useful, as auxiliars to Lakes; for if the whole quantity of water which falls upon the mountains in time of storm were poured down upon the plains without intervention, in some quarters, of such receptacles, the habitable grounds would be much more subject than they are to inundation. But, as some of the collateral brooks spend their fury, finding a free course toward and also down the channel of the main stream of the vale before those that have to pass through the higher tarns and lakes have filled their several basins, a gradual distribution is effected; and the waters thus reserved, instead of uniting, to spread ravage and deformity, with those which meet with no such detention, contribute to support, for a length of time, the vigour of many streams without a fresh fall of rain. Tarns are found in some of the vales, and are numerous upon the mountains. A Tarn, in a *Vale*, implies, for the most part, that the bed of the vale is not happily

* See that admirable Idyllium, the Catillus and Salia, of Landor.

formed; that the water of the brooks can neither wholly escape, nor diffuse itself over a large area. Accordingly, in such situations, Tarns are often surrounded by an unsightly tract of boggy ground; but this is not always the case, and in the cultivated parts of the country, when the shores of the Tarn are determined, it differs only from the Lake in being smaller, and in belonging mostly to a smaller valley, or circular recess. Of, this class of miniature lakes, Loughrigg Tarn, near Grasmere, is the most beautiful example. It has a margin of green firm meadows, of rocks, and rocky woods, a few reeds here, a little company of water-lilies there, with beds of gravel or stone beyond; a tiny stream issuing neither briskly nor sluggishly out of it; but its feeding rills, from the shortness of their course, so small as to be scarcely visible. Five or six cottages are reflected in its peaceful bosom; rocky and barren steeps rise up above the hanging enclosures; and the solemn Pikes of Langdale overlook, from a distance, the low cultivated ridge of land that forms the northern boundary of this small, quiet, and fertile domain. The *mountain* Tarns can only be recommended to the notice of the inquisitive traveller who has time to spare. They are difficult of access and naked; yet some of them are, in their permanent forms, very grand; and there are accidents of things which would make the meanest of them interesting. At all events, one of these pools is an acceptable sight to the mountain wanderer; not merely as an incident that diversifies the prospect, but as forming in his mind a centre or conspicuous point to which objects, otherwise disconnected or insubordinated, may be referred. Some few have a varied outline, with bold heath-clad promontories; and, as they mostly lie at the foot of a steep precipice, the water, where the sun is not shining upon it, appears black and sullen; and, round the margin, huge stones and masses of rock are scattered; some defying conjecture as to the means by which they came thither; and others obviously fallen from on high—the contribution of ages! A not unpleasing sadness is induced by this perplexity, and these images of decay; while the prospect of a body of pure water unattended with groves and other cheerful rural images, by which fresh water is usually accompanied, and unable to give furtherance to the meagre vegetation around it—excites a sense of some repulsive power strongly put forth, and thus deepens the melan-

choly natural to such scenes. Nor is the feeling of solitude
often more forcibly or more solemnly impressed than by the side
of one of these mountain pools : though desolate and forbidding,
it seems a distinct place to repair to ; yet where the visitants
must be rare, and there can be no disturbance. Water-fowl
flock hither ; and the lonely angler may here be seen ; but the
imagination, not content with this scanty allowance of society,
is tempted to attribute a voluntary power to every change
which takes place in such a spot, whether it be the breeze that
wanders over the surface of the water, or the splendid lights of
evening resting upon it in the midst of awful precipices.

> There, sometimes does a leaping fish
> Send through the tarn a lonely cheer;
> The crags repeat the raven's croak
> In symphony austere :
> Thither the rainbow comes, the cloud,
> And mists that spread the flying shroud,
> And sunbeams, and the sounding blast.

It will be observed that this country is bounded on the south
and east by the sea, which combines beautifully, from many
elevated points, with the inland scenery; and, from the bay of
Morecamb, the sloping shores and back-ground of distant mountains are seen, composing pictures equally distinguished for
amenity and grandeur. But the æstuaries on this coast are in
a great measure bare at low water;* and there is no instance
of the sea running far up among the mountains, and mingling
with the lakes, which are such in the strict and usual sense of
the word, being of fresh water. Nor have the streams, from
the shortness of their course, time to acquire that body of water
necessary to confer upon them much majesty. In fact, the most
considerable, while they continue in the mountain and lake-
country, are rather large brooks than rivers. The water is perfectly pellucid, through which in many places are seen, to a
great depth, their beds of rock, or of blue gravel, which give to
the water itself an exquisitely cerulean colour : this is particu-

---

* In fact there is not an instance of a harbour on the Cumberland side of the
Solway frith that is not dry at low water; that of Ravenglass, at the mouth of
the Esk, as a natural harbour is much the best. The Sea appears to have been
retiring slowly for ages from this coast. From Whitehaven to St. Bees extends
a tract of level ground, about five miles in length, which formerly must have
been under salt water, so as to have made an island of the high ground that
stretches between it and the Sea.

larly striking in the rivers Derwent and Duddon, which may be compared, such and so various are their beauties, to any two rivers of equal length of course in any country. The number of the torrents and smaller brooks is infinite, with their water-falls and water-breaks ; and they need not here be described. I will only observe that, as many, even of the smallest rills, have either found, or made for themselves, recesses in the sides of the mountains or in the vales, they have tempted the primitive inhabitants to settle near them for shelter; and hence, cottages so placed, by seeming to withdraw from the eye, are the more endeared to the feelings.

The Woods consist chiefly of oak, ash, and birch, and here and there Wych-elm, with underwood of hazel, the white and black thorn, and hollies; in moist places alders and willows abound; and yews among the rocks. Formerly the whole country must have been covered with wood to a great height up the mountains ; where native Scotch firs* must have grown in great profusion, as they do in the northern part of Scotland to this day. But not one of these old inhabitants has existed, perhaps, for some hundreds of years; the beautiful traces, how-ever, of the universal sylvan† appearance the country formerly had, yet survive in the native coppice-woods that have been pro-tected by inclosures, and also in the forest-trees and hollies, which, though disappearing fast, are yet scattered both over the inclosed and uninclosed parts of the mountains. The same is expressed by the beauty and intricacy with which the fields and coppice woods are often intermingled : the plough of the first settlers having followed naturally the veins of richer, dryer, or less stony soil ; and thus it has shaped out an intermixture of wood and lawn, with a grace and wildness which it would have been impossible for the hand of studied art to produce. Other trees have been introduced within these last fifty years, such as beeches, larches, limes, &c. and plantations of firs, seldom with advantage, and often with great injury to the appearance of the country ; but the sycamore (which I believe was brought into this island from Germany, not more than two hundred years

* This species of fir is in character much superior to the American which has usurped its place : Where the fir is planted for ornament, let it be by all means of the aboriginal species, which can only be procured from the Scotch nurseries.

† A squirrel (so I have heard the old people of Wytheburn say) might have gone from their chapel to Keswick without alighting on the ground.

ago) has long been the favourite of the cottagers ; and, with the fir, has been chosen to screen their dwellings : and is sometimes found in the fields whither the winds or the waters may have carried its seeds.

The want most felt, however, is that of timber trees. There are few *magnificent* ones to be found near any of the lakes ; and unless greater care be taken, there will, in a short time, scarcely be left an ancient oak that would repay the cost of felling. The neighbourhood of Rydal, notwithstanding the havoc which has been made, is yet nobly distinguished. In the woods of Low-ther, also, is found an almost matchless store of ancient trees, and the majesty and wildness of the native forest.

Among the smaller vegetable ornaments must be reckoned the bilberry, a ground plant, never so beautiful as in early spring, when it is seen under bare or budding trees, that im-perfectly intercept the sun-shine, covering the rocky knolls with a pure mantle of fresh verdure, more lively than the herbage of the open fields ;—the broom, that spreads luxuriantly along rough pastures, and in the month of June interveins the steep copses with its golden blossoms ;—and the juniper, a rich ever-green, that thrives in spite of cattle, upon the uninclosed parts of the mountains :—the Dutch myrtle diffuses fragrance in moist places ; and there is an endless variety of brilliant flowers in the fields and meadows, which, if the agriculture of the country were more carefully attended to, would disappear. Nor can I omit again to notice the lichens and mosses : their profusion, beauty, and variety, exceed those of any other country I have seen.

It may now be proper to say a few words respecting climate, and 'skiey influences,' in which this region, as far as the character of its landscapes is affected by them, may, upon the whole, be considered fortunate. The country is, indeed, subject to much bad weather, and it has been ascertained that twice as much rain falls here as in many parts of the island ; but the number of black drizzling days, that blot out the face of things, is by no means *proportionally* great. Nor is a continuance of thick, flagging, damp air, so common as in the West of Eng-land and Ireland. The rain here comes down heartily, and is frequently succeeded by clear, bright weather, when every brook is vocal, and every torrent sonorous ; brooks and torrents, which are never muddy, even in the heaviest floods, except, after a drought, they happen to be defiled for a short time by waters that have swept along dusty roads, or have broken out into ploughed fields. Days of unsettled weather, with partial showers, are very frequent; but the showers, darkening, or brightning, as they fly from hill to hill, are not less grateful to the eye than finely interwoven passages of gay and sad music are touching to the ear. Vapours exhaling from the lakes and meadows after sun-rise, in a hot season, or, in moist weather, brooding upon the heights, or descending towards the valleys with inaudible motion, give a visionary character to every thing around them; and are in themselves so beautiful, as to dispose us to enter into the feelings of those simple nations (such as the Laplanders of this day) by whom they are taken for guardian deities of the mountains; or to sympathise with others who have fancied these delicate apparitions to be the spirits of their departed ancestors. Akin to these are fleecy clouds resting upon the hill-tops; they are not easily managed in picture, with their accompaniments of blue sky; but how glorious are they in Nature! how pregnant with imagination for the poet! and the height of the Cumbrian mountains is sufficient to exhibit daily and hourly instances of those mysterious attachments. Such clouds, cleaving to their stations, or lifting up suddenly their glittering heads from behind rocky barriers, or hurrying out of sight with speed of the sharpest sledge—will often tempt an inhabitant to congratulate himself on belonging to a country of mists and clouds and storms, and make him think of the blank sky of Egypt, and of the cerulean vacancy of Italy, as an unanimated and even a sad spectacle. The atmosphere, however, as in every country subject to much rain, is frequently unfavourable to landscape, especially when keen winds succeed the rain which are apt to produce coldness, spottiness, and an unmeaning or repulsive detail in the distance;—a sunless frost, under a canopy of leaden and shapeless clouds, is, as far as it allows things to be seen, equally disagreeable.

It has been said that in human life there are moments worth ages. In a more subdued tone of sympathy may we affirm, that in the climate of England there are, for the lover of Nature, days which are worth whole months,—I might say—even years. One of these favoured days sometimes occurs in spring-time, when that soft air is breathing over the blossoms and new-born verdure, which inspired Buchanan with his beautiful Ode to the first of May; the air, which, in the luxuriance of his fancy, he likens to that of the golden age,—to that which gives motion to the funereal cypresses on the banks of Lethe ;—to the air which is to salute beatified spirits when expiatory fires shall have consumed the earth with all her habitations. But it is in autumn that days of such affecting influence most frequently intervene ;—the atmosphere seems refined, and the sky rendered more crystalline, as the vivifying heat of the year abates; the lights and shadows are more delicate; the colouring is richer and more finely harmonised; and, in this season of stillness, the ear being unoccupied, or only gently excited, the sense of vision becomes more susceptible of its appropriate enjoyments. A resident in a country like this which we are treating of, will agree with me, that the presence of a lake is indispensable to exhibit in perfection the beauty of one of these days ; and he must have experienced, while looking on the unruffled waters, that the imagination, by their aid, is carried into recesses of feeling otherwise impenetrable. The reason of this is, that the heavens are not only brought down into the bosom of the earth, but that the earth is mainly looked at, and thought of, through the medium of a purer element. The happiest time is when the equinoxial gales are departed ; but their fury may probably be called to mind by the sight of a few shattered boughs, whose leaves do not differ in colour from the faded foliage of the stately oaks from which these relics of the storm depend : all else speaks of tranquillity ;—not a breath of air, no restlessness of insects, and not a moving object perceptible—except the clouds gliding in the depths of the lake, or the traveller passing along, an inverted image, whose motion seems governed by the quiet of a time, to which its archetype, the living person, is, perhaps, insensible :—or it may happen, that the figure of one of the larger birds, a raven or a heron, is crossing silently among the reflected clouds, while the voice of the real bird, from the element aloft, gently awakens in the spectator the recollection of appetites and instincts, pursuits and occupations, that deform and agitate the world,—yet have no power to prevent Nature from putting on an aspect capable of satisfying the most intense cravings for the tranquil, the lovely, and the perfect, to which man, the noblest of her creatures, is subject.

Thus far, of climate, as influencing the feelings through its effect on the objects of sense. We may add, that whatever has been said upon the advantages derived to these scenes from a changeable atmosphere, would apply, perhaps still more forcibly, to their appearance under the varied solemnities of night. Milton, it will be remembered, has given a *clouded* moon to Paradise itself. In the night-season also, the narrowness of the vales, and comparative smallness of the lakes, are especially adapted to bring surrounding objects home to the eye and to the heart. The stars, taking their stations above the hill-tops, are contemplated from a spot like the Abyssinian recess of Rasselas, with much more touching interest than they are likely to excite when looked at from an open country with ordinary undulations; and it must be obvious, that it is the *bays* only of large lakes that can present such contrasts of light and shadow as those of smaller dimensions display from every quarter. A deep contracted valley, with diffused waters, such a valley and plains level and wide as those of Chaldea, are the two extremes in which the beauty of the heavens and their connexion with the earth are most sensibly felt. Nor do the advantages I have been speaking of imply here an exclusion of the aerial effects of distance. These are insured by the height of the mountains, and are found, even in the narrowest vales, where they lengthen in perspective, or act (if the expression may be used) as telescopes for the open country.

The subject would bear to be enlarged upon: but I will conclude this section with a night-scene suggested by the Vale of Keswick. The Fragment is well known; but it gratifies me to insert it, as the Writer was one of the first who led the way to a worthy admiration of this country.

> Now sunk the sun, now twilight sunk, and night
> Rode in her zenith; not a passing breeze
> Sigh'd to the grove, which in the midnight air
> Stood motionless, and in the peaceful floods
> Inverted hung: for now the billows slept
> Along the shore, nor heav'd the deep; but spread
> A shining mirror to the moon's pale orb,
> Which, dim and waning, o'er the shadowy cliffs,
> The solemn woods, and spiry mountain tops,
> Her glimmering faintness threw: now every eye,
> Oppress'd with toil, was drown'd in deep repose,
> Save that the unseen Shepherd in his watch,

Propp'd on his crook, stood listening by the fold,
And gaz'd the starry vault, and pendant moon ;
Nor voice, nor sound, broke on the deep serene ;
But the soft murmur of swift-gushing rills,
Forth issuing from the mountain's distant steep,
(Unheard till now, and now scarce heard) proclaim'd
All things at rest, and imag'd the still voice
Of quiet, whispering in the ear of Night.*

Section Second.

ASPECT OF THE COUNTRY, AS AFFECTED BY ITS INHABITANTS.

Hitherto I have chiefly spoken of the features by which
Nature has discriminated this country from others. I will now
describe, in general terms, in what manner it is indebted to the
hand of man. What I have to notice on this subject will eman-
ate most easily and perspicuously from a description of the ancient and present inhabitants, their occupations, their condition
of life, the distribution of landed property among them, and the
tenure by which it is holden.

The reader will suffer me here to recall to his mind the
shapes of the vallies, and their position with respect to each
other, and the forms and substance of the intervening mountains. He will people the vallies with lakes and rivers : the
coves and sides of the mountains with pools and torrents ; and
will bound half of the circle which we have contemplated by the
sands of the sea, or by the sea itself. He will conceive that,
from the point upon which he stood, he looks down upon this
scene before the country had been penetrated by any inhabitants :
—to vary his sensations, and to break in upon their stillness, he
will form to himself an image of the tides visiting and re-visit-
ing the friths, the main sea dashing against the bolder shore,

* Dr. Brown, the author of this fragment, was from his infancy brought up
in Cumberland, and should have remembered that the practice of folding sheep
by night is unknown among these mountains, and that the image of the Shepherd upon the watch is out of its place, and belongs only to countries, with a
warmer climate, that are subject to ravages from beasts of prey. It is pleasing
to notice a dawn of imaginative feeling in these verses. Tickel, a man of no
common genius, chose, for the subject of a Poem, Kensington Gardens, in preference to the Banks of the Derwent, within a mile or two of which he was born.
But this was in the reign of Queen Anne, or George the first. Progress must
have been made in the interval ; though the traces of it, except in the works of
Thomson and Dyer, are not very obvious.

the rivers pursuing their course to be lost in the mighty mass of waters. He may see or hear in fancy the winds sweeping over the lakes, or piping with a loud voice among the mountain peaks; and, lastly, may think of the primeval woods shedding and renewing their leaves with no human eye to notice, or human heart to regret or welcome the change. 'When the first settlers entered this region (says an animated writer) they found it overspread with wood; forest trees, the fir, the oak, the ash, and the birch had skirted the fells, tufted the hills, and shaded the vallies, through centuries of silent solitude; the birds and beasts of prey reigned over the meeker species; and the *bellum inter omnia* maintained the balance of Nature in the empire of beasts.'

Such was the state and appearance of this region when the aboriginal colonists of the Celtic tribes were first driven or drawn towards it, and became joint tenants with the wolf, the boar, the wild bull, the red deer, and the leigh, a gigantic species of deer which has been long extinct; while the inaccessible crags were occupied by the falcon, the raven, and the eagle. The inner parts were too secluded, and of too little value, to participate much of the benefit of Roman manners; and though these conquerors encouraged the Britons to the improvement of their lands in the plain country of Furness and Cumberland, they seem to have had little connexion with the mountains, except for military purposes, or in subservience to the profit they drew from the mines.

When the Romans retired from Great Britain, it is well known that these mountain-fastnesses furnished a protection to some unsubdued Britons, long after the more accessible and more fertile districts had been seized by the Saxon or Danish invader. A few, though distinct, traces of Roman forts or camps, as at Ambleside, and upon Dunmallet, and a few circles of rude stones attributed to the Druids,* are the only vestiges that re-

---

* It is not improbable that these circles were once numerous, and that many of them may yet endure in a perfect state, under no very deep covering of soil. A friend of the Author, while making a trench in a level piece of ground, not far from the banks of the Emont, but in no connection with that river, met with some stones which seemed to him formally arranged; this excited his curiosity, and proceeding, he uncovered a perfect circle of stones, from two to three or four feet high, with a *sanctum sanctorum*,—the whole a complete place of Druidical worship of small dimensions, having the same sort of relation to Stonehenge,

main upon the surface of the country, of these ancient occupants; and, as the Saxons and Danes, who succeeded to the
possession of the villages and hamlets which had been established by the Britons, seem at first to have confined themselves
to the open country,—we may descend at once to times long
posterior to the conquest by the Normans, when their feudal
polity was regularly established. We may easily conceive that
these narrow dales and mountain sides, choaked up as they must
have been with wood, lying out of the way of communication
with other parts of the Island, and upon the edge of a hostile
kingdom, could have little attraction for the high-born and
powerful; especially as the more open parts of the country furnished positions for castles and houses of defence, sufficient to
repel any of those sudden attacks, which, in the then rude state
of military knowledge, could be made upon them. Accordingly,
the more retired regions (and to such I am now confining myself) must have been neglected or shunned even by the persons
whose baronial or signioral rights extended over them, and left,

---

Long Meg and her Daughters near the river Eden, and Karl Lofts near Shap
(if this last be not Danish), that a rural chapel bears to a stately church, or to
one of our noble cathedrals. This interesting little monument having passed,
with the field in which it was found, into other hands, has been destroyed. It
is much to be regretted, that the striking relic of antiquity at Shap has been in
a great measure destroyed also.

The DAUGHTERS of LONG MEG are placed not in an oblong, as the STONES of
SHAP, but in a perfect circle, eighty yards in diameter, and seventy-two in number, and from above three yards high, to less than so many feet: a little way out
of the circle stands LONG MEG herself—a single stone eighteen feet high.

When the Author first saw this monument, he came upon it by surprize, therefore might over-rate its importance as an object; but he must say, that though
it is not to be compared with Stonehenge, he has not seen any other remains of
those dark ages, which can pretend to rival it in singularity and dignity of appearance.

> A weight of awe not easy to be borne
> Fell suddenly upon my spirit, cast
> From the dread bosom of the unknown past,
> When first I saw that sisterhood forlorn;—
> And Her, whose strength and stature seem to scorn
> The power of years—pre-eminent, and placed
> Apart, to overlook the circle vast.
> Speak, Giant-mother! tell it to the Morn,
> While she dispels the cumbrous shades of night;
> Let the Moon hear, emerging from a cloud,
> When, how, and wherefore, rose on British ground
> That wondrous Monument, whose mystic round
> Forth shadows, some have deemed, to mortal sight
> The inviolable God that tames the proud.

doubtless, partly as a place of refuge for outlaws and robbers, and partly granted out for the more settled habitation of a few vassals following the employment of shepherds or woodlanders. Hence these lakes and inner vallies are unadorned by any remains of ancient grandeur, castles, or monastic edifices, which are only found upon the skirts of the country, as Furness Abbey, Calder Abbey, the Priory of Lannercost, Gleaston Castle,—long ago a residence of the Flemings,—and the numerous ancient castles of the Cliffords, the Lucys, and the Dacres. On the southern side of these mountains, (especially in that part known by the name of Furness Fells, which is more remote from the borders,) the state of society would necessarily be more settled; though it also was fashioned, not a little, by its neighbourhood to a hostile kingdom. We will, therefore, give a sketch of the economy of the Abbots in the distribution of lands among their tenants, as similar plans were doubtless adopted by other Lords, and as the consequences have affected the face of the country materially to the present day, being, in fact, one of the principal causes which give it such a striking superiority, in beauty and interest, over all other parts of the island.

'When the Abbots of Furness,' says an author before cited, 'enfranchised their villains, and raised them to the dignity of customary tenants, the lands, which they had cultivated for their lord, were divided into whole tenements; each of which, besides the customary annual rent, was charged with the obligation of having in readiness a man completely armed for the king's service on the borders, or elsewhere; each of these whole tenements was again subdivided into four equal parts; each villain had one; and the party tenant contributed his share to the support of the man of arms, and of other burdens. These divisions were not properly distinguished; the land remained mixed; each tenant had a share through all the arable and meadow-land, and common of pasture over all the wastes. These sub-tenements were judged sufficient for the support of so many families; and no further division was permitted. These divisions and sub-divisions were convenient at the time for which they were calculated: the land, so parcelled out, was of necessity more attended to, and the industry greater, when more persons were to be supported by the produce of it. The frontier of the kingdom, within which Furness was considered, was in a constant state of attack and defence; more hands, therefore, were necessary to guard the coast, to repel an invasion from Scotland, or make reprisals on the hostile neighbour. The dividing the lands in such manner as has been shown, increased the number of inhabitants, and kept them at home till called for: and, the land being mixed, and the several tenants united in equipping the plough, the absence of the fourth man was no prejudice to the cultivation of his land, which was committed to the care of three.

'While the villains of Low Furness were thus distributed over the land, and employed in agriculture; those of High Furness were charged with the care of flocks and herds, to protect them from the wolves which lurked in the thickets, and in winter to browze them with the tender sprouts of hollies and ash. This custom was not till lately discontinued in High Furness; and holly-trees were carefully preserved for that purpose when all other wood was cleared off; large tracts of common being so covered with these trees, as to have the appearance of a forest of hollies. At the Shepherd's call, the flocks surrounded the holly-bush, and received the croppings at his hand, which they greedily nibbled up, bleating for more. The Abbots of Furness enfranchised these pastoral vassals, and permitted them to enclose *quillets* to their houses, for which they paid encroachment rent.'—West's *Antiquities of Furness.*

However desirable, for the purposes of defence, a numerous population might be, it was not possible to make at once the same numerous allotments among the untilled vallies, and upon the sides of the mountains, as had been made in the cultivated plains. The enfranchised shepherd or woodlander, having chosen there his place of residence, builds it of sods, or of the mountain-stone, and, with the permission of his lord, encloses, like Robinson Crusoe, a small croft or two immediately at his door for such animals as he wishes to protect. Others are happy to imitate his example, and avail themselves of the same privileges: and thus a population, mainly of Danish or Norse origin, as the dialect indicates, crept on towards the more secluded parts of the vallies. Chapels, daughters of some distant mother church, are first erected in the more open and fertile vales, as those of Bowness and Grasmere, offsets of Kendal: which again, after a period, as the settled population increases, become mother-churches to smaller edifices, planted, at length, in almost every dale throughout the country. The inclosures, formed by the tenantry, are for a long time confined to the home-steads ; and the arable and meadow land of the vales is possessed in common field ; the several portions being marked out by stones, bushes, or trees ; which portions, where the custom has survived, to this day are called *dales*, from the word *deylen*, to distribute ; but, while the valley was thus lying open, enclosures seem to have taken place upon the sides of the mountains; because the land there was not intermixed, and was of little comparative value ; and, therefore, small opposition would be made to its being appropriated by those to whose habitations it was contiguous. Hence the singular appearance which the sides of many of these mountains exhibit, intersected, as they are, almost to the summit, with stone walls. When first erected, these stone fences must have little disfigured the face of the country ; as part of the lines would every where be hidden by the quantity of native wood then remaining ; and the lines would also be broken (as they still are) by the rocks which interrupt and vary their course. In the meadows, and in those parts of the lower grounds where the soil has not been sufficiently drained, and could not afford a stable foundation, there, when the increasing value of land, and the inconvenience suffered from intermixed plots of ground in common field, had induced each inhabitant to enclose his own, they were compelled to make the fences of alders, willows, and other trees. These, where the native wood had disappeared, have frequently enriched the vallies with a sylvan appearance ; while the intricate intermixture of property has given to the fences a graceful irregularity, which, where large properties are prevalent, and large capitals employed in agriculture, is unknown. This sylvan appearance is heightened by the number of ash-trees planted in rows along the quick fences, and along the walls, for the purpose of browzing the cattle at the approach of winter. The branches are lopped off and strewn upon the pastures ; and when the cattle have stripped them of the leaves, they are used for repairing the hedges or for fuel.

We have thus seen a numerous body of Dalesmen creeping into possession of their home-steads, their little crofts, their mountain-enclosures ; and, finally, the whole vale is visibly divided ; except, perhaps, here and there some marshy ground, which, till fully drained, would not repay the trouble of enclosing. But these last partitions do not seem to have been general, till long after the pacification of the Borders, by the union of the two crowns: when the cause, which had first determined the distribution of land into such small parcels, had not only ceased, —but likewise a general improvement had taken place in the country, with a correspondent rise in the value of its produce. From the time of the union, it is certain that this species of feudal population must rapidly have diminished. That it was formerly much more numerous than it is at present, is evident from the multitude of tenements (I do not mean houses, but small divisions of land) which belonged formerly each to a several proprietor, and for which separate fines are paid to the manorial lord at this day. These are often in the proportion of four to one of the present occupants. 'Sir Launcelot Threlkeld, who lived in the reign of Henry VII., was wont to say, he had three noble houses, one for pleasure, Crosby, in Westmoreland, where he had a park full of deer; one for profit and warmth, wherein to reside in winter, namely, Yanwith, nigh Penrith; and the third, Threlkeld, (on the edge of the vale of Keswick,) well stocked with tenants to go with him to the wars.' But, as I have said, from the union of the two crowns, this numerous vassalage (their services not being wanted) would rapidly diminish; various tenements would be united in one possessor; and the aboriginal houses, probably little better than hovels, like the kraels of savages, or the huts of the Highlanders of Scotland, would fall into decay, and the places of many be supplied by substantial and comfortable buildings, a majority of which remain to this day scattered over the vallies, and are often the only dwellings found in them.

From the time of the erection of these houses, till within the last sixty years, the state of society, though no doubt slowly and gradually improving, underwent no material change. Corn was grown in these vales (through which no carriage-road had yet been made) sufficient upon each estate to furnish bread for each family, and no more: notwithstanding the union of several tenements, the possessions of each inhabitant still being small, in the same field was seen an intermixture of different crops; and the plough was interrupted by little rocks, mostly overgrown with wood, or by spongy places, which the tillers of the soil had neither leisure nor capital to convert into firm land. The storms and moisture of the climate induced them to sprinkle their upland property with outhouses of native stone, as places of shelter for their sheep, where, in tempestuous weather, food was distributed to them. Every family spun from its own flock the wool with which it was clothed; a weaver was here and there found among them; and the rest of their wants was supplied by the produce of the yarn, which they carded and spun in their own houses, and carried to market, either under their arms, or more frequently on pack-horses, a small train taking their way weekly down the valley or over the mountains to the most commodious town. They had, as I have said, their rural chapel, and of course their minister, in clothing or in manner of life, in no respect differing from themselves, except on the Sabbath-day; this was the sole distinguished individual among them; every thing else, person and possession, exhibited a perfect equality, a community of shepherds and agriculturists, proprietors, for the most part, of the lands which they occupied and cultivated.

While the process above detailed was going on, the native forest must have been every where receding; but trees were planted for the sustenance of the flocks in winter,—such was then the rude state of agriculture; and, for the same cause, it was necessary that care should be taken of some part of the growth of the native woods. Accordingly, in Queen Elizabeth's time, this was so strongly felt, that a petition was made to the Crown, praying, 'that the Blomaries in High Furness might be abolished, on account of the quantity of wood which was consumed in them for the use of the mines, to the great detriment of the cattle.' But this same cause, about a hundred years after, produced effects directly contrary to those which had been deprecated. The re-establishment, at that period, of furnaces upon a large scale, made it the interest of the people to convert the steeper and more stony of the enclosures, sprinkled over with remains of the native forest, into close woods, which, when cattle and sheep were excluded, rapidly sowed and thickened themselves. The reader's attention has been directed to the cause by which tufts of wood, pasturage, meadow, and arable land, with its various produce, are intricately intermingled in the same field; and he will now see, in like manner, how enclosures entirely of wood, and those of cultivated ground, are blended all over the country under a law of similar wildness.

An historic detail has thus been given of the manner in which the hand of man has acted upon the surface of the inner regions of this mountainous country, as incorporated with and subservient to the powers and processes of Nature. We will now take a view of the same agency—acting, within narrower bounds, for the production of the few works of art and accommodations of life which, in so simple a state of society, could be necessary. These are merely habitations of man and coverts for beasts, roads and bridges, and places of worship.

And to begin with the COTTAGES. They are scattered over the vallies, and under the hill sides, and on the rocks; and, even to this day, in the more retired dales, without any intrusion of more assuming buildings;

> Cluster'd like stars some few, but single most,
> And lurking dimly in their shy retreats,
> Or glancing on each other cheerful looks,
> Like separated stars with clouds between.—MS.

The dwelling-houses, and contiguous outhouses, are, in many instances, of the colour of the native rock, out of which they have been built; but, frequently the Dwelling or Fire-house, as it is ordinarily called, has been distinguished from the barn or byer by rough-cast and white wash, which, as the inhabitants are not hasty in renewing it, in a few years acquires, by the influence of weather, a tint at once sober and variegated. As these houses have been, from father to son, inhabited by persons engaged in the same occupations, yet necessarily with changes in their circumstances, they have received without incongruity additions and accommodations adapted to the needs of each successive occupant, who, being for the most part proprietor, was at liberty to follow his own fancy: so that these humble dwellings remind the contemplative spectator of a production of Nature, and may (using a strong expression) rather be said to have grown than to have been erected;—to have risen, by an instinct of their own, out of the native rock—so little is there in them of formality, such is their wildness and beauty. Among the numerous recesses and projections in the walls and in the different stages of their roofs, are seen bold and harmonious effects of contrasted sunshine and shadow. It is a favourable circumstance, that the strong winds, which sweep down the vallies, induced the inhabitants, at a time when the materials for building were easily procured, to furnish many of these dwellings with substantial porches; and such as have not this defence, are seldom unprovided with a projection of two large slates over their thresholds. Nor will the singular beauty of the chimneys escape the eye of the attentive traveller. Sometimes a low chimney, almost upon a level with the roof, is overlaid with a slate, supported upon four slender pillars, to prevent the wind from driving the smoke down the chimney. Others are of a quadrangular shape, rising one or two feet above the roof; which low square is often surmounted by a tall cylinder, giving to the cottage chimney the most beautiful shape in which it is ever seen. Nor will it be too fanciful or refined to remark, that there is a pleasing harmony between a tall chimney of this circular form, and the living column of smoke, ascending from it through the still air. These dwellings, mostly built, as has been said, of rough unhewn stone, are roofed with slates, which were rudely taken from the quarry before the present art of splitting them was understood, and are, therefore, rough and uneven in their surface, so that both the coverings and sides of the houses have furnished places of rest for the seeds of lichens, mosses, ferns, and flowers. Hence buildings, which in their very form call to mind the processes of Nature, do thus, clothed in part with a vegetable garb, appear to be received into the bosom of the living principle of things, as it acts and exists among the woods and fields; and, by their colour and their shape, affectingly direct the thoughts to that tranquil course of Nature and simplicity, along which the humble-minded inhabitants have, through so many generations, been led. Add the little garden with its shed for bee-hives, its small bed of pot-herbs, and its borders and patches of flowers for Sunday posies, with sometimes a choice few too much prized to be plucked; an orchard of proportioned size; a cheese-press, often supported by some tree near the door; a cluster of embowering sycamores for summer shade; with a tall fir, through which the winds sing when other trees are leafless; the little rill or household spout murmuring in all seasons;—combine these incidents and images together, and you have the representative idea of a mountain-cottage in this country so beautifully formed in itself, and so richly adorned by the hand of Nature.

Till within the last sixty years there was no communication between any of these vales by carriage-roads ; all bulky articles were transported on pack-horses. Owing, however, to the population not being concentrated in villages, but scattered, the vallies themselves were intersected as now by innumerable lanes and path-ways leading from house to house and from field to field. These lanes, where they are fenced by stone walls, are mostly bordered with ashes, hazels, wild roses, and beds of tall fern, at their base ; while the walls themselves, if old, are over-spread with mosses, small ferns, wild strawberries, the geranium, and lichens : and, if the wall happen to rest against a bank of earth, it is sometimes almost wholly concealed by a rich facing of stone-fern. It is a great advantage to a traveller or resident, that these numerous lanes and paths, if he be a zealous admirer of Nature, will lead him on into all the recesses of the country, so that the hidden treasures of its landscapes may, by an ever-ready guide, be laid open to his eyes.

Likewise to the smallness of the several properties is owing the great number of bridges over the brooks and torrents, and the daring and graceful neglect of danger or accommodation with which so many of them are constructed, the rudeness of the forms of some, and their endless variety. But, when I speak of this rudeness, I must at the same time add, that many of these structures are in themselves models of elegance, as if they had been formed upon principles of the most thoughtful architecture. It is to be regretted that these monuments of the skill of our ancestors, and of that happy instinct by which consummate beauty was produced, are disappearing fast ; but sufficient specimens remain* to give a high gratification to the man of genuine taste. Travellers who may not have been

---

* Written some time ago. The injury done since, is more than could have been calculated upon.

Singula de nobis anni prædantur euntes. This is in the course of things ; but why should the genius that directed the ancient architecture of these vales have deserted them? For the bridges, churches, mansions, cottages, and their richly fringed and flat-roofed outhouses, venerable as the grange of some old abbey, have been substituted structures, in which baldness only seems to have been studied, or plans of the most vulgar utility. But some improvement may be looked for in future ; the gentry *recently* have copied the old models, and successful instances might be pointed out, if I could take the liberty.

accustomed to pay attention to things so inobtrusive, will excuse me if I point out the proportion between the span and elevation of the arch, the lightness of the parapet, and the graceful manner in which its curve follows faithfully that of the arch.

Upon this subject I have nothing further to notice, except the (PLACES OF WORSHIP,) which have mostly a little school-house adjoining.* The architecture of these churches and chapels, where they have not been recently rebuilt or modernised, is of a style not less appropriate and admirable than that of the dwelling-houses and other structures. How sacred the spirit by which our forefathers were directed! The *religio loci* is no where violated by these unstinted, yet unpretending, works of human hands. They exhibit generally a well-proportioned oblong, with a suitable porch, in some instances a steeple tower, and in others nothing more than a small belfry, in which one or two bells hang visibly. (But these objects, though pleasing in their forms, must necessarily, more than others in rural scenery, derive their interest from the sentiments of piety and reverence for the modest virtues and simple manners of humble life with which they may be contemplated. A man must be very insensible who would not be touched with pleasure at the sight of the chapel of Buttermere, so strikingly expressing, by its diminutive size, how small must be the congregation there assembled, as it were, like one family; and proclaiming at the same time to the passenger, in connection with the surrounding mountains, the depth of that seclusion in which the people live, that has rendered necessary the building of a separate place of worship for so few.) A patriot, calling to mind the images of the stately fabrics of Canterbury, York, or Westminster, will find a heart-felt satisfaction in presence of this lowly pile, as a

---

* In some places scholars were formerly taught in the church, and at others the school-house was a sort of anti-chapel to the place of worship, being under the same roof; an arrangement which was abandoned as irreverent. It continues, however, to this day in Borrowdale. In the parish register of that chapelry is a notice, that a youth who had quitted the valley, and died in one of the towns on the coast of Cumberland, had requested that his body should be brought and interred at the foot of the pillar by which he had been accustomed to sit while a school-boy. One cannot but regret that parish registers so seldom contain any thing but bare names; in a few of this country, especially in that of Loweswater, I have found interesting notices of unusual natural occurrences—characters of the deceased, and particulars of their lives. There is no good reason why such memorials should not be frequent; these short and simple annals would in future ages become precious.

monument of the wise institutions of our country, and as evidence of the all-pervading and paternal care of that venerable Establishment, of which it is, perhaps, the humblest daughter. The edifice is scarcely larger than many of the single stones or fragments of rock which are scattered near it.

We have thus far confined our observations, on this division of the subject, to that part of these Dales which runs up far into the mountains.

As we descend towards the open country, we meet with halls and mansions, many of which have been places of defence against the incursions of the Scottish borderers; and they not unfrequently retain their towers and battlements. To these houses, parks are sometimes attached, and to their successive proprietors we chiefly owe whatever ornament is still left to the country of majestic timber. Through the open parts of the vales are scattered, also, houses of a middle rank between the pastoral cottage and the old hall residence of the knight or esquire. Such houses differ much from the rugged cottages before described, and are generally graced with a little court or garden in front, where may yet be seen specimens of those fantastic and quaint figures which our ancestors were fond of shaping out in yew-tree, holly, or box-wood. The passenger will sometimes smile at such elaborate display of petty art, while the house does not deign to look upon the natural beauty or the sublimity which its situation almost unavoidably commands.

Thus has been given a faithful description, the minuteness of which the reader will pardon, of the face of this country as it was, and had been through centuries, till within the last sixty years. Towards the head of these Dales was found a perfect Republic of Shepherds and Agriculturists, among whom the plough of each man was confined to the maintenance of his own family, or to the occasional accommodation of his neighbour.* Two or three cows furnished each family with milk

---

* One of the most pleasing characteristics of manners in secluded and thinly-peopled districts, is a sense of the degree in which human happiness and comfort are dependent on the contingency of neighbourhood. This is implied by a rhyming adage common here, '*Friends are far, when neighbours are nar*' (near). This mutual helpfulness is not confined to out-of-doors work; but is ready upon all occasions. Formerly, if a person became sick, especially the mistress of a family, it was usual for those of the neighbours who were more particularly connected with the party by amicable offices, to visit the house, carrying a present; this practice, which is by no means obsolete, is called *owning* the family, and is

and cheese. ⌈ The chapel was the only edifice that presided over these dwellings, the supreme head of this pure Commonwealth; the members of which existed in the midst of a powerful empire, like an ideal society or an organised community, whose constitution had been imposed and regulated by the mountains which protected it. Neither high-born nobleman, knight, nor esquire, was here; but many of these humble sons of the hills had a consciousness that the land, which they walked over and tilled, had for more than five hundred years been possessed by men of their name and blood; and venerable was the transition, when a curious traveller, descending from the heart of the mountains, had come to some ancient manorial residence in the more open parts of the Vales, which, through the rights attached to its proprietor, connected the almost visionary mountain republic he had been contemplating with the substantial frame of society as existing in the laws and constitution of a mighty empire.

SECTION THIRD.

CHANGES, AND RULES OF TASTE FOR PREVENTING THEIR BAD EFFECTS.

SUCH, as hath been said, was the appearance of things till within the last sixty years. ⌈ A practice, denominated Ornamental Gardening, was at that time becoming prevalent over England. In union with an admiration of this art, and in some instances in opposition to it, had been generated a relish for select parts of natural scenery: and Travellers, instead of confining their observations to Towns, Manufactories, or Mines, began (a thing till then unheard of) to wander over the island in search of sequestered spots, distinguished as they might accidentally have learned, for the sublimity or beauty of the forms of Nature there to be seen.⌉—Dr. Brown, the celebrated Author of the *Estimate of the Manners and Principles of the Times*, published a letter to a friend, in which the attractions of the Vale of Keswick were delineated with a powerful pencil, and the feeling of a genuine Enthusiast. Gray, the Poet, followed: he died soon after his forlorn and melancholy pilgrimage to the Vale of Keswick, and the record left behind him of

---

regarded as a pledge of a disposition to be otherwise serviceable in a time of disability and distress.

what he had seen and felt in this journey, excited that pensive
interest with which the human mind is ever disposed to listen
to the farewell words of a man of genius. The journal of Gray
feelingly showed how the gloom of ill health and low spirits
had been irradiated by objects, which the Author's powers of
mind enabled him to describe with distinctness and unaffected
simplicity. (Every reader of this journal must have been impressed with the words which conclude his notice of the Vale
of Grasmere :—' Not a single red tile, no flaring gentleman's
house or garden-wall, breaks in upon the repose of this little
unsuspected paradise; but all is peace, rusticity, and happy
poverty, in its neatest and most becoming attire.'

What is here so justly said of Grasmere applied almost
equally to all its sister Vales. It was well for the undisturbed
pleasure of the Poet that he had no forebodings of the change
which was soon to take place; and it might have been hoped
that these words, indicating how much the charm of what *was*,
depended upon what was *not*, would of themselves have preserved the ancient franchises of this and other kindred mountain retirements from trespass; or (shall I dare to say?) would
have secured scenes so consecrated from profanation. (The
lakes had now become celebrated; visitors flocked hither from
all parts of England; the fancies of some were smitten so
deeply, that they became settlers) and the Islands of Derwent-
water and Winandermere, as they offered the strongest temptation, were the first places seized upon, and were instantly de-
faced by the intrusion.

The venerable wood that had grown for centuries round the
small house called St. Herbert's Hermitage, had indeed some
years before been felled by its native proprietor, and the whole
island planted anew with Scotch firs, left to spindle up by each
other's side—a melancholy phalanx, defying the power of the
winds, and disregarding the regret of the spectator, who might
otherwise have cheated himself into a belief, that some of the
decayed remains of those oaks, the place of which was in this
manner usurped, had been planted by the Hermit's own hand.
This sainted spot, however, suffered comparatively little injury.
At the bidding of an alien improver, the Hind's Cottage, upon
Vicar's island, in the same lake, with its embowering sycamores
and cattle-shed, disappeared from the corner where they stood;

and right in the middle, and upon the precise point of the island's highest elevation, rose a tall square habitation, with four sides exposed, like an astronomer's observatory, or a warren-house reared upon an eminence for the detection of depredators, or, like the temple of Œolus, where all the winds pay him obeisance. Round this novel structure, but at a respectful distance, platoons of firs were stationed, as if to protect their commander when weather and time should somewhat have shattered his strength. Within the narrow limits of this island were typified also the state and strength of a kingdom, and its religion as it had been, and was,—for neither was the druidical circle uncreated, nor the church of the present establishment; nor the stately pier, emblem of commerce and navigation; nor the fort to deal out thunder upon the approaching invader. The taste of a succeeding proprietor rectified the mistakes as far as was practicable, and has ridded the spot of its puerilities. The church, after having been docked of its steeple, is applied both ostensibly and really, to the purpose for which the body of the pile was actually erected, namely, a boat-house; the fort is demolished; and, without indignation on the part of the spirits of the ancient Druids who officiated at the circle upon the opposite hill, the mimic arrangement of stones, with its *sanctum sanctorum*, has been swept away.

The present instance has been singled out, extravagant as it is, because, unquestionably, this beautiful country has, in numerous other places, suffered from the same spirit, though not clothed exactly in the same form, nor active in an equal degree. It will be sufficient here to utter a regret for the changes that have been made upon the principal Island at Winandermere, and in its neighbourhood. What could be more unfortunate than the taste that suggested the paring of the shores, and surrounding with an embankment this spot of ground, the natural shape of which was so beautiful! An artificial appearance has thus been given to the whole, while infinite varieties of minute beauty have been destroyed. Could not the margin of this noble island be given back to Nature? Winds and waves work with a careless and graceful hand: and, should they in some places carry away a portion of the soil, the trifling loss would be amply compensated by the additional spirit, dignity, and loveliness, which these agents and the other

powers of Nature would soon communicate to what was left behind. As to the larch-plantations upon the main shore,—they
who remember the original appearance of the rocky steeps, scattered over with native hollies and ash-trees, will be prepared to
agree with what I shall have to say hereafter upon plantations*
in general.

But, in truth, no one can now travel through the more frequented tracts, without being offended, at almost every turn, by
an introduction of discordant objects, disturbing that peaceful
harmony of form and colour, which had been through a long
lapse of ages most happily preserved.

All gross transgressions of this kind originate, doubtless, in
a feeling natural and honourable to the human mind, viz. the
pleasure which it receives from distinct ideas, and from the
perception of order, regularity, and contrivance. Now, unpractised minds receive these impressions only from objects that are
divided from each other by strong lines of demarcation; hence
the delight with which such minds are smitten by formality
and harsh contrast. But I would beg of those who are eager
to create the means of such gratification, first carefully to study
what already exists; and they will find, in a country so lavishly
gifted by Nature, an abundant variety of forms marked out with
a precision that will satisfy their desires. Moreover, a new
habit of pleasure will be formed opposite to this, arising out of
the perception of the fine gradations by which in Nature one
thing passes away into another, and the boundaries that constitute individuality disappear in one instance only to be revived
elsewhere under a more alluring form. The hill of Dunmallet,
at the foot of Ulswater, was once divided into different portions,
by avenues of fir-trees, with a green and almost perpendicular
lane descending down the steep hill through each avenue;—
contrast this quaint appearance with the image of the same hill
overgrown with self-planted wood,—each tree springing up in
the situation best suited to its kind, and with that shape which
the situation constrained or suffered it to take. What endless
melting and playing into each other of forms and colours does
the one offer to a mind at once attentive and active; and how
insipid and lifeless, compared with it, appear those parts of the

* These are disappearing fast, under the management of the present Proprietor, and native wood is resuming its place.

former exhibition with which a child, a peasant perhaps, or a citizen unfamiliar with natural imagery, would have been most delighted !

The disfigurement which this country has undergone, has not, however, proceeded wholly from the common feelings of human nature which have been referred to as the primary sources of bad taste in rural imagery; another cause must be added, that has chiefly shown itself in its effect upon buildings. I mean a warping of the natural mind occasioned by a consciousness that, this country being an object of general admiration, every new house would be looked at and commented upon either for approbation or censure. Hence all the deformity and ungracefulness that ever pursue the steps of constraint or affectation. Persons, who in Leicestershire or Northamptonshire would probably have built a modest dwelling like those of their sensible neighbours, have been turned out of their course; and, acting a part, no wonder if, having had little experience, they act it ill. The craving for prospect, also, which is immoderate, particularly in new settlers, has rendered it impossible that buildings, whatever might have been their architecture, should in most instances be ornamental to the landscape : rising as they do from the summits of naked hills in staring contrast to the snugness and privacy of the ancient houses.

No man is to be condemned for a desire to decorate his residence and possessions; feeling a disposition to applaud such an endeavour, I would show how the end may be best attained. The rule is simple; with respect to grounds—work, where you can, in the spirit of Nature, with an invisible hand of art. Planting, and a removal of wood, may thus, and thus only, be carried on with good effect; and the like may be said of building, if Antiquity, who may be styled the co-partner and sister of Nature, be not denied the respect to which she is entitled. I have already spoken of the beautiful forms of the ancient mansions of this country, and of the happy manner in which they harmonise with the forms of Nature. Why cannot such be taken as a model, and modern internal convenience be confined within their external grace and dignity. Expense to be avoided, or difficulties to be overcome, may prevent a close adherence to this model; still, however, it might be followed to a certain

T

degree in the style of architecture and in the choice of situation, if the thirst for prospect were mitigated by those considerations of comfort, shelter, and convenience, which used to
be chiefly sought after.   But should an aversion to old fashions
unfortunately exist, accompanied with a desire to transplant
into the cold and stormy North, the elegancies of a villa formed
upon a model taken from countries with a milder climate, I
will adduce a passage from an English poet, the divine Spenser,
which will show in what manner such a plan may be realised
without injury to the native beauty of these scenes.

> Into that forest farre they thence him led,
> Where was their dwelling in a pleasant glade
> With MOUNTAINS round about environed,
> And MIGHTY WOODS which did the valley shade,
> And like a stately theatre it made,
> Spreading itself into a spacious plaine ;
> And in the midst a little river plaide
> Emongst the puny stones which seem'd to 'plaine
> With gentle murmure that his course they did restraine.

> Beside the same a dainty place there lay,
> Planted with mirtle trees and laurels green,
> In which the birds sang many a lovely lay
> Of God's high praise, and of their sweet loves teene,
> As it an earthly paradise had beene ;
> In whose *enclosed shadow* there was pight
> A fair pavillion, *scarcely to be seen,*
> The which was all within most richly dight,
> That greatest princes living it mote well delight.

Houses or mansions suited to a mountainous region, should
be 'not obvious, not obtrusive, but retired;' and the reasons
for this rule, though they have been little adverted to, are evident.   Mountainous countries, more frequently and forcibly
than others, remind us of the power of the elements, as manifested in winds, snows, and torrents, and accordingly make the
notion of exposure very unpleasing ; while shelter and comfort
are in proportion necessary and acceptable.   Far-winding vallies difficult of access, and the feelings of simplicity habitually
connected with mountain retirements, prompt us to turn from
ostentation as a thing there eminently unnatural and out of
place.   A mansion, amid such scenes, can never have sufficient
dignity or interest to become principal in the landscape, and to
render the mountains, lakes, or torrents, by which it may be

surrounded, a subordinate part of the view. It is, I grant, easy to conceive, that an ancient castellated building, hanging over a precipice or raised upon an island, or the peninsula of a lake, like that of Kilchurn Castle, upon Loch Awe, may not want, whether deserted or inhabited, sufficient majesty to preside for a moment in the spectator's thoughts over the high mountains among which it is embosomed ; but its titles are from antiquity —a power readily submitted to upon occasion as the vicegerent of Nature : it is respected, as having owed its existence to the necessities of things, as a monument of security in times of disturbance and danger long passed away,—as a record of the pomp and violence of passion, and a symbol of the wisdom of law ; it bears a countenance of authority, which is not impaired by decay.

> Child of loud-throated War, the mountain stream
> Roars in thy hearing ; but thy hour of rest
> Is come, and thou art silent in thy age !

To such honours a modern edifice can lay no claim ; and the puny efforts of elegance appear contemptible, when, in such situations, they are obtruded in rivalship with the sublimities of Nature. But, towards the verge of a district like this of which we are treating, where the mountains subside into hills of moderate elevation, or in an undulating or flat country, a gentleman's mansion may, with propriety, become a principal feature in the landscape; and, itself being a work of art, works and traces of artificial ornament may, without censure, be extended around it, as they will be referred to the common centre, the house ; the right of which to impress within certain limits a character of obvious ornament will not be denied, where no commanding forms of Nature dispute it, or set it aside. Now, to a want of the perception of this difference, and to the causes before assigned, may chiefly be attributed the disfigurement which the Country of the Lakes has undergone, from persons who may have built, demolished, and planted, with full confidence, that every change and addition was or would become an improvement.

The principle that ought to determine the position, apparent size, and architecture of a house, viz. that it should be so constructed, and (if large) so much of it hidden, as to admit of its being gently incorporated into the scenery of Nature—should also determine its colour. Sir Joshua Reynolds used to say, 'If you would fix upon the best colour for your house, turn up a stone, or pluck up a handful of grass by the roots, and see what is the colour of the soil where the house is to stand, and let that be your choice.' Of course, this precept given in conversation, could not have been meant to be taken literally. For example, in Low Furness, where the soil, from its strong impregnation with iron, is universally of a deep red, if this rule were strictly followed, the house also must be of a glaring red; in other places it must be of a sullen black; which would only be adding annoyance to annoyance. The rule, however, as a general guide, is good; and, in agricultural districts, where large tracts of soil are laid bare by the plough, particularly if (the face of the country being undulating) they are held up to view, this rule, though not to be implicitly adhered to, should never be lost sight of;—the colour of the house ought, if possible, to have a cast or shade of the colour of the soil. The principle is, that the house must harmonise with the surrounding landscape : accordingly, in mountainous countries, with still more confidence may it be said, 'look at the rocks and those parts of the mountains where the soil is visible, and they will furnish a safe direction.' Nevertheless, it will often happen that the rocks may bear so large a proportion to the rest of the landscape, and may be of such a tone of colour, that the rule may not admit, even here, of being implicitly followed. For instance, the chief defect in the colouring of the Country of the Lakes (which is most strongly felt in the summer season) is an over-prevalence of a bluish tint, which the green of the herbage, the fern, and the woods, does not sufficiently counteract. If a house, therefore, should stand where this defect prevails, I have no hesitation in saying, that the colour of the neighbouring rocks would not be the best that could be chosen. A tint ought to be introduced approaching nearer to those which, in the technical language of painters, are called *warm :* this, if happily selected, would not disturb, but would animate the landscape. How often do we see this exemplified upon a small scale by the native cottages, in cases where the glare of white-wash has been subdued by time and enriched by weather-stains ! No harshness is then seen; but one of these cottages, thus coloured, will often form a central point to a landscape by which the whole shall be connected, and an influence of pleasure diffused over all the objects that compose the picture. But where the cold blue tint of the rocks is enriched by the iron tinge, the colour cannot be too closely imitated; and it will be produced of itself by the stones hewn from the adjoining quarry, and by the mortar, which may be tempered with the most gravelly part of the soil. The pure blue gravel, from the bed of the river, is, however, more suitable to the mason's purpose, who will probably insist also that the house must be covered with rough-cast, otherwise it cannot be kept dry; if this advice be taken, the builder of taste will set about contriving such means as may enable him to come the nearest to the effect aimed at.

The supposed necessity of rough-cast to keep out rain in houses not built of hewn stone or brick, has tended greatly to injure English landscape, and the neighbourhood of these Lakes especially, by furnishing such apt occasion for whitening buildings. That white should be a favourite colour for rural residences is natural for many reasons. The mere aspect of cleanliness and neatness thus given, not only to an individual house, but, where the practice is general, to the whole face of the country, produces moral associations so powerful, that, in many minds, they take place of all others. But what has already been said upon the subject of cottages, must have convinced men of feeling and imagination, that a human dwelling of the humblest class may be rendered more deeply interesting to the affections, and far more pleasing to the eye, by other influences, than a sprightly tone of colour spread over its outside. I do not, however, mean to deny, that a small white building, embowered in trees, may, in some situations, be a delightful and animating object—in no way injurious to the landscape; but this only where it sparkles from the midst of a thick shade, and in rare and solitary instances; especially if the country be itself rich and pleasing, and abound with grand forms. On the sides of bleak and desolate moors, we are indeed thankful for the sight of white cottages and white houses plentifully scattered, where, without these, perhaps every thing would be cheerless: this is said, however, with hesitation, and with a wilful sacrifice of some higher enjoyments. But I have certainly seen such buildings glittering at sunrise, and in wandering lights, with no common pleasure. The continental traveller also will remember, that the convents hanging from the rocks of the Rhine, the Rhone, the Danube, or among the Appenines, or the mountains of Spain, are not looked at with less complacency when, as is often the case, they happen to be of a brilliant white. But this is perhaps owing, in no small degree, to the contrast of that lively colour with the gloom of monastic life, and to the general want of rural residences of smiling and attractive appearance, in those countries.

The objections to white, as a colour, in large spots or masses in landscape, especially in a mountainous country, are insurmountable. (In Nature, pure white is scarcely ever found but in small objects, such as flowers : or in those which are transitory, as the clouds, foam of rivers, and snow. Mr. Gilpin, who notices this, has also recorded the just remark of Mr. Locke, of N—, that white destroys the *gradations* of distance; and, therefore, an object of pure white can scarcely ever be managed with good effect in landscape-painting. Five or six white houses, scattered over a valley, by their obtrusiveness, dot the surface, and divide it into triangles, or other mathematical figures, haunting the eye, and disturbing that repose which might otherwise be perfect.) I have seen a single white house materially impair the majesty of a mountain; cutting away, by a harsh separation, the whole of its base, below the point on which the house stood. Thus was the apparent size of the mountain reduced, not by the interposition of another object in a manner to call forth the imagination, which will give more than the eye loses; but what had been abstracted in this case was left visible; and the mountain appeared to take its beginning, or to rise, from the line of the house, instead of its own natural base. But, if I may express my own individual feeling, it is after sunset, at the coming on of twilight, that white objects are most to be complained of. The solemnity and quietness of Nature at that time are always marred, and often destroyed by them. When the ground is covered with snow, they are of course inoffensive; and in moonshine they are always pleasing—it is a tone of light with which they accord : and the dimness of the scene is enlivened by an object at once conspicuous and cheerful. I will conclude this subject with noticing, that the cold, slaty colour, which many persons, who have heard the white condemned, have adopted in its stead, must be disapproved of for the reason already given. The flaring yellow runs into the opposite extreme, and is still more censurable. Upon the whole, the safest colour, for general use, is something between a cream and a dust-colour, commonly called stone colour;—there are, among the Lakes, examples of this that need not be pointed out.*

The principle taken as our guide, viz. that the house should be so formed, and of such apparent size and colour, as to admit of its being gently incorporated with the works of Nature, should also be applied to the management of the grounds and plantations, and is here more urgently needed; for it is from abuses in this department, far more even than from the introduction of exotics in architecture (if the phrase may be used), that this country has suffered. Larch and fir plantations have been spread, not merely with a view to profit, but in many instances for the sake of ornament. To those who plant for profit, and are thrusting every other tree out of the way, to make room for their favourite, the larch, I would utter first a regret, that they should have selected these lovely vales for their vegetable manufactory, when there is so much barren and irreclaimable land in the neighbouring moors, and in other parts of the island, which might have been had for this purpose at a far cheaper rate. And I will also beg leave to represent to them, that they ought not to be carried away by flattering promises from the speedy growth of this tree; because in rich soils and sheltered situations, the wood, though it thrives fast, is full of sap, and of little value; and is, likewise, very subject to ravage from the attacks of insects, and from blight. Accordingly, in Scotland, where planting is much better understood, and carried on upon an incomparably larger scale than among us, good soil and sheltered situations are appropriated to the oak, the ash, and other deciduous trees; and the larch is now generally confined to barren and exposed ground. There the plant, which is a hardy one, is of slower growth; much less liable to injury; and the timber is of better quality. But the circumstances of many permit, and their taste leads them, to plant with little regard to profit; and there are others, less wealthy, who have such a lively feeling of the native beauty of these scenes, that they are laudably not

---

* A proper colouring of houses is now becoming general. It is best that the colouring material should be mixed with the rough-cast, and not laid on as a *wash* afterwards.

unwilling to make some sacrifices to heighten it. Both these classes of persons, I would entreat to inquire of themselves wherein that beauty which they admire consists. They would then see that, after the feeling has been gratified that prompts us to gather round our dwelling a few flowers and shrubs, which from the circumstance of their not being native, may, by their very looks, remind us that they owe their existence to our hands, and their prosperity to our care ; they will see that, after this natural desire has been provided for, the course of all beyond has been predetermined by the spirit of the place. Before I proceed, I will remind those who are not satisfied with the restraint thus laid upon them, that they are liable to a charge of inconsistency, when they are so eager to change the face of that country, whose native attractions, by the act of erecting their habitations in it, they have so emphatically acknowledged. And surely there is not a single spot that would not have, if well managed, sufficient dignity to support itself, unaided by the productions of other climates, or by elaborate decorations which might be becoming elsewhere.

Having adverted to the feelings that justify the introduction of a few exotic plants, provided they be confined almost to the doors of the house, we may add, that a transition should be contrived, without abruptness, from these foreigners to the rest of the shrubs, which ought to be of the kinds scattered by Nature, through the woods—holly, broom, wild-rose, elder, dogberry, white and black thorn, &c.—either these only, or such as are carefully selected in consequence of their being united in form, and harmonising in colour with them, especially with respect to colour, when the tints are most diversified, as in autumn and spring. The various sorts of fruit-and-blossom-bearing trees usually found in orchards, to which may be added those of the woods,—namely, the wilding, black cherry tree, and wild cluster-cherry (here called heck-berry)—may be happily admitted as an intermediate link between the shrubs and the forest trees; which last ought almost entirely to be such as are natives of the country. Of the birch, one of the most beautiful of the native trees, it may be noticed, that, in dry and rocky situations, it outstrips even the larch, which many persons are tempted to plant merely on account of the speed of its growth. The Scotch fir is less attractive during *its* youth than any other plant; but, when full grown, if it has had room to spread out its arms, it becomes a noble tree; and, by those who are disinterested enough to plant for posterity, it may be placed along with the sycamore near the house; for, from their massiveness, both these trees unite well with buildings, and in some situations with rocks also; having, in their forms and apparent substances, the effect of something intermediate betwixt the immoveableness and solidity of stone, and the spray and foliage of the lighter trees. If these general rules be just, what shall we say to whole acres of artificial shrubbery and exotic trees among rocks and dashing torrents, with their own wild wood in sight—where we have the whole contents of the nurseryman's catalogue jumbled together—colour at war with colour, and form with form?—among the most peaceful subjects of Nature's kingdom, everywhere discord, distraction, and bewilderment! But this deformity, bad as it is, is not so obtrusive as the small patches and large tracts of larch-plantations that are overrunning the hill sides. To justify our condemnation of these, let us again recur to Nature. The process, by which she forms woods and forests, is as follows. Seeds are scattered indiscriminately by winds, brought by waters, and dropped by birds. They perish, or produce, according as the soil and situation upon which they fall are suited to them: and under the same dependence, the seedling or the sucker, if not cropped by animals, (which Nature is often careful to prevent by fencing it about with brambles or other prickly shrubs) thrives, and the tree grows, sometimes single, taking its own shape without constraint, but for the most part compelled to conform itself to some law imposed upon it by its neighbours. From low and sheltered places, vegetation travels upwards to the more exposed; and the young plants are protected, and to a certain degree fashioned, by those that have preceded them. The continuous mass of foliage which would be thus produced, is broken by rocks, or by glades or open places, where the browzing of animals has prevented the growth of wood. As vegetation ascends, the winds begin also to bear their part in moulding the forms of the trees; but, thus mutually protected, trees, though not of the hardiest kind, are enabled to climb high up the mountains. Gradually, however, by the quality of the ground, and by increasing exposure, a stop is put to their ascent; the hardy trees only are left: those also, by little and little, give way—and a wild and irregular boundary is established, graceful in its outline, and never contemplated without some feeling, more or less distinct, of the powers of Nature by which it is imposed./

Contrast the liberty that encourages, and the law that limits, this joint work of Nature and Time, with the disheartening necessities, restrictions, and disadvantages, under which the artificial planter must proceed, even he whom long observation and fine feeling have best qualified for his task. In the first place his trees, however well chosen and adapted to their several situations, must generally start all at the same time; and this necessity would of itself prevent that fine connection of parts, that sympathy and organisation, if I may so express myself, which pervades the whole of a natural wood, and appears to the eye in its single trees, its masses of foliage, and their various colours, when they are held up to view on the side of a mountain; or when, spread over a valley, they are looked down upon from an eminence. It is therefore impossible, under any circumstances, for the artificial planter to rival the beauty of Nature. But a moment's thought will show that, if ten thousand of this spiky tree, the larch, are stuck in at once upon the side of a hill, they can grow up into nothing but deformity; that, while they are suffered to stand, we shall look in vain for any of those appearances which are the chief sources of beauty in a natural wood.

It must be acknowledged that the larch, till it has outgrown the size of a shrub, shows, when looked at singly, some elegance in form and appearance, especially in spring, decorated, as it then is, by the pink tassels of its blossoms; but, as a tree, it is less than any other pleasing: its branches (for *boughs* it has none) have no variety in the youth of the tree, and little dignity, even when it attains its full growth: *leaves* it cannot be said to have, consequently neither affords shade nor shelter. In spring the larch becomes green long before the native trees; and its green is so peculiar and vivid, that, finding nothing to harmonise with it, wherever it comes forth, a disagreeable speck is produced. In summer, when all other trees are in their pride, it is of a dingy, lifeless hue; in autumn of a spiritless unvaried yellow, and in winter it is still more lamentably distinguished from every other deciduous tree of the forest, for they seem only to sleep, but the larch appears absolutely dead. If an attempt be made to mingle thickets, or a certain proportion of other forest-trees, with the larch, its horizontal branches intolerantly cut them down as with a scythe, or force them to spindle up to keep pace with it. The terminating spike renders it impossible that the several trees, where planted in numbers, should ever blend together so as to form a mass or masses of wood. Add thousands to tens of thousands, and the appearance is still the same—a collection of separate individual trees, obstinately presenting themselves as such; and which, from whatever point they are looked at, if but seen, may be counted upon the fingers. Sunshine, or shadow, has little power to adorn the surface of such a wood; and the trees not carrying up their heads, the wind raises among them no majestic undulations. It is indeed true, that, in countries where the larch is a native, and where, without interruption, it may sweep from valley to valley, and from hill to hill, a sublime image may be produced by such a forest, in the same manner as by one composed of any other single tree, to the spreading of which no limits can be assigned. For sublimity will never be wanting, where the sense of innumerable multitude is lost in, and alternates with, that of intense unity; and to the ready perception of this effect, similarity and almost identity of individual form and monotony of colour contribute. But this feeling is confined to the native immeasurable forest; no artificial plantation can give it.

The foregoing observations will, I hope, (as nothing has been condemned or recommended without a substantial reason) have some influence upon those who plant for ornament merely. To such as plant for profit, I have already spoken. Let me then entreat that the native deciduous trees may be left in complete possession of the lower ground; and that plantations of larch, if introduced at all, may be confined to the highest and most barren tracts. Interposition of rocks would there break the dreary uniformity of which we have been complaining; and the winds would take hold of the trees, and imprint upon their shapes a wildness congenial to their situation.

Having determined what kinds of trees must be wholly rejected, or at least very sparingly used, by those who are unwilling to disfigure the country; and having shown what kinds ought to be chosen; I should have given, if my limits had not already been overstepped, a few practical rules for the manner in which trees ought to be disposed in planting. But to this subject I should attach little importance, if I could succeed in banishing such trees as introduce deformity, and could prevail upon the proprietor to confine himself, either to those found in the native woods, or to such as accord with them. This is, indeed, the main point; for, much as these scenes have been injured by what has been taken from them—buildings, trees, and woods, either through negligence, necessity, avarice, or caprice—it is not the removals, but the harsh *additions* that have been made, which are the worst grievance—a standing and unavoidable annoyance. Often have I felt this distinction, with mingled satisfaction and regret; for, if no positive deformity or discordance be substituted or superinduced, such is the benignity of Nature, that, take away from her beauty after beauty, and ornament after ornament, her appearance cannot be marred—the scars, if any be left, will gradually disappear before a healing spirit; and what remains will still be soothing and pleasing.—

> Many hearts deplored
> The fate of those old trees; and oft with pain
> The traveller at this day will stop and gaze
> On wrongs which Nature scarcely seems to heed:
> For sheltered places, bosoms, nooks, and bays,
> And the pure mountains, and the gentle Tweed,
> And the green silent pastures, yet remain.

There are few ancient woods left in this part of England upon which such indiscriminate ravage as is here 'deplored,' could now be committed. But, out of the numerous copses, fine woods might in time be raised, probably without sacrifice of profit, by leaving, at the periodical fellings, a due proportion of the healthiest trees to grow up into timber.—This plan has fortunately, in many instances, been adopted; and they, who have set the example, are entitled to the thanks of all persons of taste. As to the management of planting with reasonable attention to ornament, let the images of Nature be your guide, and the whole secret lurks in a few words; thickets or underwoods—single trees—trees clustered or in groups—groves—unbroken woods, but with varied masses of foliage—glades—invisible or winding boundaries—in rocky districts, a seemly proportion of rock left wholly bare, and other parts half hidden—disagreeable objects concealed, and formal lines broken—trees climbing up to the horizon, and, in some places, ascending from its sharp edge, in which they are rooted, with the whole body of the tree appearing to stand in the clear sky—in other parts, woods surmounted by rocks utterly bare and naked, which add to the sense of height, as if vegetation could not thither be carried, and impress a feeling of duration, power of resistance, and security from change!

The author has been induced to speak thus at length, by a wish to preserve the native beauty of this delightful district, because still further changes in its appearance must inevitably follow, from the change of inhabitants and owners which is rapidly taking place.—About the same time that strangers began to be attracted to the country, and to feel a desire to settle in it, the difficulty, that would have stood in the way of their procuring situations, was lessened by an unfortunate alteration in the circumstances of the native peasantry, proceeding from a cause which then began to operate, and is now felt in every house. [The family of each man, whether *estatesman* or farmer, formerly had a twofold support; first, the produce of his lands and flocks; and, secondly, the profit drawn from the employment of the women and children, as manufacturers; spinning their own wool in their own houses (work chiefly done in the winter season), and carrying it to market for sale. Hence, however numerous the children, the income of the family kept pace with its increase. But, by the invention and universal application of machinery, this second resource has been cut off; the gains being so far reduced, as not to be sought after but by a few aged persons disabled from other employment. Doubtless, the invention of machinery has not been to these people a pure loss; for the profits arising from home-manufactures operated as a strong temptation to choose that mode of labour in neglect of husbandry. They also participate in the general benefit which the island has derived from the increased value of the produce of land, brought about by the establishment of manufactories, and in the consequent quickening of agricultural industry. But this is far from making them amends; and now that home-manufactures are nearly done away, though the women and children might, at many seasons of the year, employ themselves with advantage in the fields beyond what they are accustomed to do, yet still all possible exertion in this way cannot be rationally expected from persons whose agricultural knowledge is so confined, and, above all, where there must necessarily be so small a capital. The consequence, then, is— that proprietors and farmers being no longer able to maintain themselves upon small farms, several are united in one, and the buildings go to decay, or are destroyed; and that the lands of the *estatesmen* being mortgaged, and the owners constrained to part with them, they fall into the hands of wealthy purchasers, who in like manner unite and consolidate; and, if they wish to become residents, erect new mansions out of the ruins of the ancient cottages, whose little enclosures, with all the wild graces that grew out of them, disappear. The feudal tenure under which the estates are held has indeed done something towards checking this influx of new settlers; but so strong is the inclination, that these galling restraints are endured; and it is probable, that in a few years the country on the margin of the Lakes will fall almost entirely into the possession of gentry, either strangers or natives. It is then much to be wished, that a better taste should prevail among these new proprietors; and, as they cannot be expected to leave things to themselves, that skill and knowledge should prevent unnecessary deviations from that path of simplicity and beauty along which, without design and unconsciously, their humble predecessors have moved. In this wish the author will be joined by persons of pure taste throughout the whole island, who, by their visits (often repeated) to the Lakes in the North of England, testify that they deem the district a sort of national property, in which every man has a right and interest who has an eye to perceive and a heart to enjoy.

MR. WEST, in his well-known Guide to the Lakes, recommends, as the best season for visiting this country, the interval from the beginning of June to the end of August; and, the two latter months being a time of vacation and leisure, it is almost exclusively in these that strangers resort hither. But that season is by no means the best; the colouring of the mountains and woods, unless where they are diversified by rocks, is of too unvaried a green; and, as a large portion of the vallies is allotted to hay-grass, some want of variety is found there also. The meadows, however, are sufficiently enlivened after hay-making begins, which is much later than in the southern part of the island. A stronger objection is rainy weather, setting in sometimes at this period with a vigour, and continuing with a perseverance, that may remind the disappointed and dejected traveller of those deluges of rain which fall among the Abyssinian mountains, for the annual supply of the Nile. The months of September and October (particularly October) are generally attended with much finer weather; and the scenery is then, beyond comparison, more diversified, more splendid, and beautiful; but, on the other hand, short days prevent long excursions, and sharp and chill gales are unfavourable to parties of pleasure out of doors. Nevertheless, to the sincere admirer of Nature, who is in good health and spirits, and at liberty to make a choice, the six weeks following the 1st of September may be recommended in preference to July and August. For there is no inconvenience arising from the season which, to such a person, would not be amply compensated by the *autumnal* appearance of any of the more retired vallies, into which discordant plantations and unsuitable buildings have not yet found entrance.— In such spots, at this season, there is an admirable compass and proportion of natural harmony in colour, through the whole scale of objects; in the tender green of the after-grass upon the meadows, interspersed with islands of grey or mossy rock, crowned by shrubs and trees; in the irregular inclosures of standing corn, or stubble-fields, in like manner broken; in the mountain-sides glowing with fern of divers colours; in the calm blue lakes and river-pools; and in the foliage of the trees, through all the tints of autumn,—from the pale and brilliant yellow of the birch and ash, to the deep greens of the unfaded oak and alder, and of the ivy upon the rocks, upon the trees, and the cottages. Yet, as most travellers are either stinted, or stint themselves, for time, the space between the middle or last week in May, and the middle or last week of June, may be pointed out as affording the best combination of long days, fine weather, and variety of impressions. Few of the native trees are then in full leaf; but, for whatever may be wanting in depth of shade, more than an equivalent will be found in the diversity of foliage, in the blossoms of the fruit-and-berry-bearing trees which abound in the woods, and in the golden flowers of the broom and other shrubs, with which many of the copses are in-terveined. In those woods, also, and on those mountain-sides which have a northern aspect, and in the deep dells, many of the spring-flowers still linger; while the open and sunny places are stocked with the flowers of the approaching summer. And, besides, is not an exquisite pleasure still untasted by him who has not heard the choir of linnets and thrushes chaunting their love-songs in the copses, woods, and hedge-rows of a moun-tainous country; safe from the birds of prey, which build in the inaccessible crags, and are at all hours seen or heard wheel-ing about in the air? The number of these formidable crea-tures is probably the cause, why, in the *narrow* vallies, there are no skylarks; as the destroyer would be enabled to dart upon them from the near and surrounding crags, before they could descend to their ground-nests for protection. It is not often that the nightingale resorts to these vales; but almost all the other tribes of our English warblers are numerous; and their notes, when listened to by the side of broad still waters, or when heard in unison with the murmuring of mountain-brooks, have the compass of their power enlarged accordingly. There is also an imaginative influence in the voice of the cuckoo, when that voice has taken possession of a deep mountain valley, very different from any thing which can be excited by the same sound in a flat country. Nor must a circumstance be omitted, which here renders the close of spring especially interesting; I mean the practice of bringing down the ewes from the mountains to yean in the vallies and enclosed grounds. The herbage being thus cropped as it springs, *that* first tender emerald green of the season, which would otherwise have lasted little more than a fortnight, is prolonged in the pastures and meadows for many weeks: while they are farther enlivened by the multitude of lambs bleating and skipping about. These sportive creatures, as they gather strength, are turned out upon the open mountains, and with their slender limbs, their snow-white colour, and their wild and light motions, beautifully accord or contrast with the rocks and lawns, upon which they must now begin to seek their food. And last, but not least, at this time the traveller will be sure of room and comfortable accommodation, even in the smaller inns. I am aware that few of those who may be inclined to profit by this recommendation will be able to do so, as the time and manner of an excursion of this kind are mostly regulated by circumstances which prevent an entire· freedom of choice. It will therefore be more pleasant to observe, that, though the months of July and August are liable to many objections, yet it often happens that the weather, at this time, is not more wet and stormy than they, who are really capable of enjoying the sublime forms of Nature in their utmost sublimity, would desire. For no traveller, provided he be in good health, and with any command of time, would have a just privilege to visit such scenes, if he could grudge the price of a little confinement among them, or interruption in his journey, for the sight or sound of a storm coming on or clearing away. Insensible must he be who would not congratulate himself upon the bold bursts of sunshine, the descending vapours, wandering lights and shadows, and the invigorated torrents and water-falls, with which broken weather, in a mountainous region, is accompanied. At such a time there is no cause to complain, either of the monotony of midsummer colouring, or the glaring atmosphere of long, cloudless, and hot days.

Thus far concerning the respective advantages and disadvantages of the different seasons for visiting this country. As to the order in which objects are best seen—a lake being composed of water flowing from higher grounds, and expanding itself till its receptacle is filled to the brim,—it follows, that it will appear to most advantage when approached from its outlet, especially if the lake be in a mountainous country; for, by this way of approach, the traveller faces the grander features of the scene, and is gradually conducted into its most sublime recesses. Now, every one knows, that from amenity and beauty the transition to sublimity is easy and favourable; but the reverse is not so; for, after the faculties have been elevated, they are indisposed to humbler excitement.*

It is not likely that a mountain will be ascended without disappointment, if a wide range of prospect be the object, unless either the summit be reached before sun-rise, or the visitant remain there until the time of sun-set, and afterwards. The precipitous sides of the mountain, and the neighbouring summits, may be seen with effect under any atmosphere which allows them to be seen at all; but *he* is the most fortunate adventurer, who chances to be involved in vapours which open and let in an extent of country partially, or, dispersing suddenly, reveal the whole region from centre to circumference.

A stranger to a mountainous country may not be aware that his walk in the early morning ought to be taken on the eastern side of the vale, otherwise he will lose the morning light, first touching the tops and thence creeping down the sides of the opposite hills, as the sun ascends, or he may go to some central eminence, commanding both the shadows from the eastern, and the lights upon the western mountains. But, if the horizon line in the east be low, the western side may be taken for the sake of the reflections, upon the water, of light from the rising sun. In the evening, for like reasons, the contrary course should be taken.

After all, it is upon the *mind* which a traveller brings along with him that his acquisitions, whether of pleasure or profit, must principally depend.—May I be allowed a few words on this subject?

Nothing is more injurious to genuine feeling than the prac-

---

* The only instances to which the foregoing observations do not apply, are Derwent-water and Lowes-water. Derwent is distinguished from all the other Lakes by being *surrounded* with sublimity: the fantastic mountains of Borrowdale to the south, the solitary majesty of Skiddaw to the north, the bold steeps of Wallow-crag and Lodore to the east, and to the west the clustering mountains of Now-lands. Lowes-water is tame at the head, but towards its outlet has a magnificent assemblage of mountains. Yet as far as respects the formation of such receptacles, the general observation holds good: neither Derwent nor Lowes-water derive any supplies from the streams of those mountains that dignify the landscape towards the outlets.

tice of hastily and ungraciously depreciating the face of one
country by comparing it with that of another. True it is Qui
bene distinguit bene *docet ;* yet fastidiousness is a wretched travelling companion ; and the best guide to which, in matters of
taste, we can entrust ourselves, is a disposition to be pleased.
For example, if a traveller be among the Alps, let him surrender
up his mind to the fury of the gigantic torrents, and take delight
in the contemplation of their almost irresistible violence, without
complaining of the monotony of their foaming course, or being
disgusted with the muddiness of the water—apparent even where
it is violently agitated. In Cumberland and Westmorland, let
not the comparative weakness of the streams prevent him from
sympathising with such impetuosity as they possess; and,
making the most of the present objects, let him, as he justly may
do, observe with admiration the unrivalled brilliancy of the
water, and that variety of motion, mood, and character, that
arises out of the want of those resources by which the power of
the streams in the Alps is supported.—Again, with respect to
the mountains; though these are comparatively of diminutive
size, though there is little of perpetual snow, and no voice of
summer-avalanches is heard among them; and though traces
left by the ravage of the elements are here comparatively rare
and unimpressive, yet out of this very deficiency proceeds a
sense of stability and permanence that is, to many minds, more
grateful—

> While the hoarse rushes to the sweeping breeze
> Sigh forth their ancient melodies.

Among the Alps are few places that do not preclude this
feeling of tranquil sublimity. Havoc, and ruin, and desolation,
and encroachment, are everywhere more or less obtruded; and
it is difficult, notwithstanding the naked loftiness of the *pikes,*
and the snow-capped summits of the *mounts,* to escape from the
depressing sensation, that the whole are in a rapid process of
dissolution ; and, were it not that the destructive agency must
abate as the heights diminish, would, in time to come, be
levelled with the plains. Nevertheless, I would relish to the
utmost the demonstrations of every species of power at work to
effect such changes.

From these general views let us descend a moment to detail.
A stranger to mountain imagery naturally on his first arrival

looks out for sublimity in every object that admits of it; and is almost always disappointed. For this disappointment there exists, I believe, no general preventive; nor is it desirable that there should. But with regard to one class of objects, there is a point in which injurious expectations may be easily corrected. It is generally supposed that waterfalls are scarcely worth being looked at except after much rain, and that, the more swoln the stream, the more fortunate the spectator; but this however is true only of large cataracts with sublime accompaniments; and not even of these without some drawbacks. In other instances, what becomes, at such a time, of that sense of refreshing coolness which can only be felt in dry and sunny weather, when the rocks, herbs, and flowers glisten with moisture diffused by the breath of the precipitous water? But, considering these things as objects of sight only, it may be observed that the principal charm of the smaller waterfalls or cascades consists in certain proportions of form and affinities of colour, among the component parts of the scene; and in the contrast maintained between the falling water and that which is apparently at rest, or rather settling gradually into quiet in the pool below. The beauty of such a scene, where there is naturally so much agitation, is also heightened, in a peculiar manner, by the *glimmering*, and, to-wards the verge of the pool, by the *steady*, reflection of the surrounding images. Now, all those delicate distinctions are destroyed by heavy floods, and the whole stream rushes along in foam and tumultuous confusion. A happy proportion of component parts is indeed noticeable among the landscapes of the North of England; and, in this characteristic essential to a perfect picture, they surpass the scenes of Scotland, and, in a still greater degree, those of Switzerland.

As a resident among the Lakes, I frequently hear the scenery of this country compared with that of the Alps; and therefore a few words shall be added to what has been incidentally said upon that subject.

If we could recall, to this region of lakes, the native pine-forests, with which many hundred years ago a large portion of the heights was covered, then, during spring and autumn, it might frequently, with much propriety, be compared to Switzerland,—the elements of the landscape would be the same—one country representing the other in miniature. Towns, villages, churches, rural seats, bridges and roads : green meadows and arable grounds, with their various produce, and deciduous woods of diversified foliage which occupy the vales and lower regions of the mountains, would, as in Switzerland, be divided by dark forests from ridges and round-topped heights covered with snow, and from pikes and sharp declivities imperfectly arrayed in the same glittering mantle : and the resemblance would be still more perfect on those days when vapours, resting upon, and floating around the summits, leave the elevation of the mountains less dependent upon the eye than on the imagination. But the pine-forests have wholly disappeared; and only during late spring and early autumn is realised here that assemblage of the imagery of different seasons, which is exhibited through the whole summer among the Alps,—winter in the distance,— and warmth, leafy woods, verdure and fertility at hand, and widely diffused.

Striking, then, from among the permanent materials of the landscape, that stage of vegetation which is occupied by pine-forests, and, above that, the perennial snows, we have mountains, the highest of which little exceed 3000 feet, while some of the Alps do not fall short of 14,000 or 15,000, and 8000 or 10,000 is not an uncommon elevation. Our tracts of wood and water are almost diminutive in comparison; therefore, as far as sublimity is dependent upon absolute bulk and height, and atmospherical influences in connection with these, it is obvious, that there can be no rivalship. But a short residence among the British Mountains will furnish abundant proof, that, after a certain point of elevation, viz. that which allows of compact and fleecy clouds settling upon, or sweeping over, the summits, the sense of sublimity depends more upon form and relation of objects to each other than upon their actual magnitude; and that an elevation of 3000 feet is sufficient to call forth in a most impressive degree the creative, and magnifying, and softening powers of the atmosphere. Hence, on the score even of sublimity, the superiority of the Alps is by no means so great as might hastily be inferred;—and, as to the *beauty* of the lower regions of the Swiss Mountains, it is noticeable—that, as they are all regularly mown, their surface has nothing of that mellow tone and variety of hues by which mountain turf, that is never touched by the scythe, is distinguished. On the smooth and steep slopes of the Swiss hills, these plots of verdure do indeed agreeably unite their colour with that of the deciduous trees, or make a lively contrast with the dark green pine-groves that define them, and among which they run in endless variety of shapes—but this is most pleasing *at first sight*; the permanent gratification of the eye requires finer gradations of tone, and a more delicate blending of hues into each other. Besides, it is only in spring and late autumn that cattle animate by their presence the Swiss lawns; and, though the pastures of the higher regions where they feed during the summer are left in their natural state of flowery herbage, those pastures are so remote, that their texture and colour are of no consequence in the composition of any picture in which a lake of the Vales is a feature. Yet in those lofty regions, how vegetation is invigorated by the genial climate of that country! Among the luxuriant flowers there met with, groves, or forests, if I may so call them, of Monks-hood are frequently seen; the plant of deep, rich blue, and as tall as in our gardens; and this at an elevation where, in Cumberland, Icelandic moss would only be found, or the stony summits be utterly bare.

We have, then, for the colouring of Switzerland, *principally* a vivid green herbage, black woods, and dazzling snows, presented in masses with a grandeur to which no one can be insensible; but not often graduated by Nature into soothing harmony, and so ill suited to the pencil, that though abundance of good subjects may be there found, they are not such as can be deemed *characteristic* of the country; nor is this unfitness confined to colour: the forms of the mountains, though many of them in some points of view the noblest that can be conceived, are apt to run into spikes and needles, and present a jagged outline which has a mean effect, transferred to canvass. This must have been felt by the ancient masters; for, if I am not mistaken, they have not left a single landscape, the materials of which are taken from the *peculiar* features of the Alps; yet Titian passed his life almost in their neighbourhood; the Poussins and Claude must have been well acquainted with their aspects; and several admirable painters, as Tibaldi and Luino, were born among the Italian Alps. A few experiments have lately been made by Englishmen, but they only prove that courage, skill, and judgment, may surmount any obstacles;

and it may be safely affirmed, that they who have done best in this bold adventure, will be the least likely to repeat the attempt. But, though our scenes are better suited to painting than those of the Alps, I should be sorry to contemplate either country in reference to that art, further than as its fitness or unfitness for the pencil renders it more or less pleasing to the eye of the spectator, who has learned to observe and feel, chiefly from Nature herself.

Deeming the points in which Alpine imagery is superior to British too obvious to be insisted upon, I will observe that the deciduous woods, though in many places unapproachable by the axe, and triumphing in the pomp and prodigality of Nature, have, in general,* neither the variety nor beauty which would exist in those of the mountains of Britain, if left to themselves. Magnificent walnut-trees grow upon the plains of Switzerland ; and fine trees, of that species, are found scattered over the hillsides : birches also grow here and there in luxuriant beauty ; but neither these, nor oaks, are ever a prevailing tree, nor can even be said to be common ; and the oaks, as far as I had an opportunity of observing, are greatly inferior to those of Britain. Among the interior vallies the proportion of beeches and pines is so great that other trees are scarcely noticeable ; and surely such woods are at all seasons much less agreeable than that rich and harmonious distribution of oak, ash, elm, birch, and alder, that formerly clothed the sides of Snowdon and Helvellyn ; and of which no mean remains still survive at the head of Ulswater. On the Italian side of the Alps, chesnut and walnut-trees grow at a considerable height on the mountains ; but, even there, the foliage is not equal in beauty to the ' natural product' of this climate. In fact the sunshine of the South of Europe, so envied when heard of at a distance, is in many respects injurious to rural beauty, particularly as it incites to the cultivation of spots of ground which in colder climates would be left in the hands of Nature, favouring at the same time the culture of plants that are more valuable on account of the fruit they produce to gratify the palate, than for affording pleasure to the eye, as materials of landscape. Take, for instance, the Promontory of Bellagio, so fortunate in its command of the three branches of the Lake of Como, yet the ridge of the Promontory

* The greatest variety of trees is found in the Valais.

itself, being for the most part covered with vines interspersed with olive-trees, accords but ill with the vastness of the green unappropriated mountains, and derogates not a little from the sublimity of those finely contrasted pictures to which it is a fore-ground.   The vine, when cultivated upon a large scale, not-withstanding all that may be said of it in poetry,* makes but a dull formal appearance in landscape ; and the olive-tree (though one is loth to say so) is not more grateful to the eye than our common willow, which it much resembles ; but the hoariness of hue, common to both, has in the aquatic plant an appropriate delicacy, harmonising with the situation in which it most de-lights.   The same may no doubt be said of the olive among the dry rocks of Attica, but I am speaking of it as found in gardens and vineyards in the North of Italy.   At Bellagio, what English-man can resist the temptation of substituting, in his fancy, for these formal treasures of cultivation, the natural variety of one of our parks—its pastured lawns, coverts of hawthorn, of wild-rose, and honeysuckle, and the majesty of forest trees?—such wild graces as the banks of Derwent-water shewed in the time of the Ratcliffes ; and Gowbarrow Park, Lowther, and Rydal do at this day.

As my object is to reconcile a Briton to the scenery of his own country, though not at the expense of truth, I am not afraid of asserting that in many points of view our LAKES, also, are much more interesting than those of the Alps ; first, as is im-plied above, from being more happily proportioned to the other features of the landscape ; and next, both as being infinitely more pellucid, and less subject to agitation from the winds.† Como, (which may perhaps be styled the King of Lakes, as Lu-

---

* Lucretius has charmingly described a scene of this kind.

> Inque dies magis in montem succedere sylvas
> Cogebant, infráque locum concedere cultis :
> Prata, lacus, rivos, segetes, vinetaque laeta
> Collibus et campis ut haberent, atque olearum
> *Caerula* distinguens inter *plaga* currere posset
> Per tumulos, et convalleis, campósque profusa :
> Ut nunc esse vides vario distincta lepore
> Omnia, quae pomis intersita dulcibus ornant,
> Arbustisque tenent felicibus obsita circûm.

† It is remarkable that Como (as is probably the case with other Italian Lakes) is more troubled by storms in summer than in winter.   Hence the pro-priety of the following verses :

gano is certainly the Queen) is disturbed by a periodical wind blowing *from* the head in the morning, and *towards* it in the afternoon. The magnificent Lake of the four Cantons, especially its noblest division, called the Lake of Uri, is not only much agitated by winds, but in the night time is disturbed from the bottom, as I was told, and indeed as I witnessed, without any apparent commotion in the air ; and when at rest, the water is not pure to the eye, but of a heavy green hue—as is that of all the other lakes, apparently according to the degree in which they are fed by melted snows. If the Lake of Geneva furnish an exception, this is probably owing to its vast extent, which allows the water to deposit its impurities. The water of the English lakes, on the contrary, being of a crystalline clearness, the reflections of the surrounding hills are frequently so lively, that it is scarcely possible to distinguish the point where the real object terminates, and its unsubstantial duplicate begins. The lower part of the Lake of Geneva, from its narrowness, must be much less subject to agitation than the higher divisions, and, as the water is clearer than that of the other Swiss Lakes, it will frequently exhibit this appearance, though it is scarcely pos· sible in an equal degree. During two comprehensive tours among the Alps, I did not observe, except on one of the smaller lakes between Lugano and Ponte Tresa, a single instance of those beautiful repetitions of surrounding objects on the bosom of the water, which are so frequently seen here: not to speak of the fine dazzling trembling net-work, breezy motions, and streaks and circles of intermingled smooth and rippled water, which make the surface of our lakes a field of endless variety. But among the Alps, where every thing tends to the grand and the sublime, in surfaces as well as in forms, if the lakes do not court the placid reflections of land objects those of first-rate magnitude make compensation, in some degree, by exhibiting those ever-changing fields of green, blue, and purple shadows or

Lari ! margine ubique confragoso
Nulli coelicolum negas sacellum
Picto pariete saxeoque tecto ;
Hinc miracula multa navitarum
Audis, nec placido refellis ore,
Sed nova usque paras, Noto vel Euro
Aestivas quatientibus cavernas,
Vel surgentis ab Adduae cubili
Caeco grandiuis imbre provoluto.　　　　LANDOR.

lights, (one scarcely knows which to name them) that call to mind a sea-prospect contemplated from a lofty cliff.

The subject of torrents and water-falls has already been touched upon ; but it may be added that in Switzerland, the perpetual accompaniment of snow upon the higher regions takes much from the effect of foaming white streams ; while, from their frequency, they obstruct each other's influence upon the mind of the spectator ; and, in all cases, the effect of an individual cataract, excepting the great Fall of the Rhine at Schaffhausen, is diminished by the general fury of the stream of which it is a part.

Recurring to the reflections from still water, I will describe a singular phenomenon of this kind of which I was an eye-witness.

Walking by the side of Ulswater upon a calm September morning, I saw, deep within the bosom of the Lake, a magnificent Castle, with towers and battlements : nothing could be more distinct than the whole edifice. After gazing with delight upon it for some time, as upon a work of enchantment, I could not but regret that my previous knowledge of the place enabled me to account for the appearance. It was in fact the reflection of a pleasure-house called Lyulph's Tower—the towers and battlements magnified and so much changed in shape as not to be immediately recognised. In the meanwhile, the pleasure-house itself was altogether hidden from my view by a body of vapour stretching over it and along the hill-side on which it stands, but not so as to have intercepted its communication with the lake ; and hence this novel and most impressive object, which, if I had been a stranger to the spot, would, from its being inexplicable, have long detained the mind in a state of pleasing astonishment.

Appearances of this kind, acting upon the credulity of early ages, may have given birth to, and favoured the belief in, stories of sub-aqueous palaces, gardens, and pleasure-grounds—the brilliant ornaments of Romance.

With this *inverted* scene I will couple a much more extraordinary phenomenon, which will show how other elegant fancies may have had their origin, less in invention than in the actual processes of Nature.

About eleven o'clock on the forenoon of a winter's day, coming suddenly, in company of a friend, into view of the Lake of Grasmere, we were alarmed by the sight of a newly-created Island; the transitory thought of the moment was, that it had been produced by an earthquake or some other convulsion of Nature. Recovering from the alarm, which was greater than the reader can possibly sympathise with, but which was shared to its full extent by my companion, we proceeded to examine the object before us. The elevation of this new island exceeded considerably that of the old one, its neighbour; it was likewise larger in circumference, comprehending a space of about five acres; its surface rocky, speckled with snow, and sprinkled over with birch-trees; it was divided towards the south from the other island by a narrow frith, and in like manner from the northern shore of the lake; on the east and west it was separated from the shore by a much larger space of smooth water.

Marvellous was the illusion! Comparing the new with the old Island, the surface of which is soft, green, and unvaried, I do not scruple to say that, as an object of sight, it was much the more distinct. 'How little faith,' we exclaimed, 'is due to one sense, unless its evidence be confirmed by some of its fellows! What Stranger could possibly be persuaded that this, which we know to be an unsubstantial mockery, is *really* so; and that there exists only a single Island on this beautiful Lake?' At length the appearance underwent a gradual transmutation; it lost its prominence and passed into a glimmering and dim *inversion*, and then totally disappeared; leaving behind it a clear open area of ice of the same dimensions. We now perceived that this bed of ice, which was thinly suffused with water, had produced the illusion, by reflecting and refracting (as persons skilled in optics would no doubt easily explain) a rocky and woody section of the opposite mountain named Silver-how.

Having dwelt so much upon the beauty of pure and still water, and pointed out the advantage which the Lakes of the North of England have in this particular over those of the Alps, it would be injustice not to advert to the sublimity that must often be given to Alpine scenes, by the agitations to which those vast bodies of diffused water are there subject. I have witnessed many tremendous thunder-storms among the Alps, and the most glorious effects of light and shadow; but I never happened to be present when any Lake was agitated by those hurricanes which I imagine must often torment them. If the commotions be at all proportionable to the expanse and depth of the waters, and the height of the surrounding mountains, then, if I may judge from what is frequently seen here, the exhibition must be awful and astonishing.—On this day, March 30, 1822, the winds have been acting upon the small Lake of Rydal, as if they had received command to carry its waters from their bed into the sky; the white billows in different quarters disappeared under clouds, or rather drifts, of spray, that were whirled along, and up into the air by scouring winds, charging each other in squadrons in every direction, upon the Lake. The spray, having been hurried aloft till it lost its consistency and whiteness, was driven along the mountain tops like flying showers that vanish in the distance. Frequently an eddying wind scooped the waters out of the basin, and forced them upwards in the very shape of an Icelandic Geyser, or boiling fountain, to the height of several hundred feet.

This small Mere of Rydal, from its position, is subject in a peculiar degree to these commotions. The present season, however, is unusually stormy;—great numbers of fish, two of them not less than 12 pounds weight, were a few days ago cast on the shores of Derwent-water by the force of the waves.

Lest, in the foregoing comparative estimate, I should be suspected of partiality to my native mountains, I will support my general opinion by the authority of Mr. West, whose Guide to the Lakes has been eminently serviceable to the Tourist for nearly 50 years. The Author, a Roman Catholic Clergyman, had passed much time abroad, and was well acquainted with the scenery of the Continent. He thus expresses himself: 'They who intend to make the continental tour should begin here; as it will give, in miniature, an idea of what they are to meet with there, in traversing the Alps and Appenines; to which our northern mountains are not inferior in beauty of line, or variety of summit, number of lakes, and transparency of water; not in colouring of rock, or softness of turf, but in height and extent only. The mountains here are all accessible to the summit, and furnish prospects no less surprising, and with more variety, than the Alps themselves. The tops of the highest Alps are inaccessible, being covered with everlasting snow, which commencing at regular heights above the cultivated tracts, or wooded and verdant sides, form indeed the high-. est contrast in Nature. For there may be seen all the variety of climate in one view. To this, however, we oppose the sight of the ocean, from the summits of all the higher mountains, as it appears intersected with promontories, decorated with islands, and animated with navigation.'—West's *Guide*, p. 5.

It was my intention, several years ago, to describe a regular tour through this country, taking the different scenes in the most favourable order; but after some progress had been made in the work it was abandoned from a conviction, that, if well executed, it would lessen the pleasure of the Traveller by anticipation, and, if the contrary, it would mislead him. The Reader may not, however, be displeased with the following extract from a letter to a Friend, giving an account of a visit to a summit of one of the highest of these mountains; of which I am reminded by the observations of Mr. West, and by reviewing what has been said of this district in comparison with the Alps.

Having left Rosthwaite in Borrowdale, on a bright morning in the first week of October, we ascended from Seathwaite to the top of the ridge, called Ash-course, and thence beheld three distinct views;—on one side, the continuous Vale of Borrowdale, Keswick, and Bassenthwaite,—with Skiddaw, Helvellyn, Saddle-back, and numerous other mountains—and, in the distance, the Solway Frith and the Mountains of Scotland;—on the other side, and below us, the Langdale Pikes—their own vale below *them ;*—Windermere,—and, far beyond Windermere, Ingleborough in Yorkshire. But how shall I speak of the deliciousness of the third prospect! At this time, *that* was most favoured by sunshine and shade. The green Vale of Esk—deep and green, with its glittering serpent stream, lay below us; and, on we looked to the Mountains near the Sea,—Black Comb pre-eminent,—and, still beyond, to the Sea itself, in dazzling brightness. Turning round we saw the Mountains of Wastdale in tumult; to our right, Great Gavel, the loftiest, a distinct, and *huge* form, though the middle of the mountain was, to our eyes, as its base.

We had attained the object of this journey; but our ambition now mounted higher. We saw the summit of Scaw-fell, apparently very near to us; and we shaped our course towards it; but, discovering that it could not be reached without first making a considerable descent, we resolved, instead, to aim at another point of the same mountain, called the *Pikes*, which I have since found has been estimated as higher than the summit bearing the name of Scawfell Head, where the Stone Man is built.

The sun had never once been overshadowed by a cloud during the whole of our progress from the centre of Borrowdale. On the summit of the Pike, which we gained after much toil, though without difficulty, there was not a breath of air to stir even the papers containing our refreshment, as they lay spread out upon a rock. The stillness seemed to be not of this world :—we paused, and kept silence to listen ; and no sound could be heard : the Scawfell Cataracts were voiceless to us ; and there was not an insect to hum in the air. The vales which we had seen from Ash-course lay yet in view ; and, side by side with Eskdale, we now saw the sister Vale of Donnerdale terminated by the Duddon Sands. But the majesty of the mountains below, and close to us, is not to be conceived. We now beheld the whole mass of Great Gavel from its base,—the Den of Wastdale at our feet —a gulf immeasurable : Grasmire and the other mountains of Crummock—Ennerdale and its mountains ; and the Sea beyond ! We sat down to our repast, and gladly would we have tempered our beverage (for there was no spring or well near us) with such a supply of delicious water as we might have procured, had we been on the rival summit of Great Gavel ; for on its highest point is a small triangular receptacle in the native rock, which, the shepherds say, is never dry. There we might have slaked our thirst plenteously with a pure and celestial liquid, for the cup or basin, it appears, has no other feeder than the dews of heaven, the showers, the vapours, the hoar frost, and the spotless snow.

While we were gazing around, 'Look,' I exclaimed, 'at yon ship upon the glittering sea !' 'Is it a ship ?' replied our shepherd-guide. 'It can be nothing else,' interposed my companion ; 'I cannot be mistaken, I am so accustomed to the appearance of ships at sea.' The Guide dropped the argument ; but, before a minute was gone, he quietly said, 'Now look at your ship ; it is changed into a horse.' So indeed it was,—a horse with a gallant neck and head. We laughed heartily ; and, I hope, when again inclined to be positive, I may remember the ship and the horse upon the glittering sea ; and the calm confidence, yet submissiveness, of our wise Man of the Mountains, who certainly had more knowledge of clouds than we, whatever might be our knowledge of ships.

I know not how long we might have remained on the summit of the Pike, without a thought of moving, had not our Guide warned us that we must not linger; for a storm was coming. We looked in vain to espy the signs of it. Mountains, vales, and sea were touched with the clear light of the sun. 'It is there,' said he, pointing to the sea beyond Whitehaven, and there we perceived a light vapour unnoticeable but by a shepherd accustomed to watch all mountain bodings. We gazed around again, and yet again, unwilling to lose the remembrance of what lay before us in that lofty solitude; and then prepared to depart. Meanwhile the air changed to cold, and we saw that tiny vapour swelled into mighty masses of cloud which came boiling over the mountains. Great Gavel, Helvellyn, and Skiddaw, were wrapped in storm; yet Langdale, and the mountains in that quarter, remained all bright in sunshine. Soon the storm reached us; we sheltered under a crag; and almost as rapidly as it had come it passed away, and left us free to observe the struggles of gloom and sunshine in other quarters. Langdale now had its share, and the Pikes of Langdale were decorated by two splendid rainbows. Skiddaw also had his own rainbows. Before we again reached Ash-course every cloud had vanished from every summit.

I ought to have mentioned that round the top of Scawfell-PIKE not a blade of grass is to be seen. Cushions or tufts of moss, parched and brown, appear between the huge blocks and stones that lie in heaps on all sides to a great distance, like skeletons or bones of the earth not needed at the creation, and there left to be covered with never-dying lichens, which the clouds and dews nourish; and adorn with colours of vivid and exquisite beauty. Flowers, the most brilliant feathers, and even gems, scarcely surpass in colouring some of those masses of stone, which no human eye beholds, except the shepherd or traveller be led thither by curiosity: and how seldom must this happen! For the other eminence is the one visited by the adventurous stranger; and the shepherd has no inducement to ascend the PIKE in quest of his sheep; no food being *there* to tempt them.

We certainly were singularly favoured in the weather; for when we were seated on the summit, our conductor, turning his eyes thoughtfully round, said, 'I do not know that in my whole life, I was ever, at any season of the year, so high upon the mountains on so *calm* a day.' (It was the 7th of October.) Afterwards we had a spectacle of the grandeur of earth and heaven commingled; yet without terror. We knew that the storm would pass away;—for so our prophetic Guide had assured us.

Before we reached Seathwaite in Borrowdale, a few stars had appeared, and we pursued our way down the Vale, to Rosthwaite, by moonlight.

Scawfell and Helvellyn being the two Mountains of this region which will best repay the fatigue of ascending them, the following Verses may be here introduced with propriety. They are from the Author's Miscellaneous Poems.

To ————.

ON HER FIRST ASCENT TO THE SUMMIT OF HELVELLYN.

Inmate of a Mountain Dwelling,
Thou hast clomb aloft, and gazed,
From the watch-towers of Helvellyn;
Awed, delighted, and amazed!

Potent was the spell that bound thee
Not unwilling to obey;
For blue Ether's arms, flung round thee,
Stilled the pantings of dismay.

Lo! the dwindled woods and meadows!
What a vast abyss is there!
Lo! the clouds, the solemn shadows,
And the glistenings—heavenly fair!

And a record of commotion
Which a thousand ridges yield;
Ridge, and gulf, and distant ocean
Gleaming like a silver shield!

—Take thy flight;—possess, inherit
Alps or Andes—they are thine!
With the morning's roseate Spirit,
Sweep their length of snowy line;

Or survey the bright dominions
In the gorgeous colours drest
Flung from off the purple pinions,
Evening spreads throughout the west!

Thine are all the coral fountains
Warbling in each sparry vault
Of the untrodden lunar mountains;
Listen to their songs!—or halt,

To Niphate's top invited,
Whither spiteful Satan steered;
Or descend where the ark alighted,
When the green earth re-appeared:

For the power of hills is on thee,
As was witnessed through thine eye
Then, when old Helvellyn won thee
To confess their majesty!

Having said so much of *points of view* to which few are likely
to ascend, I am induced to subjoin an account of a short excursion through more accessible parts of the country, made at a
time when it is seldom seen but by the inhabitants. As the
journal was written for one acquainted with the general features
of the country, only those effects and appearances are dwelt upon,
which are produced by the changeableness of the atmosphere, or
belong to the season when the excursion was made.

A.D. 1805.—On the 7th of November, on a damp and gloomy
morning, we left Grasmere Vale, intending to pass a few days on
the banks of Ullswater. A mild and dry autumn had been unusually favourable to the preservation and beauty of foliage; and,
far advanced as the season was, the trees on the larger Island of
Rydal-mere retained a splendour which did not need the height-
ening of sunshine. We noticed, as we passed, that the line of
the grey rocky shore of that island, shaggy with variegated
bushes and shrubs, and spotted and striped with purplish brown
heath, indistinguishably blending with its image reflected in the
still water, produced a curious resemblance, both in form and
colour, to a richly-coated caterpillar, as it might appear through
a magnifying glass of extraordinary power. The mists gathered
as we went along: but, when we reached the top of Kirkstone,
we were glad we had not been discouraged by the apprehension
of bad weather. Though not able to see a hundred yards before
us, we were more than contented. At such a time, and in such
a place, every scattered stone the size of one's head becomes a
companion. Near the top of the Pass is the remnant of an old
wall, which (magnified, though obscured, by the vapour) might
have been taken for a fragment of some monument of ancient

grandeur,—yet that same pile of stones we had never before even observed. This situation, it must be allowed, is not favourable to gaiety; but a pleasing hurry of spirits accompanies the surprise occasioned by objects transformed, dilated, or distorted, as they are when seen through such a medium. Many of the fragments of rock on the top and slopes of Kirkstone, and of similar places, are fantastic enough in themselves; but the full effect of such impressions can only be had in a state of weather when they are not likely to be *sought* for. It was not till we had descended considerably that the fields of Hartshope were seen, like a lake tinged by the reflection of sunny clouds: I mistook them for Brothers-water, but, soon after, we saw that lake gleaming faintly with a steelly brightness,—then, as we continued to descend, appeared the brown oaks, and the birches of lively yellow—and the cottages—and the lowly Hall of Hartshope, with its long roof and ancient chimneys. During great part of our way to Patterdale, we had rain, or rather drizzling vapour; for there was never a drop upon our hair or clothes larger than the smallest pearls upon a lady's ring.

The following morning, incessant rain till 11 o'clock, when the sky began to clear, and we walked along the eastern shore of Ullswater towards the farm of Blowick. The wind blew strong, and drove the clouds forward, on the side of the mountain above our heads;—two storm-stiffened black yew-trees fixed our notice, seen through, or under the edge of, the flying mists,—four or five goats were bounding among the rocks;—the sheep moved about more quietly, or cowered beneath their sheltering places. This is the only part of the country where goats are now found;* but this morning, before we had seen these, I was reminded of that picturesque animal by two rams of mountain breed, both with Ammonian horns, and with beards majestic as that which Michael Angelo has given to his statue of Moses.—But to return; when our path had brought us to that part of the naked common which overlooks the woods and bush-besprinkled fields of Blowick, the lake, clouds, and mists were all in motion to the sound of sweeping winds;—the church and cottages of Patterdale scarcely visible, or seen only by fits between the shifting vapours. To the northward the scene was less visionary;—Place Fell steady and bold;—the whole lake driving onward like a

* A.D. 1835. These also have disappeared.

great river—waves dancing round the small islands.   The house at Blowick was the boundary of our walk ; and we returned, lamenting to see a decaying and uncomfortable dwelling in a place where sublimity and beauty seemed to contend with each other.   But these regrets were dispelled by a glance on the woods that clothe the opposite steeps of the lake. How exquisite was the mixture of sober and splendid hues!   The general colouring of the trees was brown—rather that of ripe hazel nuts ; but towards the water, there were yet beds of green, and in the highest parts of the wood, was abundance of yellow foliage, which, gleaming through a vapoury lustre, reminded us of masses of clouds, as you see them gathered together in the west, and touched with the golden light of the setting sun.

After dinner we walked up the Vale ; I had never had an idea of its extent and width in passing along the public road on the other side.   We followed the path that leads from house to house ; two or three times it took us through some of those copses or groves that cover the little hillocks in the middle of the vale, making an intricate and pleasing intermixture of lawn and wood.   Our fancies could not resist the temptation ; and we fixed upon a spot for a cottage, which we began to build : and finished as easily as castles are raised in the air.—Visited the same spot in the evening.   I shall say nothing of the moonlight aspect of the situation which had charmed us so much in the afternoon ; but I wish you had been with us when, in returning to our friend's house, we espied his lady's large white dog, lying in the moonshine upon the round knoll under the old yew-tree in the garden, a romantic image—the dark tree and its dark shadow—and the elegant creature, as fair as a spirit !   The torrents murmured softly : the mountains down which they were falling did not, to my sight, furnish a back-ground for this Ossianic picture ; but I had a consciousness of the depth of the seclusion, and that mountains were embracing us on all sides ; ' I saw not, but I *felt* that they were there.'

Friday, November 9th.—Rain, as yesterday, till 10 o'clock, when we took a boat to row down the lake.   The day improved, —clouds and sunny gleams on the mountains.   In the large bay under Place Fell, three fishermen were dragging a net,— a picturesque group beneath the high and bare crags !   A raven was seen aloft ; not hovering like the kite, for that is not the habit of the bird; but passing on with a straight-forward perseverance, and timing the motion of its wings to its own croaking. The waters were agitated; and the iron tone of the raven's voice, which strikes upon the ear at all times as the more dolorous from its regularity, was in fine keeping with the wild scene before our eyes. This carnivorous fowl is a great enemy to the lambs of these solitudes; I recollect frequently seeing, when a boy, bunches of unfledged ravens suspended from the church-yard gates of H——, for which a reward of *so* much a head was given to the adventurous destroyer.—The fishermen drew their net ashore, and hundreds of fish were leaping in their prison. They were all of the kind called skellies, a sort of fresh-water herring, shoals of which may sometimes be seen dimpling or rippling the surface of the lake in calm weather. This species is not found, I believe, in any other of these lakes; nor, as far as I know, is the chevin, that *spiritless* fish, (though I am loth to call it so, for it was a prime favourite with Isaac Walton,) which must frequent Ullswater, as I have seen a large shoal passing into the lake from the river Eamont. *Here* are no pike, and the char are smaller than those of the other lakes, and of inferior quality; but the grey trout attains a very large size, sometimes weighing above twenty pounds. This lordly creature seems to know that 'retiredness is a piece of majesty;' for it is scarcely ever caught, or even seen, except when it quits the depths of the lake in the spawning season, and runs up into the streams, where it is too often destroyed in disregard of the law of the land and of Nature.

Quitted the boat in the bay of Sandwyke, and pursued our way towards Martindale along a pleasant path—at first through a coppice, bordering the lake, then through green fields—and came to the village, (if village it may be called, for the houses are few, and separated from each other,) a sequestered spot, shut out from the view of the lake. Crossed the one-arched bridge, below the chapel, with its 'bare ring of mossy wall,' and single yew-tree. At the last house in the dale we were greeted by the master, who was sitting at his door, with a flock of sheep collected round him, for the purpose of smearing them with tar (according to the custom of the season) for protection against the winter's cold. He invited us to enter, and view a room built by Mr. Hasell for the accommodation of his friends at the annual chase of red deer in his forests at the head of these dales. The

room is fitted up in the sportsman's style, with a cupboard for
bottles and glasses, with strong chairs, and a dining-table; and
ornamented with the horns of the stags caught at these hunts
for a succession of years—the length of the last race each had run
being recorded under his spreading antlers.   The good woman
treated us with oaten cake, new and crisp; and after this welcome
refreshment and rest, we proceeded on our return to Patterdale
by a short cut over the mountains.   On leaving the fields of
Sandwyke, while ascending by a gentle slope along the valley of
Martindale, we had occasion to observe that in thinly-peopled
glens of this character the general want of wood gives a peculiar interest to the scattered cottages embowered in sycamore.
Towards its head, this valley splits into two parts; and in one
of these (that to the left) there is no house, nor any building to
be seen but a cattle-shed on the side of a hill, which is sprinkled
over with trees, evidently the remains of an extensive forest.
Near the entrance of the other division stands the house where
we were entertained, and beyond the enclosures of that farm
there are no other.   A few old trees remain, relics of the forest,
a little stream hastens, though with serpentine windings, through
the uncultivated hollow, where many cattle were pasturing.   The
cattle of this country are generally white, or light-coloured; but
these were dark brown, or black, which heightened the resemblance this scene bears to many parts of the Highlands of Scotland.—While we paused to rest upon the hill-side, though well
contented with the quiet every-day sounds—the lowing of cattle,
bleating of sheep, and the very gentle murmuring of the valley
stream, we could not but think what a grand effect the music of
the bugle-horn would have among these mountains.   It is still
heard once every year, at the chase I have spoken of; a day of
festivity for the inhabitants of this district except the poor deer,
the most ancient of them all.   Our ascent even to the top was
very easy; when it was accomplished we had exceedingly fine
views, some of the lofty Fells being resplendent with sunshine,
and others partly shrouded by clouds.   Ullswater, bordered by
black steeps, was of dazzling brightness; the plain beyond
Penrith smooth and bright, or rather gleamy, as the sea or sea
sands.   Looked down into Boardale, which, like Stybarrow, has
been named from the wild swine that formerly abounded here;
but it has now no sylvan covert, being smooth and bare, a long,

narrow, deep, cradle-shaped glen, lying so sheltered that one would be pleased to see it planted by human hands, there being a sufficiency of soil; and the trees would be sheltered almost like shrubs in a green-house.—After having walked some way along the top of the hill, came in view of Glenriddin and the mountains at the head of Grisdale.—Before we began to descend turned aside to a small ruin, called at this day the chapel, where it is said the inhabitants of Martindale and Patterdale were accustomed to assemble for worship. There are now no traces from which you could infer for what use the building had been erected; the loose stones and the few which yet continue piled up resemble those which lie elsewhere on the mountain; but the shape of the building having been oblong, its remains differ from those of a common sheep-fold; and it has stood east and west. Scarcely did the Druids, when they fled to these fastnesses, perform their rites in any situation more exposed to disturbance from the elements. One cannot pass by without being reminded that the rustic psalmody must have had the accompaniment of many a wildly-whistling blast; and what dismal storms must have often drowned the voice of the preacher! As we descend, Patterdale opens upon the eye in grand simplicity, screened by mountains, and proceeding from two heads, Deepdale and Hartshope, where lies the little lake of Brotherswater, named in old maps Broaderwater, and probably rightly so; for Bassenthwaite-mere at this day is familiarly called Broadwater; but the change in the appellation of this small lake or pool (if it be a corruption) may have been assisted by some melancholy accident similar to what happened about twenty years ago, when two brothers were drowned there, having gone out to take their holiday pleasure upon the ice on a new-year's day.

A rough and precipitous peat track brought us down to our friend's house.—Another fine moonlight night; but a thick fog rising from the neighbouring river, enveloped the rocky and wood-crested knoll on which our fancy cottage had been erected; and, under the damp cast upon my feelings, I consoled myself with moralising on the folly of hasty decisions in matters of importance, and the necessity of having at least one year's knowledge of a place before you realise airy suggestions in solid stone.

Saturday, November 10th.—At the breakfast-table tidings reached us of the death of Lord Nelson, and of the victory at

Trafalgar. Sequestered as we were from the sympathy of a crowd, we were shocked to hear that the bells had been ringing joyously at Penrith to celebrate the triumph. In the rebellion of the year 1745, people fled with their valuables from the open country to Patterdale, as a place of refuge secure from the incursions of strangers. At that time, news such as we had heard might have been long in penetrating so far into the recesses of the mountains; but now, as you know, the approach is easy, and the communication, in summer time, almost hourly: nor is this strange, for travellers after pleasure are become not less active, and more numerous than those who formerly left their homes for purposes of gain. The priest on the banks of the remotest stream of Lapland will talk familiarly of Buonaparte's last conquests, and discuss the progress of the French revolution, having acquired much of his information from adventurers impelled by curiosity alone.

The morning was clear and cheerful after a night of sharp frost. At 10 o'clock we took our way on foot towards Pooley Bridge, on the same side of the lake we had coasted in a boat the day before.—Looked backwards to the south from our favourite station above Blowick. The dazzling sunbeams striking upon the church and village, while the earth was steaming with exhalations not traceable in other quarters, rendered their forms even more indistinct than the partial and flitting veil of unillumined vapour had done two days before. The grass on which we trod, and the trees in every thicket, were dripping with melted hoar-frost. We observed the lemon-coloured leaves of the birches, as the breeze turned them to the sun, sparkle, or rather *flash*, like diamonds, and the leafless purple twigs were tipped with globes of shining crystal.

The day continued delightful, and unclouded to the end. I will not describe the country which we slowly travelled through, nor relate our adventures: and will only add, that on the afternoon of the 13th we returned along the banks of Ullswater by the usual road. The lake lay in deep repose after the agitations of a wet and stormy morning. The trees in Gowbarrow park were in that state when what is gained by the disclosure of their bark and branches compensates, almost, for the loss of foliage, exhibiting the variety which characterises the point of time between autumn and winter. The hawthorns were leafless; their round heads covered with rich scarlet berries, and adorned with arches of green brambles, and eglantines hung with glossy hips; and the grey trunks of some of the ancient oaks, which in the summer season might have been regarded only for their venerable majesty, now attracted notice by a pretty embellishment of green mosses and fern intermixed with russet leaves retained by those slender outstarting twigs which the veteran tree would not have tolerated in his strength. The smooth silver branches of the ashes were bare; most of the alders as green as the Devonshire cottage-myrtle that weathers the snows of Christmas.—Will you accept it as some apology for my having dwelt so long on the woodland ornaments of these scenes—that artists speak of the trees on the banks of Ullswater, and especially along the bays of Stybarrow crags, as having a peculiar character of picturesque intricacy in their stems and branches, which their rocky stations and the mountain winds have combined to give them?

At the end of Gowbarrow park a large herd of deer were either moving slowly or standing still among the fern. I was sorry when a chance-companion, who had joined us by the way, startled them with a whistle, disturbing an image of grave simplicity and thoughtful enjoyment; for I could have fancied that those natives of this wild and beautiful region were partaking with us a sensation of the solemnity of the closing day. The sun had been set some time; and we could perceive that the light was fading away from the coves of Helvellyn, but the lake under a luminous sky, was more brilliant than before.

After tea at Patterdale, set out again:—a fine evening; the seven stars close to the mountain-top; all the stars seemed brighter than usual. The steeps were reflected in Brotherswater, and, above the lake, appeared like enormous black perpendicular walls. The Kirkstone torrents had been swoln by the rains, and now filled the mountain pass with their roaring, which added greatly to the solemnity of our walk. Behind us, when we had climbed to a great height, we saw one light, very distinct, in the vale, like a large red star—a solitary one in the gloomy region. The cheerfulness of the scene was in the sky above us.

Reached home a little before midnight. The following verses (from the Author's Miscellaneous Poems,) after what has just

been read may be acceptable to the reader, by way of conclusion
to this little Volume.

ODE.

The Pass of Kirkstone.

I.

Within the mind strong fancies work,
A deep delight the bosom thrills,
Oft as I pass along the fork
Of these fraternal hills:
Where, save the rugged road, we find
No appanage of human kind;
Nor hint of man, if stone or rock
Seem not his handy-work to mock
By something cognizably shaped;
Mockery—or model roughly hewn,
And left as if by earthquake strewn,
Or from the Flood escaped:
Altars for Druid service fit;
(But where no fire was ever lit,
Unless the glow-worm to the skies
Thence offer nightly sacrifice;)
Wrinkled Egyptian monument;
Green moss-grown tower; or hoary tent;
Tents of a camp that never shall be raised;
On which four thousand years have gazed!

II.

Ye plough-shares sparkling on the slopes!
Ye snow-white lambs that trip
Imprisoned 'mid the formal props
Of restless ownership!
Ye trees, that may to-morrow fall
To feed the insatiate Prodigal!
Lawns, houses, chattels, groves, and fields,
All that the fertile valley shields;
Wages of folly—baits of crime,—
Of life's uneasy game the stake,
Playthings that keep the eyes awake
Of drowsy, dotard Time;
O care! O guilt!—O vales and plains,
Here, 'mid his own unvexed domains,
A Genius dwells, that can subdue
At once all memory of You,—
Most potent when mists veil the sky,
Mists that distort and magnify;
While the hoarse rushes, to the sweeping breeze,
Sigh forth their ancient melodies!

III.

List to those shriller notes!—*that* march
Perchance was on the blast,
When through this Height's inverted arch,
Rome's earliest legion passed!
—They saw, adventurously impelled,
And older eyes than theirs beheld,
This block—and yon, whose Church-like frame
Gives to the savage Pass its name.
Aspiring Road! that lov'st to hide
Thy daring in a vapoury bourn,
Not seldom may the hour return
When thou shalt be my Guide:
And I (as often we find cause,
When life is at a weary pause,
And we have panted up the hill
Of duty with reluctant will)
Be thankful, even though tired and faint,
For the rich bounties of Constraint;
Whence oft invigorating transports flow
That Choice lacked courage to bestow!

IV.

My Soul was grateful for delight
That wore a threatening brow;
A veil is lifted—can she slight
The scene that opens now?
Though habitation none appear,
The greenness tells, man must be there;
The shelter—that the perspective
Is of the clime in which we live;
Where Toil pursues his daily round;
Where Pity sheds sweet tears, and Love,
In woodbine bower or birchen grove,
Inflicts his tender wound.
—Who comes not hither ne'er shall know
How beautiful the world below;
Nor can he guess how lightly leaps
The brook adown the rocky steeps.
Farewell, thou desolate Domain!
Hope, pointing to the cultured Plain,
Carols like a shepherd boy;
And who is she?—Can that be Joy!
Who, with a sun-beam for her guide,
Smoothly skims the meadows wide;
While Faith, from yonder opening cloud,
To hill and vale proclaims aloud,
'Whate'er the weak may dread, the wicked dare,
Thy lot, O man, is good, thy portion fair!'

The Publishers, with permission of the Author, have added the following

ITINERARY OF THE LAKES,

FOR THE USE OF TOURISTS.

STAGES.	MILES.
Lancaster to Kendal, by Kirkby Lonsdale	30
Lancaster to Kendal, by Burton	22
Lancaster to Kendal, by Milnthorpe	21
Lancaster to Ulverston, over Sands	21
Lancaster to Ulverston, by Levens Bridge	35½
Ulverston to Hawkshead, by Coniston Water Head . . .	19
Ulverston to Bowness, by Newby Bridge	17
Hawkshead to Ambleside	5
Hawkshead to Bowness	6
Kendal to Ambleside	14
Kendal to Ambleside, by Bowness	15
From and back to Ambleside round the two Langdales . .	18
Ambleside to Ullswater	10
Ambleside to Keswick	16¼
Keswick to Borrowdale, and round the Lake . . .	12
Keswick to Borrowdale and Buttermere	23
Keswick to Wastdale and Calder Bridge	27
Calder Bridge to Buttermere and Keswick	29
Keswick, round Bassenthwaite Lake	18
Keswick to Patterdale, Pooley Bridge, and Penrith . .	38
Keswick to Pooley Bridge and Penrith	24
Keswick to Penrith	17½
Whitehaven to Keswick	27
Workington to Keswick	21
Excursion from Penrith to Hawes Water	27
Carlisle to Penrith	18
Penrith to Kendal	26

*Inns and Public Houses, when not mentioned, are marked thus *.*

LANCASTER to KENDAL, by Kirkby Lonsdale, 30 miles.

MILES.			MILES.	MILES.			MILES.
5	Caton	. . . . . .	5	2	Tunstall	. . . . .	13
2	Claughton	. . . . .	7	2	Burrow	. . . . . .	15
2	Hornby*	. . . . .	9	2	Kirkby Lonsdale	. . .	17
2	Melling	. . . . .	11	13	Kendal	. . . . .	30

INNS—*Lancaster :* King's Arms, Commercial Inn, Royal Oak. *Kirkby Lonsdale :* Rose and Crown, Green Dragon.

LANCASTER to KENDAL, by Burton, 21¾ miles.

MILES.		MILES.	MILES.		MILES.
10¾	Burton	10¾	¼	End Moor*	16
4¾	Crooklands*	15½	5¾	Kendal	21¾

INNS—*Kendal:* King's Arms, Commercial Inn. *Burton:* Royal Oak, King's Arms.

LANCASTER to KENDAL, by Milnthorpe, 21¼ miles.

2¾	Slyne*	2¾	½	Beethom*	12½
1¼	Bolton-le-Sands*	4	1¼	Milnthorpe	13¾
2	Carnforth*	6	1¼	Heversham*	15
2	Junction of the Milnthorpe and Burton roads	8	1½	Levens-Bridge	16½
4	Hale*	12	4¾	Kendal	21¼

INN—*Milnthorpe:* Cross Keys.

LANCASTER to ULVERSTON, over Sands, 21 miles.

3½	Hest Bank*	3½	1¼	Flookburgh*	15
¼	Lancaster Sands	3¾	¾	Cark	15¾
9	Kent's Bank	12¾	¼	Leven Sands	16
1	Lower Allithwaite	13¾	5	Ulverston	21

INNS—*Ulverston:* Sun Inn, Bradyll's Arms.

LANCASTER to ULVERSTON, by Levens-Bridge, 35½ miles.

12	Hale*	12	3	Lindal*	23
½	Beethom*	12½	2	Newton*	25
1¼	Milnthorpe	13¾	2	Newby-Bridge*	27½
1¼	Heversham*	15	2	Low Wood	29½
2¼	Levens-Bridge	16½	3	Greenodd	32½
4	Witherslack*	20½	3	Ulverston	35½

ULVERSTON to HAWKSHEAD, by Coniston Water-Head, 19 miles.

6	Lowick-Bridge	6	8	Coniston Water-Head*	16
2	Nibthwaite	8	3	Hawkshead	19

INN—*Hawkshead:* Red Lion.

ULVERSTON to BOWNESS, by Newby-Bridge, 16 miles.

3	Greenodd	3	2	Newby-Bridge	8
3	Low Wood	6	8	Bowness	16

INNS—*Bowness:* White Lion, Crown Inn.

HAWKSHEAD to AMBLESIDE, 5 miles.

HAWKSHEAD to BOWNESS, 5½ miles.

2	Sawrey	2	1½	Bowness	5½
2	Windermere-ferry*	4			

KENDAL to AMBLESIDE, 13½ miles.

5	Staveley*	5	1½	Troutbeck-Bridge*	10
1½	Ings Chapel	6½	2	Low Wood Inn	12
2	Orrest-head	8½	1½	Ambleside	13½

INNS—*Ambleside:* Salutation Hotel, Commercial Inn.

KENDAL to AMBLESIDE, by Bowness, 15 miles.

MILES.		MILES.	MILES.		MILES.
4	Crook*	4	2½	Troutbeck-Bridge . . .	11½
2	Gilpin-Bridge*	6	2	Low Wood Inn	13½
3	Bowness	9	1½	Ambleside	15

A Circuit from and back to AMBLESIDE, by Little and Great Langdale,
18 miles.

3	Skelwith-Bridge* . . .	3	2	Langdale Chapel Stile*	. 13
2	Colwith Cascade. . . .	5	5	By High Close and Rydal	
3	Blea Tarn	8		to Ambleside	18
3	Dungeon Ghyll	11			

AMBLESIDE to ULLSWATER, 10 miles.

4	Top of Kirkstone. . . .	4	3	Inn at Patterdale . . .	10
3	Kirkstone Foot	7			

AMBLESIDE to KESWICK, 16¼ miles.

1½	Rydal	1½	4	Smalthwaite-Bridge. . .	12¼
3½	Swan, Grassmere* . . .	5	3	Castlerigg	15¼
2	Dunmail Raise	7	1	Keswick	16¼
1¼	Nag's Head, Wythburn .	8¼			

EXCURSIONS FROM KESWICK.

INNS—*Keswick :* Royal Oak, Queen's Head.
To BORROWDALE, and ROUND THE LAKE, 12 miles.

2	Barrow House	2	1	Return to Grange . . .	6
1	Lowdore	3	4½	Portinscale.	10½
1	Grange	4	1½	Keswick	12
1	Bowder Stone	5			

To BORROWDALE and BUTTERMERE.

5	Bowder Stone.	5	4	Gatesgarth	12
1	Rosthwaite	6	2	Buttermere*	14
2	Seatoller	8	9	Keswick, by Newlands	. 23

Two Days' Excursion to WASTDALE, ENNERDALE, and LOWES-WATER.
First Day.

6	Rosthwaite	6	2	Wastdale-head	14
2	Seatoller	8	6	Strands,* Nether Wastdale	20
1	Seathwaite	9	4	Gosforth*	24
3	Sty-head	12	3	Calder-Bridge*	27

Second Day.

7	Ennerdale-Bridge . . .	7	2	Scale-hill*	16
3	Lamplugh Cross* . . .	10	4	Buttermere*	20
4	Lowes-Water	14	9	Keswick	29

KESWICK round BASSENTHWAITE WATER.

MILES.		MILES.	MILES.		MILES.
8	Peel Wyke*	8	3	Bassenthwaite Sandbed	. 13
1	Ouse-Bridge	9	5	Keswick	18
1	Castle Inn	10			

KESWICK to PATTERDALE, and by Pooley-Bridge to PENRITH.

10	Springfield*	10	10	Pooley - Bridge* through	
7	Gowbarrow Park . . .	17		Gowbarrow Park . . .	32
5	Patterdale*.	22	6	Penrith	38

INNS—*Penrith:* Crown Inn, the George.

KESWICK to POOLEY-BRIDGE and PENRITH.

12	Penruddock*	12	3	Pooley-Bridge	18
3	Dacre*	15	6	Penrith	24

KESWICK to PENRITH, 17½ miles.

4	Threlkeld* . . : . . .	4	3½	Stainton*	15
7½	Penruddock	11½	2½	Penrith	17½

WHITEHAVEN to KESWICK, 27 miles.

2	Moresby	2	5	Cockermouth	14
2	Distington	4	2½	Embleton	16½
2	Winscales	6	6½	Thornthwaite	23
3	Little Clifton	9	4	Keswick	27

INNS—*Whitehaven:* Black Lion, Golden Lion, the Globe. *Cockermouth:* The Globe, the Sun.

WORKINGTON to KESWICK, 21 miles.

The road joins that from Whitehaven to Keswick 4 miles from Workington.

INNS—*Workington:* Green Dragon, New Crown, King's Arms.

Excursion from PENRITH to HAWESWATER.

5	Lowther, or Askham* . .	5	5	Over Moor Dovack 'to	
7	By Bampton* to Hawes-			Pooley	21
	water	12	6	By Dalemain to Penrith .	27
4	Return by Butterswick .	16			

CARLISLE to PENRITH, 18 miles.

2½	Carlton*	2½	2	Plumpton*	13
7	Low Hesket* . . .	9½	5	Penrith	18
1½	High Hesket*	11			

INNS—*Carlisle:* The Bush Coffee-House, King's Arms.

PENRITH to KENDAL, 26 miles.

1	Eamont-Bridge*	1	6¾	Hawse Foot*	17
1½	Clifton*	2½	4	Plough Inn*	21
2	Hackthorpe*	4½	2½	Skelsmergh Stocks* . .	23½
5¾	Shap	10¼	2½	Kendal	26

INNS—*Shap:* Greyhound, King's Arms.

KENDAL AND WINDERMERE RAILWAY.

TWO LETTERS

RE-PRINTED FROM THE MORNING POST.

REVISED, WITH ADDITIONS.

KENDAL:

PRINTED BY R. BRANTHWAITE AND SON.

[1844.]

NOTE.

See Preface in Vol. I. for details on these Letters, &c.   G.

SONNET ON THE PROJECTED KENDAL AND WINDERMERE RAILWAY.

Is then no nook of English ground secure
From rash assault? Schemes of retirement sown
In youth, and mid the busy world kept pure
As when their earliest flowers of hope were blown,
Must perish;—how can they this blight endure?
And must he too the ruthless change bemoan
Who scorns a false utilitarian lure
Mid his paternal fields at random thrown?
Baffle the threat, bright Scene, from Orrest-head
Given to the pausing traveller's rapturous glance:
Plead for thy peace, thou beautiful romance
Of nature; and, if human hearts be dead,
Speak, passing winds; ye torrents, with your strong
And constant voice, protest against the wrong.

WILLIAM WORDSWORTH.

Rydal Mount, October 12th, 1844.

The degree and kind of attachment which many of the yeomanry feel to their small inheritances can scarcely be over-rated. Near the house of one of them stands a magnificent tree, which a neighbour of the owner advised him to fell for profit's sake. 'Fell it,' exclaimed the yeoman, 'I had rather fall on my knees and worship it.' It happens, I believe, that the intended railway would pass through this little property, and I hope that an apology for the answer will not be thought necessary by one who enters into the strength of the feeling.

W. W.

KENDAL AND WINDERMERE RAILWAY.

No. I.

To the Editor of the 'Morning Post.'

SIR,

Some little time ago you did me the favour of inserting a sonnet expressive of the regret and indignation which, in common with others all over these Islands, I felt at the proposal of a railway to extend from Kendal to Low Wood, near the head of Windermere. The project was so offensive to a large majority of the proprietors through whose lands the line, after it came in view of the Lake, was to pass, that, for this reason, and the avowed one of the heavy expense without which the difficulties in the way could not be overcome, it has been partially abandoned, and the terminus is now announced to be at a spot within a mile of Bowness. But as no guarantee can be given that the project will not hereafter be revived, and an attempt made to carry the line forward through the vales of Ambleside and Grasmere, and as in one main particular the case remains essentially the same, allow me to address you upon certain points which merit more consideration than the favourers of the scheme have yet given them. The matter, though seemingly local, is really one in which all persons of taste must be interested, and, therefore, I hope to be excused if I venture to treat it at some length.

I shall barely touch upon the statistics of the question, leaving these to the two adverse parties, who will lay their several statements before the Board of Trade, which may possibly be induced to refer the matter to the House of Commons; and, contemplating that possibility, I hope that the observations I have to make may not be altogether without influence upon the public, and upon individuals whose duty it may be to decide in their place whether the proposed measure shall be referred to a Committee of the House. Were the case before us an ordinary one, I should reject such an attempt as presumptuous and futile ; but it is not only different from all others, but, in truth, peculiar.

In this district the manufactures are trifling ; mines it has none, and its quarries are either wrought out or superseded ; the soil is light, and the cultivateable parts of the country are very limited ; so that it has little to send out, and little has it also to receive. Summer Tourists, (and the very word precludes the notion of a railway) it has in abundance ; but the inhabitants are so few and their intercourse with other places so infrequent, that one daily coach, which could not be kept going but through its connection with the Post-office, suffices for three-fourths of the year along the line of country as far as Keswick. The staple of the district is, in fact, its beauty and its character of seclusion and retirement ; and to these topics and to others connected with them my remarks shall be confined.

The projectors have induced many to favour their schemes by declaring that one of their main objects is to place the beauties of the Lake district within easier reach of those who cannot afford to pay for ordinary conveyances. Look at the facts. Railways are completed, which, joined with others in rapid progress, will bring travellers who prefer approaching by Ullswater to within four miles of that lake. The Lancaster and Carlisle Railway will approach the town of Kendal, about eight or nine miles from eminences that command the whole vale of Windermere. The Lakes are therefore at present of very easy access for *all* persons ; but if they be not made still more so, the poor, it is said, will be wronged. Before this be admitted let the question be fairly looked into, and its different bearings examined. No one can assert that, if this intended mode of approach be not effected, anything will be taken away that is actually possessed. The wrong, if any, must lie in the unwarrantable obstruction of an attainable benefit. First, then, let us consider the probable amount of that benefit.

Elaborate gardens, with topiary works, were in high request, even among our remote ancestors, but the relish for choice and picturesque natural *scenery* (a poor and mean word which requires an apology, but will be generally understood), is quite of recent origin. Our earlier travellers—Ray, the naturalist, one of the first men of his age—Bishop Burnet, and others who had crossed the Alps, or lived some time in Switzerland, are silent upon the sublimity and beauty of those regions; and Burnet even uses these words, speaking of the Grisons—' When they have made up estates elsewhere they are glad to leave Italy and the best parts of Germany, and to come and live among those mountains of which the very sight is enough to fill a man with horror.' The accomplished Evelyn, giving an account of his journey from Italy through the Alps, dilates upon the terrible, the melancholy, and the uncomfortable; but, till he comes to the fruitful country in the neighbourhood of Geneva, not a syllable of delight or praise. In the *Sacra Telluris Theoria* of the other Burnet there is a passage—omitted, however, in his own English translation of the work—in which he gives utterance to his sensations, when, from a particular spot he beheld a tract of the Alps rising before him on the one hand, and on the other the Mediterranean Sea spread beneath him. Nothing can be worthier of the magnificent appearances he describes than his language. In a noble strain also does the Poet Gray address, in a Latin Ode, the *Religio loci* at the Grande Chartruise. But before his time, with the exception of the passage from Thomas Burnet just alluded to, there is not, I believe, a single English traveller whose published writings would disprove the assertion, that, where precipitous rocks and mountains are mentioned at all, they are spoken of as objects of dislike and fear, and not of admiration. Even Gray himself, describing, in his Journal, the steeps at the entrance of Borrowdale, expresses his terror in the language of Dante:—' Let us not speak of them, but look and pass on.' In my youth, I lived some time in the vale of Keswick, under the roof of a shrewd and sensible woman, who more than once exclaimed in my hearing, ' Bless me! folk are always talking about prospects : when I was young there was never sic a thing neamed.' In fact, our ancestors, as every where appears, in choosing the site of their houses, looked only at shelter and convenience, especially of water, and often would place a barn or any other out-house directly in front of their habitations, however beautiful the landscape which their windows might otherwise have commanded. The first house that was built in the Lake district for the sake of the beauty of

the country was the work of a Mr. English, who had travelled
in Italy, and chose for his site, some eighty years ago, the great
island of Windermere; but it was sold before his building was
finished, and he showed how little he was capable of appreciat-
ing the character of the situation by setting up a length of high
garden-wall, as exclusive as it was ugly, almost close to the
house. The nuisance was swept away when the late Mr.
Curwen became the owner of this favoured spot. Mr. English
was followed by Mr. Pocklington, a native of Nottinghamshire,
who played strange pranks by his buildings and plantations
upon Vicar's Island, in Derwentwater, which his admiration,
such as it was, of the country, and probably a wish to be a
leader in a new fashion, had tempted him to purchase. But
what has all this to do with the subject?—Why, to show that a
vivid perception of romantic scenery is neither inherent in mankind, nor a necessary consequence of even a comprehensive
education. It is benignly ordained that green fields, clear blue
skies, running streams of pure water, rich groves and woods,
orchards, and all the ordinary varieties of rural Nature, should
find an easy way to the affections of all men, and more or less
so from early childhood till the senses are impaired by old age
and the sources of mere earthly enjoyment have in a great measure failed. But a taste beyond this, however desirable it may
be that every one should possess it, is not to be implanted at
once; it must be gradually developed both in nations and individuals. Rocks and mountains, torrents and wide-spread waters,
and all those features of Nature which go to the composition of
such scenes as this part of England is distinguished for, cannot,
in their finer relations to the human mind, be comprehended,
or even very imperfectly conceived, without processes of culture
or opportunities of observation in some degree habitual. In
the eye of thousands and tens of thousands, a rich meadow,
with fat cattle grazing upon it, or the sight of what they would
call a heavy crop of corn, is worth all that the Alps and Pyrenees
in their utmost grandeur and beauty could show to them; and,
notwithstanding the grateful influence, as we have observed, of
ordinary Nature and the productions of the fields, it is noticeable what trifling conventional prepossessions will, in common
minds, not only preclude pleasure from the sight of natural
beauty, but will even turn it into an object of disgust. 'If I

had to do with this garden,' said a respectable person, one of my neighbours, ' I would sweep away all the black and dirty stuff from that wall.' The wall was backed by a bank of earth, and was exquisitely decorated with ivy, flowers, moss, and ferns, such as grow of themselves in like places; but the mere notion of fitness associated with a trim garden-wall prevented, in this instance, all sense of the spontaneous bounty and delicate care of Nature. In the midst of a small pleasure-ground, immediately below my house, rises a detached rock, equally remarkable for the beauty of its form, the ancient oaks that grow out of it, and the flowers and shrubs which adorn it. ' What a nice place would this be,' said a Manchester tradesman, pointing to the rock, ' if that ugly lump were but out of the way.' Men as little advanced in the pleasure which such objects give to others are so far from being rare, that they may be said fairly to represent a large majority of mankind. This is a fact, and none but the deceiver and the willingly deceived can be offended by its being stated. But as a more susceptible taste is undoubtedly a great acquisition, and has been spreading among us for some years, the question is, what means are most likely to be beneficial in extending its operation? Surely that good is not to be obtained by transferring at once uneducated persons in large bodies to particular spots, where the combinations of natural objects are such as would afford the greatest pleasure to those who have been in the habit of observing and studying the peculiar character of such scenes, and how they differ one from another. Instead of tempting artisans and labourers, and the humbler classes of shopkeepers, to ramble to a distance, let us rather look with lively sympathy upon persons in that condition, when, upon a holiday, or on the Sunday, after having attended divine worship, they make little excursions with their wives and children among neighbouring fields, whither the whole of each family might stroll, or be conveyed at much less cost than would be required to take a single individual of the number to the shores of Windermere by the cheapest conveyance. It is in some such way as this only, that persons who must labour daily with their hands for bread in large towns, or are subject to confinement through the week, can be trained to a profitable intercourse with Nature where she is the most distinguished by the majesty and sublimity of her forms.

For further illustration of the subject, turn to what we know of a man of extraordinary genius, who was bred to hard labour in agricultural employments, Burns, the poet. When he had become distinguished by the publication of a volume of verses, and was enabled to travel by the profit his poems brought him, he made a tour, in the course of which, as his companion, Dr. Adair, tells us, he visited scenes inferior to none in Scotland in beauty, sublimity, and romantic interest; and the Doctor having noticed, with other companions, that he seemed little moved upon one occasion by the sight of such a scene, says—'I doubt if he had much taste for the picturesque.' The personal testimony, however, upon this point is conflicting; but when Dr. Currie refers to certain local poems as decisive proofs that Burns' fellow-traveller was mistaken, the biographer is surely unfortunate. How vague and tame are the poet's expressions in those few local poems, compared with his language when he is describing objects with which his position in life allowed him to be familiar! It appears; both from what his works contain, and from what is not to be found in them, that, sensitive as they abundantly prove his mind to have been in its intercourse with common rural images, and with the general powers of Nature exhibited in storm and in stillness, in light or darkness, and in the various aspects of the seasons, he was little affected by the sight of one spot in preference to another, unless where it derived an interest from history, tradition, or local associations. He lived many years in Nithsdale, where he was in daily sight of Skiddaw, yet he never crossed the Solway for a better acquaintance with that mountain; and I am persuaded that, if he had been induced to ramble among our Lakes, by that time sufficiently celebrated, he would have seldom been more excited than by some ordinary Scottish stream or hill with a tradition attached to it, or which had been the scene of a favourite ballad or love song. If all this be truly said of such a man, and the like cannot be denied of the eminent individuals before named, who to great natural talents added the accomplishments of scholarship or science, then what ground is there for maintaining that the poor are treated with disrespect, or wrong done to them or any class of visitants, if we be reluctant to introduce a railway into this country for the sake of lessening, by eight or nine miles only, the fatigue or expense of their journey to Windermere?—

And wherever any one among the labouring classes has made even an approach to the sensibility which drew a lamentation from Burns when he had uprooted a daisy with his plough, and caused him to turn the 'weeder-clips aside' from the thistle, and spare 'the symbol dear' of his country, then surely such a one, could he afford by any means to travel as far as Kendal, would not grudge a two hours' walk across the skirts of the beautiful country that he was desirous of visiting.

The wide-spread waters of these regions are in their nature peaceful; so are the steep mountains and the rocky glens; nor can they be profitably enjoyed but by a mind disposed to peace. Go to a pantomime, a farce, or a puppet-show, if you want noisy pleasure—the crowd of spectators who partake your enjoyment will, by their presence and acclamations, enhance it; but may those who have given proof that they prefer other gratifications continue to be safe from the molestation of cheap trains pouring out their hundreds at a time along the margin of Windermere; nor let any one be liable to the charge of being selfishly disregardful of the poor, and their innocent and salutary enjoyments, if he does not congratulate himself upon the especial benefit which would thus be conferred on such a concourse.

> O, Nature, a' thy shows an' forms,
> To feeling pensive hearts hae charms!

So exclaimed the Ayrshire ploughman, speaking of ordinary rural Nature under the varying influences of the seasons, and the sentiment has found an echo in the bosoms of thousands in as humble a condition as he himself was when he gave vent to it. But then they were feeling, pensive hearts; men who would be among the first to lament the facility with which they had approached this region, by a sacrifice of so much of its quiet and beauty, as, from the intrusion of a railway, would be inseparable. What can, in truth, be more absurd, than that either rich or poor should be spared the trouble of travelling by the high roads over so short a space, according to their respective means, if the unavoidable consequence must be a great disturbance of the retirement, and in many places a destruction of the beauty of the country, which the parties are come in search of? Would not this be pretty much like the child's cutting up his drum to learn where the sound came from?

Having, I trust, given sufficient reason for the belief that the imperfectly educated classes are not likely to draw much good from rare visits to the Lakes performed in this way, and surely on their own account it is not desirable that the visits should be frequent, let us glance at the mischief which such facilities would certainly produce. The directors of railway companies are always ready to devise or encourage entertainments for tempting the humbler classes to leave their homes. Accordingly, for the profit of the shareholders and that of the lower class of inn-keepers, we should have wrestling matches, horse and boat races without number, and pot-houses and beer-shops would keep pace with these excitements and recreations, most of which might too easily be had elsewhere. The injury which would thus be done to morals, both among this influx of strangers and the lower class of inhabitants, is obvious; and, supposing such extraordinary temptations not to be held out, there cannot be a doubt that the Sabbath day in the towns of Bowness and Ambleside, and other parts of the district, would be subject to much additional desecration.

Whatever comes of the scheme which we have endeavoured to discountenance, the charge against its opponents of being selfishly regardless of the poor, ought to cease. The cry has been raised and kept up by three classes of persons—they who wish to bring into discredit all such as stand in the way of their gains or gambling speculations; they who are dazzled by the application of physical science to the useful arts, and indiscriminately applaud what they call the spirit of the age as manifested in this way; and, lastly, those persons who are ever ready to step forward in what appears to them to be the cause of the poor, but not always with becoming attention to particulars. I am well aware that upon the first class what has been said will be of no avail, but upon the two latter some impression will, I trust, be made.

To conclude. The railway power, we know well, will not admit of being materially counteracted by sentiment; and who would wish it where large towns are connected, and the interests of trade and agriculture are substantially promoted, by such mode of intercommunication? But be it remembered, that this case is, as has been said before, a peculiar one, and that the staple of the country is its beauty and its character of retirement. Let then the beauty be undisfigured and the retirement unviolated, unless there be reason for believing that rights and interests of a higher kind and more apparent than those which have been urged in behalf of the projected intrusion will compensate the sacrifice. Thanking you for the judicious observations that have appeared in your paper upon the subject of railways,

I remain, Sir,

Your obliged,

WM. WORDSWORTH.

Rydal Mount, Dec. 9, 1844.

NOTE.—To the instances named in this letter of the indifference even of men of genius to the sublime forms of Nature in mountainous districts, the author of the interesting Essays, in the *Morning Post*, entitled Table Talk has justly added Goldsmith, and I give the passage in his own words.

'The simple and gentle-hearted Goldsmith, who had an exquisite sense of rural beauty in the familiar forms of hill and dale, and meadows with their hawthorn-scented hedges, does not seem to have dreamt of any such thing as beauty in the Swiss Alps, though he traversed them on foot, and had therefore the best opportunities of observing them. In his poem " The Traveller," he describes the Swiss as loving their mountain homes, not by reason of the romantic beauty of the situation, but in spite of the miserable character of the soil, and the stormy horrors of their mountain steeps—

Turn we to survey
Where rougher climes a nobler race display,
Where the bleak Swiss their stormy mansion tread,
And force a churlish soil for scanty bread.
No produce here the barren hills afford,
But man and steel, the soldier and his sword:
No vernal blooms their torpid rocks array,
But winter lingering chills the lap of May;
No Zephyr fondly sues the mountain's breast,
But meteors glare and stormy glooms invest.
Yet still, *even here*, content can spread a charm,
Redress the clime, and all its rage disarm.'

In the same Essay, (December 18th, 1844,) are many observations judiciously bearing upon the true character of this and similar projects.

No. II.

To the Editor of the 'Morning Post.'

SIR,

As you obligingly found space in your journal for observations of mine upon the intended Kendal and Windermere Railway, I venture to send you some further remarks upon the same subject. The scope of the main argument, it will be recollected, was to prove that the perception of what has acquired the name of picturesque and romantic scenery is so far from being intuitive, that it can be produced only by a slow and gradual process of culture; and to show, as a consequence, that the humbler ranks of society are not, and cannot be, in a state to gain material benefit from a more speedy access than they now have to this beautiful region. Some of our opponents dissent from this latter proposition, though the most judicious of them readily admit the former; but then, overlooking not only positive assertions, but reasons carefully given, they say, 'As you allow that a more comprehensive taste is desirable, you ought to side with us;' and they illustrate their position, by reference to the British Museum and National Picture Gallery. 'There,' they add, 'thanks to the easy entrance now granted, numbers are seen, indicating by their dress and appearance their humble condition, who, when admitted for the first time, stare vacantly around them, so that one is inclined to ask what brought them hither? But an impression is made, something gained which may induce them to repeat the visit until light breaks in upon them, and they take an intelligent interest in what they behold.' Persons who talk thus forget that, to produce such an improvement, frequent access at small cost of time and labour is indispensable. Manchester lies, perhaps, within eight hours' railway distance of London; but surely no one would advise that Manchester operatives should contract a habit of running to and fro between that town and London, for the sake of forming an intimacy with the British Museum and National Gallery? No, no; little would all but a very few gain from the opportunities

which, consistently with common sense, could be afforded them
for such expeditions. Nor would it fare better with them in
respect of trips to the lake district; an assertion, the truth of
which no one can doubt, who has learned by experience how
many men of the same or higher rank, living from their birth in
this very region, are indifferent to those objects around them in
which a cultivated taste takes so much pleasure. I should not
have detained the reader so long upon this point, had I not heard
(glad tidings for the directors and traffickers in shares!) that
among the affluent and benevolent manufacturers of Yorkshire
and Lancashire are some who already entertain the thought of
sending, at their own expense, large bodies of their workmen,
by railway, to the banks of Windermere. Surely those gentlemen will think a little more before they put such a scheme into
practice. The rich man cannot benefit the poor, nor the superior
the inferior, by anything that degrades him. Packing off men
after this fashion, for holiday entertainment, is, in fact, treating them like children. They go at the will of their master, and
must return at the same, or they will be dealt with as trans-
gressors.

A poor man, speaking of his son, whose time of service in the
army was expired, once said to me, (the reader will be startled
at the expression, and I, indeed, was greatly shocked by it), ' I
am glad he has done with that *mean* way of life.' But I soon
gathered what was at the bottom of the feeling. The father
overlooked all the glory that attaches to the character of a British
soldier, in the consciousness that his son's will must have been
in so great a degree subject to that of others. The poor man
felt where the true dignity of his species lay, namely, in a just
proportion between actions governed by a man's own inclinations
and those of other men; but, according to the father's notion,
that proportion did not exist in the course of life from which his
son had been released. Had the old man known from experience
the degree of liberty allowed to the common soldier, and the
moral effect of the obedience required, he would have thought
differently, and had he been capable of extending his views, he
would have felt how much of the best and noblest part of our
civic spirit was owing to our military and naval institutions, and
that perhaps our very existence as a free people had by them
been maintained. This extreme instance has been adduced to

show how deeply seated in the minds of Englishmen is their sense of personal independence. Master-manufacturers ought never to lose sight of this truth. Let them consent to a Ten Hours' Bill, with little or, if possible, no diminution of wages, and the necessaries of life being more easily procured, the mind will develope itself accordingly, and each individual would be more at liberty to make at his own cost excursions in any direction which might be most inviting to him. There would then be no need for their masters sending them in droves scores of miles from their homes and families to the borders of Windermere, or anywhere else. Consider also the state of the lake district; and look, in the first place, at the little town of Bowness, in the event of such railway inundations. What would become of it in this, not the Retreat, but the Advance, of the Ten Thousand? Leeds, I am told, has sent as many at once to Scarborough. We should have the whole of Lancashire, and no small part of Yorkshire, pouring in upon us to meet the men of Durham, and the borderers from Cumberland and Northumberland. Alas, alas, if the lakes are to pay this penalty for their own attractions !

—Vane could tell what ills from beauty spring,
And Sedley cursed the form that pleased a king.

The fear of adding to the length of my last long letter prevented me from entering into details upon private and personal feelings among the residents, who have cause to lament the threatened intrusion. These are not matters to be brought before a Board of Trade, though I trust there will always be of that board members who know well that as we do ' not live by bread alone,' so neither do we live by political economy alone. Of the present Board I would gladly believe there is not one who, if his duty allowed it, would not be influenced by considerations of what may be felt by a gallant officer now serving on the coast of South America, when he shall learn that the nuisance, though not intended actually to enter his property, will send its omnibuses, as fast as they can drive, within a few yards of his modest abode, which he built upon a small domain purchased at a price greatly enhanced by the privacy and beauty of the situation. Professor Wilson (him I take the liberty to name), though a native of Scotland, and familiar with the grandeur of his own country, could not resist the temptation of settling long ago among our mountains. The place which his public duties have compelled him to quit as a residence, and may compel him to part with, is probably dearer to him than any spot upon earth. The reader should be informed with what respect he has been treated. Engineer agents, to his astonishment, came and intruded with their measuring instruments, upon his garden. He saw them; and who will not admire the patience that kept his hands from their shoulders? I must stop.

But with the fear before me of the line being carried, at a day not distant, through the whole breadth of the district, I could dwell, with much concern for other residents, upon the condition which they would be in if that outrage should be committed; nor ought it to be deemed impertinent were I to recommend this point to the especial regard of Members of Parliament who may have to decide upon the question. The two Houses of Legislature have frequently shown themselves not unmindful of private feeling in these matters. They have, in some cases, been induced to spare parks and pleasure grounds. But along the great railway lines these are of rare occurrence. They are but a part, and a small part; here it is far otherwise. Among the ancient inheritances of the yeomen, surely worthy of high respect, are interspersed through the entire district villas, most of them with such small domains attached that the occupants would be hardly less annoyed by a railway passing through their neighbour's ground than through their own. And it would be unpardonable not to advert to the effect of this measure on the interests of the very poor in this locality. With the town of Bowness I have no *minute* acquaintance; but of Ambleside, Grasmere, and the neighbourhood, I can testify from long experience, that they have been favoured by the residence of a gentry whose love of retirement has been a blessing to these vales; for their families have ministered, and still minister, to the temporal and spiritual necessities of the poor, and have personally superintended the education of the children in a degree which does those benefactors the highest honour, and which is, I trust, gratefully acknowledged in the hearts of all whom they have relieved, employed, and taught. Many of those friends of our poor would quit this country if the apprehended change were realised, and would be succeeded by strangers not linked to the neighbourhood, but flitting to and fro between their fancy villas aod the homes where their wealth was accumulated and accumulating by trade and manufactures. It is obvious that persons, so unsettled, whatever might be their good wishes and readiness to part with money for charitable purposes, would ill supply the loss of the inhabitants who had been driven away.

It will be felt by those who think with me upon this occasion that I have been writing on behalf of a social condition which no one who is competent to judge of it will be willing to subvert, and that I have been endeavouring to support moral sentiments and intellectual pleasures of a high order against an enmity which seems growing more and more formidable every day; I mean 'Utilitarianism,' serving as a mask for cupidity and gambling speculations. My business with this evil lies in its reckless mode of action by Railways, now its favourite instruments. Upon good authority I have been told that there was lately an intention of driving one of these pests, as they are likely too often to prove, through a part of the magnificent ruins of Furness Abbey—an outrage which was prevented by some one pointing out how easily a deviation might be made; and the hint produced its due effect upon the engineer.

Sacred as that relic of the devotion of our ancestors deserves to be kept, there are temples of Nature, temples built by the Almighty, which have a still higher claim to be left unviolated. Almost every reach of the winding vales in this district might once have presented itself to a man of imagination and feeling under that aspect, or, as the Vale of Grasmere appeared to the Poet Gray more than seventy years ago. 'No flaring gentleman's-house,' says he, 'nor garden-walls break in upon the repose of this little unsuspected *paradise*, but all is peace,' &c., &c. Were the Poet now living, how would he have lamented the probable intrusion of a railway with its scarifications, its intersections, its noisy machinery, its smoke, and swarms of pleasure-hunters, most of them thinking that they do not fly fast enough through the country which they have come to see. Even a broad highway may in some places greatly impair the characteristic beauty of the country, as will be readily acknowledged by those who remember what the Lake of Grasmere was before the new road that runs along its eastern margin had been constructed.

Quanto praestantias esset
Numen aquae viridi si margina clauderet undas
Herba—

As it once was, and fringed with wood, instead of the breast-work of bare wall that now confines it. In the same manner has the beauty, and still more the sublimity of many Passes in the Alps been injuriously affected. Will the reader excuse a quotation from a MS. poem in which I attempted to describe the impression made upon my mind by the descent towards Italy along the Simplon before the new military road had taken the place of the old muleteer track with its primitive simplicities ?

> Brook and road
> Were fellow-travellers in this gloomy Pass,
> And with them did we journey several hours
> At a slow step. The immeasurable height
> Of woods decaying, never to be decayed,
> The stationary blasts of waterfalls,
> And in the narrow rent, at every turn,
> Winds thwarting winds bewildered and forlorn,
> The torrents shooting from the clear blue sky,
> The rocks that muttered close upon our ears,
> Black drizzling crags that spake by the way-side
> As if a voice were in them, the sick sight
> And giddy prospect of the raving stream,
> The unfettered clouds and region of the heavens,
> Tumult and peace, the darkness and the light,
> Were all like workings of one mind, the features
> Of the same face, blossoms upon one tree,
> Characters of the great Apocalypse,
> The types and symbols of Eternity,
> Of first, and last, and midst, and without end.
>
> 1799.

Thirty years afterwards I crossed the Alps by the same Pass : and what had become of the forms and powers to which I had been indebted for those emotions ? Many of them remained of course undestroyed and indestructible. But, though the road and torrent continued to run parallel to each other, their fellow-ship was put an end to. The stream had dwindled into com-parative insignificance, so much had Art interfered with and taken the lead of Nature ; and although the utility of the new work, as facilitating the intercourse of great nations, was readily acquiesced in, and the workmanship, in some places, could not but excite admiration, it was impossible to suppress regret for what had vanished for ever. The oratories heretofore not unfrequently met with, on a road still somewhat perilous, were gone; the simple and rude bridges swept away; and instead of travellers proceeding, with leisure to observe and feel, were pilgrims of fashion hurried along in their carriages, not a few of them perhaps discussing the merits of ' the last new Novel,' or poring over their Guide-books, or fast asleep. Similar remarks might be applied to the mountainous country of Wales; but there too, the plea of utility, especially as expediting the communication between England and Ireland, more than justifies the labours of the Engineer. Not so would it be with the Lake District. A railroad is already planned along the sea coast, and another from Lancaster to Carlisle is in great forwardness: an intermediate one is therefore, to say the least of it, superfluous. Once for all let me declare that it is not against Railways but against the abuse of them that I am contending.

How far I am from undervaluing the benefit to be expected from railways in their legitimate application will appear from the following lines published in 1837, and composed some years earlier.

STEAMBOATS AND RAILWAYS.

Motions and Means, on sea, on land at war
With old poetic feeling, not for this
Shall ye, by poets even, be judged amiss!
Nor shall your presence, howsoe'er it mar
The loveliness of Nature, prove a bar
To the mind's gaining that prophetic sense
Of future good, that point of vision, whence
May be discovered what in soul ye are.
In spite of all that Beauty must disown
In your harsh features, Nature doth embrace
Her lawful offspring in man's Art; and Time,
Pleased with your triumphs o'er his brother Space,
Accepts from your bold hand the proffered crown
Of hope, and welcomes you with cheer sublime.

I have now done with the subject. The time of life at which I have arrived may, I trust, if nothing else will, guard me from the imputation of having written from any selfish interests, or from fear of disturbance which a railway might cause to myself. If gratitude for what repose and quiet in a district hitherto, for the most part, not disfigured but beautified by human hands, have done for me through the course of a long life, and hope that others might hereafter be benefited in the same manner and in the same country, *be* selfishness, then, indeed, but not otherwise, I plead guilty to the charge. Nor have I opposed this undertaking on account of the inhabitants of the district *merely*, but, as hath been intimated, for the sake of every one, however humble his condition, who coming hither shall bring with him an eye to perceive, and a heart to feel and worthily enjoy. And as for holiday pastimes, if a scene is to be chosen suitable to them for persons thronging from a distance, it may be found elsewhere at less cost of every kind. But, in fact, we have too much hurrying about in these islands ; much for idle pleasure, and more from over activity in the pursuit of wealth, without regard to the good or happiness of others.

> Proud were ye, Mountains, when, in times of old,
> Your patriot sons, to stem invasive war,
> Intrenched your brows; ye gloried in each scar:
> Now, for your shame, a Power, the Thirst of Gold,
> That rules o'er Britain like a baneful star,
> Wills that your peace, your beauty, shall be sold,
> And clear way made for her triumphal car
> Through the beloved retreats your arms enfold !
> Heard YE that Whistle? As her long-linked Train
> Swept onwards, did the vision cross your view?
> Yes, ye were startled ;—and, in balance true,
> Weighing the mischief with the promised gain,
> Mountains, and Vales, and Floods, I call on you
> To share the passion of a just disdain.

WILLIAM WORDSWORTH.

NOTES AND ILLUSTRATIONS.

ÆSTHETICAL AND LITERARY.

I. *Of Literary Biography and Monuments.*

(a) *A Letter to a Friend of Robert Burns,* 1816.

P. 5, l. 1. James Gray, Esq. Wordsworth was justified in naming Gray a 'friend' of Burns. He was originally Master of the High School, Dumfries, and associated with the Poet there. Transferred to the High School of Edinburgh, he taught for well-nigh a quarter of a century with repute. Disappointed of the Rectorship, he retired from Edinburgh to an academy at Belfast. Later, having entered holy orders, he proceeded to India as a chaplain in the East India Company's service. He was stationed at Bhooj, in Cutch, near the mouth of the Indus; and the education of the young Rao of that province having been intrusted to the British Government, Gray was selected as his instructor—being the first Christian honoured with such an appointment in the East. He died at his post in 1830, deeply regretted. He was author of 'Cuna of Cheyd' and the 'Sabbath among the Mountains,' and many other things, original and editorial. He left a MS. poem, entitled 'India,' and a translation of the Gospels into the Cutch dialect of Hindoostanee. He will hold a niche in literature as the fifteenth bard in the 'Queen's Wake' who sings of 'King Edward's Dream.' He married a sister of Mrs. Hogg.

P. 5, footnote. Peterkin was a laborious compiler; but his Lives of Burns and Fergusson are written in the most high-flown and exaggerated style imaginable. He died in 1847.

P. 5, l. 9. 'Mr. Gilbert Burns .... a favourable opportunity,' &c. This excellent, common-sensed, and humble man's contributions to the later impressions (1804, &c.) of Dr. Currie's edition of Burns are of permanent value—very much more valuable than later brilliant productions that have displaced them. In Peterkin's Burns there is a letter from Gilbert Burns to him, dated September 29th, 1814.

P. 7. Verse-quotation from Burns. From 'Address to the Unco Guid, or the Rigidly Righteous' (closing stanzas).

P. 15. Verse-quotation. From Burns' 'A Bard's Epitaph.'

P. 17, footnote. Long before Wordsworth, Thomas Watson, in his 'Epistle to the Frendly Reader' prefixed to his 'ΕΚΑΤΟΜΠΑΘΙΑ (1582), wrote: 'As for any *Aristarchus,* Momus, or Zoilus, if they pinch me more than is reasonable, thou, courteous Reader, which arte of a better disposition, shalt rebuke them in my behalfe; saying to the first [Aristarchus], that my birdes are al of mine own hatching,' &c.

P. 21, ll. 30-37, Chatterton; ll. 38-40, &c., Michael Bruce. Both of the suggested monuments have been raised; Chatterton's at Bristol, and Bruce's over his grave. A photograph of the latter is given in our quarto edition of his Poems.

II. *Upon Epitaphs.*

P. 27, l. 10. Camden. Here and throughout the quotations (modernised) are from ' Remaines concerning Britain: their

Languages,
Names,
Surnames,
Allusions,
Anagrammes,
Armories,
Monies,

Empreses,
Apparell,
Artillarie,
Wise Speeches,
Prouerbs,
Poesies,
Epitaphs.

Written by William Camden, Esquire, Clarenceux King of Armes, surnamed the Learned. The sixth Impression, with many rare Antiquities never before imprinted. By the Industry and Care of John Philpot, Somerset Herald: and W. D. Gent. London, 1657, 4to. Epitaphes, pp. 355-409.' It has not been deemed necessary to point out the somewhat loose character of the quotations from Camden by Wordsworth; nor, with so many editions available, would it have served any good end to have given the places in the 'Epitaphes.' While Wordsworth evidently read both Camden and Weever, his chief authority seems to have been a book that appeared on the sale of his library, viz. 'Wit's Recreations; containing 630 Epigrams, 160 *Epitaphs*, and variety of Fantasies and Fantastics, good for Melancholy Humours. 1641.'

P. 27, l. 16. This verse-rendering of 'Mæcenas' is by Wordsworth, not Camden—the quotation from whom here ought to have been marked with an inverted comma (') after *relictos*.

P. 27, l. 22. Weever. The title in full is as follows: 'Ancient Fvnerall Monvments within the Vnited Monarchie of Great Britaine, Ireland, and the Islands adiacent, with the dissolued Monasteries therein contained: their Founders, and what eminent Persons haue beene in the same interred. As also the Death and Bvriall of Certaine of the Blood Royall, the Nobilitie and Gentrie of these Kingdomes entombed in forraine Nations. A work reuiuing the dead memorie of the Royal Progenie, the Nobilitie, Gentrie, and Communaltie of these his Maiesties Dominions. Intermixed and Illustrated with variety of Historicall obseruations, annotations, and briefe notes, extracted out of approued Authors, infallible Records, Lieger Bookes, Charters, Rolls, old Manuscripts, and the Collections of iudicious Antiquaries. Whereunto is prefixed a Discourse of Funerall Monuments. Of the Foundation and Fall of Religious Houses. Of Religious Orders. Of the Ecclesiasticall estate of England. And of other occurrences touched vpon by the way, in the whole passage of these intended labours. Composed by the Studie and Trauels of John Weever. Spe labor leuis. London. 1631, folio.' As with Camden, Wordsworth quotes Weever from memory (apparently) throughout.

P. 27, l. 23. Query—' or fore-feeling'?

P. 32, l. 6. ' Pause, Traveller.' The ' Siste viator' was kept up long after such roadside interments were abandoned. Crashaw's Epitaph for Harris so begins; e.g. ' Siste te paulum, viator,' &c. (Works, vol. ii. p. 378, Fuller Worthies' Library.)

P. 33. John Edwards; verse-quotation. Query—the author of ' Kathleen' (1808), ' Abradates and Panthea' (1808), &c.?

P. 40. At close; verse-quotation. From Milton, Ep. W. Sh.

P. 41. Verse-heading. From Gray's ' Elegy.' *En passant*, be it noted that on 1st June 1875, at Sotheby's, the original MS. of this Elegy was sold for upwards of 300 guineas to Sir William Fraser.

P. 45, l. 28. Read ' mearely'=merrily, as ' merrely' onward.

P. 49, ll. 7-14. On these lines, alleged to have been written by Montrose, see Dr. Hannah's ' Courtly Poets' (1870), p. 207, and numerous references. It may be noted that in line 2 Wordsworth changes ' too rigid' into.' so rigid;' and l. 7, ' trumpet' into ' trumpets.'

P. 49, ll. 30-2. Verse-quotation. Milton, ' Paradise Lost,' book vi. ll. 754-6.

P. 66 (bottom). Epitaph on Mrs. Clark—*i.e.* Mrs. Jane Clarke. In l. 1,

Gray wrote, not 'the,' but 'this ;' which in the light of the criticism it is important to remember.

P. 73-75. Long verse-quotation. From the 'Excursion,' book vii. ll. 400-550. Note the 'Various Readings.'

III. *Essays, Letters, and Notes elucidatory and confirmatory of the Poems.*

(a) *Of the Principles of Poetry and the ' Lyrical Ballads.'*

P. 85. Verse-quotation. From Gray's Poems, 'Sonnet on the Death of Mr. Richard West.'

P. 99, l. 30. Sir Joshua Reynolds. For Wordsworth's critical verdict on his literary work as well as his painting, see Letters in present volume, pp. 153-157, *et alibi.*

(c) *Poetry as a study.*

P. 112, ll. 6-7. Quotation from Spenser, 'Fairy Queen,' b. i. c. i. st. 9, l. 1.

P. 113, footnote. Hakewill. The work intended is ' An Apologie or Declaration of the Power and Providence of God in the Government of the World.' Oxford, 1627 (folio), and later editions. He was George Hakewill, D.D., Archdeacon of Surrey. Died 1649.

P. 115, ll. 36-7. '1623 to 1664 ... only two editions of the Works of Shakspeare.' The second folio of 1632 and that of 1663 (same as 1664) are here forgotten, and also the abundant separate reprints of the separate Plays and Poems.

P. 123, l. 6. Mr. Malcom Laing, a historian of Scotland ' from the Union of the Crowns to the Union of the Kingdoms in the Reign of Queen Anne' (4th edition, 1819, 4 vols.), who, in an exhaustive and drastic style, disposed of the notorious ' Ossian' fictions of Macpherson.

P. 130, ll. 12-14. Verse-quotation. From the 'Prelude.'

(d) *Of Poetry as Observation and Description.*

P. 134, ll. 3-4 (at bottom). Verse-quotation. From 'A Poet's Epitaph' (VIII. ' Poems of Sentiment and Reflection').

P. 136, ll. 7-8. Verse-quotation. From Shakspeare, 'Lear,' iv. 6.

P. 136, ll. 17-24. Verse-quotation. From Milton, 'Paradise Lost,' book ii. ll. 636-43.

P. 139, ll. 10-11. Verse-quotation. Ibid. book vi. ll. 767-8.

P. 140, ll. 10-11. Verse-quotation. From Shakspeare, 'Lear,' iii. 2.

P. 141, ll. 1-2. Verse-quotation. Ibid. ' Romeo and Juliet,' i. 4.

P. 142, ll. 7-8. 12-13. Verse-quotation. From Milton, 'Paradise Lost,' book ix. 1002-3.

P. 143. Long verse-quotation. Charles Cotton, the associate ' Angler' of Walton ' for all time,' and of whom, as a Poet, Abp. Trench, in his ' Household Book of English Poetry,' has recently spoken highly yet measuredly.

P. 152, footnote *. *Various Readings.* (1) ' Sonnet composed at ——.' Such is the current heading of this Sonnet in the Poems (Rossetti, p. 177). In the MS. it runs, ' Written at Needpath (near Peebles), Mansion of the Duke of Queensbury' (*sic*) ; and thus opens :

> ' Now, as I live, I pity that great lord !
> Whom pure despite of heart,' &c. ;

instead of,

> ' Degenerate Douglas ! oh, the unworthy lord !
> Whom mere,' &c.

(2) To the Men of Kent, October 1803. In l. 3, the MS. reads :

> ' Her haughty forehead 'gainst the coast of France,'

for ' brow against.' Line 7, ' can' for ' may.' (3) ' Anticipation,' October 1803. Line 12 in MS. reads :

'The loss and the sore prospect of the slain,'

for,

'And even the prospect of our brethren slain.'

In l. 14:

'True glory, everlasting sanctity,'

for,

'In glory will they sleep and endless sanctity.'

P. 161, l. 22. 'Milton compares,' &c. In 'Paradise Lost,' ii. 636-7.

P. 163, l. 2. 'Duppa is publishing a Life of Michael Angelo,' &c. It appeared in 1806 (4to) ; reprinted in Bohn's 'Illustrated Library.'

P. 163, footnote *. Alexander Wilson, who became the renowned 'Ornithologist' of America, was for years a 'pedlar,' both at home and in the United States. His intellectual ability and genius would alone have given sanction to Wordsworth's conception ; but as simple matter-of-fact, the class was a peculiarly thoughtful and observant one, as the Biographies of Scotland show.

P. 167, ll. 30-1. 'A tale told,' &c. From Shakspeare, 'Macbeth,' v. 5.

P. 170, l. 34. 'Houbraken,' &c. Reissued from the old copper-plates.

P. 171, l. 30. 'I have never seen the works,' &c. In the Fuller Worthies' Library I have collected the complete Poems of Sir John Beaumont, 1 vol.

Pp. 178-9. Quotation (bottom). From Milton, 'Paradise Lost,' book iv. ll. 604-9 ; but 'How' is inadvertently substituted for 'Now.'

P. 196, l. 35. John Dyer. Wordsworth's repeated recognition and lofty estimate of Dyer recalls the fact that a collection of his many-sided Writings is still a *desideratum* that the present Editor of Wordsworth's Prose hopes some day to supply—invited to the task of love by a lineal descendant.

(*h*) *Of the Principles of Poetry and his own Poems.*

P. 211, ll. 24-5. Verse-quotation from Cowper : more accurately it reads :

'The jay, the pie, and even the boding owl
That hails the rising moon, have charms for me.'

('The Task,' b. i. ll. 205-6.)

IV. DESCRIPTIVE.

(*a*) *A Guide through the District of the Lakes.*

P. 217. It seems somewhat remarkable that Wordsworth nowhere mentions the following work : 'Remarks made in a Tour from London to the Lakes of Westmoreland and Cumberland in the Summer of MDCCXCI., originally published in the *Whitehall Evening Post*, and now reprinted with additions and corrections. . . . By A. Walker, Lecturer,' &c. 1792, 8vo. Wordsworth could not have failed to be interested in the descriptions of this overlooked book. They are open-eyed, open-eared, and vivid. I would refer especially to the Letters on Windermere, pp. 58-60, and indeed all on the Lakes. Space can only be found for a short quotation on Ambleside (Letter xiii., August 18, 1791) : 'We now leave Low Wood, and along the verge of the Lake have a pleasing couple of miles to Ambleside. This is a straggling little market-town, made up of rough-cast white houses, but charmingly situated in the centre of three radiant vallies, *i.e.* all issuing from the town as from a centre. This shows the propriety of the Roman station situated near the west end of this place, called Amboglana, commanding one of the most difficult passes in England. . . . Beautiful woods rise half-way up the sides of the mountains from Ambleside, and seem wishful to cover the naked asperities of the country ; but the Iron Works calling for them in the character of charcoal every fourteen or fifteen years, exposes the nakedness of the country. Among these woods and mountains are many frightful precipices and roaring cascades. In a still evening several are heard at once, in various keys, forming a kind of savage music ; one, half a mile above the town in a wood, seems upwards of a hundred feet fall.—About as much water as is in the New River precipitates itself over a perpendicular rock into a natural bason, where it seems to recover from its fall before it takes a second and a third tumble over huge stones that break it into a number of streams. It suffers not this outrage quietly, for it grumbles through hollow glens and stone cavities all the way, till it meets the Rothay, when it quietly enters the Lake' (pp. 71-3). It is odd that a book so matterful, and containing many descriptions equal to this of Ambleside, should be so absolutely gone out of sight. It is a considerable volume, and pp. 1-114 are devoted to the Lake region. Walker, in 1787, issued anonymously 'An Hasty Sketch of a Tour through Part of the Austrian Netherlands, &c. . . . By an English Gentleman.'

P. 264. Quotation from (cheu! cheu!) the still unpublished poem of 'Grasmere.'

P. 274. Quotation from Spenser, 'Fairy Queen,' b. iii. c. v. st. 39-40. In st. 39, l. 8, 'puny' is a misprint for 'pumy'=pumice; in st. 40, l. 3, 'sang' similarly misreads 'song'=sung, or were singing.

P. 284. Verse-quotation. From 'Sonnet on Needpath Castle,' as *ante*.

P. 296, footnote °. Lucretius, ii. 772 seq.; and cf. v. 482 seq.

(b) *Kendal and Windermere Railway.*

P. 331. Quotation from Burns,—Verse-letter to William Simpson, st. 14.

P. 336. Is this from Dryden? G.

END OF VOL. II.

O

LONDON:
ROBSON AND SONS, PRINTERS, PANCRAS ROAD, N.W.

www.ingramcontent.com/pod-product-compliance
Lightning Source LLC
Chambersburg PA
CBHW021112270326
41929CB00009B/850